MAĀSIR-I-'ĀLAMGIRI

MAĀSIR-I-'ĀLAMGIRI

A History of the Emperor Aurangzib-'Ālamgir (reign 1658-1707 AD)

of

SĀQI MUST'AD KHAN

Translated into English and annotated by

SIR JADUNATH SARKAR

MANOHAR
2026

First published 1947
Reprinted 2022, 2023, 2024, 2025, 2026

ISBN 978-93-94262-02-7

Published by
Ajay Kumar Jain *for*
Manohar Publishers & Distributors
4753/23 Ansari Road, Daryaganj
New Delhi 110 002

Printed at
Replika Press Pvt. Ltd.

CONTENTS

TRANSLATOR'S PREFACE

I

THE Emperor Akbar (reign 1556-1605 A.D.) set the example of having a detailed history of his reign written by official command. The result was the *Ākbar-nāmah* or 'Book of Akbar' of Ābul Fazl (completed by other hands after that author's death). Then came the Emperor Jahāngir, who dictated his own memoirs, known as the *Tuzuk-i-Jahāngiri,* and therefore no official *Jahāngir-nāmah* had to be written about him. This book, however, combines the literary characteristics of an autobiography with those of an official history, or in other words, it gives the Emperor's own reflections and feelings as well as an objective record of the events of his reign. Indeed, in this reign, the literary type of the Mughal official histories was determined for the future, as was exemplified by the *Pādishāhnāmah* (Shāh Jahān), the *'Ālamgir-nāmah* (of Aurangzib, completed by the *Maāsir-i-Ālamgiri*), the *Bahādur Shāh-nāmah* (Shāh Ālam I) and later attempts like the *Tārikh-i-Āhmad Shāhi* and the *Tārikh-i-'Ālamgir Sāni.*

In all these works, or *Nāmahs* proper, the events are built upon a rigid skeleton of dates chronologically arranged ; there is an accurate but tiresome assemblage of minute names of persons and places in the course of every month's narrative of occurrences, and the mechanical division of the book into a chapter for each regnal year is followed. Such a collection of facts, if it is to be correct, requires a basis of written official records, and this basis was supplied by the *waqāi'* or official reports of occurrences regularly sent from every province to the central Government of Delhi. By an order issued in the 24th year of his reign (1580), Akbar appointed in each province of his empire a uniform set of officers, one of whom was the Waqāi'-navis or Recorder of Events. (*Akbar-nāmah,* Bev. tr., iii. 413, also 559). Jahangir continued the system. As he writes, "It had been made a rule that the events of the subahs should be reported according to the boundaries of each, and news-writers from the Court had been appointed for this duty. This being the rule that my revered father had laid down, I also observe it, ... and information is thus acquired about the world and its inhabitants." (*Tuzuk,* Roger's tr. i. 247, see also *Bahāristān-i-Ghayibi,* Borah's tr. i. 209.) But the system of appointing secret news-writers to the provinces was really borrowed by the Indian Mughals from the 'Abbāsid Khālifs who had borrowed it from the ancient Irānian empire. The different classes of these news-reporters and their method of work are fully described in my book, *Mughal Administration,* ch. IV. sec. 6.

When this State intelligence-department was fully developed with the expansion of the Mughal Empire under Shah Jahān and Aurangzib, (1627-1707), a huge collection of reports, written on small slips of paper and transmitted to the capital in bamboo cylinders (*nalo*) at regular weekly or fortnightly intervals,—came to be formed in the archives at the capital. Besides these there were the *ākhbārāt-i-darbār-i-mu'ala,* or reports of everything that was done or said in public at the Court or camp where the Emperor was present in person. These were written daily,—sometimes twice a day, when (as usual) there were morning levees and evening Courts held by His Majesty. Such *ākhbārāts* or manuscript news-letters were sent to the vassal princes, provincial governors, and generals out on campaign by their paid agents at the imperial Court, and differed only in their place of origin from the letters coming in a contrary direction, namely the letters of the Government spies in the mufassil which supplemented the more open reports of the official *waqāi'-navis*.

On this accumulated mass of accurate, detailed, and absolutely contemporary records of occurrences, some Persian author, known for his mastery of polished courtierly prose, was selected by the Emperor to work and write the *Nāmah* or official annals of his reign. The book was read to the Emperor and corrected under the royal direction before being passed for publication,—the term 'publication' here meant, the release of the book for being copied for presentation to the princes and high nobles. The Emperor, after one or two trial hearings, delegated the work of revision to his wazir.

These official annals, in addition to being full of nauseating flattery of the author's patron and his "sacred" offspring, were extremely verbose ; for example the record of the first 20 years of Shah Jahan's reign occupies 1662 printed pages of 22 lines each (or 83·1 pages for a single year on the average); the history of the first decade of Aurangzib's reign covers 1107 pages of the same size (or 110·7 pages for one year). But their details and dates of incidents are valuable, though I have detected instances where the Nāmah has given a wrong date owing to the carelessness of the historian's clerks in making extracts from the *waqi'ā* in the imperial record office for being worked into his history. However, the survival of the *ākhbārāt* for that particular day has enabled me to correct the wrong date entered in the *Nāmah*.

It must also be conceded that the author's flattery of the Emperor, though fulsome and offensive to modern taste, is more a defect of manner than one of fact. In these official histories, no fact has been really falsified, though credit is often given to the Emperor where he did not deserve it. We shall have more patience with the courtly author and derive greater profit from his book if we remember that he is only following the *facon de parler* prevalent in Asiatic courts. And why Asiatic only? The Stuart king of England was styled "His Gracious and *Sacred Majesty*" and Napoleon's *Moniteurs* were not models of factual veracity. Thus, with a *Nāmah* in our hands, we get the true basis for a narrative of the events of that monarch's reign and can then form our own judgment of the characters and political forces. Their chief defect —and one which disqualifies them from being called histories in the modern sense of the term, is their absolute silence about the economic and social aspects of the times, and what is known as "the condition of the people"

II

The history of the first ten years of Aurangzib's reign was written, under his orders, in the form of a full-sized *Nāmah*, by Mirzā Muhammad Kāzim, under the title of *'Ālamgir-nāmah*. (Printed in the Bibliotheca Indica series by the R.A.S. Bengal.) But after the author had completed the first decade, the Emperor forbade him to continue it any further. The reason for this prohibition is given by Sāqi Musta'd Khan as, "Because this monarch of the external and internal universe preferred laying the foundations of things esoteric to displaying things external", (p. 68 of the printed Persian text.) What really happened was that when (about 1670) the history of the tenth year was completed by Kāzim, Aurangzib curtailed his State expenditure and closed the costly department of prolix official annals. There is no authority for the popular legend that he forbade the writing of his history by any one else as a crime or that Khāfi Khan's history is so entitled because it was written in secret (*khufia*) in fear of any such royal prohibition. The word *Khāfi* has nothing to do with *khufia ;* it really means 'a native of Khwāf',—a district of Khurāsān situated between Herāt and Nishābur (*Encyclopaedia of Islam,* ii. 866.)

Aurangzib's finances did not improve when the second decade of his reign ended in 1678. He now found himself too much involved with the tribes on the Afghan frontier and was soon afterwards too hard pressed by the Rajputs and the Marathas, to allow him to spend any thought or money on such non-utilitarian purposes as the compilation of a florid and verbose chronicle of his reign. And his circumstances did not improve up to the end of his life. Thus it happened that no *complete* history of his reign came to be officially composed while he lived.

After his death (in 1707), his last secretary and favourite disciple in State policy and religiosity, I'nāyetullah Khan Kashmiri, urged Sāqi Musta'd Khan to complete the history of such a model sovereign. In order to help him in this work, the State archives were thrown open to him and he made extracts of the necessary materials to be used in his book, which was completed in 1710 and entitled *Maāsir-i-'Ālamgiri.* For the career of 'Ināyetullah, see Irvine's *Later Mughals,* 1. 259 and 333 ; he rose to be Wazir under Muhammad Shah and was keen on reimposing the *jazia* on the Hindus, (*Ibid.* 1. 103-105).

Of our author Muhammad Sāqi Musta'd Khan's life, we know a few facts only, all supplied by him either in his own History of Aurangzib or in his preface to his patron Bakhtāwar Khan's book the *Mirāt-ul-'Ālam.* He was brought up by Bakhtāwar Khan (a favourite officer of Aurangzib, whose character is noted in the *Maāsir,* (p. 253 of the printed text). In this Khan's establishment our author filled the offices of *munshi* and *diwān.* He assisted his patron, during the last seventeen years of his life, in the composition of the *Mirāt-ul-'Ālam,* which Aurangzib authorised him after Bakhtāwar's death, to make public. He then passed into the imperial service with a *mansab.* He held under this Emperor in succession the posts of *mushrif* of the *jā-namāz-khānah, waqāi'navis* of Thursdays, *mushrif* of the Khawāses, and *munshi* of the *nazāral*, (text, pp. 253, 255, 407, 462.)

A gentleman of Patna City, named Babu Ram Bahadur (*alias* Chhotu Lal), has a Persian ms. named *Inshā-i-Matlub*, which contains letters written by Sāqi Musta'd Khan to his contemporaries, but it lacks pp. 9-48, and the paper is old and brittle.

The *Maāsir-i-'Ālamgiri* has been written in a very much abridged form compared with the *Nāmahs ;* on an average it gives 11 pages to one year's narrative, against 110·7 pages for one year of the same reign in the *'Ālamgirnāmah.* But the loss is really one of the flowers of rhetoric rather than of facts. Consequently in many places it reads like a dry list of official postings and promotions as in our Government Gazettes. But its other portions give valuable, sometimes interesting information, especially the few that embody the author's personal observations and reflections on events, or character-sketches.

In this translation the text has been slightly condensed. Not a single fact or date has been omitted by me, but the prolix wording of some sentences has been replaced by a plain recital of their substance, and many trite reflections and moralisations (which are conventional in Persian historical literature at the beginning of a chapter or section) have been omitted altogether ; also, verses and long laudatory phrases. But every *significant* epithet has been preserved. I have inserted the page numbers of the Persian original in the body of my translation, so that any curious reader can easily satisfy himself that this is a complete reproduction in English of the historical matter of the original text. All the Hijera dates have been converted to the Christian era according to Swami-Kannu Pillai's *Indian Ephemeris.*

This translation was made by me many years ago for my own use, and it was laid aside when my *History of Aurangzib* in 5 volumes was completed. On the Royal Asiatic Society of Bengal agreeing to print it and thus fill a long-standing gap of 51 years in the authentic sources of Mughal Indian history available in English, my translation was compared word for word with the original, revised, and in several places expanded by the addition of phrases and sentences from the original which had been omitted in my rather too utilitarian first version. Every word of the Persian text which I now consider to be significant and necessary for bringing out the author's tone and spirit, has been restored.

In this work of revision I have been very greatly helped by Professor Nirod Bhusan Roy, M.A., whom the Society has appointed to assist me in preparing the copy and seeing this (and several other books planned by the Society) through the press. He has gone through my translation with meticulous care and persistently drawn my attention to every point where he thought it better to modify my former wording or amplify a passage in order to make it correspond more closely to the original author's intentions. After discussion, I have in most cases accepted his view and made the change. After the press-copy had been thus prepared and a portion actually set in type, I was supplied, through the courtesy of Khan Sahib Sayyid

Hasan Askari, M.A. (Professor, Patna College), with an old manuscript of the Persian original, transcribed about 1750, from the Waqf Library of Diwān Nasir Ali (in Khujwān, Arrah district), which furnishes a much more correct text than the printed Bibliotheca Indica edition and fills up certain serious gaps in the latter not noticed when the text was printed. My English translation has been revised a second time by collating it with this newly found manuscript under Professor N. B. Roy's care, and a great improvement effected. Most of the emendations I have made in the printed Persian text from this manuscript and other authentic sources, are indicated by inserting in the body of the book the word *Cor* within brackets, without burdening the pages with a footnote on every variant reading. Many other obvious errors of the printed text also have been silently corrected. For this enhancement of the usefulness of the translation, the reader's gratitude is due to Professor Roy.

Owing to the present difficulty of printing, the translation has been printed with a bare minimum of the most necessary diacritical marks, namely ā, é, and the apostrophe for *'ain*. But it has been considered unnecessary to insert these marks in the case of words which occur most frequently, or continue the system to the end of the book after following the rules for several pages. Nor have I been able to maintain uniformity in the spelling of proper names throughout such a long book full of such names. This is particularly the case with regard to the final *h*.

The elaborate index has been prepared by Professor Nirod Bhusan Roy and ought to prove very helpful to the reader by reason of its accumulation of information and methodical arrangement. The glossary of obscure words has been added by me.

Jadunath Sarkar
Oct. 1947

ERRATA

P. 32, l. 9	*for* Sayyid	*read* Sa'id
,, 66, l. 10	,, ,,	,, ,,
,, 33, l. 26	,, Islām	,, Āslam
,, 37, l. 43	,, Khan and Mulla	,, Khan, Mulla
,, 39, l. 19	,, intetrviewed	,, interviewed
,, 49, l. 24	,, Saifullah	,, Saifuddin [as on p. 84 of text]
,, 67, l. 14-15	,, a silver sword-belt and *baz*	,, a sword-belt decorated with silver filigree work [*cor.*]
,, 78, l. 27	, jalau	,, jilau
,, 95, l. 7	,, Ali Tabār	,, Ala Tabār
,, 117, l. 20	,, Fāzil	,, Fazāil [*cor.*]
,, 158, l. 34	*after Qamruddin insert* Khan gained the title of Mukhtar Khan and Qamruddin,	
,, 163, l. 28	*for* Nur-ul-bahar	*read* Nur-ul-dahar
,, 207, l. 39	,, Āsam	,, Āsad
,, 247, l. 34	,, langar	,, langri
,, 250, l. 39	,, *mashk* and *matwala*	,, and *mashk*
,, 278, l. 20	,, Islampur	,, Islampuri
,, 307, l. 6	,, Mirza	,, Mirza Khan

,, 319, cancel footnote and insert—

> *Māqabl āyāt-khāndan ayti bud* [Ms. reads *āst*] *manzil dar shān-i-ān barguzidah-i-ruzgār.* The word *manzil* means a halting-place in a journey, or the point at which the reading of a section of the *Qurān* stopped on a particular day. Does the variant adopted in the printed text mean that Shāh 'Ālam at first trained himself by duly chanting only one verse a day, and after he had memorized the whole he used to recite whole sections?

For *Sakkhar* read *Sagar,* on pp. 207, 208, 218, 220, and 294.

MAĀSIR-I-'ĀLAMGIRI

CHAPTER I

WAR OF SUCCESSION BEGINS

[2] On the 6th Sept 1657/7th Zil H ; 1067 A H the Emperor Shāh Jahān, who will henceforth be designated *'Ala Hazrat*,—fell ill at Delhi, [3] and had to give up the work of government His eldest son, Dārā Shukoh, seizing the opportunity, closed the roads of the arrival of news from the provinces, and this led to great disorder in the Empire, (so that) Murād Bakhsh, the fourth son of the Emperor, and Subahdār of Gujrat, crowned himself (there), and Shāh Shuj'ā, the Emperor's second son, did the same thing in Bengal, and advanced with his army on Patna Dārā Shukoh, in his fear of Aurangzib's power, (had) tried to alienate Shāh Jahān's mind from him, and by means of various lies induced him to recall to Court the army previously sent to reinforce Aurangzib And with the design that in the Emperor's lifetime and under his protection he would get rid of Shuj'ā and Murād Bakhsh and then with peace of mind turn to the affairs of the Deccan and the removal of Aurangzib, Dārā conveyed the Emperor to Agra when his disease was at its worst He sent Raja Jai Singh with imperial and his own troops under the command of his eldest son Sulaimān Shukoh against Shuj'ā. At the same time Raja Jaswant Singh,—who being related to Shāh Jahān's mother, was greatly trusted and given the title of Mahārāja, and was one of the chief Rajas of Hindustan, was sent with a large army towards Mālwa on the way to the Deccan, in order to bar the road A separate force under Qāsim Khan was appointed to accompany the Maharaja to Ujjain, and, [4] if found politic, to start against Murād Bakhsh Through Dārā Shukoh's magic arts the Emperor's mind

---

* The *figures* within square brackets indicate the page-numbers of the Persian text as printed in the Bibliotheca Indica Series, edited by Aghā Ahmad 'Ali, Calcutta, 1871 A D All *words* within square brackets have been added by the translator, Sir Jadunath Sarkar, who has silently corrected the misprints in the text, especially about proper names,

was somewhat estranged from Aurangzib. He ordered 'Isa Beg, Aurangzib's agent (at Court), to be imprisoned for no offence, and confiscated his property; but after a time realising the shamefulness of this act released him. Among the villainous ways of Dārā Shukoh—what became the chief cause of Aurangzib's wrath was the inclination of his heart to the principles (or practices) of the Hindus and the spreading of disregard of Islamic religious prohibitions (*Ibahāt* and *Ilhād*). Therefore, considering it necessary to defend the faith and the State, Āurangzib determined to go to Shāh Jahān and to carry (with himself) Murād Bakhsh, who after doing some foolish acts, had at this time submissively begged the patronage of Aurangzib. As it was probable that Jaswant Singh and Qāsim Khan would fight, Aurangzib prudently collected the means of war, and on Monday, the 25th January, 1658/1st Jamad A., 1068 A.H., started from Aurangabād towards Burhānpur, where he arrived on Thursday, the 18th February/25th Jamad A., and whence he sent a letter to Shāh Jahān (begging permission) to visit him in his illness. No reply came in one month, but alarming news continued to arrive. Jaswant, at the instigation of Dārā Shukoh, displayed aggression. On the 20th March/25th Jamad S., Aurangzib started for Agra, and on Wednesday, the 14th April/21st Rajab, when marching from Dipalpur [5] he met on the way Murād Bakhsh, who had come from Ahmadābād to see him. Aurangzib halted at Dharmātpur (situated 7 *kos* from Ujjain), one *kos* off from which village Jaswant Singh and Qāsim Khan had encamped for the purpose of fighting. The enemy stepped beyond their limits and prepared for fight. On Thursday, the 15th April 1658/22nd Rajab, Aurangzib marshalled his army in battle order, and beat his drums for battle. Jaswant, too, drew up his troops and rode (out) to fight, and the two armies clashed together. Though the Hindus were very numerous they were slaughtered, and at last Jaswant took to flight with a small party towards his 'home' Marwar.

[6] Qāsim Khan and other imperial soldiers considered it fortunate to fly with their lives from such destruction. Aurangzib gained the victory and captured all the property of the enemy. At the Prince's order nearly six thousand dead bodies of the enemy were counted.

On Sunday the 23rd May 1658/1st Ramzan, Aurangzib crossed the Chambal and heard that Dārā

Shukoh had advanced from Dholpur. On Friday, the 28th May/6th Ramzan, he arrived near the army of Dārā and halted at a distance of 1½ *kos*. Dārā on horseback advanced that day a little in front of his camp, but not daring to step further in his fear of Aurangzib, he tormented his soldiers, who were all fully armed, by keeping them all the day in the burning wind. Vast numbers perished of excessive hunger and thirst. At the end of the day he retired to his place. The following day, Aurangzib ordered his army to advance towards Agra. That morning, the 29th May 1658/7th Ramzan, Dārā drew up his army on the ground he had taken up the day before and advanced against the army of Aurangzib. A violent battle followed; it began with the roar of guns and muskets on both sides; and the fire of slaughter blazed forth. Rustam Khan, Rao Chhatra Sāl, Raja Rāi Singh Rāthor and other chiefs of Dārā's army were slain, and although [7] he still had a (large) body of troops with himself, his firmness was shaken; he descended from his elephant and mounted his horse. At this untimely move on his part his soldiers were disturbed in mind and took to flight. The breeze of victory blew on Aurangzib's banners. One of the wonderful signs of Aurangzib's fortune was this, that, while so many commanders of Dārā Shukoh were slain that the like was not seen in any other battle,—not to speak of his losses in common soldiers—not one of the leaders of the victorious army perished except 'Āzam Khan *alias* Multafat Khan, who died after the victory from the violence of the (hot) wind.

Dārā after his flight arrived at his house in Agra in the evening with his son and a few servants, and after staying for three *prahars* (quarters) of the night took the road to Delhi. Aurangzib, after rendering thanks to the Giver of Victory, reached the enemy's camp, and stayed in the tent of Dārā Shukoh, which was standing. Next day the army marched to Samugarh. This day he sent a humble letter of apology to Shāh Jahān, excusing himself for the occurrence of the battle. On Tuesday the 1st June/10th Ramzan, he reached the garden of Nurmanzil situated in Agra. Shāh Jahān sent a reply to the letter, and on the day following presented to him a sword [8] named Alamgir. The high grandees and other imperial officers came in troops to the Court of Aurangzib in hope (of his patronage) and each received favours suited to his rank. On Friday, the 11th

June/20th Ramzan he entered the city and occupied Dārā Shukoh's palace. On the 12th June/21st Ramzan he learnt that Dārā Shukoh had arrived at Delhi on the 5th June/14th Ramzan. Although Aurangzib's aim was to see Shāh Jahān, yet Dārā had by secret letters filled the Emperor's mind with distrust of Aurangzib. Therefore he gave up his design and on Sunday the 13th June/22nd Ramzan started for Delhi. On Tuesday, the 15th June/24th Ramzan, he received at Ghātsāmi the news of Dārā's flight from Delhi. On the 21st June/30th Ramzan, Bahadur Khan was appointed to pursue Dārā. As Murād Bakhsh was violently preparing for rebellion and was waiting for an opportunity to carry out his futile plans, Aurangzib made him a prisoner at Mathurā, on Wednesday the 23rd June/2nd Shawwal, and thus freed the people from mischief and tumult; the captive was sent to the fort of Delhi under Shaikh Mir. On learning that Dārā Shukoh had started for Lahore, Aurangzib decided to set out for the Panjāb.

FIRST CORONATION

As astrologers indicated Wednesday the 21st July/1st Zil Q., as an auspicious day for the accession, [9] and no time was left to go to Delhi and make preparations for the ceremony, Aurangzib stayed for a few hours in the garden of Aghrābād [=Shālamār], and sat on the throne at the above-mentioned auspicious time. The presents which were made to the Princes, the high grandees, the mansabdārs and other officers, are beyond numbering. 'Abdur Rashid Tatawi found the date of accession in the Quranic text, *Ati'u-allah,* &c.

PURSUIT OF DĀRĀ

As this coronation ceremony was decided to be short, many of the rites of accession were put off to the second (year's) ceremony, e.g., reading the *khutba,* stamping coins, and settling the Emperor's title were not carried out on this occasion but kept in abeyance.

Before the accession, an army was sent under Khalil-ullah Khan to join Bahādur Khan, reach the Satlej, and arrange for crossing that river. Aurangzib now learnt that Sulaimān Shukoh had hastened towards Hardwār from the other side of the Ganges river, intending to join his father by the road of Sahāranpur. Aurangzib appointed Amirul-umārā *alias* Shāista Khan and Shaikh Mir and other chiefs to engage in the expedition against him. On Thursday, the 22nd July/2nd Zil Q., [10] he ordered his tents to be pitched outside, for the march to the Panjāb. On Wednesday, the 4th August/15th Zil Q., a letter was received from Bahādur Khan announcing the crossing of the Satlej by the imperial army and the flight of Dara's men. At this time Sulaimān Shukoh fled into the hills of Kashmir and so the Emperor ordered the force sent against him to return.

Dārā after reaching Lahore collected nearly 20,000 troopers, and on hearing the news of Bahādur Khan and Khalillullah Khan's crossing the Satlej, he posted a large force under Dāud Khan on the Biās river to bar their way, and sent Sipihr Shukoh after him. Thereupon the Emperor wisely ordered Raja Jai Singh and a few other chiefs to join the first detachment. Dārā learning of it found that he could not resist, and started from Lahore towards Multān. At this time Maharaja Jaswant Singh came from his country and rubbed his forehead in humility and shame at the threshold of the Court. The Emperor graciously pardoned his faults, showed him imperial favours and sent him to Delhi.

On Sunday, the 12th Sept./24th Zil. H., the Emperor came to know from Khalilullah Khan and other nobles at Haibatpuri Pati that Dārā Shukoh had come out of Lahore with adequate equipment and was intending to fight the imperial forces, and that on seeing this the imperial officers had slackened their pursuit. Thereupon, the Emperor sent Prince 'Azam from this station, with the unnecessary soldiers and baggage [11] to Lahore, while he himself decided to make a forced march. When he learnt that Dārā Shukoh, without standing firmly even in Multān, had started for Bhakkar and that many of his followers had left him, and the causes of his trouble were on the increase, the Emperor gave up his forced march and travelled by easy stages to Multān, without halting anywhere. Although Saf Shikan Khan had left Multān on Wednesday, the 22nd Sept./4th Muharram, in pursuit of Dārā, yet for greater caution Shaikh Mir too was sent with 9,000 troopers on the same errand. At this time the Emperor heard that his brother Shāh Shuj'ā to whom he had been strongly attached before his accession, had come out of Bengal with hostile intentions.

Hence Aurangzib set out from Multān on Thursday the 30th Sept./12th Muharram, and arrived in Delhi fort on Saturday, the 20th Nov./4th Rabi. A., News of Shuj'ā's disturbance came in succession. The Emperor had intended to overlook (Shuj'ā's conduct) as far as possible, but when Shuj'ā audaciously advanced to the frontier of Benares, he determined to fight. The Emperor had no help but to order Prince Muhammad Sultān to march out of Agra in that direction on Saturday, the 4th Dec./18th Rabi. A. As it was repeatedly learnt that Shāh Shuj'ā wished to advance beyond the limits of Benares, the Emperor considered it politic to go to the hunting-lodge of Soron and wait for the news about Shuj'ā, so that if he returned towards Patna the Emperor would recall his deputed troops, otherwise he would fully engage in the expedition against him. [12]

Therefore, on Thursday the 2nd Dec. 1658/16th Rabi. A., he left Delhi. On the 6th/20th Rabi. A., news came that the deputed troops had reached Etawah on the 5th. The Emperor advanced hunting and reached Soron on Sunday, 19th Dec./3rd Rabi. S. As his design was to make a peaceful end to the affair of Shuj'ā, he sent him a letter full of good counsels to learn the details of his intentions. But when he learnt for certain that gentleness and mercy would be thrown away on him, he set out from Soron on Tuesday the 21st Dec./5th Rabi. S., to put him down. Order was sent to Muhammad Sultān and the detachment not to force an encounter but wait for junction with the Emperor.

On Sunday the 2nd January, 1659/17th Rabi. S., the imperial tents were pitched outside the village of Korra, where Prince Muhammad Sultān was staying with the advanced detachment, and four *kos* from which Shuj'ā was waiting. Mu'azzam Khan, who had been summoned by command from Khandesh, arrived in the imperial camp on this day.

BATTLE WITH SHAH SHUJ'Ā AT KHAJWA

Shuj'ā, planting his artillery in front, wished to marshal his ranks in battle array. On Tuesday, the 4th January/19th Rabi. S., the third day following the Emperor's arrival at Korra, it was ordered that the artillery should not be carried in front but made to fire opposite the army of Shuj'ā, and the imperial army should bravely engage in battle. [13] At the imperial order, waves upon waves of troops rushed forward, while nearly 90,000 horsemen prepared themselves for action. It was ordered that the Emperor's camp and tents should remain where they were.

That day Shuj'ā, too was engaged in marshalling his troops. After four *gharis* of the day had passed, the Emperor traversed the distance separating (his camp) from Shuj'ā's, and when three *prahars* had passed he drew up his ranks a mile from Shuj'ā's army. Shuj'ā without advancing, sent some pieces of cannon in front and there was a hot fight till nightfall, when Shuj'ā withdrew his artillery. After taking steps for precaution and watchfulness, strengthening the entrenchments, and urging his troops to be on the alert, the Emperor retired to a small pavilion, pitched on the battle-field.

Towards the end of that night an event happened which short-sighted men regarded as a catastrophe, and which caused a dispersion in the imperial army. It was as follows. The wicked Maharaja Jaswant Singh, who outwardly professed obedience but at heart sought for some occasion for mischief, at the very time when the Emperor had given him the command of the right wing, planned to take to flight and informed Shuj'ā of his design. At the end of the night, he turned back with all his own troops and another body of Rajputs, and first plundered the camp of Muhammad Sultān which was in his way; great oppression [14] was committed on the camp; alarming news spread; mischievous people laid hands on the imperial effects and the property of the nobles and soldiers. When the Emperor heard of it, he did not stir from his place. Although nearly half of his army had dispersed, yet the Emperor relying on Providence did not pay any heed to his smallness of number, but set out for the battle-field. This day Shuj'ā changed the formation he had adopted the day before, and drew up his troops in another manner.

The firing of rockets, guns and muskets began between the two sides. This day many serious reverses befell the imperial army; the Emperor had not more than 2,000 cavalry round himself, yet in whatever side he turned his face or made a firm stand, the damage was repaired. And at the sight of his intrepidity and valour, his Bahrām-like soldiers by their heroic exertions made such a terrible destruction of their enemy that Shuj'ā's ranks were broken. He fled from the field, and the imperialists gained this wonderful victory solely through the aid of Heaven and not through their own efforts. [15]

The Emperor thanked the Giver of Victories, and, passing with his army through the camp of Shuj‘ā which was near the tank of Khajwa, halted. That very day he sent Prince Muhammad Sultān from the place in pursuit of Shuj‘ā, and himself stayed there till Tuesday, 11th January/26th Rabi. S. On Wednesday, the 12th he marched from the environs of Khajwa and on Friday the 14th/29th Rabi. S., he came to the river Ganges. At that stage Mu'azzam Khan and other great nobles were deputed to join Prince Muhammad Sultān in pursuing Shuj‘ā.

PURSUIT OF DĀRĀ SHUKOH CONTINUED

I shall now write about the army detached under Shaikh Mir and Saf Shikan Khan to pursue Dārā. On Wednesday, the 22nd Sept./4th Muharram Saf Shikan Khan hastened from Multān in pursuit of Dārā, crossed the Biās river and heard that Dārā had gone further on. The Khan, therefore, advanced and after a few days' halt in expectation of Shaikh Mir and Dilir Khan was joined by their army. News came that Dārā had crossed the river at Bhakkar and halted at Sakkar. The imperial officers thought it best that Shaikh Mir and Dilir Khan should cross the river with their soldiers and march along the other bank towards Sakkar, while Saf Shikan with his troops should hasten along this side towards Bhakkar, so that the enemy might be crushed between the two sides.

Next day according to the plan Saf Shikan Khan [16] parted from Shaikh Mir and started for Bhakkar. Shaikh Mir crossed the river in two days and arrived within 12 *kos* of Sakkar on Saturday, the 23rd Oct./5th Safar, his army reaching Sakkar on the 24th. Three days before this Saf Shikan Khan had arrived at Bhakkar but had marched away the day before Shaikh Mir's arrival. It was found that Dārā had gone forward on the 18th Oct./30th Muharram, leaving his heavy baggage in the fort of Bhakkar, the rest of his treasures and property were in boats while he himself was travelling through the jungles. Dāud Khan and other leaders among his followers having deserted him, (Dārā) wanted to go from Sakkar towards Qandāhār, but at the desertion of his followers and the refusal of his women he had started for Tatta. Saf Shikan Khan left Āghar Khan with a force at Bhakkar to press the siege hard and himself went towards Siwistān. A letter of Muhammad Sālih Tarkhān, qiladār of the place, now reached him saying that Dārā had come within 5 *kos* of the fort, and that Saf Shikan Khan should come up quickly and bar the path of his treasure boats. The Khan sent his relation Muhammad Ma'sum in advance with a force, to pass beyond Dārā's boats and entrench on the bank of the river. He himself marched at night, passed 3 *kos* from the front of Dārā's army, waited for the enemy's boats, and wished to cross the river and attack the enemy. As Dārā's boats advanced and opposed the arrival of the boats accompanying Saf Shikan, he sent a message to Muhammad Sālih to send boats from that side and also oppose Dārā. As Muhammad Sālih was not divinely guided to carry out this order, he sent to say that on this side the water ([17] was waist-deep, and so the boats would pass by the other side; therefore Saf Shikan Khan did not cross over. Next day it became evident from the dust-cloud on the other side that Dārā was marching and removing his boats by that side. Thus a splendid victory was frustrated through the duplicity of Muhammad Sālih.

In short, Dārā crossed the low hill of Siwistān, and Saf Shikan Khan marched two stages in pursuit of him on that very side of the river. Shaikh Mir arriving on the other bank sent a message saying that it was better that Saf Shikan Khan should cross the river and come over to his side, so that the two might carry on the pursuit together. Therefore Saf Shikan Khan crossed the river, and learnt that Dārā had reached Tatta and intended to go to Gujrāt. Saf Shikan Khan hastening before Shaikh Mir came within one *kos* of the river at Tatta, but Dārā marched away towards Gujrāt from the other bank of the river. Saf Shikan Khan crossed the river, by building a bridge in seven days.

Meantime an order was sent to Shaikh Mir, Dilir Khan, and Saf Shikan Khan to give up the pursuit and return to the Emperor. When the Emperor heard of Dārā's going to Gujrāt, he returned from Allahabad. On Saturday, the 15th January, 1659/1st Jamad. A., while encamped on the bank of the Ganges he learnt from Muhammad Sultān's despatches of the capture of Allahabad. As it was necessary to punish Jaswant Singh, who wanted to join Dārā, he sent Muhammad Āmin Khan, Mir Bakhshi, with 9,000 cavalry from Ghātampur on the 16th January/2nd Jamad. A., to destroy him.

As the Emperor wished [18] to march without delay for the punishment of Jaswant Singh and the suppression of Dārā, he did not go to Agra but on Friday, the 4th February/21st Jamad. A., started from the garden of Nur Manzil towards Ajmir. On the 8th/25th Jamad. A., when he marched out of the hunting-lodge of Rupbās, Shaikh Mir and Dilir Khan, having returned from the pursuit of Dārā, joined the Emperor.

As the return of the army was the cause of Dārā's enjoying repose, he stepped into the wilderness and reached Cutch and thence Gujrāt. Shāh Nawāz Khan Safavi, the father of the late imperial consort Dilras Bānu Begam, who had been appointed by the Emperor Subahdār of this province, joined Dārā out of lack of spirit. Dārā after passing one month and seven days in Gujrāt, gathered together 22,000 cavalry, issued from it on Monday, the 14th February/1st Jamad. S., and receiving on the way Jaswant Singh's letters inviting him to go to Ajmir, was emboldened to advance. On Sunday, the 20th February/7th Jamad S., the Emperor encamped near Hindáun; and no halt was made from here to the village of Tuda. On Monday the 28th February/15th Jamad. S., Āmir Khan, brother of Shaikh Mir, who had, by order, taken Murād Bakhsh from Delhi fort to Gwalior, joined the Emperor.

SECOND BATTLE WITH DĀRĀ AND HIS FLIGHT

Dārā Shukoh after reaching Ajmir got ready for battle. On Wednesday, the 9th March/24th Jamad. S., the Emperor encamped 6 *kos* from the tank of Rāmeshwar, [19] and there ordered the marshalling of his army for battle. Dārā strengthened by the hope of the arrival of Jaswant Singh, acted boldly. Just then Raja Jai Singh, taking pity on the sinful Jaswant Singh and getting his offences pardoned through the Emperor's graciousness, wrote him a letter giving him the glad news of his being pardoned and dissuading him from his wish to join Dārā. When he got it, he turned back from a distance of 20 *kos* from Jodhpur. Dārā urged him to come and sent his son Sipihr Shukoh to him, but to no effect. Meantime the imperial army had arrived near Ājmir; Dārā was therefore, compelled to set his heart on battle, but as he was not strong enough to fight an open battle with the imperial army, he entrenched the hill-pass of Ajmir across its breadth. The imperial army stayed at Deorāi, 3 *kos* from Ajmir, which was at a short distance from Dārā's station.

Next day, the imperial army advanced half a *kos* and halted. The Emperor ordered his artillery to be carried forward to play upon the enemy. The enemy returned the fire with cannon and musket.

That day and night and up to the 3rd *prahar* (quarter) of the next day, the flame of battle raged between the two sides. Shāh Nawāz Khan Safavi, Muhāmmad Sharif, [20] Mir Bakhshi of Dārā Shukoh, and other leaders of his army were slain. Among the imperialists, Shaikh Mir fell shot through the chest with a musket-ball. But Mir Hāshim, a fellow-clansman of Shaikh Mir, who sat behind him on the *howdah* of his elephant, very carefully propped him up in his arms, so that none knew of his death till the end of the battle. Dārā beholding the heroic exertions of the imperialists, took to flight inspite of his trenches being still intact, and turned towards Gujrāt. Such a crowning victory adorned the country and the people. The Emperor on hearing of it thanked God, the true Giver of Victories.

It is well-known that few kings had to fight so many royal battles and lordly encounters in such a period, as this Emperor had to do with powerful enemies in a single year. But through God's grace he achieved victory everywhere by dint of his strong arm and sharp sword. But inspite of his great valour and activity, so great was his humility that he never ascribed these victories to his own powers, but always spoke of them as miracles wrought by God, and ever rendered his thanks to the Creator for this great good fortune by adoration of Allah, the establishment of the Holy Law of the Prophet, and the extinction of all traces of illegal and prohibited practices. [21] Inspite of his splendour and power, not for a moment did he yield up his body to repose or slackness, but added a lustre to the throne by his constant vigilance, devotion to God, dispensation of justice, promotion of the public happiness, and attention to the condition of the peasantry and the soldiery and the rules of justice and equity. I hope that the spiritual and material worlds may always be resplendent through the rule of this religious king.

Next day, Monday, the 14th March 1659/29th Jamad S., he sent Raja Jai Singh and Bahādur Khan to pursue Dārā, and being free from anxiety on the score of

Dārā, set out on Monday, the 18th March/4th Rajab on return from Ajmir.

A despatch from Prince Muhammad Sultān brought the news that Shāh Shuj'ā had halted for a few days in Mungir wishing to reside there for some time, but through fear of the approach of the imperial army had fled towards Jahāngirnagar, and Mu'azzam Khan had entered the fort of Mungir. On Thursday, the 7th April/24th Rajab, the Emperor reached Fathpur, and on Tuesday, the 19th April/6th Shaban he started for Delhi. He learnt from Muhammad Sultān's despatches that Shāh Shuj'ā, who had gone to Rājmahal before this, had removed his baggage to boats when the imperial army approached that city, and Rājmahal, too, was occupied by the imperialists.

News came that Dārā after leaving Ajmir had gone to Gujrāt [=Ahmadabad] and wished to seize it a second time, but Sardār Khan, one of the officers of the local reinforcements [22] opposed him, and Dārā, giving up the desire of capturing the city, fled for refuge to Kanhji Kuli. On Monday the 2nd May, the Emperor reached the palace of Khizirābād. A halt of eleven days was made here, and on Thursday the 12th May/29th Shaban, he entered the Delhi fort.

CHAPTER II

SECOND CORONATION, MAY 1659

At the first auspicious coronation celebrations had been greatly curtailed on account of the expedition into the Panjab and also want of leisure, the reading of the *khutba,* the stamping of coins, and the proclamation of the Emperor's title had been postponed. Now that the work of conquest had been completed, he ordered his officers to make preparations for the coronation celebrations, and they did their best. On Sunday, 5th June 1659/24th Ramzan, when the Emperor was 40 years 7 months and 13 days (solar) or 41 years 10 months and 2 days (lunar) old, he sat on the throne. . . .

[23] An eloquent *khātib* ascended the pulpit and read an impressive *khutbah,* and he was rewarded to his heart's content. Such quantities of gold and silver coins were distributed in the name of the Emperor that the wide bag of hope was filled by picking them up. The courtiers bowed to do honour, and sang the praises of and prayed for the Emperor. The doors of imperial treasuries were opened to all people; and the expectations of all, young and old, were fulfilled.

In former times the sacred Quranic *credo* (*Kalma*) used to be stamped on gold and silver coins, and such coins were constantly touched with the hands and feet of men; Aurangzib said that it would be better to stamp some other words on coins. At this time Mir 'Abdul Bāqi, surnamed *Suhbāi,* showed the following couplet of his own composition :—

"King Aurangzib 'Ālamgir
Stamped coins, in the world, like the bright
full moon."

The Emperor liked it and ordered that one face of mohars and rupees should be stamped with this verse and the other with the name of the mint-city and the year of accession (in which they would be coined).

The Emperor's title on the grand seal was ordered to be engraved as Abul Zafar Muhi-ud-din Muhammad Aurangzib Bahādur 'Ālamgir Pādishāh Ghāzi. It was ordered that edicts should be issued announcing the accession and the happy news [24] of protection and happiness to all parts of the Empire. The Emperor with openhanded liberality gave grand rewards to the princes, begams and imperial handmaids; every one of the nobles and faithful servants received promotion and title according to his rank; pious and religious men, poets, musicians and singers received suitable rewards and gifts.

The Emperor ordered that these entertainments should continue on the same scale up to Friday, the 19th August/10th Zil H., (the date of Id-uz-buha) and be joined to the latter, so that during the whole period the desires of the people might be gratified and their long-standing hopes realised. Mullā Shāh of Badakshān found the date of the accession in the chronogram—*Zill-al-Haq*, "The Shadow of Truth".

Another scholar found the date in *Pādishāh-i-mulk-i-haft-iqlim*, and a third in *Zeb-i-āurang wa tāj-i-pādishāhān*. Mullā 'Azizullah, son of Mullā Taqi of Isfahān [25] found the chronogram in the words of God, *Innāl-mulk-lilla yutiyia man yishshā*.

As the Emperor's (first) victories were gained in the month of Ramzan, he ordered that in official records the first day of this month should be counted as the commencement of every year of his reign.

As the preceding sovereigns, following the practice of Jamshid and Naushirwān, used to regard the first day of the month of Farwardi as a day of great rejoicing and to celebrate it with festivity, this pious faith-protecting Emperor ordered that, in the place of the (Persian) new year's (*nauroz*) celebration, an imperial festivity should be held every year in the month of Ramzan and continued to the *Id-ul-fitr* (on the 1st Shawwāl), and that this celebration should be called the *nishāt-āfroz jashan*.

In order to put down forbidden practices and vices, Mullā 'Auz Wajih, the chief of the learned men, was appointed Censor, and instead of an annual stipend of 15,000 rupees he was given the *mansab* of a *hazāri* (100 tr.) Thank God that even now, owing to the piety of the Emperor, the whole of Hindustan is free from the filth of innovation and heresy.

At this time the Emperor learnt from the news-letter of Bengal that Prince Muhammad Sultān who had been deputed with Mu'azzam Khan to crush Shuj'ā, had;

through the instigation of the latter, gone away on Wednesday the 8th June 1659/27th Ramzan with a few servants by boat with the intention of joining Shuj'ā and was showing hostility to the imperial cause.

FATE OF DĀRĀ SHUKOH

On Saturday the 2nd July/21st Shawwal, news came to Court of the capture of Dārā Shukoh with his son Sipihr Shukoh, on Friday the 10th June/29th Ramzan by Malik Jiwan, the zamindar of Dādar and [26] of the hastening of Bahādur Khan on receipt of the letter of the said Malik and his taking over charge of both the prisoners. The Amir-ul-umārā was appointed Subahdār of the Deccan *vice* Prince Muhammad Mu'azzam, 'Aqidat Khan was made commandant of Daulatābād *vice* 'Āqil Khan, who with Wazir Khan was ordered to come to Court in the company of the prince. Saturday, the 2nd July, 1659/21st Shawwal, was the 6th (solar) birthday of prince Muhammad 'Azam. He was presented with a jewelled *sarpech,* a dagger with a pearl-set strap, and five horses. Malik Jiwan was rewarded for Dārā's capture by a robe of honour being sent him, and the rank of a *hazāri* (200 tr.) and the title of Bakhtiār Khan being conferred on him. Qābil Khan Munshi wanted to retire to seclusion; he was given an annual stipend of 5,000 rupees. Raja Rājrup was sent to the hills of Srinagar, to hold before Prithvipat, the zamindar of that place, hopes and fears and thus induce him to surrender Sulaimān Shukoh. News came from Bengal that Shah Shuj'ā while going from Ākbarnagar to Tānda had suspected from Ālawardi Khan's actions a wish to desert him, and had therefore slain him and his son Saifullah. At this time an order was issued to build a *Shir Hāji* wall around the fort of Agra, and in three years the work was completed under the supervision of 'Itibār Khan.

On Tuesday, the 2nd August/23rd Zil.Q., took place the ceremony of weighing the Emperor on his 42nd lunar birthday; gold of the Emperor's weight was distributed among the poor; and all men, far and near, were rendered happy by the granting of robes, promotion of rank, and the gift of jewels, horses, and elephants.

[27] At this time Bahādur Khan brought Dāra Shukoh to the exalted Court. He was kept in the palace of Khizirābād. As it was necessary for various reasons to

remove the dust of his life from the plain of the world of the living, on the night of Tuesday, the 30th August/21st Zil.H., the lamp of his life was quenched, and he was buried in Humāyun's tomb. Saif Khan was ordered to convey Sipihr Shukoh to the fort of Gwalior, and then return to Agra and be its Subahdar. Raja Jai Singh who had lagged behind Bahādur Khan arrived at Court and was honoured with favours. As owing to their many forced marches the Raja and Bahādur Khan had lost many horses, the Emperor graviously presented the Raja with 200 and the Khan with 100 horses.

At this time, according to his usual generosity the collection of road-toll (*rāhdāri*) on the transit of grains and other articles was abolished for ever. On this account the Crown-lands made a sacrifice to the amount of 25 lakhs of rupees a year; and what was given up for the whole Empire cannot be imagined.

At this time Zulfiqār Khan Qarāmānlu died. The Emperor graciously consoled his son Āsad Khan and his son-in-law Nāmdār Khan by the grant of robes of honour. Bakhtiār Khan zamindar of Dādar was sent back to his estate. Mu'azzam Khan during his service under Qutb-ul-mulk had conquered the country of Karnātik; one of its strong forts, Kanji Kota, (Gandi Kota) [28] was held by the men of the Khan, but Qutb-ul-mulk coveted it. Mir Ahmad Khwāfi with the title of Mustafa Khan was sent to govern this country. News came from the province of Kabul that Sherullah [=Sher Beg], son of S'ādat Khan, grandson of Tarbiyat Khan deceased, had slain his father with a dagger. The Emperor ordered Mahābat Khan the nāzim to imprison him, and appointed Shamshir Khan as commandant of Kabul fort *vice* the murdered man.

Now came from Turān-land that love had changed into quarrel between Subhān Quli Khan, ruler of Balkh, and his brother Qāsim Sultān, who held command of the fort and that Subhān Quli Khan had got rid of him by clever devices.

The going over of Prince Muhammad Sultān to Shuj'ā was a great calamity to the army in Bengal. Though the Emperor felt reassured from Mu'azzam Khan's commanding the army, yet after the celebration of the weighing ceremony at the commencement of the 41st solar year of his life,—when the desires of the people were satiated with gifts—he set out as a measure of precaution with the army towards the bank of the Ganges on Sunday, the 13th Nov./8th Rabi.A. Raja Jai Singh was rewarded with one lakh of rupees: Raja Jaswant Singh was pardoned and restored to the title of Mahārāja.

Mir Ibrāhim, son of the late Mir Numān, was deputed to convey articles worth 6 lakhs and 30,000 rupees to the Sharifs of Mecca and Medina. On Thursday the 24th November/19th Rabi.A., the Emperor reached Garhmukteshwar. On Sunday the 27th/22nd Rabi. A., Prince Muhammad Mu'azzam with Wazir Khan having arrived from the Deccan, [29] had audience of the Emperor. On Tuesday the 20th December/15th Rabi.S., the Prince was married to a high-born lady of Khurāsan. On Saturday, the 7th January, 1660/4th Jamad.A., the Emperor marched from Garhmukteshwar towards Allahabad. At this time a despatch came from Mu'azzam Khan stating that he had crossed the Ganges, determined to end the war with Shuj'ā, while Shuj'ā had left Tānda which was his military base for Dacca. As the real object of this march of the Emperor was to strengthen the army of Bengal, and as his mind was quieted about that affair, he returned from [Mau] Shamsābād towards Delhi, the fort of which he entered on Monday, the 13th February, 1660/11th Jamad.S.

As it was the pious Emperor's intention to offer obligatory prayers in congregation, by the side of his retiring place, he laid the foundation of a small mosque of marble with carvings of plants and fret-work of various kinds. It was completed in the space of 5 years at an expenditure of one lakh and 60,000 rupees. 'Āqil Khan found the chronogram in the holy verse, *Innāl-masājid-illa falā tad'uāma'-allah.*

At this time news came from Bengal that prince Muhammad Sultān [30] at the time of Shuj'ā's flight to Dacca had repented of his conduct, come back to Akbarnagar in the same way that he had left it, and joined Islām Khan. Muhammad Mirak, macebearer, carried to him a robe with rarities from the Emperor, and Fidāi Khan was ordered to bring the Prince to Court. When he arrived near the capital, Álah Yār Khan went forward on Thursday, the 26th April, 1660/25th Shaban, and conveyed him by water to Salimgarh, his custody being given to Mu'atamad Khan.

CHAPTER III

THIRD YEAR OF REIGN: (1070 A.H.)

1st May, 1660—19th April, 1661

Now began the month of Ramzan. On Thursday, the 24th May, 1660/24th Ramzān, 1070 A.H., a charming and grand assembly was held, and joyous music was played.

On this auspicious day news came from Bengal that Shuj'ā, unable to make a stand at Dacca, had fled to Arakan, on Sunday, the 6th May/6th Ramzan and that Mu'azzam Khan had entered Dacca.

It had been ordered that the celebrations should begin on the 24th Ramzan, the date of the 2nd accession, and be carried on to the 'Id-ul-fitr. During this period all officers of the Court far and near, great and small, were [31] gratified with gifts by the Emperor. On the morning of the 'Id day the Emperor went to the mosque, and for two days after the 'Id the festivities and banquets were continued.

I shall now leave the account of the incidents of the Court, but this small book cannot hold even an abridged history of the occurrences of Bengal and the exertions of the imperial army, which had been deputed from Allahabad in January 1659 under the leadership of Prince Muhammad Sultān and Mu'azzam Khan in pursuit of Shuj'ā. Therefore I give up the attempt to describe this affair in detail. Suffice it to say that the march of the imperial army put Shuj'ā to such hard straits that none could hold with him save Sayyid 'Alam Bādah-kash, one of the Sayyids of Barha, and Sayyid Quli Uzbak with twelve Mughals and a few other men. After traversing calamitous regions, he reached the most villainous island of Arākan where he was entrapped in the snare of that land of infidels. His fate will be narrated in the proper place.

On Sunday, the 15th July, 1660/17th Zil. Q., the Emperor was weighed on his 44th lunar birthday. The people were rewarded. The princes received many kinds of favour. Mu'azzam Khan [32], the general in Bengal, was given the high titles of Khān-i-Khānān and Sipahsālār and the rank of a 7 *hazāri,* (7 *hazār doāspa* and *sehāspa*); a robe and a jewelled sword were sent to him in reward of his suppression of Shuj'ā. All kinds of reward and favour were bestowed on the commanders of the army sent to Bengal and on the viceroys and courtiers.

Najābat Khan who for some offences had incurred the imperial wrath, now got his pardon, came unarmed and was cherished with the gift of a sword. Mansur, brother of the Kāshghar chief 'Abdullah Khan and Mahdi, the brother's son of the Khan, who in fear of him had come to India by way of Badakhshān had audience and entered the imperial service. Presents from the Begam Sāhib and other begams and princes, consisting of jewels and jewelled ware, were presented to the Emperor and accepted. At the joyous 'Id-uz-zuha/7th August 1660, royal gifts were bestowed on vast numbers of people.

Rao Karn Bhurtia [of Bikanir], at Dārā's instigation had come home from the Deccan without permission. Āmir Khan was now sent to that quarter to take the frightened and humiliated man with himself if he begged pardon, otherwise to boldly extirpate him. When the Khan reached the frontier of Bikanir, the Rao came and waited on him and through the Khan's intercession was introduced to the forgiving Emperor and received gifts.

On Sunday, 2nd September/7th Muharram [33], Ikhlas Khan Khweshgi, who brought the treasures, jewels, other effects and women of Shuj'ā from Bengal, had audience. At this time the fort of Chākna situated in Konkan was conquered by the Amir-ul-umārā, viceroy of the Deccan, who had been sent out to put down the wicked Shivā and to capture his strong places, which he had seized owing to changes (decay) in the Bijapur administration and the slaughter of Āfzal, the Bijapuri leader. The Khan after properly punishing Shivā's men, established outposts in some places.

At this time took place the festivity of the weighing of the Emperor on his 43rd solar birthday and vast numbers of men were gratified with favours.

At this time Parenda was captured without a blow. Ghālib, the 'Adil Shāhi commandant of the fort, proposed to the Āmir-ul-umārā the surrender of the fort, with a view to entering the imperial service. The Āmirulumārā sent Mukhtār Khan as qil'adār and summoned Ghālib to himself, and on behalf of the Emperor gave him the rank of 4 *hazāri*, the title of Khan and other rewards. At this time Prithvi Singh, zamindār of the Srinagar hills, wrote a letter to Raja

Jai Singh begging pardon for his offences and offering to surrender Sulaimān Shukoh. At the Raja's request, his son Kumār Rām Singh was given leave to depart for bringing away Sulaimān, and he brought him to Delhi on Thursday, the 27th December, 1660/5th Jamad. A. He was kept in Salimgarh. On Tuesday, the 15th Jan. 1661/24th Jamad. A. Murtaza Khan conveyed him and prince Muhammad Sultān to Gwalior and entrusted them to Mu'atamad Khan, its qiladār.

When the Emperor learnt from the news-letters of the port of Surat [34] that Husain Pāshā, governor of Basra, had sent with his servant Qāsim Āqā, a letter of congratulation on his accession with horses of the Persian breed for the Emperor, an order was issued on Mustafa Khan collector (mutasaddi) of the port of Surat to give Qāsim Āqā 4,000 rupees for his expenses, and send him to the Court. At this time Ibrāhim Beg, envoy of Subhān Quli Khan ruler of Balkh, arrived at Court with a special letter and presents of Turān-land. As he had an old ailment, he died in a few days; his companions were given robes and 20,000 rupees and sent away.

As famine appeared in many places of the Empire, it was ordered that in addition to the permanent alms-houses ten more should be opened in Delhi and twelve others in the parganahs around it for the relief of the poor. Similar arrangements were made in Lahore. In addition to the amounts customarily spent in the months of Muharram, Rajab, Sha'bān, Ramzān, Rabi'-ul-awwal, and Zilhijj, this year double the amount was distributed. Orders were issued to the grandees down to commanders of a thousand that they should practise charity on their own account, and this alms-giving continued until the scarcity was turned into plenty.

CHAPTER IV

FOURTH YEAR OF THE REIGN. (1071 A.H.)

20 April 1661—9 April 1662

With the month of Ramzan [35] began the 4th year of the reign. The 24th of Ramzan was the anniversary of the Coronation, and last year the celebrations began on that date. But as owing to the fast the people had no liking for entertainment, the commencement of this celebration was postponed to the day of 'Id (1st Shawwal) and it was given a duration of ten days. A son was born to Prince Muhammad Mu'azzam, and named Sultān Muhammad Mui'zuddin.

The Emperor learnt that Budāq Beg, ambassador of Shāh 'Abbās II, king of Persia, had entered Multān on Friday, the 19th April, 1661/29th Shaban. Tarbiyat Khan, the Subahdār, had entertained him hospitably and presented him with 5,000 rupees and nine pieces of cloth. At Lahore Khalilullah Khan very hospitably treated him and gave him 20,000 rupees, an enamelled sword and dagger, and seven pieces of cloth from among the rarities of India. When he arrived at Sarāi Bāoli, food from the Emperor's own table was sent to him, and he was ordered to have audience on the 22nd May/3rd Shawwāl.

When the month of Shawwāl began, preparations were made for the royal festivities, as ordered before. The Emperor went to the 'Idgāh. (20th May 1661, 'Id-ul-fitr.) After his return from that place he engaged in gratifying the desires of the world : the Princes, nobles, Rajas, amirs, all received rewards and gifts beyond their desire.

Qāsim Āqā Rumi at interview presented five Arab horses as an offering from Husain Pāshā [36], and some horses and Georgian slaves also on his own account. He was favoured with a robe and 5,000 rupees. When Budāq Beg, envoy of Persia, came to the outskirts of Delhi, on the 3rd day from the 'Id, 22nd or 23rd May, Āsad Khan, Saif Khan and Multafat Khan conducted him from outside the city to the Presence. The interview was ordered to take place in the Hall of Audience. After bowing he presented the Shāh's letter of congratulation on the Emperor's accession. A robe, a turban-jewel (*jigha*), a jewelled dagger, a festive *ārgaja* with a gold cup and saucer, and betels with a gold betel-casket and tray, were presented to him. The mansion of Rustam Khan was assigned for his residence, and Mir 'Aziz Badakhshi as his care-taker. On Sunday the 26th May/7th Shawwāl, the Shāh's presents were offered to the Emperor; these included 66 horses, one round pearl weighing 37 carat, and these were valued in all at four lakh and 22,000 rupees.

On Saturday the 6th July, 1661/19th Zil. Q., the Emperor was weighed on his 45th lunar birthday, in the customary way; all people, great and small, at Court and in the provinces received presents. On Saturday, the 27th July/10th Zil, H., the 'Id-uz-zuha took place. The Emperor gave *conge* to the Persian envoy, with a reward of one lakh of rupees, robes, an enamelled dagger, with a pearl strap, a horse with gold saddle and bridle, an elephant with gold litter and silver trappings, a gold-embroidered housing, one *dariāi* elephant, and a *pālki* with gold trappings. It was stated that a reply to the Shāh's letter would be soon [37] sent. From first to last 5 lakhs of rupees were bestowed on the ambassador and 35 thousand rupees on his companions. 'Āqil Khan begged permission to go into retirement; an annual subsistence of 9,000 rupees was settled on him.

The Emperor was weighed on his 44th solar birthday, and conferred favours on all. Qāsim Āqā, an officer of Husain Pāshā, was sent back with 12,000 rupees and a robe, and his companions got 1,000 rupees; a jewelled sword was sent for the Pāshā.

On Sunday, the 17th November/4th Rabi. S., Khwāja Ahmad, son of Khwāja Khāwand Mahmud, envoy of 'Abdul, 'Aziz Khan the ruler of Bukhārā, arrived in the environs of Delhi. Saif Khan advancing conducted him to the Emperor. He presented a letter and gifts consisting of roadster Turki horses, large two-humped male and female camels and other things, one of which being a ruby worth 24,000 rupees. The Emperor graciously gave him that day a robe, a dagger with a pearl strap, 20,000 rupees and a mansion to stay in.

At this time the daughter of Raja Rup Singh, who had been converted to Islam and brought up in the imperial harem, was married to Prince Muhammad Mu'azzam. The details of this splendid ceremony can be learnt from the honoured book (*'Ālamgirnāmah*) * * * *

As Daud Khan the Subahdār of Patna, [38] had by hard fight conquered the country of Palāmau, a dependency of the province of Bihār, a robe of honour was sent to him. Sayyid Āmir Khan, was made Subahdār of Kabul *vice* Mahābat Khan.

On Monday, the 10th February/1st Rajab, Fāzil Khan came from Agra and presented some jewels and jewelled ware sent by Shāh Jahān. On the 11th news came that Khalilullah Khan, Subahdār of Lahore, who had arrived sick at Delhi, had died. The second day from his death, the Emperor visited the house of his surviving relatives, and favoured Mir Khan, Ruhullah Khan, and 'Azizullah, his sons and other relatives with robes. An annual stipend of 50,000 rupees was granted to his widow, Hamida Banu, daughter of Malika Banu, the sister of Mumtāz-uz-zamāni.

On Saturday, the 15th February, 1662/6th Rajab, Prince Muhammad Ākbar was circumcised. Khwāja Āhmad, envoy of Bukhara, was given his *conge* with a robe, a jewelled dagger with pearl strap, and 30,000 rupees as reward. From first to last one lakh and 20,000 rupees were given to this envoy. On Wednesday, the 12th March/1st Shaban, eighty elephants of Shuj'ā, sent by the Khān-i-Khānān and two elephants from the spoils of Palāmau were presented to the Emperor.

How can I describe fully the hunting in which His Majesty often delighted? I give a little as a sample of much: This year 150 *kulangs* (large cocks or herons) were struck down by the royal falcons. There was also a hunt, in which 355 deer were driven into the net; eight of these deer [39] were brought down by the Emperor and 47 others by the party that had been given permission to hunt in the enclosure into which the game had been driven. The rest were ordered to be released. The Emperor was informed that at first many deer had come within the circle of the *qamurgha*, but in fright they fell upon the beaters (āhal-i-qamurgha) in a large body, five men were gored with horns and two men were killed. About a thousand deer escaped.

A curious incident was now reported to the Emperor; at the village of Sonepat a party of boys played at king and ministers, two of them were charged (in play) with theft and taken by the policeman to the king, who ordered punishment. This senseless (mock) policeman hit the two on the head with the stick he carried in his hand so hard that they were killed, and this game proved fatal.

ACCOUNT OF THE CONQUEST OF KUCH BIHĀR AND ĀSSĀM

Towards the end of the year 1657 A.D./1067 A.H., owing to the illness of Shāh Jahān, disturbances broke out in all the frontiers, Bhim [=Prān] Nārāin, zamindār of Kuch Bihār occupied the Kāmrup district, appertaining to the imperial dominions. Just then Jayadhwaj Singh, Raja of Assam, who considered his country safe from the inroad of the imperial army and wanted to conquer the aforesaid district deputed a large army by the land-route to the district, [40] of Kāmrup.

The Khan-i-Khanan, knowing the invasion of these two countries to be urgent, started from Khizrpur by order of the Emperor, on Friday the 1st November, 1661/18th Rabi. A. His army occupied the city of Kuch Bihar on Thursday, the 19th Dec./7th Jamad. A., and named it, 'Alamgir-nagar. On Thursday, the 9th January, 1662/28th Jamad. A., the army set out for the conquest of Assam by way of Ghorāghāt. After campaigning for five months, the Islamic standard was planted in Garhgāon, the capital of Assam, on Monday, the 17th March/6th Shaban. I cannot describe in detail what the *'Alamgirnamah* gives fully, namely, the great designs of the faithful army, their exertions and hardships in this campaign through extreme devotion and fidelity to the Emperor, the capture of countless spoils consisting of all kinds of things, money and other articles, nor describe here the wonders, rarities, strange things, and precious objects of Kuch Bihār and Assām comprising the inanimate and animate creation, the varieties of trees, fruits, and plants, plains and rivers, food and dress, forts and houses of these countries.

When the Emperor learnt the details of this famous victory from the despatches of the Khān-i-Khānān, he graciously gave the Khan's son Muhammad Amin Khan who was then at Court, a robe and sent a *farmān* full of praise, a special robe, *tumān tugh,* and a reward of 1 kror of dām (Rs. 2½ lakhs) to the faithful Khan. [41]

CHAPTER V

FIFTH YEAR OF THE REIGN (1072 A.H.)

10th April 1662—29th March 1663

The month of Ramzān was spent in the performance of the appointed religious duties. The fifth year of the reign began. The imperial officers set about preparing for the festivities and fireworks in the manner of previous years. On the day of 'Id 10th May, the Emperor after returning from the mosque conferred gifts and rewards on the courtiers, commanders in all places, and the āmirs in the subahs; tributes were offered to and accepted by him.

On Monday the 12th May, 1662, the Emperor declined in health. Too much blood-letting caused weakness and swooning. This continued till Tuesday, the 17th June/10th Zil. Q., when Hakim Muhammad Amin and Hakim Mahdi tried the best remedies. Alms were given for removing the disease and relieving the needs of the poor. On Tuesday, the 24th June/17th Zil. Q., he took the bath of recovery. On Tuesday, the 17th July/10th Zil. H, ('Id-uz-zuha) he went to the place of prayer; great and small, rich and poor on seeing him enjoyed a double 'Id. On Wednesday, the 23rd July/17th Zil. H. he was weighed on his 46th lunar birth-day.

Mahābat Khan was made subahdār of Gujrāt *vice* Maharaja Jaswant Singh, and promoted to be a 6 *hazāri* (5 *hazār* tr.). On his coming back from a life of retirement, Razavi Khan Bukhāri was created a 2,500 *zāt* (400 tr.) [42] The officers of 'Ādil Khan who had brought his tribute were dismissed with robes. Taqarrab Khan died. His son Muhammad 'Ali Khan, who too had been removed from his rank for his father's offences, was graciously presented with a mourning robe and the rank of 1,500 (200 tr.). Saif Khan, who had retired, came from Sirhind and received a robe, and a sword, and the rank of two *hazāri* (1,500 tr.).

On Tuesday, the 2nd December, 1662/1st Jamad. A., the Emperor was weighed on his 45th solar birthday, all men received gifts according to their desires. Najābat Khan who had been punished for some offence in the first year, was again created a 5 *hazāri* (4,000 tr.). On Monday, the 8th December/7th Jamad. A. the Emperor started for Lahore. At Karnāl Fāzil Khan, Mir-i-Sāmān, was sent to proceed with the surplus camp-followers and baggage by the direct route to Lahore, while the Emperor advanced hunting in the direction of Mukhlispur, and reached Lahore on Sunday the 8th February, 1663/10th Rajab. As it was the imperial wish to visit Kashmir, he sent Khidmatgār Khan to make roads. On Friday the 13th February/15th Rajab, Qutbuddin Khan Khweshgi, faujdār of Junāgarh, slew the wicked Rāi Singh, uncle of Chhatra Sāl, zamindar of the country of Jām, who had raised disturbances and had dispossessed his nephew after the death of the latter's father Rāi Mal [=Ran Mal] with one son, an uncle and other relatives, numbering in all 300 men. [43] The Emperor ordered the country to be named Islāmnagar, in recognition of the bravery of the Khan.

THE CONCLUSION OF THE AFFAIRS OF ASSAM

When the Khān-i-Khānān took up his residence at Mathurāpur for passing the rainy season and water covered the whole land, the Assamese began to act boldly. As the Mughal troops could not ride out, the audacity of the Assamese passed all limits. Their Raja too came down from the hills of Nāmrup. The Mughal outposts were withdrawn; no other place than Garhgāon and Mathurāpur remained in the possession of the imperialists. Provisions were exhausted. The poisonous air caused a pestilence which carried off vast numbers. This affected the whole land of Assam, and vast crowds of the enemy, too, in the hills went to hell. During this period the food of the soldiers and the cattle was rice and beef, large quantities of which had been captured from the enemy. There was no alternative but to wait patiently for the end of the rains. In the middle [of the month of Safar/mid September] the rains decreased and boats of provisions too arrived at that time.

By the end of Rabi-ul-awwal, as the land reappeared, the Mughals sallied forth on all sides and made a terrible slaughter of the enemy in the same way as before. The Raja fled to the hills, and made overtures of peace, but the Khan did not agree and started for Nāmrup.

In the meantime many acute diseases attacked the Khan. The soldiers, worn out with labour and sufferings, were shaken in mind by the fear of his dying in such a (terrible) country and wished [44] to desert him, and go back to Bengal. The Khan on learning of it was grieved and on Friday the 5th December, 1662/4th Jamad. A. he advanced one stage. Necessity now compelled him to decide on peace and return. The Raja, who saw his own capture imminent, made Dilir Khan his mediator, and the latter induced the Khān-i-Khānān to agree to the Raja's proposal.

On Monday the 5th January, 1663/5th Jamad. S., the agents of the Raja arrived, and brought to the imperial camp a tribute of 20,000 *tolahs* of gold, 1 lakh and 8 thousand *tolahs* of silver, 20 elephants for the Emperor, 15 for the Khān-i-Khānān, and 5 for Dilir Khan, as well as the daughter of the Raja, the daughter of another Raja of a part of the country of Assam (a near relative of the chief Raja), four sons of the nobles of the Raja's Court (who were to stay in Bengal as hostages for the arrival of the balance of the tribute, *i.e.*, what had been promised over and above what was now delivered.)

On Saturday, the 10th January/10th Jamad. S., the Khān-i-Khānān, marched from the mouth of the Nāmrup hill and returned towards Bengal, arriving at Lakhugarh on Thursday, the 22nd/22nd Jamad. S.; on Wednesday, the 11th February/13th Rajab he marched out of Kajli and arrived at Pāndu opposite Gauhati on the further side of the river, sending away Rashid Khan as faujdar of Kāmrup. At this time his illness became past remedy. When he found himself in this plight, he deputed 'Askar Khan to reconquer Kuch Bihār, which Bhim [=Prān] Nārāyan had recovered, and himself started for Khizrpur. On 31st March 1663/2nd Ramzan, he died within 2 *kos* of Khizrpur. [45]

CHAPTER VI

SIXTH YEAR OF THE REIGN. 1073 A.H.

30th March, 1663—18th March 1664

On Thursday, the 23rd April, 1663/25th Ramzan, the Court officers made preparations for the celebration of the coronation anniversary in the Dilkasha garden situated on the other bank of the Rāvi. The Emperor, starting on that day for the trip to Kashmir, halted in the garden. That very day the news of the Khān-i-Khānān's death arrived. Prince Muhammad Mu'azzam went to the house of Muhammad Amin Khan and conducted him to the Emperor, who consoled him with a robe. The 'Id prayer (29th April) was performed in the chapel of the camp. Princes and nobles, of the Court and the provinces, received favours.

On Friday, the 1st May/3rd Shawwal the Emperor resumed his journey. One of the occurrences of this period was the night attack of the infernal Shivā on the camp of the Āmir-ul-umārā, the cutting off of his forefinger during the encounter, and the slaughter of his son Ābul Fath Khan. As this incident was due to the negligence of this premier noble, the Emperor punished him by transferring him from the viceroyalty of the Deccan (which was given to prince Muhammad Mu'azzam) to that of Bengal *vice* the deceased Mu'azzam Khan. On Tuesday, the 14th May/14th Shawwal, the Emperor reached Bhimbar, which is the gateway to Kashmir. As during his stay in Lahore the snow in the Pir Panjāl route had disappeared, the imperial party was to proceed by it. It was ordered that Raja Jai Singh and Najābat Khan [46] should stay on the banks of the river Chenāb with the surplus camp-followers. Tāhir Khan was permitted to depart to his jagir with some other āmirs. Saf Shikan was ordered to stay at the foot of the pass of Bhimbar with a party in order to guard the mouth of the hills. Some nobles and servants attended on the Emperor, while Muhammad Āmin Khan and Fāzil Khan were to come three stages behind the imperial party.

On Thursday, the 14th May/16th Shawwal, he marched out of Bhimbar. While crossing the terrible Pir Panjāl pass a frightened elephant turned back from the front and stampeded towards Bhimbar like a sudden calamity or a whirlwind; a terrible confusion befell the men and animals in that narrow pass. Some female elephants and some porters of the government fell into the pit of destruction and were so thoroughly crushed by the attack of this moving mountain that not to the speak of the men, not a bone of the elephants could be seen. On the occurrence of this terrible accident, the heart of the humble-cherishing Emperor was greatly grieved, and from that very time he resolved never again to visit Kashmir. In short, on Thursday, the 28th May/1st Zil. Q., he entered the city of Srinagar. Raja Raghunāth, mutasaddi (Superintendent) of the revenue department, died. On Sunday, the 7th June/11th Zil. Q., the post of Wazir was entrusted to Fāzil Khan, Iftikhār Khan becoming Khān-i-Sāmān.

During the reign of Shāh Jahān, every year 79,000 rupees were distributed in five months through the Sadr-us-Sadur, but in the other seven months no expenditure was made (on charity). Now the Emperor ordered that during five months the existing practice should be followed, and during the remaining seven months 10,000 rupees were to be distributed every month so that in all every year one lakh [47] and 49,000 rupees were to be spent on the needy.

On Saturday, the 13th June/17th Zil. Q., the Emperor was weighed on his 47th lunar birthday; presents were given to all the nobles of the Court and the provinces. Fāzil Khan, on obtaining the post of Diwān fell severely ill and died. On Tuesday, the 23rd June/27th Zil. Q., the Emperor condoled with his brother's son Burhānuddin who had recently come from Persia, by presenting him with a robe and kindly undertook to bring him up.

After enjoying the scenery of all the places of Kashmir, he set out from that abode of pleasure on the 16th August/22nd Muharram on return towards Lahore. J'afar Khan, Subahdār of Mālwa, was summoned to Court to receive the Wazirship, Najābat Khan being appointed in his place. The Emperor reached Lahore on Tuesday, the 29th September/7th Rabi. A. On Monday, the 2nd November/11th Rabi. S., he was weighed on his 46th solar birthday. 'Āqil Khan who was living in retirement at Lahore, was again taken into service as a two *hazāri* (700 tr.). Tarbiyat Khan was sent to Irānland as envoy to carry a reply to the letter of Shāh 'Abbās brought by Budāq Beg, with precious things and rarities worth seven lakhs of rupees. On the 9th November, the Emperor started for Delhi. J'afar Khan had audience at Pānipat, and was created Wazir. On Friday the 20th November/29th Rabi. S., the Emperor arrived in the environs of Delhi. [48]

CHAPTER VII

SEVENTH YEAR OF THE REIGN : 1074 A.H.

18th March 1664—7th March 1665

With the approach of Ramzan, festive arrangements were made. After returning from the mosque, the Emperor sat on the throne and gratified with his royal gifts the hearts of the princes and nobles, the rich and the poor. Presents were made to him and accepted.

On Sunday, the 5th June/21st Zil. Q., he was weighed on his 48th lunar birthday. A letter was received from Prince Muhammad Mu'azzam reporting the birth of a son to the mother of Muhammad Mu'izuddin; the child was named 'Izzuddin. Mustafa Khan Khafi was sent as envoy to Turān-land. A letter composed by Dānishmand Khan along with certain rare jewelled ware worth one lakh 50,000 rupees was sent with him to 'Abdul 'Aziz Khan, ruler of Bukhārā, and another letter with presents worth one lakh of rupees to Subhān Quli Khan, ruler of Balkh.

Although Maharaja Jaswant Singh greatly exerted himself to root out Shivā, to desolate his country, and to conquer his forts, yet no result satisfactory to the imperialists was produced. Therefore, Raja Jai Singh was appointed with other famous commanders to put him down. On Friday, the 30th September, 1664/19th Rabi. A., the Emperor was weighed on his 47th solar birthday; imperial favours were conferred on the princes and nobles.

The Emperor learnt that Najābat Khan Subahdār of Mālwa had died; Wazir Khan Subahdār of Khāndesh was appointed to succeed him [49] and Dāud Khan one of the assistants of Raja Jai Singh, was made Subahdār of Khāndesh; but a *farmān* was sent to him to leave one of his kinsmen at Burhānpur and himself set out for his destination [the Maratha country].

A letter was received from Prince Muhammad Mu'azzam reporting the birth of a son on Monday, the 5th December, 1664/26th Jamad. A., to the daughter of Rup Singh Rāthor; the child was named Sultan Muhammad 'Azim,

CHAPTER VIII

EIGHTH YEAR OF THE REIGN : 1075 A.H.

8th March, 1665—24th February, 1666

With the month of Ramzan began the 8th year of the reign. Preparations for the celebration were made. After returning from the mosque on the 'Id-ul-fitr the Emperor gratified the hearts of all with many acts of goodness and favour.

Hāji Āhmad Sayyid, who in the fourth year of the reign had been sent to convey six lakh and 60,000 rupees worth of presents to the Holy Cities, now (on return) had audience, and presented 14 Arab horses as *peshkash* (offering). Sayyid Yahia, envoy of the Sharif of Mecca was granted an interview and presented a supplicatory letter, three Arab horses and some sacred relics. He was rewarded with a robe and 6,000 rupees. Siddi Kāmil, envoy of the king of Abyssinia, and Sayyid 'Abdullah, representative of the ruler of Hazramaut (in Arabia), arrived at Court with letters and presents; they were shown high honour by the grant of robes and cash. Nine Arab steeds which Imām [50] Ism'ail, ruler of Yemen, had sent were presented to the Emperor. This celebration continued for five days.

News reached the Court that 'Itibār Khan, commandant of Agra, had died. R'adāndāz Khan, faujdār of the environs (of Agra) succeeded him, while the latter's office was given to Hushdār Khan, the Subāhdar.

On Saturday, the 13th May, 1665/8th Zil. Q., Maharaja Jaswant Singh came from the Deccan and had audience.

On Sunday, the 23rd April/17th Shawwal, the Emperor was weighed on his 49th lunar birthday; imperial gifts and honours glorified the servants at Court and the provinces. The envoys of Mecca, Abyssinia and Hazramaut were given *conge,* after being presented with suitable rewards in cash and kind. On Wednesday, the 14th June/ 10th Zil. H., was the 'Id-uz-zuha. On Friday, the 23rd occurred the festival of 'Id-i-Gulābi, when the princes and nobles presented jewelled or enamelled goblets.

The Emperor learnt that, through the exertions of Raja Jai Singh, Dilir Khan, and other heroes, Purandar,

Rudramāl, and other forts of Shivā were captured, and the latter knowing that his end would be extirpation, had very prudently sent messengers to the Raja to beg for safety, and having been freed from despair by the Raja's promise and agreement [51] had surrendered twenty-three forts to the imperial officers. On Monday, the 12th June, 1665/8th Zil. H., he came unarmed and interviewed the Raja, who embraced and made him sit near him, promised him safety of life and property, and presenting a jewelled sword and dagger urged him to put on the arms, and then sent him to Dilir Khan, who too treated him with many favours. In the terms of the Raja's request, a *farmān* was sent to him (Shivā) containing pardon and a gracious robe from the Emperor. His son Sambhā was made a five *hazāri* (same tr.). The Raja Jai Singh was made a seven *hazāri* (same tr. do-aspa seh-aspa) in recognition of his excellent services. His son, Rām Singh, who was at Court, Dilir Khan, Dāud Khan, Rāi Singh, Kirat Singh and others too received many kinds of favour. As 'Ādil Khan of Bijapur had delayed in paying his tribute and tried to help Shivā, an imperial order was sent to Raja Jai Singh saying that, after settling the country and forts gained from Ṣhivā, he should hasten to attack the Bijāpur territory and destroy the enemy without engaging himself in the siege of the fort. Muhammad Zāhid, son of Qāzi Islām, was appointed Censor of the Court. The high minister J'afar Khan had built a nice mansion on the bank of the Jamunā. The Emperor visited it and that premier noble performed the etiquette of spreading the carpet before the door (pā-āndāz), supplication (*niāz*) and offered valuable presents consisting of rarities and wonderful articles. This year a reply to the letter of 'Abdullah Khan, ruler of Kāshghar [52] was sent with Khwāja Ishāq along with certain precious articles.

On Wednesday, the 25th October, 1665/25th Rabi. S., the Emperor was weighed on his 48th solar birthday; presents were given to the nobles at Court and the provinces. At the request of Raja Jai Singh, a *farmān* was issued summoning Mulla Āhmad Navāyet, the chief noble of 'Ādil Khan, who had come to the Raja to promote the interests of his master, and being desirous of entering the imperial service was waiting for an opportunity to do it. He was granted the rank of a 6-*hazāri* (same tr.).

On Saturday, 9th December/11th Jamad. S., the Emperor learnt from the despatches of Saif Khan, Subahdār of Kashmir, that in accordance with the imperial order Daldal Muhamal,,* zamindār of Greater Tibet, had accepted Islam, the *khutba* had been read in the Emperor's name in the country, imperial coins issued and a high mosque built there. The Khan who had wisely managed this affair was rewarded with a promotion of rank and the grant of a robe. Murād Khan, a zamindar of Lesser Tibet, who had shown great friendliness in this expedition was given a robe of honour.

On Wednesday, the 3rd January, 1666/7th Rajab, Prince Muhammad Mu'azzam, having come from the Deccan, had audience. News came from the Deccan that Mulla Āhmad Navāyet, who had started for the Court, had died. An order was issued to send his son Āsad and the other surviving members of his family to His Majesty. [53] From the letters of news-reporters in Agra it was learnt that Shāh Jahān was seized with strangury on the 8th January, 1666/12th Rajab and that his illness was increasing in severity, and the doctors had withdrawn their hands from applying remedies as they declared the disease to be beyond cure. The Emperor wished to march in that direction. As a measure of precaution, Prince Muhammad Mu'azzam was sent in advance on Friday, the 19th January/23rd Rajab. Early in the night of Monday, the 22nd January, 1666 A.D./26th Rajab, Shāh Jahān succumbed to the disease and gave up the ghost. On the occurrence of this tragic event, R'adāndāz Khan, Khwāja Phul (Bahlol), Sayyid Muhammad Kānauji and Qāzi Qurbān entered the *Ghusalkhāna* at the wish of Begam Sāhib [Jahānārā] and engaged in making the necessary preparations for the funeral and the burial. The corpse was carried out of the fort through the door of the octangular (*musamman*) tower. Hushdār Khan Subahdār, joined (the procession), took the coffin across the Jamunā, and carried it to the mausoleum of Mumtāz-uz-zamāni built by His late Majesty. After reading the funeral prayer, they consigned the body to the earth under the dome. The chronograms for the death of Shāh Jahān are "Shāh Jahān died", and "Raziullah" (by Āshraf Khan). He had lived 76 years and 3 months, and reigned 31 years and 2 months. The prince got the news at a distance of 7 *kos* at the end of the night of his decease.

---

* *Daldal* is a misreading for *Dalai*. *Muhamal* does not resemble any of the titles of the ruler of Tibet, and I can only conjecture that it is a mistake for *Mahāmuni*.

Early in the day of burial he arrived at the city and performed the ceremony of condolence. [54] On the arrival of the sad news, the Emperor, the Princes and the Begams put on mourning. It was ordered that in letters and edicts Shāh Jahān's title should be given as *Firdaus Āshiāni*. On Sunday, the 4th February/9th Shab'ān the Emperor started by boat towards Agra in order to visit his father's tomb. On Friday, the 23rd/28th Shab'ān, he alighted at the mansion of Dārā Shukoh, and visited the tomb. The next day and the day following he went to the fort and made kind inquiries of and gave solace to the Begam Sāhib and all the other ladies of the harem, and made them all quit their robes of mourning. For certain works it was necessary for him to stay (in Agra) for a few days; so he summoned the ladies of his harem from Delhi.

At this time the fort of Chātgāon was conquered through the efforts of the Āmir-ul-umārā; his son Buzurg Ummed Khan and other commanders were honoured and gladdened with many favours.

CHAPTER IX

NINTH YEAR OF THE REIGN (1076 A.H.)

25th February, 1666—14th February, 1667

With the month of Ramzan began the ninth year of the reign. The Court was decorated for the 'Id. On Tuesday, the 27th March/1st Shawwāl, joyous music was played. After returning from the place of prayer, the Emperor sat on the throne. The Begam Sāhib was given a reward of one lakh of gold coins, and her annual pension, formerly 12 lakhs of rupees, was increased by five lakhs of rupees. [55] Pur Hunar Bānu Begam and Gauharārā Begam each received one lakh of rupees.

At this time the imperial treasury, which the officers had in the fifth year of the reign removed from Agra fort to Delhi fort, was again transferred to Agra. As Raja Jai Singh had sent Shivā to the Court and the latter had arrived in the environs of Agra, Kumār Rām Singh and Mukhlis Khan were ordered to advance and meet him and bring him to His Majesty. On Saturday, the 12th May, 1666/18th Zil. Q., the Emperor was weighed on his 50th lunar birthday. Shiva with his son Sambhā was honoured with an audience. He presented 1500 *āshrafi* as *nazar* and 6,000 rupees as *nisār*. As Raja Jai Singh had sent Shivā at his request to the Court, the Emperor overlooking his former offences wished to confer on him favours and give him permission to depart after a few days. On the day of interview he stood at the proper place along with the high āmirs. But this wild animal of the wilderness of ignorance, who knew not the etiquette of the imperial court, went into a corner and made improper expressions of dissatisfaction and complaint to Kumār Rām Singh. His brainless head led him to make a tumult. The Emperor ordered that he should return to his lodging, that Kumār Rām Singh should make him alight in a house near his own pavillion and bring his son Sambhā with himself to the audience, and that Fulād Khan should watch him in view of the fraud and satanic trickery of this arch-deceiver.

A royal letter containing all these matters was sent to Raja Jai Singh [56] asking him to write what he considered politic, so that Shivā might be treated accordingly. After two or three days, this knave in terror of the Emperor's wrath, turned to contriving some remedy; and beseeching the intercession of the nobles, he professed submission and repentance. About this time the despatch of Jai Singh was received, saying "I have given him promise and assurance of safety and he is engaged in our warfare in this region. Pardoning his offences would be advisable". Therefore Fulād Khan was ordered to remove the guards from his house. Kumār Rām Singh, too, slackened his watch. This artful cheat feigning sickness fled with his son on Sunday, the 19th August/27th Safar. Thereupon, Kumār Rām Singh was dismissed from his *mansab*. An order was sent to Raja Jai Singh saying that the trouble-maker Ṅetāji, who was related to Shivā and had been created a 5-*hazāri* (same tr.) at the Raja's request and was staying with him, should be arrested by cunning and sent to the Court.

As the Emperor had decided on going to Delhi, for transacting certain affairs, he sent in advance the Begam Sāhib and other ladies of the harem.

At this time a despatch of Tarbiyat Khan, who had been sent on an embassy to Persia was received, stating the wickedness of heart, folly, violence of temper, and unimaginable haughtiness of the wretched Shāh 'Abbās, and reporting that he wished to go to Khurāsān with a view to waging war. After Tarbiyat Khan's arrival at the Court, this matter was again communicated to the Emperor by him and other reporters. The Emperor determined to punish this empty-headed king, who wished to destroy the alliance between them without any reason. [57] Accordingly he first deputed Prince Muhammad Mu'azzam with Maharaja Jaswant Singh and declared that he himself would march to the Panjab. As Tarbiyat Khan had committed some faults in conducting the embassy, he was forbidden the Court. On Tuesday, the 9th October/19th Rabi. S., the Emperor set out by the Jamunā from Agra to Delhi, which was reached in 14 stages.

On Saturday, the 27th October/8th Jamad. A., he was weighed on his 49th solar birthday. Āmir Khan, nāzim of Kabul had arrested and sent some Mughals to the Court on the suspicion of their being spies. The Emperor appointed 'Itimād Khan and Mullā 'Abdul Qawi to investigate their case. The Khan took one of them without chains or handcuffs to his private room. Suddenly the man rushed out of the room, went to the servant who stood outside with his weapons, snatched away his sword, and returning struck the Khan and killed him. The people around cut the man down. The Emperor was grieved to hear of the death of such a faithful old servant, and gave robes and promotions to his sons and other relatives. He visited the mansion of J'afar Khan the premier noble, who offered presents of jewels and jewelled ware.

Khwāja Ishāq who had gone last year on an embassy to Kāshghar, returned (from the way) on hearing of disturbances in that country. But now on hearing of the settlement of peace in that country he was sent a second time. [58]

As the King of Persia was going from Farrukhābād to Isfahān he was attacked with an inflammation of the throat owing to exposure and died at Khārsammān on Wednesday, the 22nd August/1st Rabi. A. His minister placed his eldest son Mirzā Safi on the throne. On Wednesday, the 12th December/24th Jamad. S., Aurangzib learnt this news at his private hunting-lodge (*khās shikār*) from the letters of reporters on the frontiers, and said "My wish was different (from this). But as the True Avenger has punished him for his sins, it would not be generous and heroic to send an army against the country of Irān". So an order was sent to Prince Muhammad Mu'azzam not to advance beyond Lahore, but stay there for a few days.

Bahādur Khan, an officer sent with the Prince, returned from the way to the Court, and was sent to Allahabad as Subahdār. Raja Jai Singh, after arresting Shivā's relation Netaji sent him to the Court. He was made over to Fidāi Khan and accepted Islām.

As Raja Jai Singh after concluding the expedition against Shivā, had gone with the imperial army to punish 'Ādil Khān, Abul Muhammad, grandson of Bahlol, one of the 'Ādil Shāhi chiefs joined the Raja, after two stages had been passed. The new-comer was created a 5-*hazāri* (same number of troopers) at the Raja's request and appointed to assist in the war. At the Raja's command and through the exertions and services of Shivā and his general Netāji [59] the forts Phaltan, Thāthwara, Khāwan, and Mangalbeda were captured. During this period many heroic attacks and fights took place with Ābul Muhammad, Khawās Khan and their countless army. The imperial army triumphed; all the villages adjacent to Bijāpur were repeatedly overrun and harried by our troops. In short, the imperial army arrived within five kos of Bijāpur. 'Ādil Khan after strengthening the fort of Bijāpur, cut the banks of his tanks, filled up the surrounding wells with briars, razed to the ground the homesteads outside the fort, stood a siege, and appointed his army to repel the imperial forces. As the Raja did not design to conquer the fort of Bijāpur and had not brought with himself siege-materials, he halted for some days, and then marched away. On Saturday, the 20th January, 1666/24th Rajab, he crossed the river Bhimā. Diānat Rāi, the trusted servant of 'Ādil Khan, brought a message to the Raja begging pardon and professing submission, with some jewelled ware. As the rainy season arrived, and the Raja got a letter from the Emperor ordering him to pass the monsoon at Āurangābād, he gave up the campaign and returned.

At this time Dilir Khan by imperial command first went to the kingdom of Chānda : Mānji Mallār, the zamindār, intetrviewed the Khan, gave him five lakhs of rupees, and agreed to pay one kror of rupees as fine to the imperial Government, and two lakhs of rupees as his permanent annual tribute. Then the Khan went to the kingdom of Deogarh. Kok (Kukia) Singh, the ruler of the place agreed to pay 15 lakhs of rupees as the balance (of tribute) for the past with an additional three lakhs [60] of rupees every year. After having gained composure about the affairs of these places, the Khan again marched with his army by command to the Deccan, and was created a 5-*hazāri* (same tr. *do āspa seh-āspa*).

CHAPTER X

TENTH YEAR OF THE REIGN. 1077 A. H.

15th February 1667—3rd February, 1668

The month of Ramzan led to the increase of charity and good deeds. The Court officers made preparations for the celebration.

On Sunday, the 24th February/10th Ramzan a prince was delivered by Udipuri Mahal, and he was named Muhammad Kāmbakhsh. Prince Muhammad Mu'azzam, on return from Lahore, had audience. On Sunday, the 17th March/1st Shawwāl, the Emperor, after returning from the place of prayer, sat on the throne, and conferred favours on the princes and nobles.

Shivā's relation Netā, who had accepted Islām, was raised after circumcision to the rank of a 3-*hazāri* (2,000 tr.) with the title of Muhammad Quli Khan. Mir 'Imāduddin, diwān of the bayutāt, got the title of Rahmat Khan, and 'Azizuddin that of Bahrāmand Khan. On Saturday, the 23rd March/7th Shawwāl, Prince Muhammad Mu'azzam was given *conge* as Subahdār of the Deccan; by an increment of 5-*hazār*, [61] he was created a 20-*hazāri* (12-*hazār* tr.). Maharaja Jaswant Singh, Rāi Singh, Saf Shikan Khan and Sarbuland Khan were appointed under him, and given favours. Raja Jai Singh was recalled to Court.

DISTURBANCES CAUSED BY THE YUSUFZAI ĀFGHĀNS

When the Emperor learnt of the rising of the Yusufzai Āfghāns, their exalting as their commander a silly beggar under the name of Muhammad Shāh, the disturbances caused by the exertions of that deceitful impostor the wicked Mullā Chālāk, and the leadership of the black-faced Bhāgu, he sent orders to Kāmil Khan, faujdār of Attock, to gather together the faujdārs and jāgirdārs of the environs of the river Nilāb, and engage in crushing the rebels as far as possible.

Order was sent to Āmir Khan, Subahdār of Kābul, to depute Shamshir Khan, with five thousand men to put them down. Kāmil Khan in his eagerness, did not wait for the arrival of Shamshir Khan, but fought a severe engagement with the enemy, overpowered them, and recovered the imperial outposts. On Thursday, the 2nd May/18th Zil. Q. Shamshir Khan after crossing the river Nilāb, came towards Attock, and entered the enemy's territory on the other side of the river opposite the Yusufzai country. The enemy went away to the hills and waited for an opportunity.

On that day, Muhammad Āmin Khan Mir Bakhshi, with Āmir Khan, Qubād Khan and other commanders, and 9,000 troopers in all, was sent from the Court to punish these rebels. Before the arrival of this Khan, Shamshir Khan had repeatedly fought great battles and engagements. [62]. Three hundred of the leading maliks of the tribes were taken prisoner. On hearing of it the Emperor honoured Shamshir Khan and Kāmil Khan with imperial favours.

On Thursday, the 9th May, 1667/25th Zil. Q., the Emperor was weighed on his 51st lunar birthday. During this celebration Prince Muhammad 'Azam was made a 15-*hazāri* (7 *hazār* tr.) by an increment of 3-*hazār*. Prince Muhammad Akbar was made a 8-*hazāri* (2 *hazār* tr.) and granted the *tumān tugh*, kettledrum, and umbrella. 'Umdatul Mulk J'afar Khan and the officers at Court and the provinces were cherished with various favours. Rustam Bey and Khushi Bey, the envoys of the Kings of Bukhārā and Balkh respectively, were presented with robes and cash and given *conge*. From first to last two lakhs of rupees were spent on the envoy of Bukhārā, and one lakh and 50 thousand rupees on that of Balkh. Razavi Khan of Bukhārā was appointed Sadr *vice* 'Ābid Khan. Tarbiyat Khan's offences were pardoned, and he was sent to Orissa as Subahdār *vice* Khān-i-Daurān deceased. It was learnt from the letters of the reporters of Burhānpur that Raja Jai Singh was coming from Aurangabad to the Court when on arriving there he died on the 28th of Muharram.* The Emperor cherished his son Kumār Rām Singh, who had so long been under punishment, by giving him the title of Raja and many favours.

Muhammad Āmin Khan after arriving in the Afghān country harried and desolated their homes as far as possible;

* This date is incorrect. The writer's sole authority, the *Ālamgirnāmah* (p. 1051) merely states—"On the 28th [month not given] from the news-letters of Burhānpur the Emperor learnt that Raja Jai Singh has died in that city." The dynastic list maintained by the Jaipur State gives 28th August 1667 (18th Rabi A) as the date of his death, and therefore the news of it may have reached the Emperor on the 28th of Rabi-ul-awwal, and not possibly on that day of the month of Muharram (=10 July).

the Emperor ordered him to leave Shamshir Khan there and come to Lahore, [63] and be its Subahdār *vice* Ibrāhim Khan.

On Monday, the 2nd December, 1667/25th Jamad. S., the Emperor was weighed for his 50th solar birthday. From the letters of the news-writers of the province of Kashmir and the despatch of Murād Khan, zamindār of [Lesser] Tibet, the Emperor learnt that 'Abdullah Khan the ruler of Kāshghar, after being overpowered by his son Bulbars Khan, had with his family and dependants and a few of his servants in a plundered and destitute condition, turned his face in this direction with a view to seeking refuge with the Emperor. It was also learnt that Khwāja Ishāq, who had been sent to him as envoy, had interviewed him in this condition and helped him to be released from this difficulty, and that they would soon reach Kashmir.

On hearing this news the Emperor in his extreme kindness and appreciation of worth, deputed Khwāja Sādiq of Badakhshān and Saifullah to act as guest-superintendent to this noble King; one dagger, one jewelled *jigha,* one hundred and nine Arab, Persian and Turki horses, some of which had jewelled and gold trappings, two elephants, some gold and silver vessels, a certain number of suits of dress, nice robes, tents, pavilions, precious carpets, and all other articles of splendour, were sent with them; and the above officers were ordered to hasten to Kashmir, meet the noble Khan there, and act as his caretakers till his arrival at the Court. An order was sent to Mumtāz Khan, Subahdār of Kashmir, directing that when 'Abdullah Khan, [64] would reach that pleasant land, he should be supplied by the imperial government with all his necessaries, and given 50,000 rupees from the provincial treasury, and that when he would start for the Court, the Subahdār should accompany and conduct him to His Majesty.

An order was issued to Muhammad Āmin Khan, Subahdār of Lahore, that when 'Abdullah Khan would come within the limits of that province he should treat him with every respect and care, properly perform the rites of hospitality, and give him 50,000 rupees from the public revenue, and a large amount and some articles on his own behalf. Similarly, orders were issued to all the governors and faujdārs on his route to perform the rites of hospitality in their respective places, and conduct him over their jurisdictions in the most excellent manner.

On Thursday, the 19th December/13th Rajab, Dānishmand Khan was made Mir Bakshi *vice* Muhammad Āmin Khan, and presented with a special robe and a jewelled pen-case. At this time Khwāja Bahlol was appointed commandant of Gwalior *vice* Muhammad Mu'atamad Khan and received a robe, a horse, a dagger, and the title of Khidmatgār Khan, while the title of Khidmatgār Khan was changed to Khidmatguzār Khan. At this time it was learnt from the news-reports of Bengal that the wretched Assamese had a second time audaciously crossed their own frontier and attacked Gauāhati on the boundary of Bengal, with a vast army and a large flotilla; and that as reinforcement had not reached Sayyid Firuz Khan, the thānadār of the place, the enemy had conquered Gauāhati, and the aforesaid Khan had bravely [65] sacrificed his life with many of his comrades in devotion (to duty). The Emperor decided that one of the great and eminent nobles of the Court should be deputed to Bengal with an army from His Presence to put down the enemy and that he should join this force to some of the troops serving in Bengal, and engage in chastising this wicked tribe. Therefore, Raja Rām Singh was appointed to perform this exploit. On Friday, the 27th December, 1667/21st Rajab he was sent off with a robe, a horse with gold trappings and a jewelled dagger with pearl strap. Nasiri Khan, Kesari Singh Bhurtia [Rathor], Raghunāth Singh Mairtia, Brahmadeo Sisodiā and many other nobles and mansabdārs, 1,500 *āhadis,* and 500 *barqāndāzes* were appointed under him.

Here ends my abridgment of the history of the first ten years.

CHAPTER XI

AUTHOR'S PREFACE

[Twenty-two lines of trite remarks *omitted*.]

[67] Be it known to the reader that the *'Alamgirnāmah,* giving the incidents of the first ten years of the reign of the Emperor Ābul Zafar Muhiuddin Muhammad Aurangzib 'Ālamgir Ghāzi, was written by * * * [68] Mirzā Muhammad Kāzim. The Emperor forbade the writer to continue the history thereafter. * * *

After the death of this Emperor, in the reign of Ābul Nasar Qutbuddin Shāh 'Ālam Bahādur Pādishāh Ghāzi, 'Ināyetullah Khan, chief of the wazir's diwān and personal disciple of 'Ālamgir, urged this worthless fool Muhammad Must'ad Khan that many of the occurrences and incidents, sayings and acts of Aurangzib during the (last) forty years of his reign were hidden from our knowledge and that 'Ālamgir's deeds had not been collected in a history. "You have tasted the cup of meaning, and possess sufficient ability to express the praise of Ālamgir, and to discharge this task."

I pleaded, "This is [69] a difficult task, beyond the capacity of man full of defects such as I am. The execution of such works depends upon the demand of leaders appreciative of merit and right-minded masters expert in handling words. In their absence, the work produced would be consigned to the niche of forgetfulness. If the sheets of the news-letters of the Court and the provinces be collected, then the work of the composition may be accomplished with ease. A passionate friend has no other thought than to realise his desire by any means whatsoever, and (thus) to leave a memorial for all times." [But] my entreaty produced no effect (on his mind).

This humble servant, who considered it his duty to be true to the salt of the virtuous Emperor, and had been all his life one of the knot of servants standing outside the door of His Majesty's Court, recorded what he had seen, and what he had learnt on inquiry from the trusty friends who had borne office during that reign. As this book of fortunate victories contains the triumphs of the Emperor 'Ālamgir,

I considered "*Maāsir-i-'Ālamgiri*" as its proper title, that phrase being its title as well as giving its date (year of completion), 1120 A. H./1708 A. D. [70]

11TH YEAR OF THE REIGN: 1078 A. H.

4th February, 1668—22nd January, 1669

With the month of Ramzan, the 11th year began. The courtiers set about making preparations for the (annual coronation) festivity. The month of Ramzan was spent in fasting during the day and remaining quiet at night. On Thursday, the 5th March/1st Shawwal, the Emperor went to the mosque to perform the two-fold prayers of 'Id-ul-fitr, and on his return sat on the throne in the Public Audience Hall. The Princes and peers made their salutations and were granted promotions, robes of honour, and titles.

Coronation Gazette: Muhammad 'Azam got a robe and a jewelled *dhup*, and Muhammad Kāmbakhsh a robe. Umdat-ul-mulk J'afar Khan was given a robe and a silver-hilted dagger, Dānishmand Khan, Mir Bakhshi, a robe, an elephant, and promotion to the rank of a 5-*hazāri* (2,000 tr.), The imperial physician, gained promotion to the rank of 2,500 *zāt*, (100 tr.), [71] Himmat Khan to the rank of 2½ *hazāri* (1,200 tr.), and Lutfullah Khan to that of 1½ *hazāri* (500 tr.), Muhammad Ism'ail, son of Āsad Khan, got his appointment to the rank of 3-*sadi*. Muhammad Y'aqub, son of Shaikh Mir, formerly a 4-*sadi* (100 tr.) now got an increment of 200 troopers. Ibrāhim Khan was appointed Subahdār of Bihār, *vice* Lashkar Khan and raised to the rank of a 5-*hazāri* (5,000 tr.) Mahābat Khan, Subahdār of Ahmadābād Gujrāt, had audience, and was created Subahdār of Kabul *vice* Sayyid Āmir Khan.

As the Emperor had no liking for pleasure, and his devotion to duty left him no time for festivity, he ordered that the chief musician Khush-hāl Khan, Bisrām Khan, Ras-bin, and others might come to the Court, but must not make music. Gradually (music) was entirely forbidden.

On Thursday, the 12th March/8th Shawwal, 'Abdullah Khan (the expelled King of Kāshghar), who had come to the environs of Delhi, alighted in one of the gardens. The Emperor ordered arrangements to be made for his hospitable reception. On Sunday, the 15th March/11th Shawwal, Umdat-ul-mulk J'afar Khan and Āsad Khan went outside the city to bring him to His Majesty. While riding he shook hands with the two, came to the door of the Halls of Audience on horseback, thence reached the red barrier (*kathra*) in a *palki,* [72] and the silver barrier on foot. Sitting down near the golden barrier, he partook of the Emperor's own bread and water, which had been presented to him. He then kissed the jewelled staff presented to him and took it in his arms. After one *prahar* and six *gharis* he went to see the *ghusalkhāna,* and then sat on the river-side. After an hour, the Emperor appeared; the Khan went up to him, made his salutation, and shook hands with His Majesty. The Emperor took him by the hand to the mosque. After half an hour he was permitted to depart. Ekkātāz Khan, Mubāriz Khan, and Khwāja Muhammad Sādiq conducted him to the *haveli* of the late Rustam Khan, a charming house which had been furnished afresh with carpets and other things from the Emperor's personal furniture department. He was now presented with 11 lakhs of rupees in cash, 20,000 rupees in kind, and 18 horses with trappings of jewel, gold and silver, and gold-embroidered horse-cloth, which had been assembled in the Audience Hall. He with his ladies passed the whole of the next day in visiting and merry-making in the garden of Sāhibābād. [73] On behalf of the Begam Sāhib he was presented with 20,000 rupees, eighteen *thāns* of cloth, a jewelled dagger with *phul-katāra,* a jewelled betel-case with a gold tray, an enamelled spittoon, a crystal *chaughara,* and 200 dishes of food with *ārgajah* and *pān.* On the 29th March/25th Shawwal, when the Emperor after rising (from the throne) was standing near the fountain of the Court, 'Umdat-ul-mulk brought the Khan with himself to the Presence. There was not a yard's distance between them: The Khan bowed, the Emperor laid his hand on his gracious breast. At his command, he stood in front of the Emperor near the fountain and was presented with a *tuighun* falcon. 'Umdat-ul-mulk was commanded to entertain the Khan with an elephant-fight and to sit with him there, while the Emperor went to his Khawābgāh (sleeping room).

On Saturday, the 25th April/23rd Zil. Q., the Emperor was weighed in the ghusal-khāna, in the customary manner: the 52nd lunar year of his life began. The Princes and the grandees received many gifts; while the Begam Sāhib and other ladies and princes sent presents to the Emperor. On Sunday, the 3rd May/1st Zil. H., Rahmat Bānu, daughter of the King of Assam, was married to Muhammad 'Azam: the bride's settlement was 1 lakh, 80,000 rupees.

It was reported from the province of Tatta, that the village of Samāwāni, in the jurisdiction of the port of Lāri [74], had sunk down with 30,000 residents, owing to an earthquake.

On Tuesday, the 12th May/10th Zil. H., the Emperor went to say his two-fold 'Iduzzaha prayers. On Friday, the 17th July/17th Safar Muhammad 'Azam was contracted to Jahānzeb Bānu Begam,* the daughter of Dārā Shukoh and

* Akbar
- Salim
  - Khurram
    - Aurangzeb
      - Azam+Jahānzeb
        - Bidar Bakht.
  - Parviz+Jahān Bānu
    - Dara+Nādira
      - Jahānzeb Bānu
- Murād
  - Jahān Bānu
    - Nādira

Nādira Bānu Begam, who was the daughter of Jahān Bānu Begam, who was the daughter of Sultan Murād (4th son of Ākbar) and wife of Sultān Parwiz, the elder brother of Shāh Jahān; the ceremony was performed in the house of the Emperor's elder sister Jahānārā Bānu, surnamed the Begam Sāhib, who had brought her up like her own daughter. 'Umdat-ul-mulk J'afar Khan and other nobles conceyed 1,60,000 rupees to her as nuptial present (*sāchiq*).

On Saturday, 1st August/3rd Rabi. A., Lashkar Khan was appointed Subahdār of Multān *vice* Tāhir Khan. News came from Bengal that at first the dust was raised and then a terrible apparition of great height appeared; after some hours it disappeared. Then it was found that for half a league (round it) men and animals were lying killed and wounded. On Monday, 14th September/17th Rabi. S., news came from Jaunpur that heavy rain had fallen for 22 days commencing on 7th August. Many high buildings and 22 yards of the east wall of the fort had tumbled down. In some places the lightning had struck; some men had been killed, others who had become senseless recovered consciousness with the loss of their hearing.

'Abdun Nabi Khan [75] after removal from his post in Fathpur Jhunjhnu, was created a 2-*hazāri* (1,000 tr.) and appointed faujdar of Mathurā. Muhammad 'Ali Khan was appointed diwān of Raushanārā Bānu Begam.

The Emperor ordered the Subahdārs and faujdars of the provinces of Allahabad and Oudh to search for and send manacled and fettered to the Court those men who castrated children and to regard it as a peremptory order that no one should be allowed to engage in this wicked practice.

On Wednesday, 21st October 1668/25th Jamad. A., the 51st solar year of his life began. The Emperor sat on the throne in the *ghusalkhāna,* which had been decorated for the ceremony of weighing. He stopped the practice of (birthday) weighing. * * * Muhammad 'Azam got a special robe with a half-sleeve coat and a jewelled turban. As 'Abdullah Khan after spending eight months in happiness in Delhi, wanted to visit the holy cities, [76] he received leave to depart. The imperial officers prepared the requisites of his journey. Orders were issued to the Subahdārs, magistrates and faujdārs of the road from Delhi to Surat that they should conduct the Khan through their respective jurisdictions in the best manner. 'Superintendents of guests' were appointed, as at the time of his coming. From first to last ten lakhs of rupees were spent on him.

'Ināyat Khan, the diwān of Khālsa was raised to the rank of 9-*sadi* (100 tr.), Shaikh Sulaimān was appointed dārogha of 'adālat, *vice* Mir Husaini, and a 7-*sadi* (70 tr.) Islām Quli, the master of the horse of 'Abdul 'Aziz, king of Bukhārā, was made a *hazāri.* Sayyid Āmir Khan, the dismissed Subahdar of Kābul, had audience, and presented 500 mohars and 2,000 rupees. He kissed the Emperor's feet, and the Emperor laid his gracious hand on his back.

Khush-hāl Khan and other masters of revels were given 3,000 rupees and 40 suits of *khel'at.* Sayyid 'Usmān, the messenger of the Sherif of Mecca, was allowed to depart with a robe, 9,000 rupees and a horse with silver trappings. Shaf'i Khan was appointed *diwān-i-tan vice* Kifāyet Khan; Tāhir Khan the dismissed Subahdār of Multān, had audience, and presented 100 *mohars* and 1,000 rupees. Five hundred *mohars* sent by Mahābat Khan [77] on the occasion of the birth of a son, were presented to the Emperor; the son was named Zamāna Beg. The imperial Bakhshis were ordered to dismiss all troopers up to 3-*sadis,* excepting the servants and zamindārs. Saf Shikan Khan from the service of Prince Muhammad Mu'azzam and Mukhtār Khan, the qiladār of Parenda, came and had audience of the Emperor.

The Emperor in order to obey the rules of the Holy law and to put down uncanonical innovations, ordered the removal of the two stone elephants of exactly the same size which had been made by skilful artisans and placed on the two side-posts of the fort, from which circumstance the door was called Hatiāpul.

Marriage of 'Azam. The festivities began on Monday, the 21st December, 1668/27th Rajab. On Sunday, the 3rd January, 1669/10th Shaban, the Emperor sat in the Court of Private Audience; the Prince received a robe with *chahārqab,* ten Arab and 'Irāqi horses, two elephants with gold trappings, a *talāir,* a jewelled sword worth 20,000 rupees, a turban [78] worth 60,000 rupees and cash amounting to 12 lakhs of rupees. The Begam Sāhib was presented with the elephant Sarwārganj, worth 15,000 rupees and Jahānzeb Bānu Begam with two elephants. After 5 *gharis* of night, the Prince came with pomp and show to the Emperor, who now went to the mosque. The knot was tied by Qāzi 'Abdul Wahhāb, with Mir Sayyid Muhammad Qanauji as his deputy, and Mullā 'Auz Akhsikati and Shaikh Saifullah Sirhindi as the witnesses. The marriage-portion was six lakhs of rupees. The Emperor with the prince rode on horseback to the house of the Begam Sāhib. Grandees down to commanders of 1500 formed the train of the Prince. After two *prahars* and one *ghari* of night, the Emperor and the Prince returned. Towards the morning the bride came to the Prince's house.

On Sunday, the 10th January, 1669/17th Shaban, the Emperor visited the Prince at his house. [79] All the ground from the fort to the seraglio of the prince was covered with cloth of gold, silver and plain cloth. The Emperor sat on a throne of gold. The courtiers made their bows. It was ordered that grandees down to commanders of 1500 should make their salutations for their robes of honour through the mediation of the Bakhshi and others through that of the *dārogha* of *khilat-khāna.* The Prince made a present of jewels and cloth valued at five lakhs of rupees. Then the Emperor visited the inner apartments (*mahal*) and afterwards returned to the palace. At the time of the Emperor's arrival, the Prince had advanced to receive him outside the door of the band-room. At the time of his return, he was honourably dismissed from within the *ghusalkhāna*. On Wednesday, the 6th January/13th Shaban, 'Abdur Rashid, the ambassador of Bulbāris Khan, the ruler of Kāshghar, had audience and presented his master's letter. It was made over to Khidmat Khan, the dārogha of petitions.

On the 13th January/20th Shaban, the Emperor ordered that men should not use in their garments cloth of gold, as the wearing of it was opposed to the Holy Law.

CHAPTER XII

TWELFTH YEAR OF THE REIGN. 1079 A. H.

23rd January, 1669—12th January, 1670

The Emperor passed the month of Ramzan in religious observances. The courtiers made preparations for celebrating the coronation day. [80] The moon of Shawwal became visible on Friday. On the day of 'Id the Emperor visited the 'Idgāh, and at the time of return offered his Friday prayer in the great Jām'a Mosque. [1st Shawwal was Monday, the 22nd February]. Next Tuesday, the 2nd Shawwal he sat on the jewelled throne.

Coronation Day Gazette. Prince Muhammad 'Azam got a robe and promotion to the rank of 15-*hazāri* (9,000 tr.) Prince Akbar a robe, 'Umdat-ul-mulk J'afar Khan, Muhammad Āmin Khan, Āsad Khan, Abdur Rahman Sultān son of Nazar Muhammad Khan, Nāmdār Khan, Dānishmand Khan, Sayyid Munawwar Khan and other officers, great and small, were rewarded with robes, horses, elephants, and promotions. Bad'i Sultān son of Khusrau Sultān was made a 2-*hazāri* (200 tr.). Āmir Khan, son of Khalilullah Khan, was made dārogha of mansabdārs *vice* Hasan 'Ali Khan. Mu'ataqad Khan, son of Najābat Khan, who had been removed from his *mansab* for some offence, was reinstated as a 2-*hazāri* (same tr.). Abul Muhammad [81] grandson of Bahlul Khan Miyāna, who came from the Deccan, had audience, and was created a 5-*hazāri* (4,000 tr.) with the title of Ikhlās Khan. Mukhtār Khan, the qiladār of Parenda got leave to return (to his post).

On Thursday, the 8th April, 1669/17th Zil. Q., occurred an eclipse; prayers were said and alms distributed, as was the custom.

The Lord Cherisher of the Faith learnt that in the provinces of Tatta, Multān and especially at Benares, the Brahman misbelievers used to teach their false books in their established schools, and that admirers and students both Hindu and Muslim, used to come from great distances to these misguided men in order to acquire this vile learning. His Majesty, eager to establish Islām, issued orders to the governors of all the provinces to demolish the schools and temples of the infidels and with the utmost urgency put down the teaching and the public practice of the religion of these misbelievers.

On Friday, the 9th April/18th Zil. Q., occurred the 53rd lunar birthday of the Emperor, observed with the usual celebrations at Court; His Majesty sat on the throne; but no weighing took place, as that practice was stopped from the 11th year. Musicians and singers remained excluded from the Court. The band (naubat), however, played happy strains, as formerly. Prince Muhammad 'Azam got a robe and a shield with jewelled knobs, Muhammad Akbar a robe, 'Umdat-ul-mulk J'afar Khan and other [82] courtiers were rewarded with robes. Muhammad Mu'azzam sent to the Emperor a ruby, which 'Ādil Khan King of Bijāpur had presented: it weighed 5 *tānk* and 5 *surkh;* its price was estimated at 20,000 rupees. A robe was sent by the Emperor to the Prince. Dilir Khan was made a 5-*hazāri* (same tr.) in reward for the capture of Deogarh.

News came from the province of Allahabad that Ālawardi Khan 'Alamgirshāhi had died. His brothers Hasan 'Ali Khan, Ārslān Khan, Muhammad Shah, Āmānullah Khan, Hazbar Khan, Husain 'Ali Khan, and Sanjar, were presented with robes of condolence and consoled. Mir Khan was created Subahdār of Allahabad, and a 4-*hazāri* (3,000 tr. *do-āspa*) *vice* the deceased, and given a robe. Mu'ataqad Khan was made dārogha of the servants of the retinue (*jilau*) in his place; Himmat Khan was made dārogha of the Diwān-i-Khās; Kāmgār Khan, son of J'afar Khan, was appointed dārogha of the jewel-market, Lutfullah Khan, son of the late S'adullah Khan, was appointed dārogha of *dāk chauki vice* 'Āqil Khan who had turned hermit, and he received a *bālāband;* two horses were presented to Mir Shihābuddin, messenger of the king of Bukhārā.

On Saturday, the 1st May/10th Zil. H., the Emperor went to the mosque to perform the prayers of the 'Id-uz-zuha. [83] Buland Khan from the Deccan was granted audience. Hakim Ibrāhim, who had by command accompanied 'Abdullah Khan Kāshghari to the port of Surat, returned and had audience. Mirzā Mukarram Khan Safavi, after giving up the robes of a hermit, came to the Court without arms; the Emperor presented him with a sword. It was ordered that the ranks of officers from 900 to 200 *zāt* should be reported in their absence, and those from 100 to 20 should be personally presented standing. Saif Khan was made Subahdār of Kashmir *vice* Mubāriz Khan.

On Wednesday, the 12th May/21st Zil. H., it was learnt that 'Abdun Nabi Khan, faujdār of Mathurā, in order to punish the turbulent men of the village of Tilpat had attacked and at first defeated them, but was himself killed during the fight by a musket-ball. He was a religious and benevolent man and combined administrative capacity with bravery in command. He built the lofty mosque of Mathurā. His brother's son and (own) son-in-law, Muhammad Ānwār was given a robe of condolence. His property was seized for the State: the cash amounted to 93,000 gold mohars, and 13 lakhs of rupees.

On Thursday, the 13th May/22nd Zil. H., R'adāndāz Khan, was appointed to root out the rebels near Agra [84] and received a horse with gold trappings. Sarbuland Khan was appointed Qur Begi *vice* Himmat Khan. Muhammad Āmin Khan, nāzim of Lahore got permission to return to his post. M'asum Khan reported that a counterfeit Shuj'ā had appeared in the neighbourhood of Morang and raised disturbances. Urgent orders were issued to Ibrāhim Khan and Fidāi Khan that if he raised his head within their jurisdiction, they should behead him.

Saf Shikan Khan, was appointed faujdār of Mathurā *vice* Abdun Nabi Khan and Dilir Himmat, son of Bahādur Ruhila, that of Nadarbār. Brahma Deo Sisodiā was appointed to accompany Saf Shikan Khan, Sayyid 'Abdul Wahhāb, messenger of the King of Māchin, had audience. Sālih Bahādur, macebearer, was sent to demolish the temple of Malārna.

On Thursday, the 3rd June 1669/13th Muharram, after one *prahar* of the night, the Emperor by way of the garden of Haiāt-Bakhsh, visited the porter's lodge which was assigned for the residence of the saint Shaikh Saifuddin Sirhindi. After an hour spent in talking with the saint and honouring him, he returned to the palace.

It was reported that the wandering Hindu saint, Uddhav Bairāgi, was confined in the chabutra of the police station in punishment for his seducing men to false beliefs, and that two Rajputs who were his disciples used to visit

Qāzi 'Abul Mukāram, son of Qāzi 'Abdul Wahhāb for the purpose of trying to get him released, and that finding an opportunity [85] they had fatally stabbed him on the way with daggers. The Emperor ordered all the three (Hindus) to be executed. Raghunāth Singh Sisodiā left the Rānā, joined the Emperor, was created a *hazāri* (300 tr.), and presented with a dagger worth 1,000 rupees.

ARRIVAL OF HUSAIN PĀSHĀ, LATE GOVERNOR OF BASRĀ

News-writers of Multān had before this informed the Emperor that Husain Pāshā, the governor of Basrā had quarrelled with the ruler of Turkey and been replaced by Yahia Pāshā, that as he could neither stay there nor return to his king, he chose to banish himself from his country with his family and a few servants, and at first went to Persia, where he met with no welcome, and that at last deciding to go to the imperial Court he was coming to India stage by stage. * * * *

[86] The Emperor approved of his desire, and ordered Ārtaq Beg, macebearer, to carry a robe, a *pālki,* and a female elephant to this lucky man at Sirhind, and to persuade him to visit the Emperor with perfect composure of mind. On Thursday, the 1st July/11th Safar he learnt that Husain Pāshā had arrived at Āghrābād. By the imperial command Fulād Khan the *kotwāl* met him at the salt-market. Bakhshi-ul-mulk Āsad Khan, Sadr-us-sadur 'Abid Khan and Mir Tuzuk Ekkatāz Khan waited on him at the Lahore gate of the city-wall, and conducted him to the Emperor. Bakhshi-ul-mulk Dānishmand Khan and Āsad Khan acted as his guides up to the door of the ghusalkhānā. He made the customary obeisance, was permitted to kiss the throne, and was stroked by the Emperor on the back. His sons Āfrāsiab Beg and 'Ali Beg presented 5,000 rupees and he offered a ruby worth 20,000 rupees and ten Arab horses. The Emperor gave him a special robe, a sword with jewelled *sāz* worth 6,000 rupees [87] a jewelled dagger, an elephant with silver trappings and *talāir,* 100,000 rupees in cash, and the rank of 5-*hazāri* (same tr.) with the title of Islām Khan, Āfrāsiāb Beg was created a Khan and 2-*hazāri* (1,000 tr.), and 'Ali Beg, a Khan and commander of 1,500 (500 tr.). They were given the haveli of Rustam Khan, an excellent house furnished with carpets

and other furniture, along with a carpeted boat, in which he would come by water to pay his respects to the Emperor. * * * *

News came from Attock-Benares that on Thursday, the 24th June/4th Safar, a severe earthquake had formed a pit 50 yards in length and of unfathomable depth. News came from Kashmir that on Wednesday, the 23rd June/3rd Safar the earthquake continued from evening to morning. The buildings rocked like cradles but were not damaged.

Sayyid Munawwar Khan, son of Sayyid Khān Jahān of Bārha, was appointed faujdār of Bārha. Rai Makarand after transfer from Bareli was appointed to Bengal. A baby elephant was presented to the young Prince Muhammad Kām Bakhsh. Raja Rām Singh, son of Mirzā Rāja Jai Singh, was promoted by the addition of 1,000 troopers. [88] Islām Khan received an increment of 1,000 *zāt* (same tr.), *tankhwā* for ten months, and his sons *tankhwā* for eight months in cash, and permanent exemption from the payment of the price of the food of the cattle in his case, and exemption for two years in the case of his sons. 'Abdullah Khan was restored to the rank of 2-*hazāri* (1,000 tr.) and granted a robe, an enamelled dagger, and the post of dārogha of ghusalkhāna. On Thursday, the 2nd September, 1669/15th Rabi. S., Mirzā Mukarram Khan Safavi died of a severe fever.

It was reported that, according to the Emperor's command, his officers had demolished the temple of Viswanāth at Kāshi.

On Saturday, the 18th September/2nd Jamad. A., Ekkatāz Khan and Giridhardās Sisodiā had a fight in the course of their watch before the Lahore gate. The Hindu went to hell; the Khan received five wounds, and among his clientele (*birādari*) some Mughals were wounded. Iftikhār Khan, Khan-i-Sāmān, was ordered to make a review of camels, cows, and mules twice every year. On Saturday, the 2nd October/16th Jamad. A., after the Emperor had sat down in the audience hall, Multafat Khan, Himmat Khan, and Ruhullah Khan were conversing together, when Dildār, son of Ulfat Khan (Muhammad Tāhir) and grandson of Daulat Khan, who bore ill will to Multafat Khan, suddenly struck his sword on the back of the Khan with both his hands. As soon as he faced round, the assailant struck three other blows; Multafat Khan received them on his shield, and thrust at him with his sword. Meantime Himmat Khan struck at him with his sword, Fazlullah Khan, Mir-Tuzuk hit him on the head with a rod. Getting perplexed and [89] receiving blows with sticks from Bahramand Khan and others, the assailant ran up to the marble stool. Jamil Beg Khawās who used to fan the Emperor with a *chāmar,* stabbed him in the armpit with a dagger. He was despatched, and his corpse was taken up and thrown outside. The men of the left hand group (*dangal-i-chap*) and the slaves of that day's guard, both high and low, were degraded in rank. Two kror *dām* from the chakla of Hisār which had been assigned as jāgir to Prince Muhammad Mu'azzam was granted as *in'ām,* and instead of it a *jāgir* was assigned to him in the Deccan.

On Monday, the 11th October/25th Jamad. A., it was learnt that when four *gharis* of the night had passed, a star on the east shot out of the sky and fell towards the west, lighting up houses, as with moonlight, and then a sound like the rumbling of thunder was heard. By the gracious favour of the Emperor J'afar Khan was ordered to visit the gardens of Āgharābād and Nulbāri, and he did so.

On Monday, the 26th October/10th Jamad. S., began the 52nd solar year of the Emperor's life. Festivity, presents from and to princes and grandees. [90] Islām Khan was presented with 100 pieces of gold-embroidery, Fazlullah Khan and Hazbar Khan conducted Shādmān Khwāja, the messenger of Balkh, from the door of the ghusalkhāna. He presented the respects of Subhān Quli Khan, and received a robe and 10,000 rupees. Safi Khan was sent as Subahdār of Orissa vice Tarbiyat Khan. On Sunday and Monday, 31st October and 1st November/15th and 16th Jamad. S., the Emperor visited the tombs of Humāyun, Shaikh Nizāmuddin Āulia, and Khwāja Qutbuddin Bakhtiār Kāki Tushi. Rewards in cash were given to the attendants of the three shrines and they showed the sacred relics. Muhammad Yār, son of 'Itiqād Khan, was first appointed a 4-*sadi*. 'Ali Akbar, messenger of the king of Golconda, had audience, and offered a tribute of 1,000 mohars and 15 elephants. Mir Shihābuddin, son of 'Ābid Khan came to the Court from *Vilāyet;* the Khan presented a shield ornamented with enamelled flowers. The Mir was made a 3-*sadi* (70 tr.) Khwāja Muhammad Y'aqub, about whom [91] something will be written afterwards, narrated to the author, "Subhān Quli Khan took me with him on a visit to his melon-ground.

Rustam Bé Atāliq and I were sitting together on one side, when Mir Shihābuddin came to me and said, "My father calls me, but I am not getting my master's permission to go". At this time the Atāliq and I supported this request saying that a letter might be kept written so that after the permission was given there might not be the delay of writing. We went to him at the time of his meal, made the request, and got his permission. On that occasion Shihābuddin, too, presented to the Khan some pieces of *shawl* sent by his father. The letter received the royal seal and the Khan offered prayers for his journey. When he had gone some steps, the Khan called him back and said, "You are going to Hindustān where you will become a big man. I hope you will not forget me."

THE EMPEROR'S JOURNEY TO AGRA FOR PUTTING DOWN REBELS

On Sunday, the 28th November, 1669/14th Rajab, the imperial tents [92] were pitched near the Jamunā, and the army set out towards Agra at the appointed hour. The Emperor hunted on most of the days of the journey. On Saturday, the 4th December/20th Rajab, while riding out to hunt, he learnt the circumstances of the rebellion in the villages of Rewāra, Chandarkha, and Sarkhud. By order of the Emperor Hasan 'Ali Khan attacked them. They fought up to noon with bows and muskets; and then, being unable to resist any longer, many of them performed the *jauhar* of their women, and rushed to fight at close quarters; many of the imperialists including the companions of Hasan 'Ali Khan attained martyrdom, while 300 of the infidels went to hell and 250 persons, male and female, were made prisoners. The Khan returned to the Emperor at sunset and reported on the battle. The prisoners were ordered to be made over to Sayyid Zain-ul-'Ābidin, jāgirdār of the place.

Saf Shikan Khan faujdār of Mathurā, came to interview. An order was issued that he should appoint 200 horsemen from among his servants to guard the crops of the villages and to prevent the soldiers from oppressing any one or taking any child prisoner. Nāmdār Khan, faujdār of Murādābād, came to interview, by command. He offered 100 mohars, 1,000 rupees and two black hawks. Hasan 'Ali Khan was appointed faujdār of Mathura *vice* Saf Shikan

Khan, [93] and made a commander of 3,500 *zāt* (2,000 tr.) and was given a robe, a sword, a horse. Āmānullah, son of Ālawardi Khan 'Alamgirshāhi, the faujdār of the environs of Agra, got an increment of 300 troopers and was ordered to help the aforesaid Khan. Under the Khan were placed 2,000 *barqāndāz* troopers, 1,000 archers, 1,000 musketeers, 1,000 rocket-men, 25 pieces of cannon, 1,000 *beldars* and 1,000 *tabardars* (pioneers and sappers). Hushdār Khan governor of Agra came to interview.

On Wednesday, the 15th December/1st Shaban a letter accompanied by 1,000 mohars was received from Prince Muhammad Mu'azzam giving news of the birth of a son to the daughter of Rup Singh Rāthor. The child was named Daulatāfzā; a letter and jewels worth 100,000 rupees were sent to the child and its parents. On Friday, the 31st December/17th Shaban, the Emperor visited the tombs of Shāh Jahān and Mumtāz-uz-zamāni, and presented 44,000 rupees to the officers of the tombs on behalf of himself and the two princes.

On Saturday, the 1st January, 1670/18th Shaban the Emperor took up his residence in the palace of Agra fort.

Goklā Jāt, the accursed rebel and the ring-leader of the disturbance in the country of Tilpat, who was the cause of the killing of 'Abdun Nabi Khan and had plundered the pargana of S'adābād, [94] was captured through the valour and efforts of Hasan 'Ali Khan and his *peshkār* Shaikh Raziuddin. The Khan sent him and his comrade Sonki to the Emperor in charge of Shaikh Qawm. By imperial order, his limbs were hacked off one after another in the *chabutra* of the *kotwāli*. His son and daughter were made over to Jawāhir Khan, *nāzir,* for being brought up (as Muslims). The daughter was married to Shāh Quli Chelah (slave), an intimate servant of high rank. The son became a memoriser of the Qurān with the name of Fāzil, and in the opinion of the Emperor surpassed in correctness all other memorisers, and he had the happiness of hearing His Majesty's chanting of the Qurān.

Shaikh Raziuddin, a very learned and high-born man of Bhāgalpur in Bihār, was among the scholars engaged in compiling the *Fatāwa-i-'Ālamgiri,* and got a daily stipend of three rupees. He had many other accomplishments such as military skill, administrative capacity, pleasantness of speech, and knowledge about most places. His merits were reported to the Emperor by Qāzi Muhammad Husain Jaunpuri, Censor of the Court, and Bakhtāwar Khan a personal attendant. He was given the rank of a *sadi* and gradually through the help of Hasan 'Ali Khan, rose to be an Amir and then a Khan and did splendid services. At last he sank into sleep in the cradle of death. [95]

CHAPTER XIII

THIRTEENTH YEAR OF THE REIGN. (1080 A.H.)

13th January, 1670—1st January, 1671.

On Thursday, 27th January/15th Ramzan, the justice-loving Emperor ordered that complainants should not be excluded from the side of the window of *darsan* : the harem-officers were to draw up their petitions by means of ropes and show them to His Majesty. During this month of Ramzan abounding in miracles, the Emperor as the promoter of justice and overthrower of mischief, as a knower of truth and destroyer of oppression, as the zephyr of the garden of victory and the reviver of the faith of the Prophet, issued orders for the demolition of the temple situated in Mathurā, famous as the Dehra of Kesho Rāi. In a short time by the great exertions of his officers, the destruction of this strong foundation of infidelity was accomplished, and on its site a lofty mosque was built at the expenditure of a large sum. This temple of folly was built by that gross idiot Birsingh Deo Bundela. Before his accession to the throne, the Emperor Jahāngir was displeased with Shaikh Ābul Fazl. [96] This infidel became a royal favourite by slaying him, and after Jahāngir's accession was rewarded for this service with the permission to build the temple, which he did at an expense of thirty-three lakhs of rupees.

Praised be the august God of the faith of Islām, that in the auspicious reign of this destroyer of infidelity and turbulence, such a wonderful and seemingly impossible work was successfully accomplished. On seeing this instance of the strength of the Emperor's faith and the grandeur of his devotion to God, the proud Rajas were stifled, and in amazement they stood like images facing the wall. The idols, large and small, set with costly jewels, which had been set up in the temple, were brought to Agra, and buried under the steps of the mosque of the Begam Sāhib, in order to be continually trodden upon. The name of Mathurā was changed to Islāmābād.

On 12th February, 1670, the day of 'Id, the Emperor rode out on a huge elephant, with Prince Muhammad 'Azam seated behind him, and dismounted at the 'Idgāh.

[97] Next day, he sat on the throne of gold presented by Āmirul-umārā 'Ali Mardān Khan and placed in the middle of the hall of the palace. Princes Muhammad 'Azam and Akbar received robes. 'Umdat-ul-mulk J'afar Khan got an increment of 1,000 troopers and 1 kror of dam as reward. Raja Rām Singh, who was a 4-*hazāri* (4,000 tr. *do-āspa, seh-āspa*), was raised higher by 1,000 troopers on condition of serving in Assām. Kumār Kishan Singh, son of Rām Singh, was given a jewelled turban. Hasan 'Ali Khan's conditional rank of 1,500 was made unconditional, and he was granted kettle-drums. Āshraf Khan and Himmat Khan were promoted by 500 troopers; Mir Taqi was made a 3-*hazāri,* Multafat Khan and Mughal Khan were promoted by 500, and so made 2-*hazāris*.

Sazāwar Khan and Fazlullah Khan were each given 100 troopers. Bakhshi-ul-mulk Āsad Khan and Faizullah Khan were presented with two riding horses of great speed. 'Abdur Rahmān Sultān and Bahrām Sultān each got 10,000 rupees as reward. Shādmān Khwāja, ambassador of Balkh got leave to depart, with 25,000 rupees in cash, a robe, a jewelled sword worth 5,000 rupees, an elephant with a silver saddle, a flowered shawl, 150 pieces of cannon, Āghābāni turban, and Gujrāti *fota* of the same value; his followers received 10,000 rupees as reward. Muhammad 'Ābid, son of Zāhid Khan Panjābi got the rank of 1½-*hazāri* (300 tr.) [98] and the title of Nawāzish Khan. Dārāb Khan, dārogha of the Emperor's own musket-room, became dārogha of the ghusalkhāna *vice* 'Abdullah Khan. The *bayutāt* of Agra thus reported the price of grain to the Emperor: fine Sukhdās rice at 14 seers, wheat 35 seers, pulse 1 md. 2 seers, ghee (*raughan*) 4 seers, for a rupee and the prices of other articles were also according to this standard.

On Sunday, the 27th March 1670/15th Zil. Q., the 54th lunar year of the Emperor's life began. Festive decorations were suspended. The officers of the band-room were ordered that the music of the ceremony which used to be played all day was (henceforth) to be played after the passing of one *prahar,* as at the festivity on Sundays. Bakhtāwar Khan, dārogha of the khawāses, was presented with a dagger having a crystal handle. Sayyid Āmjad Khan, son of Mir Sayyid Muhammad Qanauji, was appointed Censor of the imperial camp *vice* Qāzi Muhammad Husain, deceased.

The courtiers who used to salute each other by raising the hand to the head, were now ordered to say [simply] *salām 'alekum.*

On Wednesday, 20th April/9th Zil. H., Mullā 'Abdul 'Aziz 'Izzat, son of Mullā 'Abdul Rashid Akbarābādi, had [99] audience in the mosque through the mediation of Himmat Khan and Bakhtāwar [cor.] Khan. He, after acquiring knowledge of both the traditional and rational branches of learning alike and attaining to the high rank of a master of all the sciences, was spending his days in a life of seclusion in his house contented with a daily stipend of three rupees only, and never bowed his head down in supplication to any of the powerful grandees. As fortune had destined him for celebrity and advancement, his great intellectual powers, wisdom, mastery of meaning, elegance of language, sound understanding and agreeable nature, judicious speech and power of devising plans became the cause of his being taken up for training and favour at the Court of the Emperor, who discovers and discerns all merit. The Shaikh at first got a *mansab* of 400, a robe, 5 horses, a sword, a dagger, a spear, a decorated *palki* and other articles. On the fourth day, when the grants were reported a second time for confirmation, he got an increment of 100 (30 tr.) and the post of *dārogha-i-'arz-i-mukarrar, vice* Lutfullah Khan. He was elevated by being given the right of private audience, and that of not having to raise his hand to his head before anybody,—*'salām 'alek'* being enough for him.

News came from the Deccan that Shivāji after seizing the fort of Purandar had captured the qiladār, Raziuddin. Bakhtāwar Khan issued orders to the diwāni officers that they should report to the Emperor the income and expenditure at the end of the year and should bring to the ghusalkhāna, (every) Wednesday the registers of the Diwāns of the *tankhwa* and the Crown-land departments. 'Ināyet Khan reported that since the reign of Shāh Jahān the public expenditure had exceeded the income by 14 lakhs of rupees. It was ordered that the privy purse (*khālsa*) income should be fixed at four krores of rupees, and the expenditure the same. After looking over the accounts of disbursements, His Majesty retrenched many items of the expenditure of the Emperor, the Princes, and the begams.

It was reported that Hasan 'Ali Khan was sparing no exertion in slaying and capturing the infidel rebels, plundering their houses, destroying their families and demolishing their strong forts, and had planted Shāh Muhammad Nawāz, Sidam Baluch, Shaikh Raziuddin, L'al Muhammad, Nazar Muhammad and others in full control over the *mahāls* of the *zamindāri*; he was ordered to come to Court. On Wednesday, the 6th April/25th Zil. Q., he had audience and was highly praised. On Saturday, the 9th April, 1670/ 28th Zil. Q., news came from Delhi of the death of Badrunnisā Begam, daughter of the Emperor. The father greatly loved her for her Rābi'a-like piety, memorisation of the Quran, good character and manners.

News came that Prince Muhammad Mu'azzam had been instigated by flatterers to act in a self-willed and independent manner. [101] The Emperor's letters of advice producing no effect, he summoned the Prince's mother, Nawāb Bāi from Delhi, in order to send her to her son for bringing him back to the right path if any trace of recalcitrancy was found in him. Iftikhār Khan was sent to the Prince, with a verbal message of mingled kindness and reproach. The Khan speedily went to his destination and discharged his mission. As the Prince's character was full of devotion to the Emperor and the reports against him were utterly false, he replied very submissively, expressing grief and regret. His Majesty, therefore, renewed his favour to the Prince, and became very angry with Iftikhār Khan for his error of judgment. When the Khan returned he and his brother Multafat Khan [102] were deprived of their ranks and titles. Sher Beg, macebearer, conducted Sultān Husain across the river of Attock and brought Mir Ibrāhim Husain to Lahore, under his strict escort (*sazāwali*). Āshraf Khan was made Khān-i-sāmān *vice* Iftikhār Khan and Mughal Khan was made dārogha of the macebearers *vice* Āshraf Khan. Hāji Āhmad S'aid Khan became dārogha of *'arz-i-mukarrar vice* Mughal Khan. On Tuesday, the 29th March/17th Zil. Q., news came that Dilir Khan after reinstating the zamindār of Deogarh in his zamindāri had returned to Aurangabad. Nawāb Bāi, summoned from Delhi, reached Sikandāra on Thursday, the 13th April/2nd Zil. Q. Prince Muhammad Akbar, Bakhshiulmulk Āsad Khan and Bahramand Khan advanced to meet her, and conducted her to the imperial harem.

On Thursday, the 21st April/10th Zil. H., occurred the 'Id-uz-zuha. The Emperor visited the 'Idgah for prayer and sacrifice. Dost Muhammad, the *Khutba*-reader was rewarded with a robe and 500 rupees and Ni'amat Khan Bakāwal (superintendent of the kitchen) with a knife, according to the fixed custom. Robes and jewelled daggers were sent by a macebearer to Dilir Khan and Dāud Khan. Hāji Shaf'i Khan became diwān of the Deccan *vice* Mukarramat Khan, Kifāyet Khan diwān-i-tan *vice* the Hāji, Shāh Khwāja dārogha of the departments of branding and muster (*dāgh* and *tashiha*) *vice* Kifāyet Khan. Nawāb Bāi started for Aurangabad. She was commanded to spend two days at Gwalior with her eldest son, Muhammad Sultān who was imprisoned there. [103] Sarbuland Khan was to conduct her to Prince Muhammad Mu'azzam in the Deccan, and then return.

As the illness of 'Umdatulmulk J'afar Khan became severer, the Emperor twice went to his house, at first to comfort the sick man and the second time to condole with his relatives. On Friday the 6th May, 1670/25th Zil. H., he died. In his character were united all graciousness of heart and grandeur of behaviour. The Emperor mourned the death of such a devoted servant, and ordered that for 3 days 120 dishes of food should be sent to the bereaved family. Princes Muhammad 'Azam and Akbar were ordered to go to the houses of his sons, Nāmdār Khan and Kāmgār Khan to make the customary inquiries and to console their mother, Farzāna Begam. Special robes were sent to both and a *tora* to her. Akbar, after having raised them from the posture of mourning, brought them both to the Emperor who honoured them with jewelled daggers having pearl *ilaqas* and many other favours and kind words. Mourning robes were presented to Bakshiulmulk Āsad Khan, Mirzā Bahrām, and his sons Bahramand Khan and Sharfuddin, to Iltifāt Khan, Muftakhar, Mufākhar, Raushandil and others. Āsad Khan was appointed deputy diwān and presented with a jewelled dagger and two packets of betels from the Emperor's own hand. The Emperor ordered that [on Āsad Khan's letter of appointment] should be written through the mediation (rasālatun) of Prince Md. Mu'azzam [104] and that the seal of the Prince should be affixed by Diānat Khan. On Sunday, the 8th May/27th Zil. H., Ekkatāz Khan was sent as envoy to Bukhārā, and presented with a horse worth 100 *mohars,* an elephant worth 4,000 rupees, a jewelled dagger, a jewelled sword, a jewelled *jigna*. He was a 1½ *nazāri* (500 tr.) and now got an increment of 500 (100 tr.).. For 'Abdul 'Aziz, the king of Bukhārā, there were sent with him, besides presents and rarities of Hindustān worth more than 2 lakhs of rupees, five *tāzi* and four Cutchi horses. Mughal Khan was made Mirtuzuk *vice* Ekkatāz Khan and given a gold mace (*'asa*), Mubāriz Khan became governor of Multān *vice* Lashkar Khan, Jahāngir Quli Khan was appointed *nāib* (deputy) of Muhammad 'Azam in the faujdārship of the chakla of Sambal. A *farmān* was sent to Muhammad Āmin Khan appointing him Subahdār of Kābul *vice* Mahābat Khan, Tarbiyat Khan was made Subahdār of Oudh *vice* Fidāi Khan who came to the Court and was sent to reside at Gwalior, as was considered expedient. R'adāndāz Khan, dārogha of the *topkhāna* accompanying the Emperor, Raja Devi Singh, Yaḥia Khan Deccani, Sayyid 'Ali Akbar, Rumi Khan, Kārtalb Khan Miwāti, Badi 'Sultān of Balkh, Mirzā Sadruddin, son of Mirzā Sultān, and his companions were rewarded with promotion, robes, horses, swords, and [105] daggers, according to their ranks. Jāni Khan was made *nāib* of R'adāndāz Khan, in the dārogha-ship of the *topkhāna* accompanying the Emperor.

On Thursday, the 4th August, 1670/27th Rabi. A., a son was born to Muhammad 'Azam and Jahānzeb Bānu Begam. The Emperor named him Bidār-bakht, and presented him with a cap worth 10,000 rupees, and the Begam with a pearl necklace worth 10,000 rupees, and a *smarani* worth 7,000 rupees. Āmānat Khan, *alias* Sayyid Āhmad Khattāb got the title of Khan, and was sent to Bengal as diwān. 'Abdullah Khan of Kāshghar, after visiting the holy cities, returned to the Court, he was presented with 1 lakh of rupees from the revenue of Surāt and Mālwa. News came that Dānishmand Khan, Mir Bakhshi, the nāzim and qiladār of Delhi, had died on Monday, the 18th July/10th Rabi. A. He was one of the greatest scholars of the age and his life was devoted to charity and piety. Lashkar Khan, Subahdār of Multān, who had come to Court, was appointed the first Bakhshi *vice* the deceased; he got a lift of 1000 (same tr.) on his rank of 4-*hazāri* (same tr.) Himmat Khan, the third Bakhshi, was made second Bakhshi *vice* Āsad Khan, Nāmdar Khan was appointed Subahdār of Delhi, and Mu'atamad Khan commandant of the fort. Sayyid Āmir Khan who [106] after resigning his rank was living in Delhi, died on 3rd September, 1670/27th Rabi. S. The Emperor gave robes of mourning and words of consolation to Muhammad Ibrāhim, Muhammad Ishāq, and Muhammad Y'aqub, the sons of his brother Shaikh Mir. News came from Peshāwar that Muhammad Āmin Khan had reached that place on Wednesday, the 17th August/10th Rabi. S. Riding coats for the rainy season were presented to Āsad Khan, Murtaza Khan, 'Ābid Khan, Hasan 'Ali Khan, Tāhir Khan, and other officers at Court and the provinces. Hāji Āhmad Sayyid Khan was appointed diwān of Begam Sāhib. Lutfullah Khan was appointed *dārogha* of *'arz-i-mukarrar vice* him. Faizullah Khan was made faujdār of Sambal *vice* the agents of Prince 'Azam, and Sarbuland Khan was made Qushbegi (master of the hunt) *vice* him.

On Saturday, the 29th October/24th Jamad. S., [the 53rd] solar year of the Emperor's life began. He sat on the throne of gold. * * * R'adāndāz Khan who had gone with Fidāi Khan was summond to the Court and had the honour of audience.

It was learnt that on Sunday, the 2nd October, 1670/27th Jamad.A., the accursed Shivā had attacked Surat, burnt and plundered the town for some hours, and then retired. A letter with 1000 mohars came from Prince Muhammad Mu'azzam announcing the birth of a son to him and Nurunnisā Begam, [107] the daughter of Sanjar, Najam-i-Sāni. Mirzā Muhammad, the agent of the Prince presented them to the Emperor, who gave the baby the name of Rafi'-ush-shān. Sarbuland Khan who had gone to the Deccan as escort of Nawāb Bāi, now returned and had audience. Mahābat Khan, the ex-Subahdār of Kabul, came and had audience, the Emperor remarking "You are welcome". On Monday, the 28th November/25th Rajab he was sent on the Deccan expedition, and presented with a robe with half-sleeve and collar, a horse with gold trappings, and an elephant with *talāir*. His son Bahrām got a jewelled dagger. Rao Rup Singh, son of Rao Karn, Raja Amar Singh, son of Kishan Singh, Dilir Himmat, brother and Suhrāb, brother's son of Mahābat, and other officers of that Khan's army received presents.

It was ordered that ribbon frills in the European style should not be attached to the boats and *palkis* of the princes and peers.

CHAPTER XIV

FOURTEENTH YEAR OF THE REIGN: 1081 A.H.

2nd January,—21st December, 1671.

With the month of Ramzan commenced the 14th year of the reign. * * * * * * [108] On Wednesday the 1st February, occurred the 'Id-ul-fitr. After returning from the mosque, the Emperor sat on the throne. * * *

Āsad Khan was made the first Bakhshi *vice* Lashkar Khan deceased. Hasan 'Ali Khan, after receiving a robe and a horse, hastened back to his post. Muhammad Sharif, envoy of Bukhārā, got a present of 25,000 rupees and a robe and a horse with gold trappings. Shaikh 'Usmān, the agent of the Sharif of Mecca, placed before the Emperor his master's presents consisting of two Arab horses, a silver sword-belt and *bāz*. He received a jewelled dagger, 10,000 rupees and a gold coin weighing 100 *mohars* and a rupee weighing 100 rupees. Twenty thousand rupees were entrusted to him for the Sharif of Mecca. Sayyid Muhammad Rumi, the envoy of Abyssinia, presented his master's gifts. At his first interview he got a robe, and at his leave taking a robe and 10,000 rupees. Yalangtosh Khan Bahadur was given a sword, a dagger, a spear, and a shield. Irādat Khan was made Ākhta Begi *vice* Ruhullah Khan, S'ādat Khan Qāqshāl who had come to the Court, went back to his post.

On Monday, 10th April/10th Zil. H., took place the 'Id-uz-zuha. Five thousand mohars were presented to Purhunar Bānu Begam and Gauharārā Begam each. On Monday, the 12th June/14th Safar, Muhammad Āmin Khan reached the Court by command [109]; Lutfullah Khan met him at the gate of the fort and Āsad Khan at the door of the ghusalkhāna. He presented four Arab and 'Iraqi horses. The Emperor gave him a robe and made kind inquiries. On Sunday, the 21st May/22nd Muharram Nauras Bānu Begam, wife of Shāh Nawāz Khan Safavi died. Mourning robes were presented to Dārāb Khan and Khānazād Khan, the sons of Mirzā Ābu S'aid, sister's son of Nur Jahān Begam. The Amir-ul-umārā's tribute of 2 lakhs 30,000 rupees, consisting of elephants and other presents and rare things, was placed before the Emperor. Shādkām Chela, an old slave of His Majesty, died. Posts and dresses were conferred on his relatives. Maharaja Jaswant Singh was appointed thānahdār of Jamrud, and given a overcoat for the rainy season (*farghal-i-bārāni*) and a horse worth 500 mohars. Bisrām Khan the chief musician died. Robes were given to Bhupat, his son, and Khushhāl Khan (musician). Ziāuddin Husain, Yādgar Husain, and Muhammad Husain, daughter's sons of Āshraf Khan, had audience and were given robes. As they were very stout, the Emperor ordered that one of them was to be brought to the Court every day.

Muhammad 'Ali Beg, son of Amirulumārā 'Ali Mardān Khan came from Persia, had audience, and received a robe, a sword, a jewelled dagger with a pearl *ilaqa,* and 10,000 rupees. On Saturday, the 29th July/2nd Rabi. S., Mir Muhammad brother of Asālat Khan, who had newly arrived from Persia, interviewed the Emperor [110] and received a jewelled dagger and 7,000 rupees. Hushdār Khan was appointed nāzim of Burhānpur *vice* Dāud Khan who after interview was made nāzim of Allahabad, *vice* Mir Khan and received a special robe, a horse with gold trappings, and an elephant with bronze trappings. 'Ināyet Khan, daftardār of khālsa (crownlands) got the faujdāri of the chakla of Bareli. Āmānat Khan *alias* Mirak Mu'inuddin got his post and an inkpot of crystal stone. Muhammad Yār, son of 'Itiqād Khan, got a robe on his marriage with the daughter of Farrukh Fāl. Muhammad 'Ali Beg got the title of 'Aliquli Khan and the rank of 2-*hazāri* (same tr.), a standard, kettle-drums, and gold and silver articles worth 30,000 rupees.

Yahia Pāshā, who had been appointed by the ruler of Turkey, to govern Basrā *vice* Husain Pāshā, did not occupy his office owing to some change in his fortunes, came to the imperial Court, and received a special robe with buttons of gold thread, a jewelled sword and dagger, 10,000 rupees and the rank of 1500 (700 tr.) Bārāni (rain) robes were presented to the princes and the grandees, high and low, at the Court and in the provinces. 'Ābid Khan was made Subahdār of Multān *vice* Mubāriz Khan. On Monday, the 11th September, 1671/17th Jamad. A., Rushanārā Begam, the Emperor's sister died [111]. She had noble qualities and admirable traits, and greatly loved her brother. The Emperor gave away large sums in charity for the benefit of her soul, and conferred favours on her male and female servants.

Muhammad Āmin Khan was invited to Court to take up the duties of Wazir. True, he was unique in counsel and honesty, but his nature contained the vile characteristics of self-will and pride. As by making some improper requests, he alienated the equable mind of the Emperor, on Friday, the 15th September/21st Jamad. A., he was sent to Kabul as Subahdār, and presented with a special robe, a dagger set with jasper and having a pearl *'ilaqa,* and a tall elephant, with silver trappings. Iftikhār Khan's and Multafat Khan's faults were pardoned and they were restored to their ranks [112] and titles. The first was sent to Kashmir as Subahdār *vice* Saif Khan who had turned hermit and been removed from his rank. The second was appointed qiladār of Delhi *vice* Mu'atamad Khan. On Thursday, the 28th September/4th Jamad.S., Mir Khan, the ex-Subahdār of Allahabad had audience. Lutfullah Khan received a robe on his marriage with the daughter of Lashkar Khan. Kāmgār Khan was sent to the Amir-ul-umārā. Sufi Bahadur was sent as envoy to Ānusha Khan, ruler of Urganj, and received a robe, a jewelled *jigha,* a sword, a quiver, and a shield. Nāmdār Khan was appointed Subahdār of Agra and Mu'atamad Khan commandant of Agra fort. The Emperor learnt that 'Abdūllah Khan after returning from his pilgrimage, was coming to the imperial court; he bestowed on him 1,000 mohars and a silver tray and cover

THE EMPEROR'S JOURNEY FROM AGRA TO DELHI.

On Thursday, the 2nd November/10th Rajab, he started from Agra, hunting on the way. He reached Khizrābād on Thursday the 23rd/1st Shaban. On Sunday, the 26th/4th Shaban, after visiting the tombs of Khwāja Qutbuddin and Shaikh Nasiruddin, the Lamp of Delhi [113] and presenting 1500 rupees to the residents of the two places, he arrived at the palace. On Monday, the 18th December, 1671/26th Shaban, Prince Muhammad 'Azam sent 1000 mohars on account of the birth of a son to his begam. He was named Jawān-bakht. Kāmyāb Khan Safavi, who had been dismissed, was reinstated in his rank. 'Abdullah Khan who had arrived at Delhi before the Emperor, was conducted to the Court by Āsad Khan and

Bahramand Khan and had the honour of being received in audience. 2,000 mohars and fifty trays of food were sent to his house. Dismissed Mir Khan was restored to his rank, Mir Mahmud got the rank of a *hazāri* (400 tr.) and the title of 'Aqidat Khan. On 16th December/24th Shaban, the Emperor received the peshkash of Muhammad Āmin Khan consisting of 280 pearls worth 1 lakh and 5,000 rupees, and 50 horses.

CHAPTER XV

FIFTEENTH YEAR OF REIGN : 1082 A.H.

22nd December 1671—10th December 1672.

[Month of Ramzan and the Emperor's gifts] * * * [114] 'Aqidat Khan got a robe on his marriage with the daughter of Ruhullah Khan. On the death of Hushdār Khan, son of Multafat Khan 'Alamgiri and grandson of 'Azam Khan Jahāngiri, Kāmgār and J'afar, sons of Hushdār (deceased) had audience.

The astonishing occurrence of the suppression of the Satnāmis who are (also) called Mundiyas.

Those who observe the wondrous works of Heaven have been filled with astonishment at the occurrence of this affair in which a rebellious horde of low people like goldsmiths, carpenters, scavengers, tanners [115] and members of other menial professions, who are naturally weak and fore-doomed to slaughter, took I know not what into their heads so that they were filled with a spirit of obstinate self-will, as if in their rebellious pride they felt their heads to be an untolerable burden on their shoulders and wilfully walked into the trap of their destruction. The detailed account of this affair is as follows :

A large body of wicked mischief-makers of the Miwāt district suddenly sprang out of the ground like termites (winged ants) and descended from the sky like locusts. It was said that these wicked people considered themselves immortal, and believed that if one of them was slain, seventy others would spring up in his place. They defied the imperial authority and caused disturbances near Nārnol, in a body of about 5,000 men, and plundered the villages and parganahs. Tāhir Khan the faujdār, being unable to resist them came to the Presence, and the Emperor formed the resolution of crushing the despicable infidels. On Friday, the 15th March, 1672/26th Zil. Q., R'adāndāz Khan with the artillery, Hāmid Khan with the troops of Khās chauki and 500 troops of his father Sayyid Murtaza Khan, Yahia Khan Rumi, Najib Khan, Rumi Khan, Kamāluddin, son of Dilir Khan, Purdil son of Firuz Khan Miwāti, and Āsfandiyār, the bakhshi of Prince Akbar with a body of the Prince's troops, were ordered to set out against these infidels. When the imperial troops reached the place, the enemy resolving to fight advanced inspite of their lack of war materials; [116] they acted the battle described in old Hindu books called in the Hindu tongue the *Mahābhārat,* which means the slaying of elephants in the field. The Muslim heroes charged and reddened their pitiless swords in the blood of the rebels. A terrible battle was fought. R'adāndāz Khan, Hāmid Khan and Yahiya Khan greatly distinguished themselves. Many of the Muslims were slain, and many others wounded. At last the enemy took to flight, and many of them were slain by the victors in the pursuit, very few escaped; our generals won the victory and the tract was cleared of the infidels. The victors were granted audience and congratulated by the Emperor. R'adāndāz Khan was given the title of Shujā'et Khan and made a 3500 (2000 tr.) Hāmid Khan, Yahia Khan, Rumi Khan, Najib Khan and all other warriors, high and low, got promotions and robes.

On Friday, the 29th March/10th Zil. H., occurred the 'Id-uz-zuha. [117] *Disaster to Muhammad Āmin Khan, and retreat from the Khyber Pass* : * * *

Muhammad Āmin Khan wanted to go to govern Kabul and encounter the turbulent Afghans. On Sunday the 21st April, 1672/3rd Muharram, though he had got the news that the Afghans had blocked the pass of Khyber before the day on which he had planned to cross it, he proceeded on without paying any heed to it or considering it necessary to dislodge them. At the time of crossing the same disorder took place among his troops which had happened in Akbar's time to Hakim Abul Fath, Zain Khan Kokah and Raja Birbal. The Afghans crowded on all sides, and began to hurl arrows and stones. The troops were scattered and [118] the horses, elephants, and men were mixed up in confusion. At this crisis, although several thousand men had lost their lives by falling from the summit of the hills into the abyss, Muhammad Āmin Khan from his high sense of honour wanted to sacrifice his life in fight. But his servants seized his bridle and brought him away from the place of danger. After losing 'Abdullah Khan, the young and faithful son of the Khan, and without gaining any honour, he galloped back to Peshāwar in a wretched condition. The Emperor got this news on the 30th April/12th Muharram.

On Saturday, the 18th May/30th Muharram, Fidāi Khan left Lahore for Peshāwar. On 8th May, 1672/20th

Muharram, Sarbuland Khan was made Subahdār of Agra *vice* Nāmdār Khan, Multafat Khan dārogha of the imperial retinue *vice* Sarbuland Khan. Faizullah after receiving a special dress and a horse with gold trappings, started for Morādābād. 'Abdullah Khan received 20,000 rupees, Saif Khan, the 'hermit'* was granted interview, a sword, and restoration to his rank.

MARRIAGE OF MUHAMMAD AKBAR WITH SALIMA BĀNU BEGAM.

She was the daughter of Sulaimān Shukoh, whom Gauhar-Ārā Begam had adopted [119] as her daughter and brought up. The Prince got a present of 4 lahks of rupees, a special robe with half-sleeves, a *kalgi,* a jewelled *dhup*, a necklace and a *sahra* (bridegroom's veil) of pearls, and two Arab and 'Irāqi horses. On Tuesday, the 18th June, 1672/2nd Rabi. A., the knot was tied in the mosque, through the agency of 'Abdul Wahhāb, the chief Qāzi. Five lakhs of rupees were fixed as the marriage-portion. Everyone present pronounced benediction. The Prince, after five *gharis* of night, set out on horseback in a grand procession; Muhammad 'Azam, Bakhshi-ul-mulk Āsad Khan, Mir Khan, Nāmdār Khan and other high grandees, accompanied him. On both sides of the road from the Delhi gate to the mansion of the Begam, wooden structures were set up for illumination. * * *

News arrived that Prince Muhammad Mu'azzam was coming to interview the Emperor. On Thursday, the 25th July/9th Rabi. S., [120] he had audience, and received a special robe, a sword with jewelled trapping, a pearl necklace, an *arsi* set with jewels, and 1 lakh of rupees. Princes Muhammad Mu'izuddin and Muhammad 'Azim [-ud-din] received neck-pendent.

On Sunday, 15th September/2nd Jamad. S., Muhammad Sālih, son of Khwāja Tāhir Naqshbandi was married to Āsāish Bānu Begam, daughter of Murād Bakhsh, and received a robe, a horse with gold trappings, a jewelled dagger and a *kalgi,* and a female elephant. The knot was tied in the presence of Sarbuland Khan, Qāzi Abdul Wahhāb, and Mullā Muhammad Y'aqub.

* 'Hermit' is a Persian word conventionally used to mean 'retired to private life and unemployment after voluntarily resigning some public office.'

On Wednesday, the 9th October/26th Jamad. S., Wazir Khan and Muhammad Tāhir, the latter an old and devoted servant, died. Mir Khan got the subahdārship of Malwa *vice* Wazir Khan. Sarbuland Khan became second Bakhshi, *vice* Himmat Khan, who got Sarbuland's post *viz.* subahdāri of Agra. Mughal Khan became Qushbegi *vice* him (Himmat), Muhammad Tāhir, an old servant of the period before the Emperor's accession, who held the diwāni of the household of Hasan 'Ali Khan by command, was accused of the sin of cursing the first three caliphs. According to the canonical law and the insistence of the chief of the Ulemā, Mullā 'Auz Wajih, he was beheaded on the 3rd November/22nd Rajab.

Izid Bakhsh, the son of Murād Bakhsh, who had been brought to the Court from the prison of Gwalior, was married on Wednesday, the 27th November/16th Shaban to Mihrunnisā Begam, the Emperor's daughter, in the presence of Qāzi 'Abdul Wahhāb, Shaikh Nizām, Bakhtāwar Khan, and Darbār Khan. [121]

Multafat Khan, who had gone to Gwalior to bring Muhammad Sultān and Sipihr Shukoh, had audience on Sunday, the 8th December 1672/27th Shaban. Places were assigned in the fort of Salimgarh for the residence of both. On Tuesday, the 10th December/29th Shaban the Emperor visited the house of Prince Muhammad Mu'azzam, a gold-embroidered carpet and other things were spread as foot-cloth from the tower near the bridge gate of Salimgarh to the mansion of the Prince. Prince Muhammad Akbar was a 20-*hazāri* (2,000 tr.); he now got a promotion of 2,000 *zat*. On Thursday, the 5th December/24th Shaban, Khwāja Jawāhir Khan, treasurer (*tahvildār*) of the Emperor's private jewel department, died. He was an old slave of the Emperor and very kind to the poor. On Saturday, the 18th May/30th Muharram, Fidāi Khan started from Lahore for Peshāwar. Muhammad Āmin Khan was appointed Subahdār of Āhmadābād Gujrāt on the 11th June, and degraded from a 6-*hazāri* (5000 tr.) to a 5-*hazāri* (same tr.). He was ordered to go to his post without being granted an interview. Mahābat Khan who had come to the Emperor at Agra and been appointed on the Deccan expedition, was in view of his connection with the Afghans, ordered not to come to Court.

Islām Khan, on account of his delay in summoning to India his family and third son, Mukhtār Beg, had been dismissed and forbidden the Court, and was staying at Ujjain. At the prayer of 'Umdat-ul-mulk [122] Bahādur Khan, he was restored to his rank and appointed to the army of the Khan. He summoned his son and family from Basrā.

CHAPTER XVI

SIXTEENTH YEAR OF THE REIGN : 1083 A.H.

11th December 1672—29th November, 1673.

On the 10th January/1st Shawwal took place the 'Id-ul-fitr, with rejoicing in the palace. As usual, the two halls of audience and ghusalkhāna were decorated. The princes and courtiers attended at the palace to accompany the Emperor who went to the 'Idgāh in a high chair. [123] On Saturday, the 11th January/2nd Shawwal he sat on the throne in the palace-hall. Muhammad Mu'azzam got a robe with half-sleeves, a pearl necklace, one lakh of rupees, and an elephant with gold trappings worth 5000 rupees. Muhammad 'Azam got a robe with half-sleeves, and Muhammad Akbar, a *tora,* (jewelled turban-end).

Bakhshi-ul-mulk Āsad Khan and other officers, great and small, were rewarded with a variety of things, such as jewels, robes, horses, elephants and promotion of rank. Muhammad Mu'azzam was a 20-*hazāri* (15,000 tr.). He now got a reward of three krors of dam and an increment of 10,000 (5,000 tr.) Sultan Mu'izzuddin who was getting a daily allowance of 150 rupees, now received an increment of 50 rupees, Sultan Muhammad 'Azim was getting 100 rupees daily; it was now increased by 50 rupees. The Princes and grandees of the Court and the provinces sent *peshkash* worth about 50 lakhs of rupees. The envoy of Sikandar 'Ādil Khan, king of Bijāpur, presented jewels and embroidery worth four lakhs of rupees. The envoy of 'Abdullah Qutb-ul-mulk, king of Haidarābad, presented articles, gems, and China-ware vases of Golkonda. The Emperor ordered these presents to be considered as equivalent to three lakhs of rupees. Bahādur Khan [124] became Subahdār of the Deccan *vice* the agents of Prince Muhammad Mu'azzam, and got the title of Khan Jahān Bahādur; a special robe and a jewelled dagger were sent to him through a mace-bearer. He was a 6-*hazāri* (5,000 tr.) *do-āspā* and *seh-āspā,* and now got an increment of 1,000 troopers. Mir Ibrāhim, son-in-law of Safiyyah Bānu Begam's Kokah, was given the faujdāri of Miwāt with the title of Kārtalb Khan, while Murshid Quli Khan became dārogha of *dāgh* and *tashiha* in his place. Diānat Khan, who had no equal in the art of astrological calculations, "went to visit the celestial heavens". His sons, Diw-āfkan, Sher-āfkan and Rustam, got promotions and mourning robes.

On Monday, the 16th December, 1672, the Emperor ordered that Dārāb Khan should bring Muhammad Sultān and Sipihr Shukoh into the khwābgāh (sleeping chamber) of His Majesty. Both of them had audience; after interview they received robes and emerald *sarpeches*. Muhammad Sultān was married to Dostdār Bānu Begam, the daughter of Murād Bakhsh, and presented with a robe, a sword, a jewelled *muttaka,* and a horse with a jewelled saddle. In the khwābgāh the Emperor put a pearl chaplet on the Prince's head with his own hands and took him to the mosque. The Qāzi-ul-quzāt Abdul Wahhāb, with Mullā Muhammad Y'aqub as his agent, and Mir Sayyid Muhammad Qanauji and Mullā 'Auz Wajih as witnesses, tied the knot. Two lakhs of rupees were settled as the marriage-portion. Shujā'et Khan, Shaikh Nizām, [125] Darbār Khan, Bakhtāwar Khan and Khidmatgār Khan were present.

On Thursday, 30th January, 1673/21st Shawwal, Zubdat-un-nisā Begam was married to Sipihr Shukoh the son of Dārā Shukoh. Four lakhs of rupees was fixed as the marriage-portion. The knot was tied in the mosque, in the presence of His Majesty, Qāzi 'Abdul Wahhāb, Mullā 'Auz Wajih, Mullā Y'aqub, Darbār Khan and Bakhtawār Khan. Sipihr Shukoh was presented with a jewelled dagger, a jewelled *sarpech,* a pearl necklace and a pearl chaplet. Gauharārā Begam and Hāmida Bānu Begam, arranged the marriage ceremonies.

Iftikhār Khan, after removal from Kashmir, was sent to Peshāwar. Prince Muhammad Sultān got a yearly allowance of 12,000 rupees, Sipihr Shukoh of 6,000 rupees, and 'Izid Bakhsh of 4,000 rupees. On Tuesday, the 11th February, 1673/4th Zil. Q., Saifullah, inspector (mushrif) of the Qushkhānah* reported that a hunt-superintendent (mir-shikar) dreamed in sleep that a man with a drawn sword was encountering him; and when he awoke he found himself wounded and his sword lying bare by him. On Sunday, the 23rd February/16th Zil. Q., Prince

* *Qushkhāna*--the place where beasts of prey (*e.g.*, cheetah, falcon etc.) are kept.

Muhammad Mu'azzam, by command, visited the tomb of Khwāja Qutbuddin, and presented 1,000 rupees to the shrine. On Tuesday, the 25th March/16th Zil. H., Prince Muhammad Sultān too, visited the shrine, and presented 500 rupees. On Monday, the 10th March/1st Zil. H., Āsad Khan resigned the post of deputy diwān [126]. The Emperor ordered that Āmānat Khan, the diwān of the Khālsa, and Kifāyet Khan, the diwān-i-tan, should affix their seals a little below that of the high diwān, and transact the diwāni affairs.

Farjām Birlās had agreed to marry his daughter to his sister's son, aged 15 or 14. But in the end the match was broken off, on account of his sister being the greatest shrew of the age. At this time he came to the Court after his removal from the faujdāri of Attock, and the sister instigated her son saying, "If you do not kill this shameless wretch in the Court, I shall not give you a quittance for my milk". Then flinging her veil at his head, she cried out, "Wear it and stay within doors". The son obeying his mother's command reached the place where Farjām was standing during the bustle and noise caused by the Emperor's taking his seat in the Hall of Audience, slew him with one stab and then tried to run away. But he was captured and thrown into prison. On Thursday, the 13th March/4th Zil. H., he was executed in accordance with the Qāzi's decision at the reservoir of the *jalaukhāna* in front of the Hall of Audience, in the presence of the heirs of the deceased, *viz,* his wife and his daughter who was married to 'Ali Quli Birlās. The Emperor had expressed a wish that they would renounce their 'right of blood', but they did not agree. The corpse was made over to his mother who was waiting at the gate of the fort in a chariot (*rath*).

[127] On Wednesday, the 19th March/10th Zil. H., occurred the 'Id-uz-zuha. The Emperor went to the mosque for the two-fold prayers of 'Id, accompanied by the four Princes, and sacrificed a sheep. Prince Muhammad Sultān sacrificed a camel, by command. During the return journey a mad man coming up to the equipage flung a stick. It hit the corner of the royal Sedan chair (*takht*) and fell on the Emperor's knee. The macebearers arrested him. But His Majesty ordered him to be released without doing him any injury.

On Sunday, the 23rd March/14th Zil. H., Kām Bakhsh was circumcised. Mān Singh, Mahā Singh and Anup

Singh, the sons of Rāi Singh, came to Court after their father's death and were granted audience, and received robes. Mirzā Jān Minu-chehr, faujdār of Irich died. The Emperor said, "I grant the *māhi* and *marātib* to Khan Jahān Bahādur. He should get them made." Ruhullah Khan, son of Khalilullah Khan, became faujdār of Dhāmuni. Bāqi Khan, bakhshi of the subah of the Deccan, died, and Murshid Quli Khan, got his place. On Wednesday, the 23rd April, 1673/16th Muharram, news came that Mahābat Khan had started from Zafarbāgh near Peshāwar towards Kabul. Sarbuland Khan was ordered to take charge of the records of the Wālāshāhi department, in addition to his own.

On Monday, the 16th June/11th Rabi. A., it was learnt that two hours before noon a halo appeared round the sun like a rainbow and lasted for seven *gharis*.

On Friday, [128] the 18th July/13th Rabi. S., Muhammad Mu'azzam's wife, the daughter of 'Abdul Mumin, died. After returning from the Jām'a mosque, the Emperor paid a visit to the house of the Prince, read the *fātiha,* and then returned to the palace by boat. On Saturday, 2nd August/28th Rabi. S., news came from the Deccan that Kirāt Singh, the son of [Mirza Raja] Jai Singh, had died. On Wednesday, the 20th August/17th Jamad. A., a son was born to Prince Akbar, and named 'Abdul Wahhāb. On Wednesday, the 24th September/22nd Jamad. S., a son was born to Prince Muhammad Mu'azzam, and named Khujistah Ākhtar. The alarm caused to the zamindār of Kumāon by the march of the imperial army across his kingdom, was removed by the mediation of Sayyid Murtaza Khan, and he was pacified. He requested Hāmid Khan to conduct his son to the Court. He did so on the 3rd October/2nd Rajab, and the prince at the time of his audience presented 1,000 mohars and 3,000 rupees as *nazar*, and got a robe. News came from Persia that the cities of Nishāpur, Herāt, and Sabzawār, had sunk in the ground. Khan Jahān Bahādur, after a forced march of 60 *kos*, severely defeated the rebel Shivāji, took a large booty, and sent it with Dalpat Kumār [129] to the Emperor, who viewed the things on Wednesday, the 22nd October/21st Rajab. The Khan showed a three-legged *bagla* (a kind of heron) brought from the hills of Kumāon. Faizullah Khan came from Morādābād to interview. Mahābat Khan neglected to chastise the Āfghān rebels, and went to Kabul by a secret understanding with them that neither side was to harm the other. The Emperor was highly displeased at this. On Monday, the 17th November/17th Shaban, Shuj'āet Khan was sent to punish the Afghans with a large army and plenty of war-materials, and was presented with a special robe, a *jigha* of jasper set with jewels, an Arab steed with gold trappings, and an increment of 500 *zāt* (same troopers). Sarfarāz Khan was made the nāib of the topkhana, Khidmatgār Khan deputy qiladār, and Darbār Khan, nāib of the ghusalkhāna. His (Darbār Khan's) followers too got robes, swords, horses, elephants and promotions.

CHAPTER XVII

17TH YEAR OF THE REIGN. 1084 A. H.

30th November, 1673—18th November, 1674

[130] On the 30th December, the day of the 'Id-ul-fitr, the Emperor visited the mosque; presents, rewards, and promotions were given as usual. Fortune led Mir Qawām-uddin, the *Sadr* of Persia, and brother of Khalifa Sultān, the Wazir of the king of that country, to come to India. On Sunday, the 4th January, 1674/6th Shawwal he had audience and received many favours, a special robe, a jewelled dagger with *phul-katāra* and pearl *ilaqa,* a sword with a gold saz, a shield wrought with roses, a mace (asa), *kalgi* of jasper, 10,000 rupees in cash, the rank of 3-hazāri (1,500 tr.) and the title of Khan. His son Sadruddin was given a robe, a sword with a gold *saz,* and the rank of 700 (100 tr.). Mir Ibrāhim, the son of Shaikh Mir returned to the Court after a visit to Mecca and was restored to his rank of 1,500 (1,000 tr.). Hakim Sālih Khan died. Mourning robes were presented to Hakim Muhasan, and to the other sons and relatives of the deceased. [131] Muhammad 'Ali Khan, son of Taqarrab Khan was made dārogha of the *kirkirāq-khānah vice* him. Mir 'Abdur Rahmān, son of the late Islām Khan, was sent as an envoy to Haidarābād. The 8th March/10th Zil. H., was the day of the 'Id-uz-zuha, when the Emperor visited the mosque for the two-fold prayers.

SHUJ'ĀET KHAN'S DEATH, THE EMPEROR GOES TO HASAN ĀBDĀL

The Emperor learnt that on Saturday, the 14th February/18th Zil. Q., Shuj'āet Khan after crossing the Gundāb had drawn up his forces for crossing the *kotāl* (pass) of Kharāpa. The Āfghāns, who were waiting for an opportunity, hemmed him round in the narrow pass. Though the imperial troops fought valiantly and were untiring in their exertions, yet as Providence had willed it otherwise they failed to carry the day and Shuj'āet fell in the course of the fight. The rest, who had saved their lives from the stone-showering Āfghāns, fled broken to Peshāwar. The Emperor decided to go there in person [132], and started on the 7tł April, 1674/11th Muharram, for Hasan Ābdāl. Himma Khan was made dārogha of the ghusalkhāna and Saf Shikar Khan that of the topkhāna *vice* Shuj'āet Khan deceased Safi Khan nāzim of Agra, was appointed nāzim of Delhi Mu'atamad Khan got the subahdāri of Agra in addition to the qiladāri of Agra fort. Faizullah Khan went back to Morādābad. Ihtamām Khan, dārogha of buildings, and other officers of Delhi went back to their posts. Qawāmuddin Khan and his son were ordered to go to the Emperor after two months. Shaikh 'Abdul 'Aziz, faujdār of the chakla of Sirhind, got the title of Dilāwar Khan. Sarbuland Khan was ordered to advance along the foot of the hills, with 2,500 troopers and the artillery. Nāmdār Khan, having incurred the royal displeasure, was removed from his rank and granted a pension of 4,000 rupees a year. Muhammad Sālih, son of Fidāi Khan, got the title of Khan and was sent to his father. Rahmat Khan bayutāt, was sent to Lahore to arrange for celebrating the anniversary of the death of the Prophet. Mir Khan, son of Khalilullah Khan was removed from his rank for refusing to take up the faujdāri of Irich; Ism'ail Hut, zamindār of Multān, was sent back to his home on Tuesday, the 23rd June/29th Rabi. A., and received the title of Khan and a horse.

Iftikhār Khan and 'Aqidat Khan were sent to reinforce Fidāi Khan in the expedition to Jammu. [133] Raja 'Ināyetullah, zamindar of Rajāor, was given leave to depart. On Friday, the 12th June/18th Rabi. A. Bakhshi-ul-mulk Sarbuland Khan was sent to Peshāwar with Bad'i Sultān, Nāmdār Khan and a strong force. On Sunday, the 14th June/20th Rabi. A., Maharaja Jaswant Singh, thānadār of Jamrud, advancing from his charge, had audience with the Emperor at Rāwalpindi and received a special robe and an *arsi* worth 7,000 rupees, and at the time of departure a sword with jewelled *sāz* and an elephant with *talāir*. On Friday, the 26th June/2nd Rabi. S., the Emperor reached [the palace at] Hasan Ābdāl.

A charming anecdote is told of the virtue and kindness of His Majesty, the vice-gerent of God the Giver. Two or three days after his arrival at the above place he visited the garden of Hasan Ābdāl. The author's servants complained that under the wall of the palace an old man used to work a water-mill, which was turned by the water that issued from the garden and fell into a *nālā*. As the place was in charge of the palace *nāzir's* officers, they had closed the path of water. As a consequence the people had difficulty in grinding flour, and the old man too found it hard to secure his livelihood. [134] I reported the whole matter to Bakhtāwar Khan, and he in his turn to the Emperor, who ordered him to go and personally open the water-course, and issued strict orders so that none should hinder the old man's work. In accordance with the Emperor's order it was done. At night, when the Khan returned to his quarters after 1½ *prahars,* His Majesty who was then seated at his table entrusted two dishes of food and five *āshrafis* to Shaikh Abul Khair, son of the great scholar and courtier Shaikh Nizām, saying, "Carry these to Bakhtāwar Khan, he will guide you to the house of the old man, as he may possibly know it. Convey my salām to the poor man and beg his pardon saying (on my behalf), You are my neighbour, and my arrival has caused you hardship. Pardon me." The Shaikh came to the Khan, and after inquiries and exertions learnt from a footman that there was a village on another hillock, where the old man had his hut. The footman guided the Shaikh to the place at midnight, awakened the old man, tendered the apology, and secured the absolution.

Next day Darbār Khan the *nāzir* was ordered to send the Emperor's *pālki* to him and bring him to the mahal. The old man, who had never before in his life heard the name of *pālki,* not to speak of his seeing a *pālki* with poles of silver, was brought in. The Emperor inquired into his circumstances. He replied that he had two unmarried daughters and two sons with bare heads and feet, and that his wife was living. Two hundred rupees were presented to him. He passed two nights in the mahal, and received money, ornaments, and dresses from all [135]. As he had heard from some one that I had pressed his suit on Bakhtāwar Khan, he came and stood before my tent, with a *do-shāla* on his back, a gown (*peshwāz*) with a *dāman* (hem) on his body, a scarf with gold thread (*dāman-badla*) on his head, *kinkhāb* drawers on his legs, his lap full of gold coins, rupees, and gold ornaments, and a face full of a hundred wrinkles and bleared eyes. I asked "Who art thou?" He replied "I am the man, who has come to such a good fortune through the help of you and your Khan." "Be you blessed!" I rejoined, and took him to the Khan, who also made him some presents. After two or three days, the Emperor again ordered the *nāzir* to bring him with his daughters. The eunuchs took the *pālkis* and fetched them. This time he got 1,000 rupees for dowry (*kanyādān*). The people of the mahal gave him money, ornaments and dresses, double those of the first occasion. He was granted water for a second mill in the neighbourhood. Order was issued to the *nāzir* to give him *sanads* from the imperial *daftar* exempting him from the payment of taxes and molestation for any of the prohibited cesses (*ābwāb*).

Hakim Sanjāk went by command to the old man's house to treat his eye. Afterwards the man was taken to the houses of Princes Muhammad Sultān, Muhammad 'Azam, Muhammad Mu'azzam, Muhammad Akbar, Āsad Khan and Yalangtosh Khan and favoured by them. His daughters were married. His sons put on cloaks of gold embroidery. His wife, having passed through the beauty and vigour of youth, was known as the old crone and leader of the villagers. But it was seen as a fact that this old woman Zulekhā-like grew youthful again through the grace of the Yusuf of the Age. It is no exaggeration to say that the wrinkles [136] on her face disappeared and gave place to loveliness. Her bleared eyes sparkled again. * * *

Āghar Khan was sent with Nusrat Khan, Mirzā Sultān and a force with the necessary equipments to chastise the Āfghāns of Jamrud and Khyber. Rāi La'l Chand was sent to investigate the affairs of the Crownlands of the Subah of Kabul. The Emperor decided that Prince Akbar and Āsad Khan should hasten to Kabul by way of Kohāt. On Tuesday, the 15th September/24th Jamad. S., the Prince received a special robe, a *kalgi* of heron's feather (*par-i-kalang*), a sword and a jewelled shield, 50 Arab, 'Iraqi, hill-breed and Turki horses, and an elephant with silver *sāz;* Āsad Khan was given a special robe, a sword, a horse, and an elephant. Shahāmat Khan, Ghairat Khan, Sayyid Munawwar Khan, Mubāriz Khan, Siādat Khan, Muftakhar Khan, Sazāwar Khan, Kāmyāb Khan, Muhammad Isma'il the son of Āsad Khan, 'Ināyet Khan, Mufākhar Khan, Bahramand Khan, Hayāt Beg, Dilir the son of Bahādur Khan, Kumār Kishan Singh the son of Raja Rām Singh, and other officers were appointed to posts and commands and received presents. On Sunday, the 27th September/7th Rajab, Fidāi Khan was appointed Subahdār of Kabul *vice* Mahābat Khan and a strong force with abundant material [137] was sent with him. He was directed, through

Bakhtāwar Khan, that when his force would enter the *kotāl*, at first the van should cross and halt on the further side, next day the centre should cross, the rear halting on this side, and if the right wing did not get space enough, it should march with the van, and the left wing with the rear.

On Monday the 16th November/27th Shaban, Mahābat Khan had audience and was sent against Bir Singh, grandson of Bithaldās Gaur. Shaikh 'Abdul 'Aziz, dārogha of *'arz-i-mukarrar,* had reached the rank of 7-*sadi* (200 tr.), but owing to his extravagance he had difficulty in securing his livelihood, even though he was granted some *jāgirs* and cash rewards. He began to show laxity in discharging his work and attending at the Court, and as if it were the will of God that he would not come out of this plight, he applied to be permitted to go to Lahore for some time. The Emperor assented after repeating the verse :

> "Don't have your hand tied to your neck, nor open it entirely."
> (Be neither niggardly nor extravagant.)

It was ordered that Lutfullah Khan as his deputy should present the officers to the Emperor and Bakhtāwar Khan should bring the secret papers for His Majesty's signature. After arriving at Lahore, the Shaikh wrote the following *ghazal* to Bakhtāwar Khan. [138] Omitted. * * *

CHAPTER XVIII

18TH YEAR OF THE REIGN : [1085 A.H.]

19th November, 1674—8th November, 1675.

* * * *

'Id-ul-fitr, on Saturday, the 19th December/1st Shawwal; the customary celebrations at Court. *Peshkash* presented by Princes and Peers. Promotions and gifts bestowed on them.

[139] Prince Muhammad Sultān was made a 20-*hazāri* (10,000 tr.) and presented with a robe with half-sleeves, a pearl necklace, a neck-pendent of ruby worth 14,000 rupees, one lakh of rupees in cash, two horses with gold and enamel *sāz,* two elephants with silver *sāz,* kettledrums, *tugh,* and banner. Prince Muhammad Mu'azzam was given a robe, a pearl necklace, a ruby neck-pendent a jewelled turban-end, and five lakhs of rupees in cash. Muhammad 'Azam was given a robe with half-sleeves, and Muhammad Akbar and Sultān Mu'izzuddin the same, Sultan Muhammad 'Azim got a robe; the last two got the rank of 7-*hazāri,* (2,000 tr.) *tugh,* banners, and kettledrums. A special robe, a jewelled dagger, and a gracious *farmān* (letter) were sent to Rānā Rāj Singh and a special robe to Maharaja Jaswant. Himmat Khan, Āshraf Khan the Khan-i-sāmān, Sadr-us-sadur Razavi Khan, Sayyid Murtaza Khan, Tarbiyat Khan, Saf Shikan Khan and other courtiers great and small, got robes of honour. Bakhshi-ul-mulk Sarbuland Khan got an increment of 5-*sadi* and became a 4-*hazāri* (2,500 tr.) Mir Khan previously dismissed, was now given the title of Āmir Khan and the rank of 4-*hazāri* (3,000 tr.) Qawāmuddin Khan got an increment of 5-*sādi* and became a 3,500 (1,500 tr.) [140] Kāmgār Khan and Muhammad 'Ali Khan each got an increment of 500 and became a 2-*hazāri* (500 tr.) Khwāja Shāh got the title of Sharif Khan and Kamāluddin, son of Dilir Khan and Baqr Khan each got an increment of 2-*sadi* and became a *hazāri* (700 tr.) Qābil Khan Burhānuddin, brother's son of Fāzil Khan deceased, got the title of 'Itimād Khan. Muhammad Sharif munshi, dārogha of *dāk* and the letter-

office (*dār-ul-inshā*), brother of Abul Fath Qābil Khan, an old wālāshāhi servant, got that title (Qābil Khan), and an increment of 100. Bakhtāwar Khan, was raised to the rank of a *hazāri* (250 tr.) Sayyid 'Ali, envoy of the Sharif of Mecca and Muhammad Āmin, master of the horse (*sālār-i-āspān*) got permission to depart with 5,000 rupees for each. The chief of the Khwājas of Juibār, Khwāja Muhammad Y'aqub, the son-in-law of Nazar Muhammad Khan king of Balkh, was presented with 10,000 rupees. It was ordered that this amount should be sent to the Khwāja's house at the beginning of every month. Dilir Khan had audience and was made Subahdār of Multān *vice* 'Ābid Khan and Husain Beg Khan, son-in-law of 'Ali Mardān Khan, was made faujdār of Jaunpur. Prithvi Singh, zemindār of Jammu, was appointed to accompany Ludi Khan in the Kabul expedition. Muhammad Wafā, son of 'Abdullah Khan deceased, was sent as thānahdār of Guzar-rishi and Kohat. The letter of Bahrām and Farjām [141] sons of Mahābat Khan informed the Emperor that he had died at Amanābad, on Tuesday, the 22nd December, 1674/4th Shawwal. They were summoned to Court.

Raghudās Jhālā, an officer of the Rānā, came to the Emperor and got the rank of 7-*sadi* (500 tr.) Muhtasham Khan, Mir Ibrāhim, eldest son of Shaikh Mir, was appointed faujdār of Langarkot *vice* Multafat Khan and received a robe, a banner, and a horse with gold trappings. On Tuesday, the 9th March, 1675/22nd Zil. H., 'Ābid Khan on transfer from Multān came and waited on the Emperor. Mir 'Abbās, brother of Sayyid Sultān Karbalāi, son-in-law of Muhammad Āmin Khan, who had applied for permission to go home, received a robe and 2,000 rupees as present. Āurang Khwāja Chaurāghāsi, when leaving for Bukhārā, received a robe, a jewelled *jigha,* a female elephant, and 10,000 rupees. Khwāja Muhammad Tāhir Naqshbandi, father of Khwāja Muhammad Sālih and son-in-law of Murād Bakhsh, got leave to go home and a present of 500 *mohars*. Bikram Singh of Gwālior was confirmed as a thanahdar and given a robe, a jewelled dagger, and a horse with gold trappings. He was ordered to bring with himself 2,500 hill-infantry. 'Ināyet Khan became faujdār of Khairābad *vice* Mujāhid Khan. On Monday, the 24th May/9th Rabi A., Saf Shikan Khan died. [142] Multafat Khan replaced him as dārogha of topkhāna. A robe was sent to him with a macebearer.

As Khan Jahān Bahādur had defeated the infernal Shivā by repeated attacks and many forced marches and greatly exerted himself in chastising the other rebels of the Deccan, Bijāpur and Haidarābād, on Wednesday, the 7th July/23rd Rabi. S., the Emperor rewarded him by giving him the titles of Khan Jahān Bahādur Zafar Jang Kokaltāsh, and promoted him to be a 7-*hazāri* (same tr.) by an increment of *hazāri zāt,* and presented him with 1 kror of *dām*. His servant Muhammad Sālih, who had brought the cash, horses and elephants of the tribute, got a robe, and his companions a reward of 1,000 rupees. Muhammad Mirak, macebearer, carried to Zafar Jang and his sons splendid robes, high promotions, titles, and a *farmān* of praise. At Zafar Jang's request Sambhā, the son of Shivā, was granted the rank of 6-*hazāri* (same tr.), eighty lakhs of *dām* as present, kettle-drums, and banner; a robe and a *farmān* were sent with the macebearer. Āshraf Khan, Khan-i-sāmān, [143] condoled with the Sadr Razavi Khan, for the death of his brother and brought him to Court. A mourning robe and permission to go to Delhi were given him.

On Thursday, the 22nd July/9th Jamad. A., a son was born to Muhammad 'Āzam, named Sikandar-Shān. The Prince was given a robe, the baby a pearl necklace, and Jahānzeb Bānu Begam 10,000 rupees. This year 'Abid Khan was appointed Mir-i-haj for conveying to Mecca and Medina the gift (*nazar*) which used to be sent there every year. Qāzi-ul-quzāt 'Abdul Wahhāb having fallen ill, started for Delhi. Sayyid Ali Ākbar, Qāzi of Lahore, became his deputy. 'Abdullah Khan of Kāshghar, who had been living happily on the Emperor's bounty at Delhi, died on Wednesday, the 20th October/10th Shaban. Mourning robes were presented to Nāsir Khan and other relatives of the deceased.

On Monday, the 8th November, 1675/29th Shaban, news came that 'Abdullah Qutb-ul-mulk, king of Haidarābād, had died, and been succeeded by Abul Hasan, his brother's son and own son-in-law. Nāmdār Khan was restored to the rank of 4-*hazāri* (2,000 tr.) and made Subahdār of Oudh *vice* S'aādat Khan; Mukhtār Beg, the third son of Islām Khan, who had arrived with the Khan's family at Ujjain, was created a 7-*sadi* (200 tr.) Āmānat Khan [144] resigned his post of *peshdast* of the khālsa and became commandant of Lahore. Kifāyet Khan *peshdast* of the *daftar-i-tan,* got the vacant office in addition to his own. Khan Zamān, son of 'Āzam Khan deceased, became nāzim of Berār and a 5-*hazāri* (3,000 tr.) Ābul Hasan, king of Haidarābād, sent with his envoy Qawām-ud-din tribute of nine lakhs of rupees, jewels, and elephants. Robes were given to the envoy at arrival and departure. Ruhullah Khan was reinstated in the grade of 1,500 (400 tr.) and made faujdār of Sahāranpur. Tarbiyat Khan became dārogha of the Emperor's retinue *vice* Mukarram Khan Muhammad Ishāq, the second son of Shaikh Mir.

Mukarram Khan with his younger brother Shamshir Khan, Muhammad Y'aqub and a strong force, was ordered to punish the Āfghāns near the *kotāl* of Khāpash. On Friday, the 11th June/27th Rabi. A., it was learnt that he had repeatedly fought with the enemy, plundered many of their houses, and taken many prisoners. One day, at first a few Āfghāns appeared. The Khan despising their number, flung himself on the enemy, and at first defeated them. Afterwards two countless forces, which had lain concealed in the waist of the hill, charged him. Shamshir Khan and Mir 'Azizullah, son-in-law of Shaikh Mir, boldly stood their ground and heroically [145] died, with a large number of the imperialists. Lack of water and of road on any side whatever caused the death of many horse and foot soldiers. A great defeat befell our side, and terrible hardships on high and low alike. Guided by men who knew the country Mukarram Khan with some other lucky survivors, went to 'Izzat Khan thānahdar of Bājaur. The latter, who had often defeated the Āfghāns, was firmly entrenched there with his retinue. He regarded the approach of the fugitives as a very fortunate circumstance and offered them various kinds of relief. The Emperor was very sorry to hear of the death of his servants, especially young Shamshir Khan, and praised 'Izzat Khan for his services. He ordered Mukarram Khan to come to Court. A letter of condolence and a mourning robe were sent to Muhtasham Khan. On Monday, the 14th June/30th Rabi. A., Bakhshi-ul-mulk Sarbuland Khan was sent with a large army (in all 9,000 tr.) and a vast quantity of material in order to deal effectively with the enemy. Āghar Khan was made thānahdār of Jalālābād, Hazbar Khan of Jagdalak, Farāq Khan of Lamghānāt, Āllahdād of Gharib-Khānah, Suhrāb son of Garshāsp, faujdār of Dānki, Khanjar Khan that of Bangashāt. The Emperor ordered Sufid Khāk to be called

Mughalabad and Bāzārak Fatihābād. The news-writer of the force of Fidāi Khan reported that on Thursday, the 1st July/17th Rabi S., the Khan [146] had started from Pesh-Bulāq towards Kabul. As this Khan had done his utmost in attacking the Āfghāns, plundering and destroying their homes, and his services had gained praise, he was given the title 'Āzam Khan Kokah. On Thursday, the 26th August/14th Jamad. S., news came that Hazbar Khan thānahdār of Jagdalak had fought a battle with the Āfghāns, and been slain with his son and other imperial soldiers, and that 'Abdullah Khweshgi, thanahdār of Bārangāb and Surkhāb had fled from his outpost (*thānah*), many of his companions having been slain or captured.

On Tuesday, the 19th October/9th Shaban, a letter from Āmir Khan reported that 'Ālam, Ism'āil and other Āfghān rebels of Shāhjahānpur and Kāntgolah, who after being defeated by the imperial troops had taken shelter in the fort, had been captured and that they were being sent to the Court with Ibrāhim Khan who was coming from Bengal.

Bakhtāwar Khan by order took securities from the astrologers of the Emperor and the Princes that they would not construct almanacs for the next year and orders to the same purport were sent to the provinces.

A basket fell into the well of the haveli of Muhammad Shaf'i Mir-i-sāmān of Muhammad Sultān; two men who successively descended to bring it up, died. The third shouted from midway "Take me out"! After remaining unconscious for an hour, he recovered and said "A dark goblin became visible before me at the bottom of the well and [147] cried out in a terrible voice, "Why are you coming? Get out".

News came from Delhi of the death of Purhunar Bānu Begam, who was the eldest child of Shāh Jahān and had been borne to him by Qandahāri Mahal, the daughter of Mirzā Husain Safavi. Safi Khan, the nāzim, and other officers of the Subah buried her corpse in a mausoleum (garden) which had been built by a mason under her direction.

CHAPTER XIX

19TH YEAR OF THE REIGN : 1086 A.H.

9th November, 1675—27th October, 1676.

* * * *

'Id-ul-fitr, 9th December/1st Shawwal. Saif Khan Faqirullah, son of Tarbiyat Khan, was restored to his title, and received a special robe, a sword, and a *mansab,* on returning from the life of a hermit. [148] Ābul Muhammad, daughter's son of Ibrāhim 'Ādil Khan and son of Bahar Khan, a scholar, came from Bijāpur, had audience, got a robe and was created a 3-*hazāri* (2,000 tr.) with the title of Khan and a present of 60,000 rupees. His brothers and sons got proper *mansabs*. On Friday, the 17th December/9th Shawwal, Āmir Khan from Bihār had audience, Tarbiyat Khan was appointed in his place. On Sunday, the 2nd January, 1676/27th Shawwal, Shaikh Nizām married Bāi Phupdevi [*cor.*], the daughter of the Raja of Kishtāwar to Muhammad Sultān.

THE EMPEROR'S RETURN FROM HASAN ĀBDĀL TO DELHI.

On Thursday, the 23rd December, 1675/15th Shawwal, began the return journey from Hasan Ābdāl. The first stage was Kālābāgh. Hunting at many of the stages (on the route) the Emperor arrived at the garden of Lahore on Friday, the 21st January, 15th Zil. Q., Āmānat Khan, the commandant interviewed. As Qāzi 'Ābdul Wahhāb had died at Delhi on Friday, the 26th November/18th Ramzan, his son Shaikh-ul-Islām, who was the Qāzi of Delhi, came to Court by command and received his father's post of Qāzi of the army. Maulvi 'Abdullah of Siālkot, son of Mullā 'Abdul Hakim deceased, who combined piety with scholarship, virtues with polished manners and had not so long had the satisfaction of ever meeting the Emperor, [149] had been requested from Hasan Ābdāl to come to Lahore after the Emperor's arrival there. The Maulvi reached Lahore two or three days before the Emperor and had several interviews with His Majesty. After being honoured with a robe, 200 mohars, and a female elephant, he returned home. Ekkatāz Khan who had gone as envoy to Balkh, returned after four years and three days, and was granted audience and a robe. He presented eleven horses, leather goods and a knife. Mullā Muhammad Tāhir, brother of the eminent Mullā 'Auz Wajih, and an envoy of Subhān Quli Khan, came with Ekkatāz Khan and received a robe and 7,000 rupees. Lutfullah Khan became dārogha of *filkhānah vice* Faizullah Khan, Turktāz Khan was given a robe, a horse, a quiver with a sheath (*qurtān*) and ordered to Kabul. On Saturday, the 19th February, 1676/14th Zil. H., Muhammad 'Āzam was sent as Subahdār to Multān. Khwāja Tālib conveyed to his house a robe, a jewelled sword, 200 Arab, 'Irāqi, and Turki horses, two elephants with *talāir* and silver *sāz*, and 1 kror *dām*. Sultān Bidār Bakht got a robe, a horse, and an elephant; Mullā Muhammad Tāhir, envoy of Balkh, 4,000 rupees and a *pālki*, [150] with a carpet, and his companions 2,000 rupees. The joyous news was received that a son had been born to Muhammad Muazzam (*cor*) who was named Khujista Ākhtar; Khusrau Chelā conveyed to him a pearl necklace, a pearl cap and 5 pieces (*thān*) of cloth. Dilir Khan was sent on the Deccan expedition, with a robe, a horse, an elephant, and a jewelled dagger. Ghairat Khan was made faujdār of Jaunpur *vice* Husain Beg Khan deceased. Ibrāhim Khan came from Bihār and had audience. On Wednesday, the 29th March, 1676/24th Muharram, the imperial order was issued; Ruhullah, an armed personal attendant, conveyed to the Amir-ul-umārā, a robe, a jewelled dagger, and a *farmān* praising him for the conquest of Morang, and appointing him Subahdār of Orissā *vice* Rashid Khan, with two krors of *dām* as reward. His agent too got a robe. Mullā 'Auz Wajih, who had turned hermit, was restored to the rank of a *hazāri*. Himmat Khan became Subahdār of Allahabad *vice* Hasan 'Ali Khan and was granted a robe and one lakh of rupees. 'Abdur Rahim Khan succeeded him as dārogha of ghusalkhāna, Ruhullah Khan replacing the latter, as ākhta begi. Sarbuland Khan who had been removed from his *mansab*, was reinstated; Dārāb Khan came from Ajmir, had audience, and became dārogha of topkhāna *vice* Multafat Khan; Sayyid Ahmad Khan replaced him [151] at Ajmir. Qawāmuddin Khan was sent to Kashmir as Subahdār. Prince Muhammad Sultān received a present of jewels worth seven lakhs of rupees. Muhammad Mu'azzam received a *tora* of jewelled tassels (*jhumka*) worth 9,000 rupees and a jewelled *punchi* worth 50,000 rupees. 'Abdur Rasul Khan was made qiladār of Kulbarga, which was conquered this year by the imperialists. Hamza Khan was appointed qiladār of Kaliāni, Irij Khan faujdār of Irijpur *vice* Khan Zamān, Tahmāsp Khan that of Ārapanwāra *vice* M'asum Khan.

The Emperor learnt that Islām Khan, nāzim of Malwa, who had been appointed to serve under Khan Jahān Bahādur Kokaltāsh, was standing with the vanguard on Tuesday, the 13th June/11th Rabi. S. Accidentally at a time when the battle was still evenly balanced, the gunpowder caught fire while being distributed at that spot. His elephant being panic-stricken blindly rushed into the ranks of the enemy who surrounded him, cut the girth of his *howdah,* brought him down to the ground, and cruelly cut him to pieces with his son 'Ali Beg Khan. His eldest son, Afrāsiāb Khan, was favoured by the Emperor with an increment of 5-*sadi* (same tr.) [152] and made a 2½-*hazāri* (1,500 tr.). His younger son Mukhtār Beg got 3 *sadi* (200 tr.) more and became a *hazāri* (400 tr.). His property, amounting to three lakhs of rupees, 2,000 *āshrafis* and other articles, which had been seized by the State at Ujjain and Sholāpur, was given to his sons, and they were ordered to make good the dues from their father. On Sunday, the 24th September/26th Rajab, Muhammad Ākbar was sent as Subahdār to Mālwa, on the death of Islām Khan, and received a special robe with a *bālāband* and a *sarpech* of ruby, two Arab and 'Irāqi horses with gold *sāz* and one elephant. Mullā Muhammad Tāhir, envoy, when taking leave for returning, received an elephant, 10,000 rupees and a jewelled *'asa.* On 3rd October, Sultān Mu'izzudin was married to the daughter of Mirzā Mukarram Khan Safavi. He received a robe with *chahār-qab,* a pearl necklace worth 10,000 rupees, a *smarani* worth 10,000 rupees and an elephant with *talāir.* Yalangtosh Khan Bahādur on the day of his marriage received a robe, an emerald *sarpech,* a horse with gold *sāz* and an elephant with silver *sāz.* Sultān Quli got the title of Khan and the faujdāri of Islāmābād Mathurā *vice* Mubāriz Khan Mir-kul. On Sunday, the 8th October/10th Shaban, Āsad Khan was appointed grand Wazir, and received a special robe and a jewelled ink-pot worth 5,000 rupees. [153] On Sunday, the 15th October, 1676/17th Shaban Muhammad Mu'azzam was sent on the Kabul expedition with many high commanders, artillery, treasure and material and given the title of Shāh 'Ālam Bahādur, a special robe with half-sleeves, jewels worth two lakhs of rupees, swords with jewelled *sāz,* three good Arab, 'Irāqi and Turki horses, with jewelled *sāz* and wrought saddle, and one lakh of *āshrafi*. Sultān Mu'izzuddin received a robe, a jewelled *kalgi* and *sarpech,* a horse named *Koh-i-Razm* (Rock in battle) with gold *sāz,* a sword with enamelled *sāz,* an elephant with silver *sāz,* a bow and a quiver; Sultan Muhammad 'Azim a robe, a *kalgi,* a *sarpech* and a *smarani;* Sultān Daulatāfzā a pendent of ruby; Sultān Khujistah-Ākhtar an emerald *kangan* (wristlet); Āmir Khan, Saif Khan, Raja Rām Singh, and other grandees were rewarded with gifts. Mughal Khan was removed from his rank of 2½ *hazāri* (1,400 tr.). Muhtasham Khan got the faujdāri of Sahāranpur. Himmat Khan hastened to take up his post as Subahdār of Allahabad *vice* Hasan 'Ali Khan; Muhammad Shuj'ā son of Qaiāmuddin Khan, came from Persia, had audience and was made a *hazāri* (300 tr.). An annual pension of 12,000 rupees was settled on 'Āqil Khan who had resigned his office and taken to a life of retirement. Ibrāhim Khan [154] applied for resigning his *mansab;* it was granted. Iftikhār Khan was appointed faujdār of Bangashāt.

On Friday, the 27th October, 1676/29th Ramzan, while the Emperor was returning from the Jām'a mosque, and had alighted from the boat in order to mount the movable chair (*takht-i-rawān*), an ill-fated disciple of Guru Tegh Singh threw two bricks, one of which reached the chair. He was seized by the retinue and ordered to be made over to the *kotwāl.*

[RETURN OF THE EMPEROR FROM LAHORE TO DELHI]

On Thursday, the 24th February, 1676/19th Zil. H., the Emperor left Lahore. Kamāluddin, son of Dilir Khan was created a Khan. On 21st February/16th Zil. H., Dostdār Bānu Begam, wife of Muhammad Sultān, died in the sārāi of Rustam Khan. On Monday, the 27th March/22nd Muharram, the Emperor arrived at Delhi. On Saturday, the 24th June/22nd Rabi. S., Raja Rām Singh came from Assām and had interview.

While the Emperor was mounting his horse in the square (*chauk*) before the Hall of Audience, a complainant flung a stick at him. It fell on the other side of His Majesty's umbrella; the man was made over to the *kotwāl*.

The scouts (*qarāwals*) showed a deer of pure white colour. On Thursday, the 13th July/12th Jamad. A., a son was born to Sipihr Shukoh and Zubdatunnisā Begam; he obtained the name of 'Ali Tabār. The Emperor went to Sipihr Shukoh's house to see the child. On 5th August/5th Jamad. S., [155] a son was born to Muhammad Sultān, he was named Mas'aud Bakht. On Wednesday, the 30th August/1st Rajab, Muhammad Sultān was married to the daughter of the brother of Daulatābādi Mahal. On Friday, the 1st September/3rd Rajab, Muhammad Ākbar was married to the daughter of Alah Quli, son of Murād Quli Ghakkar.

The Emperor learnt that Muhammad Muhsan, son of Khan Jahān Bahādur, had been slain in battle at the fort of Naldrug. On Thursday, the 19th October/21st Shaban, while the Emperor was mounting his horse after returning from the Jām'a mosque, a wretch came forward with an uplifted sword. The retinue arrested him; a small wound was inflicted on the finger of Mukarram Khan. The mace-bearers wanted to slay him, but the Emperor forbade it, settled on him a daily allowance of half a rupee and sent him as prisoner to Ranthambhor. On Wednesday, the 25th October/27th Shaban, a water-carrier approached the Emperor on the steps of the Jām'a mosque and cried out *salām 'alekum*. He was ordered to be made over to the *kotwāl*.

CHAPTER XX

20TH YEAR OF THE REIGN. 1087 A.H.

28th October, 1676—17th October, 1677

* * * *

The Emperor passed the month of Ramzan in fasting and prayer. On most days, especially from the 17th of that month onwards he went to the mosque of the ghusalkhānah day and night, and there held [156] the Court of Justice. On Monday, the 27th November/1st Shawwal, occurred the 'Id-ul-fitr. Shah 'Ālam Bahādur was a 40-*hazāri* (25,000 tr.); he got an increment of 5-*hazār* troopers. Muhammad 'Āzam was a 15-*hazāri* (9,000 tr.) and now received an increment of 5-*hazāri zāt*. Yalangtosh Khan Bahādur, a *hazāri* (500 tr.) received promotion of 500 (200 tr.) 'Itiqād Khan, Mir Kul, after his removal from *mansab*, was reinstated as a 2-*hazāri* (1,000 tr.). Sayyid' Mustafa, son of Sayyid Murtaza Khan, became a 5-*sadi* (100 tr.) On Monday, the 27th November, 1676/1st Shawwal, Ruhullah Khan became Khan-i-saman *vice* Āshraf Khan. Yalangtosh Khan Bahādur foolishly stabbed himself with a knife, his rank was reduced by 5-*sadi* (200 tr.). Kāmgār Khan was dismissed from his *mansab*.

Mullā 'Auz Wajih, the leading theologian died. His home was Akhsikat in Samarqand. During his study under Mir 'Auz Tāshkandi, he surpassed all his class-fellows. After having served for sometime as a teacher in Balkh, he came to the Emperor Shah Jahān's Court in the 13th year of his reign, and took service as *mufti* of the camp. In Aurangzib's reign he was Censor of the army for a short time, and exerted himself far beyond any other holder of the post in putting down vices. [157] The rest of his life he spent in teaching, being highly honoured by the nobility.

When Muhammad 'Āzam, who was coming from Multān for interview, reached Āghrābād, Māh Bānu on behalf of His Majesty conveyed to him the present of a betel-tray, a small tray, a *do-ghara*, a dish (*rikābi*), and a spitoon (*ugāldān*) of stone set with jasper. He was granted interview on Tuesday, the 16th January, 1677/22nd Zil. Q., and presented with a robe with *sarpech,* other special clothing, and nine horses. Sultān Bidār Bakht and Sikandar Shān received two *sarpeches* worth 5,000 rupees each. On Saturday, the 17th February/24th Zil. H. Mirzā Beg, a servant of Shāh 'Ālam Bahādur, brought a letter and 1,000 mohars on the occasion of the birth of a son, who was named Muhammad Humāyun. A jewelled *sarpech* for the Prince and a jewelled cap and a pearl necklace for the Sultān (grandson) were sent with him. On Monday, the 19th March/24th Muharram, at the recommendation of Shāh 'Ālam Bahādur, Āmir Khan was made Subahdār of Kabul *vice* 'Āzam Khan Kokah. Bakhshi-ul-mulk Sarbuland Khan was presented with a stone ink-pot set with jasper. Manohardās, qiladār of Sholāpur promised 50,000 rupees as *peshkash* for being given the title of Raja. The Emperor accepted it. On Friday, the 13th April, Muhammad 'Āzam was made Subahdār of Bihār *vice* Tarbiyat Khan and presented with a special robe, a dagger, a *sarpech,* a *kalgi,* two horses, and five krors of *dām* as reward. Tarbiyat Khan was made faujdār of Tirhut and Dārbhangā, *vice* Hādi Khan, Dārāb Khan made Mir Tuzuk *vice* Ruhullah Khan, [158] Mukarram Khan dārogha of mace-bearers *vice* 'Abdur Rahim Khan, Sayyid Khan faujdār of Bangashat *vice* Iftikhār Khan, Khan Zamān Subahdār and qiladār of Zafarabad Bidar. Good fortune brought Shāh Beg Khan Kāshghari to India. At interview he received a special robe, a dagger with gold hilts and pearl *'ilāqa,* a jewelled *jigha,* a shield wrought with gold flowers, a female elephant and 5,000 rupees in cash. Seven dishes and three trays of bread and a *pālki* with carpet were sent to his house. He was created a 1½ *hazāri* (200 tr.). Kishan Singh, son of Rām Singh coming from Kabul had audience, and was granted leave for four months to visit his home. 'Ināyetullah, son of S'ādullah Khan deceased, became bakhshi of *Shāgird-peshah vice* Hakim Muhammad Muhasan. A macebearer carried to Hasan 'Ali Khan a *farmān* appointing him Subahdār of Agra. Muhammad Isma'il son of Umdat-ul-mulk Āsad Khan married the daughter of Amir-ul-umārā Shāista Khan. He was presented with a robe and a horse with gilt *sāz,* and given the title of 'Itiqād Khan. He had brought his own *kalgi* and *sahrā;* the Emperor took them with his own hands and made them over to Sultān Sipihr Shukoh to be placed on his head. Kāmyāb Khan became faujdār of Sahāranpur *vice* Muhatasham Khan, and the latter that of Miwāt *vice* Fulād Khan. Hāmid Khan became Subahdār of Ajmir *vice* Sayyid Āhmad Khan. Khwāja N'amatullah, who had brought a letter from the king of Bukhārā received 400 rupees. Muhammad Qāsim Khan collector [159] of the port of Cambay, became that of Surat *vice* Ghiāsuddin Khan. Kām Bakhsh, on finishing the memorising of the *Qurān,* received a robe, two horses with gold *sāz,* a jewelled *sarpech,* a pearl necklace, a shield wrought with jewelled flowers (*gul*), a quiver, and a bow-case. Khānahzād Khan became thānadār of Ghaznin *vice* Ālah Yār Khan, and the latter got the former's post of qiladār of Kabul. 'Āzam Khan Kokah was appointed Subahdār of Bengal *vice* the Amir-ul-umārā, and received a robe, a jewelled dagger, and a horse worth 500 mohars with gold *sāz.* 'Ināyet Khan became *peshdast* of the Khālsa office *vice* Kifāyet Khan. Mughal Khan, who had been dismissed, was reinstated as a 2-*hazāri* (1,000 tr.); Fazlullah Khan, dismissed, was restored to his *mansab* and sent to serve in Bengal.

DEATH OF PRINCE MUHAMMAD SULTAN

The Prince was taken seriously ill. For a short time he remained weak and confined to bed. On Sunday, the 3rd December, 1676/7th Shawwal [160] the Emperor, at the imperial hunting-lodge of Malār, learnt of his death. Inspite of his fortitude, the Emperor wept on hearing this news. Ruhullah Khan Khan-i-sāmān, Siādat Khan, 'Ābdur Rahim Khan, Shaikh Nizām and Mullā Muhammad Y'aqub were ordered to bury him near the tomb of Khwāja Qutbuddin, and to get the whole of the *Qurān* recited and alms distributed for the peace of his soul. He was born in 1639 A.D./1049 A.H. and lived 38 years 10 months.

A letter came from Muhammad Ākbar to say that he had entered Ujjain on Saturday, the 23rd December, 1676/27th Shawwal. Sultān 'Āla Tabār, son of Sipihr Shukoh, died and the robe of mourning was given. On Sunday, the 28th January, 1677/4th Zil. H., Ākbarābādi Mahal of Shāh Jahān died. Bakhshi-ul-mulk Sarbuland Khan was ordered to abolish the tankhwā of eight and seven months, and to give the *naqdis* tankhwā for six months only. On Friday, the 30th March/5th Safar, the Emperor learnt that Fazlullah Khan, who had been appointed to Bengal, had been mortally stabbed by a servant with a dagger. On

Tuesday, the 3rd April/9th Safar, Sikandar Shān, son of Prince Muhammad 'Āzam, died. A letter came from Khan Jahān Bahādur to say that on Monday the 14th May/21st Rabi. A., Naldurg had been captured by the imperialists. On 9th June/17th Rabi. S., the death occurred of Sultān [161] Mas'aud Bakht, son of Sultān Muhammad deceased. News came from Ujjain that Kishan Singh Hādā had come to interview Prince Ākbar; while putting on the robe of honour he had a sudden altercation with the Prince, and stabbed himself to death in the stomach. His four servants slew fifteen men (of the Prince) before they were slain. On Saturday, the 4th August, 1677/14th Jamad. S., Prince Muhammad 'Āzam reached Patna; and Shāh 'Alam Bahādur reached Kābul on Thursday, the 15th August/25th Jamad. S. Qutbuddin Khan and Raja Indraman Bundela died. 'Abdur Rahman Khan, the bakhshi and news-writer of the Deccan, was informed that Khan Jahān Bahādur was summoned to the Court, and that Dilir Khan was ordered to keep watch till the arrival of another Subahdār, and that the affairs of the place were to be conducted with his advice. 'Umdat-ul-mulk Āsad Khan was sent to the Deccan with a large army and a vast store of materials.

CHAPTER XXI.

21ST YEAR OF THE REIGN : 1088 A.H.

18th October, 1677—6th October 1678.

Prince Akbar came from Ujjain, had interview on Tuesday, the 30th October/13th Ramzan, and received a robe with half-sleeves, a *bālāband,* and 5 horses. [162] On Sunday, the 18th November/2nd Shawwal, the day following the 'Id-ul-fitr, the Emperor sat on the throne; according to the custom of the celebration (of coronation) betel-leaves and scents were distributed among the persons present at Court. The Emperor ordered the few apparel that had been used in the decoration of the coronation festivity to be removed, and said to Bakhshi-ul-mulk Safi Khan, "I abolish the celebration; return the *peshkash* sent by the Amir-ul-umārā, and the other grandees are not to make any presents to me. The clerks should use inkpots of China-ware and gilt stone, instead of silver ones. The amounts of *in'ām,* which were brought into the Court on silver trays, should henceforth be brought on shields. Men who have no such drawers as are sanctioned by the canonical law, should come dressed in socks. In the *khil'at-khānah* embroidered cloth should be used instead of stuff with gold and silver flowers worked on it. The factory of *do dāmi* (extremely fine cloth) established at Chanderi should be abolished. Erect a *kathra* of lapis lazuli set in gold, in the place of the uncanonical *kathra* (railing) of gold and silver. Do not plant rose-beds in any imperial garden, except in that of Āghrābād and Nurbāri. No *mansabdār* above the 4-*sadi* should begin the construction of pucca houses without permission." [Another text adds;] "remove the gold and silver censers for burning aloe-wood which are brought into the royal residence."

On Monday, the 26th November/10th Shawwal, Kām Bakhsh was made a 8-*hazāri* (2,000 tr.) and given a *tuman,* a *tugh,* a banner, kettle-drums, an umbrella, 30 horses, and 15 elephants. [163] Winter dresses were presented to the princes and peers of the Court and the provinces. On Wednesday, the 28th November/12th Shawwal, Ibrāhim Khan was appointed Subahdār of Kashmir *vice* Qawāmuddin

Khan; Muhammad Yār Khan son of 'Itiqād Khan became dārogha of the goldsmith's department *vice* Khidmatgār Khan, Sazāwār Khan became faujdār of Qanauj. Muhammad N'aim, *mushrif* of the stable, became bakhshi of Kām Bakhsh. Khwāja Bahāuddin, son of Khwāja Pārsā, daughter's son of Subhān Quli Khan, king of Balkh, came from vilayat and received a robe, 14,000 rupees in cash, and a jewelled dagger. Khwāja Khidmat Khan became dārogha of jewellery market (*jawāhir bāzār*), *vice* 'Itiqād Khan. Mughal Khan became ākhta begi, *vice* Ruhullah Khan, Munawwar Khan was sent as faujdār of Rātha, Mahoba, and Jalālpur Khabdup, *vice* Subhakaran Bundela. Muhammad Kāzim, author of the *'Ālamgirnāmah* became dārogha of the sale department. Āi Begam, sister of Najābat Khan the son of Sarbuland Khan, died. Nāmdār Khan conducted Najābat to the Emperor to receive a robe of condolence. On Monday, the 15th April, 1678/3rd Rabi. A., Sayyid Murtaza Khan died; of high birth, charitable and brave, he used to keep [164] his soldiers on high pay and in great splendour. The Emperor sent Bakhtāwar Khan to make inquiries before his death. The Khan brought to the Emperor this prayer from the Sayyid, "I had hoped to give up my life in the service of my master. But it is not to be, hence my grief. Others present gold and gems to His Majesty, I wanted to present a few lives (of the enemy) in exchange of mine. That might probably be of use to His Majesty." After the Sayyid's death many of his servants, from *hazāris* to commanders of 80, were taken into the imperial service, and the footmen too were provided with posts in the workshop and store departments (*kārkhānazāt*).

On Thursday, the 18th April, 1678/6th Rabi. A., Shaikh 'Abdul 'Aziz died. Two days before, Bakhtāwar Khan had sent the author to him, to carry the imperial command that there should be no slackness in his treatment, and that if he wished, the Emperor was ready to send any of the Yunāni doctors that he desired to treat him. When I went, I found him reclining in bed and engaged in composition; his words were being written down by his pupils, such as Mir Hādi, Muhammad S'aid 'Ajāz, and others. On hearing the imperial message he replied to the author, "I have no prejudice for any particular system of treatment. But I have no faith in the book-knowledge of these men (*i.e.*, the Yunāni doctors of the Court). If any of them be fit for being given a call, I have no objection. I have chosen as my doctor 'Abdul Malik, on whose book-learning, diagnosis, experience, and prudence I have reliance. Life is not so precious an article that for prolonging it [*cor.*] we should make such frantic exertions. We must be drowned in water, when it rises above the head." I reported this speech to Bakhtāwar Khan, who asked me to write it down, and then read it to His Majesty. The Emperor [165] said to the Khan, "You will not believe that the greatest of scholars has said so. The fear that we feel springs from the thought of how our acts would be judged by God."

Lutfullah Khan became dārogha of *'arz-i-mukarrar vice* him. Āshraf Khan became news-reader *vice* Lutfullah, Muhammad Yār Khan became dārogha of *qurkhānah vice* Imāmwardi, who became faujdār of Sahāranpur, Muhsan Khan dārogha of chini-khānah *vice* Muhammad 'Ali Khan. On Monday, the 8th July 1678/28th Jamad. A., Hāmid Khan came to Court and received a robe of condolence and the post of dārogha of khās-chauki *vice* his deceased father. Iftikhār Khan went to Ajmir in his place. Qawāmuddin Khan came to Court from Kashmir and got a robe. 'Abdur Rahim Khan became ākhta begi *vice* Mughal Khan, Lutfullah Khan was graciously authorized to enter the fort in his *pālki.*

The news-writer of the Deccan reported that Dilir Khan had a stiff fight with the army of Golkonda; an elephant was killed by a rocket, the elephant ridden by the Khan was wounded by a musket-ball; the servant who rode on the elephant behind the Khan was killed by a rocket; the fire of the rocket even fell on the collar of the Khan, but it was extinguished with the water of his leather-bottle, many of the enemy as well as the Khan's followers were slain. Fighting and guarding his own troops he reached his tent at evening.

On Sunday, the 20th January, 1678/6th Zil. H. Shah 'Ālam Bahādur from Kābul interviewed the Emperor and received a special robe and a jewelled *jigha.* His sons and subordinate grandees [166] received robes and jewels.

24th January/10th Zil. H., the Emperor went to the mosque, to say the two-fold 'Id-uz-zuha prayers. On Wednesday, the 8th May/26th Rabi. A., he learnt of Shivāji's attack on Mungi-patan.

The news-writer of Surat reported that a mare had

delivered a colt with three legs; the third leg was close to the chest, and all the three legs were used in walking.

Murād Bakhsh's daughter was married to Khwāja Y'aqub, brother's son of Khwāja Sālih Naqshbandi; the Emperor presented a robe, a horse with gold *sāz*, a *jigha* of jasper, 4,000 rupees in cash and a female elephant. First Sarbuland Khan conveyed the groom to the *deorhi* (portico) of the Begam Sāhib for salutation. Next the knot was tied in the mosque of Ākbarābādi. The marriage settlement was two lakhs of rupees. Sulaimān Shukoh's daughter was married to Khwāja Bahāuddin, son of Khwāja Pārsā; and the same favours were conferred on him too. Sultān-ud-din, the son of Sayyid Muhammad successor of Qutb-i-'Ālam (sainted dead), brother's son and son-in-law of Sadr-us-sadur Razawi Khan, received a robe, a female elephant, and 1,000 rupees when leaving for Āhmadābād.

On Monday, the 29th April/17th Rabi. A., Qawāmud-din Khan was made Subahdar of Lahore, and Kāmgār Khan *bayutāt vice* Rahmat Khan, Sayyid Muhammad Bijāpuri, one of the sons of Ghaus-ul-'āzam, who was highly revered by all there, came to Court and received a pension of 6,000 rupees a year. On Friday, the 5th July/25th Jamad. A., Akbar was appointed Subahdār of Multān and presented with a special robe, a pearl necklace, a ruby neck-pendant, [167] two horses with gold *sāz*, and an elephant with *talāir*, Safi Khan was appointed to serve under him, 'Abdur Rahim Khan becoming his deputy. The daughter of Kirat Singh was married to Muhammad 'Azim; 63,000 rupees, jewels, a gold litter (*chaudol*), a *pālki*, and five *dolis* with silver railings, were given as dowry. On the day of marriage the Prince received a special robe, a pearl necklace and a jewelled *kalgi;* Qamruddin, son of Mukhtār Khan was created a Khan. A peshkash of eleven lakhs of rupees was received from 'Ādil Khan Bijāpuri. Amir-ul-umārā Shāista Khan, who had come from Bengal, was granted audience in the private chamber. He received a splendid robe, a dagger with its handle set with jasper, *sāz* of enamel with *'ilāqa*, and *dhup* with *sāz* of gold. He was honoured by being presented with the truncheon (*'asā*) of jasper which the Emperor carried in his own hands. The Amir-ul-umārā's peshkash amounted to thirty lakhs of rupees in cash and jewels costing four lakhs of rupees. It included a mirror, before which, if a watermelon was placed, it dried up and drops of water trickled from it. Another was a casket (*sanduq*) to one side of which a [toy] elephant was tied and to the other a goat; the elephant could not pull it away but the goat dragged away the casket and the elephant. The Amir-ul-umārā according to his request, attained to the highest point of the ambition of courtiers, and was authorized to come in a *pālki* up to the ghusalkhānah, and to sound his band (*naubat*) after that of Shāh 'Ālam Bahādur. The Khan [168] went by command to interview Shah 'Ālam Bahādur, and presented to him 200 mohars and 2,000 rupees. After embrace he was seated near the Prince's *masnad,* and presented with a robe with *chahārqub* and a dagger with handle of Jasper.

On Sunday, the 16th June, 1678/6th Jamad. A., the Amir-ul-umārā was sent as Subahdār to Agra *vice* Hasan 'Ali Khan, and rewarded with a special robe and two Arab and 'Irāqi horses. 'Abdur Rahman Khan, bakhshi and news-writer of the Deccan, was deprived of the title of Khan, because he had altered the amount that Bahādur Khan had collected from the ruler [of Bijapur] in entering it into his news-letter. When Bahādur Khan, after his removal from the subahdāri, reached the Court from the Deccan, he was punished for some serious offences and for his tyranny in extorting peshkash, by being deprived of his rank and title, —his property in cash, articles, furniture, and elephants being confiscated. The Emperor, however, graciously overlooked the offences of this old servant and granted him an interview, on Thursday, the 23rd May/11th Rabi. S., when he was restored to his former rank and title. By command, 'Āqil Khan conveyed (him) to the presence of Shah 'Ālam Bahādur, who gave him a robe and dagger worth 7,000 rupees.

News came that 'Āzam Khan Kokah, the dismissed Subahdār of Bengal was coming to Bihār, when he died at Dacca on Friday, the 24th May/12th Rabi S. The new Subahdār, Prince Muhammad 'Āzam, hastened from Patna to that side (on hearing of it). [169] Nurullah Khan was appointed deputy of the Prince for governing Orissā. Saif Khan was made Subahdār of Bihār. The Emperor condoled with Khan Jahān Bahādur, the younger brother of the deceased, and presented robes to his two sons. Robes were sent with a macebearer to Sālih Khan and other sons of the deceased. The property of the deceased—twenty-two lakhs of rupees and 1,12,000 mohars—was confiscated.

On Wednesday, the 18th September, 1678/11th Shaban, Prince Shāh 'Ālam Bahādur with a vast army was sent to govern the subahs of the Deccan, and presented with a special robe with jewelled *bālāband,* a pearl necklace, a *jigha,* three horses, an elephant with gold *sāz,* and one lakh *āshrafi* in cash; and to his original stipend of six kror *dām* was now added four kror *dām,* besides (the increase of) his *mansab*. His sons were promoted and rewarded properly, and his followers favoured with robes, horses, and elephants. Qawāmuddin Khan, Subahdār of Lahore, was entrusted with the faujdāri of Jammu in addition. Raja Jaswant Singh Bundela was sent to punish the sons of Champat Bundela [*i.e.,* Chhatra Sāl and Angad].

The Emperor learnt that grain had become dear in Lahore. He ordered the addition of another twenty rupees daily to the expense of the relief kitchen. News came from Kabul that the kings of Balkh and Bukhārā were at war with each other, and in both places grain was so dear that men [170] were eating carrion and other forbidden things. On Saturday, the 21st September/14th Shaban, news came that 'Umdat-ul-mulk Āsad Khan had started from Burhānpur for Āurangābād. Jān Beg, son of Bakhtān Beg, got the title of Ātish Khan. It was ordered that on Sundays and Thursdays 'Ināyet Khan and Kifāyet Khan should come to the Emperor for reporting the diwāni business. Āsāish Bānu, daughter of Murād Bakhsh, and wife of Khwāja Muhammad Sālih, died. Āmir Khan, Subahdār of Kabul, reached his post on Saturday, the 8th June/27th Rabi. S.

News came from Jaunpur that it began to rain on Wednesday, the 29th May/17th Rabi. S.; the lightning struck the eastern hall* where Ghairat Khan was sitting; six men died, two regained consciousness after a time; the Khan was hurt in the leg, but remained safe. On Monday, the 29th July/19th Jamad. S., Muhammad 'Āzam entered Dacca. From the papers sent by Shaf'i Khan diwān of Bengal, the Emperor learnt that the Āmir-ul-umārā had drawn (spent) one kror and thirty-two lakhs of rupees in excess of his tankhwā for twelve months. He ordered that the amount should be entered as due from the Āmir-ul- umārā.

---

* The printed text reads *Iwān-i-sharqruya*. Is it a mistake for *Sharqia*, built by the Sharqi Sultans? For Subhān the MS. reads *Bakhtān*.

CHAPTER XXII.

22ND YEAR OF THE REIGN 1089 A.D.

7th October, 1678—25th September, 1679.

*   *   *   *

[171] On Wednesday, the 16th October/10th Ramzan, he ordered Mir Mughis, who was going to Bengal as diwān, to carry to Prince Muhammad 'Āzam a jewelled *sarpech* worth 35,000 rupees. On the 12th birthday of Kām Bakhsh he was presented with a pearl necklace and shield with jewelled flowers (*gul*). Khwāja Muhammad Sālih Naqshbandi got a robe on his marriage with the daughter of Shaikh Mir deceased. Condolence robes were presented in connection with the death of Ghiās-ud-din Khan to his brothers 'Abdur Rahim Khan and 'Abdur Rahman Khan, and to his son Raziuddin. Bahramand Khan and Sharfuddin got mourning robes for the death of their mother. Ābul Muhammad Khan Bijapuri became faujdār of Oudh *vice* Tahawwar Khan; Dārāb Khan was sent with a strong force to chastise the Rajputs of Khandela and demolish the great temple of the place. Bahramand Khan became his deputy, and Khwāja Mirzā became dārogha of the elephants *vice* him.

On Wednesday, 6th November, 1678/1st Shawwal, occurred the festival of 'Id-ul-fitr. News came from Peshāwar, that Maharaja Jaswant Singh had died on Tuesday, the 10th December/6th Zil. Q. 'Id-uz-zuha took place on Monday, the 13th January, 1679. [172] Bahramand Khan became Mir Bakhshi *vice* Lutfullah Khan, Tāhir Khan was appointed faujdār and Khidmatguzār Khan qiladār of Jodhpur, the home of the deceased [Mahā-] Raja; Shaikh Ānwār became āmin and 'Abdur Rahim *kotwāl* of the place.

THE EMPEROR'S FIRST JOURNEY TO AJMIR

On Thursday, the 9th January, 1679/6th Zil. H., the Emperor marched out of Delhi for Ajmir. Kāmgār Khan was made qiladār, Fulād Khan faujdār, and 'Itimād Khan diwān of Delhi.

On Friday, the 7th February/6th Muharram, Khan Jahān Bahādur was sent with Hasan 'Ali Khan and other high āmirs to take possession of the country of the deceased [Mahā-] Raja. On the 14th February/13th Muharram, Kumār Kishan Singh, grandson of Raja Rām Singh came from home and had audience. Ruhullah Khan became ākhta begi *vice* 'Abdur Rahim Khan. On Monday, the 17th February/16th Muharram, 'Umdat-ul-Mulk Āsad Khan from the Deccan interviewed the Emperor at Kishangarh. On Wednesday, the 19th February, the Emperor arrived at Ajmir; after visiting the tomb of Khwāja Mu'inuddin, he entered the palace: On Wednesday, the 26th February/25th Muharram, the late Maharaja's agent reported that his two wives who were pregnant [173] had after reaching Lahore delivered two sons with an interval of a few hours between them. Shāista Khan from Agra had audience on the 28th February/27th Muharram. On Sunday, the 2nd March/29th Muharram, Shāhrukh, a servant of Prince 'Āzam, brought to the Court a despatch announcing the conquest of Gauhati, and received a reward of 1,000 rupees. The Emperor granted to the prince a pearl necklace of 91 beads worth two lakhs of rupees, and a jewelled turban-end worth 25,000 rupees.

On Monday, the 10th March/7th Safar, Prince Muhammad Ākbar came from Multān, had audience, and received a robe with half-sleeves and a *bālāband*. News came from Multān that 'Izzat Khan, the dismissed Subahdār of Tatta, had arrived at Multān as the deputy of Prince Ākbar, and Safi Khan had started for Lahore. Sayyid 'Abdullah was sent to fort Siwānah to attach the property of the deceased Raja. The Āmir-ul-umārā was sent back to Agra with a special half-sleeve robe, a *bālāband* and a jewelled dagger. Dārāb Khan who had been sent with a strong force to punish the Rajputs of Khandela and to demolish the great temple of the place, attacked the place on the 8th March/5th Safar, and slew the three hundred and odd men who had made a bold defence, not one of them escaping alive. The temples of Khandela and Sānula and all other temples in the neighbourhood were demolished. Tahawwar Khan became faujdār of Ajmir *vice* Iftikhār Khan. [174] The Emperor permitted the agents of Rānā Rāj Singh to present his letter. He begged that his son Kumār Jai Singh might make his bow to the Emperor; it was granted. Muhammad Na'im was ordered to act as his guide. On Tuesday, the 1st April, 1679/29th Safar, Indra Singh, son of Rāo Rāi Singh went to the tent and brought him to the Emperor. At interview the Kumār received a special robe, a necklace of pearls and emerald, an *arsi* of jasper, a jewelled punchi and a female elephant. Faizullah Khan and Mukhtār Khan, who came to the Court from Morādābād and Mālwa, were sent back to their posts. Āmānullah Khan became faujdār of Gwalior *vice* Mu'atamad Khan. On Monday, the 10th March/7th Safar the imperial camp left Ajmir for Delhi, which was reached on Wednesday, the 2nd April/1st Rabi. A.

As all the aims of the religious Emperor were directed to the spreading of the law of Islām and the overthrow of the practices of the infidels, he issued orders to the high diwāni officers that from Wednesday, the 2nd April, 1679/1st Rabi. A., in obedience to the Qurānic injunction "till they pay commutation money (*jazia*) with the hand in humility" and in agreement with the canonical traditions, *jazia* should be collected from the infidels (*zimmis*) of the capital and the provinces. Many of the honest scholars of the time were appointed to discharge the work (of collecting *jazia*). May God actuate him to do that which He loves and is pleased with, and make his future life better than the present!

[175] On Sunday, the 13th April, 12th Rabi. A., Prince Muhammad Ākbar was sent to Lahore, and presented with a special robe of half-sleeves, a quiver, a bow-case, two horses with gold *sāz*, a jewelled *sarpech*, and a *muttakā*. Muhammad Zamān Luhāni was made a Khan, and Shāh Beg Khan Kāshghari got the title of 'Abdullah Khan. Iftikhār Khan and others, after being rewarded, accompanied the Prince. On Saturday, the 19th April/18th Rabi. A., Kumār Jai Singh, son of the Rānā, was sent back to his home with a robe, a pearl *sarpech*, a ruby pendent, a jewelled turban-end, an Arab horse with gold trappings and an elephant. To the Rānā Rāj Singh were sent a *farmān*, a robe, a jewelled *sarpech* and 20,000 rupees.

On Sunday, the 25th May/24th Rabi. S., Khan Jahān Bahādur came from Jodhpur, after demolishing the temples and bringing with himself some cart-loads of idols, and had audience of the Emperor, who highly praised him and ordered that the idols, which were mostly jewelled, golden, silvery, bronze, copper or stone, should be cast in the yard (*jilaukhānah*) of the Court and under the steps of the Jām'a mosque, to be trodden on. They remained so for some time and at last their very names were lost. On Monday, the 26th May/25th Rabi. S., Indra Singh, son of Rāo Rāi Singh, grandson of Amar Singh, was appointed Raja of Jodhpur in succession to his uncle Jaswant Singh, and given the title of Raja, a special robe, a sword, [176] with jewelled *sāz,* a horse with gold *sāz,* an elephant, banner, *tugh,* and kettledrums. He presented a tribute of thirty-six lakhs of rupees which was graciously accepted. It was formerly the practice of the Emperors to apply the *tikā* with their own hands to the foreheads of the great Rajas, and in this reign Āsad Khan had by command put the *tikā* on the forehead of Raja Rām Singh. The practice was now forbidden, salutation (*taslim*) alone being declared to be enough.

'Āqil Khan became Bakhshi-i-tan *vice* Safi Khan. On Tuesday, the 24th June/25th Jamad. A., Dārāb Khan of the Bani Mukhtār (Sayyid clan) died. Mourning robes were presented to Jān-sipār Khan, his brother, to Muhammad Khalil, Muhammad Taqi and Muhammad Kāmyāb, his sons, and to his son-in-law Lashkari. Ruhullah Khan succeeded him as mir ātish; and Bahramand Khan became ākhta begi *vice* Ruhullah, 'Itiqād Khan bakhshi of the *āhadis vice* Bahramand. News came from the army of Prince Muhammad Mu'azzam that Sharzā Khan Bijāpuri had interviewed him, the Emperor created him Rustam Khan, and sent him a letter, a robe, a horse, an elephant, a banner, and kettledrums.

As Raja Jaswant Singh had left no son when he died in (the province of) Kābul, his trusted servants, *viz.* [177] Sonang, Raghunāthdās Bhātti, Ranchhor, Durgādās and others, reported to the Emperor after the Raja's death that two of his wives who were pregnant had, after their arrival at Lahore, delivered each a son. These servants after reporting the fact of the birth of the sons, begged that *mansab* and the kingdom might be conferred (on one of them). The Emperor ordered that the sons should be sent to his Court, and that when they would come of age, *mansab* and *rāj* would be granted. These shallow-brained people after reaching Delhi pressed their request with great insistence. At this time one of the two sons died. When the Emperor learnt that these wicked men mischievously wished to flee, carry the second son with the two mothers to Jodhpur, and raise a tumult there, he on Tuesday, the 15th July, 1679/16th Jamad. S., ordered both the Rānis and the child, who were living in the mansion of Rup Singh Rāthor, to be seized and placed in Nurgarh. Fulād Khan Kotwāl, Sayyid Hāmid Khan with the men of the khās chauki, Hamid Khan, son of Dāud Khan, Kamāluddin Khan son of Dilir Khan, and Khwāja Mir (who had got the title of Salābat Khan) with the servants of the cavalry (*risāla*) of the late Prince Sultān Muhammad, were ordered to make these wicked men abstain from their criminal plan, [178] and to prevent them from carrying out their crude design, and if they foolishly engaged in fight, to give them proper chastisement. The officers appointed tried counsel and friendly dissuasion; but the wretched infidels rashly took to fighting, and after slaying many of the imperialists, large numbers of the defenders perished. When the Rajputs found themselves hard pressed by the imperialists, they slew the two Rānis, who had been brought into the field in male attire, left the second son, who had been concealed in the house of a milk-vendor there, and then broke and fled. Fulād Khan who had learnt the fact about the second son, took him from the milk-vendor's house to the Court. By order he was shown to the Raja's servant-girls who had been made prisoners, and they acknowledged him to be the Raja's son. He was kept in the harem in charge of the servants of Zeb-un-nisā Begam, and named Muhammadi Rāj. The Khan next day secured the ornaments and other things of the child. In the tumult the property of the Raja, the two Rānis, and the other Rajputs was taken away by plunderers. What [179] the imperial clerks seized for the State was ordered to be delivered into the treasury (*kotha*) of the *bait-ul-māl*. The corpses of both the Rānis and of Ranchhor the Rajput chief, and the heads of thirty of their captains were counted. The rest, who had escaped from the imperial officers, reached Jodhpur on Wednesday, 23rd July/24th Jamad. S. They under the instigation of Durgādās and others imputed to Raja Jaswant Singh two counterfeit boys, one Ran-thamb (who died) and the other Ajit Singh, and caused disturbances. Tāhir Khan, faujdār of Jodhpur, who had not shown any vigour in obstructing the fugitives, was dismissed and deprived of his title of Khan. Indra Singh, who was too incompetent to rule the country and put down the disturbances, was summoned to Court.

On Sunday, the 17th August/20th Rajab, the Emperor visited the garden of Khizirābād. A strong force was sent under Sarbuland Khan to wrest Jodhpur from the Rajputs.

On Saturday, the 23rd August/26th Rajab, the Emperor learnt that Rāj Singh (Rāthor), one of the officers of the Raja, having gathered together a countless host, had encountered Tahawwar Khan faujdār of Ajmir; a severe fight was waged for three days; after the discharge of arrows and bullets, fighting at close quarters took place; mounds of the slain were formed on both sides; at last Tahawwar Khan gained the victory [180] and Rāj Singh with numberless men went to hell. Indeed, so great was the valour exhibited (by the imperialists) that the Rajputs never again came forward to fight, but hid their heads in deserts and wildernesses.

On Friday, the 29th August, 1679/2nd Sha'bān, Muhammad Ākbar from Lahore had audience; a robe and special jewels worth 77,000 rupees, were conveyed to his house by Khwāja Himmat.

THE EMPEROR'S SECOND JOURNEY FROM DELHI TO AJMIR

On Wednesday, the 3rd September/7th Shaban, the imperial camp started for punishing the rebels. That day Muhammad Ākbar was sent from the stage of the village of Pālam, to go in advance to Ajmir, and was presented with a special robe, a *bālāband,* and seven horses. His subordinates, too, received favours. 'Itimād Khan Burhānuddin became diwān of Delhi, Mir Hidāyetullah bakhshi and news-writer, Āflātun, qiladār, 'Abdullah Chalpi, bayutāt, Nur-ul-Haq, son of Qāzi 'Abdul Wahhāb became a Qāzi, Abu S'aid, son-in-law of the (deceased) Qāzi, became dārogha of the 'adālat; and other officers were appointed to various posts and sent away. [181] On Tuesday, the 9th September/13th Shaban, the Āmir-ul-umārā became Subahdār of Bengal, *vice* Prince Muhammad 'Āzam, and Safi Khan became that of Agra. *Farmāns* and robes were sent (to them) with macebearers.

On Tuesday, the 16th September/20th Shaban, Muhtasham Khan, faujdār of Miwāt, interviewed while the Emperor was riding. On Thursday, the 25th/29th Shaban, the Emperor entered the Jahāngiri palace on the bank of the Ānāsāgar lake, after visiting the tomb of Shaikh Mu'inuddin and presenting 5,000 rupees there.

CHAPTER XXIII

23RD YEAR OF THE REIGN : 1090 A. H.

26th September, 1679—14th September, 1680

* * * *

The Emperor spent the whole month of Ramzan in prayer. Himmat Khan, Subahdār of Allahabad, had audience on Friday, the 26th September/1st Ramzan, and was at once sent to serve under Prince Muhammad Akbar and presented with a special robe and a horse with gold *sāz*; a coloured *sarpech* adorned with an emerald for the Prince was entrusted to him. On the 2nd October/7th Ramzan, a letter accompanied by a *peshkash* of 400 mohars was received from Prince Muhammad 'Āzim announcing the birth of a son to the daughter of Kirat Singh. [182]. The child was named Muhammad Karim. On the 4th October/19th Ramzan, a a letter was received from Dilir Khan stating that the fort of Mangalbida had been wrested from Shivaji.

On Sunday, the 26th October, 1679/1st Shawwal, occurred the 'Id-ul-fitr. * * * A *farmān* of praise was sent to Sujan Singh for his having captured Shivaji's fort. Hāfiz Muhammad Āmin Khan, Subahdār of Ahmadābād, had audience, and was rewarded along with his companions. Fakhar Khan was sent to Delhi with a robe. Tahawwar Khan was given a robe, a quiver, a bow, and an elephant, and sent to occupy Mandal and other parganahs. Indra Singh was made thānadār of Nimbaj, Raghunāth Singh that of Siwānah and Dhāmān, and Muhakam Singh Mertiā that of the village of Pur. On the 24th November, a letter with 900 mohars was received from Muhammad Akbar, announcing the birth of a son, who was given the namē of Nekusiyar.

THE EMPEROR'S MARCH FROM AJMIR TO UDAIPUR

On Sunday, the 30th November/7th Zil. Q., the Emperor started from Ajmir to punish the Rana. Prince Akbar, coming from Mertā had audience at Deorāi. [183].

MUHAMMAD 'ĀZAM'S RAPID MARCH FROM BENGAL

Traversing this vast distance, in spite of its difficulties, in obedience to the Emperor's command, was one of the feats of this Prince. Trustworthy men who accompanied him narrate that after midnight the Prince entered a *pālki* and slept. Mustafa Kāshi, Lohrāsp Beg, Qāsim Beg and three or four officers like them, waited on the Prince by turns. From day-break to noon he rode on horseback, so that at the time of his alighting not more than two or three men were with him. Gradually the others dropped in.

He left the baggage, harem, and *kārkhānas* with Mir Hādi and 1,000 troopers at Patna with orders to follow him. From Patna to Benares, which was traversed in seven days, he was accompanied by Jahān-zeb Bānu Begam. At Benares, Mir Khan and Shāh Quli Khan Bakhshi were ordered to convey her stage by stage under escort of 2,000 troopers; they reached (Delhi) in twenty-five days, while the Prince by rapid marches finished the journey from Benares in twelve days and three hours, and had audience on Tuesday, the 16th December, 1679/23rd Zil. Q.* That day he had travelled seventy kos.

One day when he was riding on a wretched post-horse [184] he said to Qāsim Beg, "My quiver now appears to me heavy". The Khan replied "This servant may remove it". The Prince asked "What will you do with your own quiver?" He replied "I shall fasten your quiver on my back," and did so. Five hundred *Khush-āspā* troopers formed his retinue, and many men were favoured with the gift of horses. Twelve troopers, four footmen, one *chobdār*, one road-measurer (*jarib-kash*), and two time-keepers (*ghariālis*) who had been constantly in attendance, arrived with the Prince.

One day, during the journey, while the Prince and his son Bidār Bakht were riding on post-horses, under the protection of God, the Shāhzāda felt very thirsty. They reached a well near a village; a water-carrier presented a cup of water, the Prince gave him two *āshrafis*. A villain saw it and imagined that he was a macebearer carrying a large number of *āshrafis*. He barred the road and shouted

---

* 22nd October, 1679 "Recd. a letter from Dacca dated the 13th instant advising that the Prince Sultan 'Āzam had left the city on the 6th, and on the 12th began his journey towards Rajmahal." Hughly diary, quoted in *Fort St. George, Diary and consultation book* for 1679.

to the servants not to advance. The Prince did not attend to it, and the servants did not stop at his bidding. The wretch came forward violently. The Prince pierced him with an arrow through the breast. The villain fell down there and did not rise up again. The servants went on their way. Suhrāb Beg, one of the officers, who was following the Prince like a shadow, reached the place, recognised the arrow, [185] cut off the villain's head, and after extracting the arrow hastened to overtake the Prince. He showed the arrow and uttered this couplet in the place of a prayer :

> "To all four quarters will spread the fame of thy royal command,
> Even as thy arrow has reached the heart of thy foe."

After this the Prince ordered that some *charn* and two anna, four anna pieces of gold and silver, copper coins and cowries also should be kept in his pocket. At many of the stages the officers of the jāgir of Shāh 'Ālam Bahādur and other grandees brought costly horses, camels, and mules, and presented kids and fowl. But nowhere was cooked food procurable, except one day from the house of the Qāzi of Mālpur. So he (usually) lived on dry bread, dry fruits, and fried barley. One day the Shāhzāda spoke of [tasting] *khichri*. The servants went to a *sarāi*, cooked it, and brought it in a second-hand dish or *katora* of wood. Both father and son were hungry, but the Prince after a look at it, ordered his son to eat it. He in aversion refused to eat it. The Prince consoled him by saying, "God willing, we shall get food from the Emperor's own table in two or three days." * * *

On the 17th December, 1679/24th Zil. Q., Bidār Bakht was made a 8-*hazāri* (2,000 tr.), 'Ābid Khan was given the title of Qalich Khan. On Saturday, the 3rd January, 1680/11th Zil. H., when the Emperor marched from Mandal [186], it was learnt that the men of the Rānā had evacuated the pass of Debāri. Hāfiz Muhammad Āmin Khan reported that some of his servants had ascended the hill and found the other side of the pass also deserted; (evidently) the Rānā had evacuated Udaipur and fled. On the 4th January/12th Zil. H., the Emperor encamped in the pass. Hasan 'Ali Khan was sent in pursuit of the infidel. Prince Muhammad 'Āzam and Khan Jahān Bahādur were permitted to view Udaipur. Ruhullah Khan and Ekkatāz Khan went to demolish the great temple in front of the Rānā's palace, which was one of the rarest buildings of the age and the chief cause of the destruction of life and property of the despised worshippers. Twenty *māchātor** Rajputs were sitting in the temple vowed to give up their lives; first one of them came out to fight, killed some and was then himself slain, then came out another and so on, until every one of the twenty perished, after killing a large number of the imperialists including the trusted slave, Ikhlās. The temple was found empty. The hewers broke the images.

As Mir Shihābuddin's luck was in the ascendant, the Emperor summoned him when the Mir was stationed at midnight with a party of scouts (*qaghalchis*) round His Majesty's tent and said, "It is some days since Hasan 'Ali Khan entered the pass in pursuit of the infidel. No news has come of him. You should go and get the news." Without any delay he set out with the party of *qaghalchis* to execute the command. Inspite of his ignorance of the state of the strange country, [187] the ups and downs, diversity of the roads, the long distance, and the fear of robbers, he was guided by fortune to the army of the Khan. He procured news and a letter from the Khan and immediately returned, reaching the imperial camp at night, two days after his starting, and had audience. Without the mediation of Bakhshis to present him for making his bow of promotion, he received an incrlarement of 200 making him a 7-*sadi,* the title of Khan, an elephant, and a special bow and quiver, and was again sent to Hasan 'Ali Khan to convey the Emperor's orders. This was the beginning of his advancement.† I shall hereafter narrate in the proper place only one of the many instances of his promotion.

Sarbuland Khan Mir Bakhshi, after a long illness died on Saturday, the 27th December, 1679/4th Zil. H. He was a faithful officer, good inwardly and outwardly.

On Friday, the 16th January, 1680/24th Zil. H., Himmat Khan was sent to Allahabad. Akbar was presented with a *sarpech* of ruby worth 40,000 rupees and sent to Udaipur. A force with abundant materials and equipment

---

* Māchātor.—Opium-bemused Rajputs "who never rise from their beds, but to go to war". (Platt's *Hindustani Dictionary.*)

† Mir Shihābuddin, better known as Ghāzi-ud-din Firuz Jang, was the father of the first Nizām-ul-mulk Asaf Jāh. For the above incident see *Ahkām-i-'Alamgiri* (text ed. by me) § 33; Khāfi Kh., ii. 267, and *Maāsir-ul-umāra,* ii. 832.

was despatched under Hasan 'Ali Khan to punish and pursue the Rānā; his companions were rewarded when taking leave. Shaikh Raziuddin, the leader of his companions, did good service in this expedition and got the title of Khan. Ruhullah Khan became Mir Bakhshi *vice* Sarbuland Khan deceased, but the name of the post was not verbally mentioned. Salābat Khan [188] replaced him as dārogha of topkhāna, Sālih Khan becoming dārogha of ghusalkhāna *vice* Salābat. Tahawwar Khan got the title of Pādishāh Quli Khan.

News came from Lahore that Sayyid 'Ali Akbar, Qāzi of the place, never bowed to anybody on account of his honesty, bravery and spirit, but in contrast with him his sister's son Sayyid Fāzil was foolish, violent and abusive and had made the lives of the *nāzim* and *kotwāl* miserable by his words and deeds. At last they attempted his life. The Qāzi died a shameful death in the conflict with Mir Qawāmuddin Khan, the *nāzim*. He and Nizāmuddin, the *kotwāl*, were removed from their ranks and posts. The *kotwāl* was executed in Lahore and Qawāmuddin was summoned to Court. Prince Muhammad 'Āzam became Subahdār of the Panjab *vice* him, and received a turban end and jewelled *muttakā*. Lutfullah Khan became deputy Subahdār, Abu Nasr Khan becoming dārogha of *'arz-i-mukarrar vice* him. Qawāmuddin Khan on reaching the Court at Ajmir, was subjected to much disgrace in the Court of the Holy Law, till at last Sayyid 'Ali Akbar, the son of the deceased Qāzi, at the entreaty of the grandees of the Court gave up the demand for his execution in consideration of his old age. About the same time the Khan died, out of pity for his own condition.

On Saturday, the 24th January, 1680/2nd Muharram, the Emperor went to view lake Udaisāgar, constructed by the Rānā, and ordered all the three temples [189] on its banks to be demolished.

News came that Hasan 'Ali Khan having crossed the pass on Wednesday, the 21st January/9th Zil. H., had attacked the Rānā, who had fled leaving his camp and property behind. In this expedition much grain was captured by the soldiers and it led to cheapness. On the 29th January/7th Muharram, Hasan 'Ali Khan brought to the Emperor twenty camel-loads of tents and other things captured from the Rānā's palace and reported that one hundred and seventy-two other temples in the environs of Udaipur had been destroyed. The Khan received the title of Bahādur 'Alamgirshāhi. On the 31st January/9th Muharram, Khan Jahān Bahādur was sent to Bhainsror (*cor.*), and presented with a robe, a jewelled dagger, and a horse with gold *sāz*.

On Monday, the 22nd February/1st Safar the Emperor went to view Chitor; by his order sixty-three temples of the place were destroyed. On Friday, the 26th/5th Safar, Khan Jahān Bahādur came from Bhainsror and had audience at Chitor and was honoured by being presented with a half-sleeve from the Emperor's own person. On Sunday, the 28th February/7th Safar, Hāfiz Muhammad Āmin, Nāzim of Ahmadābād, was sent to his post, and given a robe, a horse, and an elephant. On the 1st March Khan Jahān Bahādur Zafar Jang Kokaltāsh Khan became Subahdār of the Deccan *vice* the eldest Prince, and was presented with a robe, a jewelled dagger, a horse, and an elephant. Shaikh Sulaimān, dārogha of *'adālat,* got the title of Fāzil Khan. On Thursday, the 4th March/12th Safar [190] Muhammad Akbar was appointed with a well-equipped force to guard the environs of Chitor, and presented with a special robe, a pearl necklace, a jewelled *jigha,* a horse, and an elephant. Hasan 'Ali Khan, Raziuddin Khan and others were rewarded with robes and sent with the Prince. Hakim Shamsā, who had reached the Court with the daughter of 'Ādil Khan Bijāpuri, received a special robe, a horse with gold *sāz,* an elephant, the rank of 3-*hazāri* (1,000 tr.), the title of Shamsuddin Khan and posting under Khan Jahān Bahādur.

THE EMPEROR'S RETURN FROM UDAIPUR TO AJMIR

On Saturday, the 6th March, 1680, he started from Udaipur. 'Abdullah Khan who had been deprived of his annual pension, was given the rank of a 2-*hazāri* (*hazār* tr.) and made qiladār of Āgra *vice* 'Abdur Rasul Khan; Mukarram Khan was sent to chastise the rebels near Ranthambhor, with a robe and an elephant.

On Tuesday, the 16th March/24th Safar, Yalangtosh Khan Bahādur was sent to bring the Emperor's consort, Aurangābādi Mahal, who had been summoned to Court along with Zeb-un-nisā Begam. Qābil Khan, brother of Abul Fath Qābil Khan, mir munshi, of Tatta, an old servant of the days of Prince-hood, who, in consideration of (his brother's) long service and intimate knowledge of the Emperor, had been brought up and favoured by His Majesty, was led astray by his evil luck. On account of his improper lapses [191] he was removed from his rank of a *hazāri* (70 tr.) and the post of being close to the Emperor's person and qānungoship of the subah of Tatta, with his son-in-law 'Abdul Wās'i. On his application the Emperor wrote "Go to Delhi". After his arrival, Fulād Khan was ordered to confiscate his house, to place him on a horse in the same state in which he would come out of his house, and to expel him from the city. It was done. During his two and a half years of close attendance on the Emperor (*taqarrab*) he had amassed twelve lakhs of rupees in cash, besides articles and a newly-built house. All these were now confiscated. He went to Lahore and died there. Fazāil Khan became dārogha of *dākchauki vice* Qābil Khan and his heart's desire was gratified. Shaikh Makhdum of Tatta, munshi of Muhammad 'Āzam, became munshi of the Emperor. He received the rank of 5-*sadi* (300 tr.), a dagger with *sādāhkār*, 2,000 rupees in cash, and ten pieces each of cloth, fotah, jāmawār, and kinkhāb. Afterwards he rose to be a 1½-*hazāri* and got the title of Fāzil Khan and the post of Sadr, which he held till his death. His post under the Prince was given to Shaikh 'Abdul Wali, son of Shaikh 'Abdus Samad J'afarkhāni.

On Monday, the 22nd March, the Emperor arrived at Ajmir, and after first visiting the tomb of Khwāja Mu'inuddin entered the palace. [192]. Mughal Khan, son of Tāhir Khan, came from the Deccan, had audience, and was made First Mir Tuzuk. Salābat Khan was removed from his rank for some offence and succeeded by Bahramand Khan in the post of dārogha of topkhāna. 'Abdur Rahim Khan replaced Bahramand as *ākhta begi*. Hayāt Beg, son of Bāqi Khan got the title of Khan, Khwāja Kamāl that of Khanjar Khan, and 'Abdul Wāhid, son of Mirzā Khan, that of Mir Khan. Kāmgār Khan, son of Hushdār Khan, who had been removed from his rank, stabbed himself in the stomach in four places, but recovered through the kind attention of his relatives.

On Wednesday, the 31st March, 1680/10th Rabi. A., Wāris Khan, news-reader, who had written the third volume of the *Pādishāhnāmah*, was killed with a pen-knife by a mad student, whom the Khan had been taking care of with a view to saving him from molestation by other men, and whom he made to sleep near himself at night. On Monday, the 5th April, 1680/15th Rabi. A., a letter was received from Shāh 'Alam Bahadur, saying that the *khutba* had been read in His Majesty's name in Bijapur, and coins stamped in gold and silver in his name. The courtiers bowed to express their congratulation.

On Thursday, the 6th May/16th Rabi. S., Muhammad 'Āzam advanced one stage, by command, to welcome his sister, and conducted her and Aurangābādi Mahal to the Emperor's harem. The Emperor learnt that [193] Nazar Bey the Atāliq of Subhān Quli Khan, King of Balkh, was coming to Court. Orders were issued to pay him 5,000 rupees from the treasury of Kabul and the same sum from that of Lahore. Qalandar Bey, envoy of Balkh, had audience and received a robe, a dagger, and 1,000 rupees in cash. Hāji Shaf'i Khan became diwān of Bengal *vice* Mir Mughis, and was succeeded by Sharif Khan as dārogha of *dāgh* and *tashiha*. Hāmid Khan was appointed to punish the rebels of Sojat and Jitāran. Muhammad Mirak, macebearer, got the title of Khan. Iftikhār Khan became faujdār of Jaunpur *vice* Shujā'et Khan, Multafat Khan who had been previously dismissed was now restored to the rank of a 3-*hazāri* (1,000 tr.) and appointed faujdār of Ghāzipur Zamānia. On Thursday, the 20th May/1st Jamad. A., Bahramand Khan, dārogha of topkhānah, who had his quarters in a garden on the other side of the lake of Ānāsāgar, was sitting in the shade of a tree, when the lightning struck (him). The Khan jumped into a reservoir, and recovered his senses after a few hours.

On Wednesday, the 9th June/21st Jamad. A., news came that Khan Jahān Bahādur had reached Aurangābād and interviewed Shāh 'Alam Bahādur, and the latter had started for the Court. On the 14th June/26th Jamad. A., Muhammad 'Āzam and Bidār Bakht after being richly rewarded started on the expedition against the Rānā. [194] Nazar Bey was given the title of Aurang Khan and the rank of 2-*hazāri* (700 tr.), Muhammad Āmin, the title of Shāh Quli Khan, and Hāji Muhammad, that of Mir Khan.

On Friday, the 25th June, Muhammad 'Āzam reached Chitor. Muhammad Akbar, after interviewing (him) during a ride, stārted from Chitor for Sojat and Jitāran.

News came from the Deccan that on Friday the 14th May, 1680/24th Rabi. S., Shivāji after returning from a journey dismounted from his horse, twice vomitted blood in the excess of heat, and sank down into the pit of hell.*

Abu Turāb, who had been sent to demolish the temples of Amber, returned to Court on Tuesday, the 10th August/24th Rajab, and reported that he had pulled down sixty-six temples. Khwāja Mu'atamad Khan, qiladār of Gwalior, died on Thursday, the 26th August/10th Shaban.

CHAPTER XXIV.

24TH YEAR OF THE REIGN. 1091 A.H.

15th September, 1680—3rd September, 1681.

* * * *

Khidmatguzār Khan was appointed bakhshi and news-writer of Chitor. On Saturday, the 25th September, 1680/11th Ramzan, Ekkatāz Khan [195] died. His sons, Mir 'Abdullah, Mir Nurullah, and 'Atāullah, received mourning robes. 'Āqil Khan, second bakhshi, became Subahdār of Delhi and received a special robe and a jewelled dagger, with pearl *'ilāqa*. On Saturday, the 16th October/2nd Shawwal, Ghaznafar Khan was sent with 400 cavalry, Muhammad Sharif khush-manzil, and *qarāwals,* to ascertain the stages from Ajmir to the lake of Rājsamudra. On Sunday, the 24th October/10th Shawwal, Himmat Khan became First Bakhshi; a robe and gold *do-patta* were sent to his house. The same day, the property of Mu'atamad Khan amounting to twelve lakhs and 50,000 rupees, besides jewels and animals, came to Court from Gwalior. On Tuesday, the 9th November/26th Shawwal, Hāmid Khan went towards Mertā to punish the Rāthor rebels. Of his comrades Shihābuddin Khan received a robe and a female elephant and the others robes. Ruhullah Khan became second bakhshi. On Saturday, the 13th November/1st Zil. Q., he received a robe, a horse, an elephant and a banner, and went to serve under Muhammad Akbar. Mughal Khan was sent to chastise the rebels of Sāmbhar and Didwāna. Mukhtār Beg, son of Islām Khan Rumi received the title of Nawāzish Khan, a robe of honour and permission to wear the customary dress of India.

On Tuesday, the 30th November/18th Zil. Q., Muhammad N'aim, bakhshi of Kāmbakhsh, and other officers of that Prince received robes from the Emperor and went to serve under Akbar. Sadruddin, son of Qawāmuddin Khan [196] received a robe for the death of his father. Udwat Singh Bhadauriya became qiladār of Chitor. To Shahāmat Khan was sent a *farmān* appointing him qiladār of Kabul, *vice* Sayyid Khan deceased.

On Saturday, the 18th December, 1680/6th Zil. H., Lutfullah Khan who had reached the Court from Lahore, became dārogha of ghusalkhāna *vice* 'Abdur Rahim Khan, who became third bakhshi and received a jasper inkpot. Sazāwar Khan became *ākhta begi vice* him. Ābul Qāsim, son of Qāzi 'Ārif, *peshdast* of the third bakhshi, received a shawl. Rāj Singh and Prithvi Singh Rāthor each got a robe and 2,000 rupees. Aghar Khan became *rāhdār* of Kabul and received kettledrums. A robe and a horse with gold *sāz* were sent to Qalich Khan with Shihābuddin Khan. Dewāfkan, son of Diānat Khan, got the title of Mu'atamad Khan, and the dāroghaship of *dāgh* and *tashiha vice* Sharif Khan. Bidār Bakht was rewarded with a pearl necklace and ruby pendant on completing the memorisation of the *Qurān*.

REBELLION OF PRINCE MUHAMMAD AKBAR

* * * *

[197] On Friday, the 7th January, 1681/26th Zil. H., the Emperor learnt from the letters of spies, approved observers and other well-informed persons that through the instigation of the Rāthors and some ungrateful imperial servants, Prince Muhammad Akbar had rebelled, promoted those of the imperial officers who agreed with him, and imprisoned those whom he suspected of being unfriendly. [198] The Emperor's heart was deeply grieved to hear of this sad occurrence. Relying on God's help he turned his attention to remedying this mischief. Bahramand Khan, Mir Atish, was ordered to dig trenches round the army, to place men to defend the passes, and to mount guns on the hillocks near the imperial abode. Orders were sent to Hāfiz Muhammad Āmin Khan, nāzim of Ahmadabad, and other chiefs, that they should assist each other and firmly guard the frontiers of their provinces. At this time when the imperial army was dispersed in the task of punishing the rebel [Rajputs], the only men with the Emperor were the servants whose total number did not exceed 10,000 troopers. The Emperor often said "The hero (Akbar) has got a fine opportunity. Why is he delaying (to attack me)?"

entrenchments of 'Umdat-ul-mulk Āsad Khan and others. 'Umdat-ul-mulk was ordered to inspect the trenches at the end of every day. Orders were sent to imprison in the fort of Garh-Bithli the agent of the Prince Akbar, the agents of Shuj'āet Khan, son of Najābat Khan, and Pādishāh Quli Khan, son-in-law of 'Ināyet Khan who had misled the Prince. Shihābuddin Khan, son of [199] Qalich Khan, had gone towards Sirohi for punishing Sonang, Durgādās and other Rāthors who wanted to go to Gujrat. At this time the enemy (Rajputs) in a large body came to the Prince and guided him in his rebellion. The Prince sent Mirak Khan to Shihābuddin to induce him with favours and gifts to join him. The Khan had a large force with him and was at some distance from the Prince's army; he very wisely marched away, rapidly covered sixty *kos* in two days, and joined the Emperor, bringing Mirak Khan with himself. Every one of his comrades down to commanders of 200 was favoured with interview; he received robes, praise, and high promotion which will be gradually set forth. Mirak Khan, who had left his tent and belongings in the Prince's camp, was presented with a robe, 2,000 rupees in cash, and an increment of 200 (50 tr.). Muhammad 'Ārif, brother of Shihābuddin Khan, got a robe and promotion. All his subordinates, of high and low rank alike, were rewarded with robes and promotion. On Monday, the 10th January/30th Zil. H., the Emperor when riding to hunt, reviewed the troops and the entrenchments. Hāmid Khan, who had been sent with the men of the *chauki-i-khās* and other troops to punish Durjan Singh of Mertā, returned by forced marches and interviewed the Emperor while he was riding [200].

On Wednesday, the 12th January/2nd Muharram, a letter was received from Shāh 'Ālam Bahādur stating that he had reached the lake of the Rānā and was soon coming to meet the Emperor. Āsad Khan, Muhammad 'Ali Khan Ābū Nasar Khan, and others went to reconnoitre in the direction of the lake of Pushkar, and returned. Himmat Khan, who was seriously ill, was left in the fort to guard Ajmir.

On the 13th January/3rd Muharram, after performing the Friday prayer and reading the *fātiha* at the tomb of Shaikh Mu'inuddin, the Emperor started from Ajmir, and stopped at the camp of Deorāi. Shihābuddin Khan, who had gone forward for scouting reported that the enemy's army was dispersed at Kurki, therefore he had stayed there during the night instead of coming to the Emperor. The High Bakhshis reported that the troops with the Emperor numbered 16,000 cavalry.* They were commanded to marshal the army :—the Centre, the Vanguard and the Front Skirmishers together numbered 10,000, the Right and Left Wings and the Advanced Reserve were together 6,000 strong.

Spies brought the news that the Prince was advancing to fight the Emperor, but his soldiers were in despair, many escaping when they got an opportunity. Kamāluddin Khan and others came and joined the Emperor's camp. After the morning prayer on Sunday, the 15th January/5th Muharram, the Emperor considering it necessary to punish the rebels, rode nearly three miles, dismounted at Doraha (*cor.*) (201), and sat down within the pavilion and cloth-screens of his touring camp (dauriya). News came in quick succession that the enemy were coming. He said, "Don't advance. Let them come on." After the zuhar prayer, Shah 'Ālam Bahadur had audience. The tent, which had been at Deorai, was brought by order and pitched for His Majesty's residence.

At one *prahar* and two *gharis* of night, the Emperor was kneeling on the prayer-carpet and Shah 'Alam Bahādur was present, when the news came that Pādishāh Quli Khan, having come from the enemy's army, had reached the door of the audience hall. Lutfullah Khan dārogha of the ghusalkhānah, was ordered to bring him in unarmed. The wretch, who had evidently some wicked intention in his mind, strongly objected to taking off his arms after reaching the *deorhi* of the ghusalkhānah. Lutfullah Khan coming in reported, "He says that he is a hereditary servant (khānahzād), and had never been made to enter anywhere deprived of his arms." The Emperor said, "He must not come in armed." Lutfullah Khan then went back to him. He was seized with despair, and wanted to run away. But his ingratitude clogged his steps. As soon as he stepped out of the screen of the door of the ghusalkhānah, the men of the imperial retinue and the slaves fell upon him. As he wore cuirass and coat of mail under it, the blows produced little effect. One struck him on the throat and silenced his disturbance.

* Text misprints *shāhzādah* for *shānzdah*.

On Saturday, the 15th January/5th Muharram, news came that Himmat Khan, the First Bakhshi, son of Islām Khan Bahādur of the days of Princeship, [202] had died. He was a good man, charitable, benevolent to all; and used to entertain in his assembly all kinds of men of learning and skill, and reward them. Both father and son had a well-balanced nature, and were expert in composing prose and verse.

Before dawn on Sunday, the 16th January, 1681/6th Muharram, the Emperor learnt that Muhammad Akbar, who had encamped one and a half kos from him (the Emperor's tent), had fled away at midnight leaving his family and children behind. * * * * [203]. The courtiers made their bows for this victory. Music of rejoicing was played for three hours. Muhammad 'Ali Khan, Khān-i-sāmān, went to confiscate his stores (kārkhānajāt). Darbār Khan, nāzir, brought to the Emperor Nekusiyar and Muhammad Āsghar, the sons, and Safiyyat-un-nisā, Zakiyyat-un-nisā and Najibat-un-nisā, the daughters, and Salimā Bānu Begam the wife (*mahal*) and other relatives of the Prince. Muhatasham Khan, the son of Shaikh Mir deceased, M'amur Khan, Muhammad N'aim Khan, and Sayyid 'Abdullah were released from the Prince's prison and interviewed the Emperor receiving robes. Shihābuddin Khan, who had gone in pursuit, killed many of the followers and fatigued stragglers of the Prince's party. Shāh 'Alam Bahādur was sent in pursuit of the Prince. Qalich Khan, Khān Zamān, Indra Singh, Rām Singh, Sujan Singh and others were appointed under him. Fifty thousand *āshrafis* were presented to Shah 'Alam Bahādur, two lakhs of rupees to Prince Mu'izzuddin, three thousand *āshrafis* to Prince Muhammad 'Azimuddin, and fifty thousand *āshrafis* to Shāh 'Alam's followers. Ruhullah Khan was ordered to carry this treasure to the Prince.

On Monday, the 17th January/7th Muharram the Emperor returned, and after visiting the tomb of Khwāja Mu'inuddin entered the palace of Ajmir. On the 19th January/9th Muharram, news came that the thānadār of Mandal had been slain and that small fort had been captured by the rebels. As for the men [204] who had joined Muhammad Akbar in revolt, it was ordered that Khwājas Manzur and Muhrim should be imprisoned in Garh-Bithli, Murtaza Quli in Alwar, Farāq (or Qazzāq) Khan in Gwalior, and Muhammad Hātim, son of Ghaznafar Khan in Kāngra,

Qāzi Khubullah, Muhammad 'Āqil, Shaikh Taiyyab, and Mir Ghulam Muhammad of Āmroha, who had affixed their seals to a decree declaring the deposition of His Majesty as demanded by religion, were sent to fort Garh-Bithli after being tied to planks and severely flogged. Many others were flogged and imprisoned. Zebunnisā Begam, whose letters to Muhammad Akbar were discovered, was deprived of her annual pension of four lakhs of rupees, her property was confiscated, and she was lodged in fort Salimgarh. On the 23rd January/13th Muharram, Kāmbakhsh was married to Fakhr-i-Jahān Khānam, daughter of Barkhurdār Beg, mansabdār. On the 26th January/16th Muharram, Aurangābādi Mahal, Salimā Bānu Begam (wife of Muhammad Akbar) and other dependents were sent to Delhi. News came from the army of Shāh 'Alam Bahādur that he had reached Jālor and Muhammad Akbar Sānchor, and that Qalich Khan was hastening in pursuit with a force.

The news-writer of the army of Muhammad 'Āzam reported that he (the Prince) having learnt that the Rānā's diwān Dayāldās wanted to make a night attack, had sent Dilāwwar Khan against that wretch. A battle ensued; [205] many of the enemy were slain; after slaying his wife he broke away; his daughter and a few other persons were taken prisoners. Qalich Khan who had come to Court without the Prince's permission, was refused audience. At first Ihtimām Khan, kotwāl, kept him under surveillance; then he was made over to Salābat Khan. Muhammad Ibrāhim surnamed Shuj'āet Khan left Akbar and came over to Shah 'Alam, who sent him to the Court, where he was made over to Salābat Khan and kept under surveillance in the Akbari palace. Hāfiz Muhammad Āmin Khan sent a letter stating that Muhammad Akbar, having advanced with the Rāthors by way of the hill of Dongar to the territory of the Rānā, wanted to go to Ahmadābād; at this time spies brought the news that after passing by Rājpiplā he had gone to the Deccan by way of Sārangarh. Sazāwar Khan was imprisoned with his son for an offence, made over to Jalāl Beg Mingbāshi. Muhammad Shaf'i mushrif of ghusalkhānah, who evidently shared his guilt, was dismissed from his rank and post. Mughal Khan became *ākhtabegi vice* him, and Bahramand Khan, Mir Tuzuk *vice* Mughal Khan. Mirzā Muhammad, son of Murshid Quli Khan got the *mushrifi* of ghusalkhānah. Tāpidās, peshdast of Ruhullah Khan, and Bālkishan his munshi were made over to the kotwāl, as they were securities for Gangārām, an *'amla* of Khān Jahān Bahādur, who had rebelled in the province of Allahabad. A letter came from Khan Jahān Bahādur stating [206] that Muhammad Akbar had passed by Burhānpur on Sunday, the 16th May, 1681/7th Jamad. A., and entered the territory of Sambhā, who had kindly and honourably given him shelter in his dominion. Muhammad Māsih and other sons, brothers and sons-in-law of Himmat Khan deceased, received mourning robes. Āshraf Khan became First Bakhshi *vice* the deceased, and Kāmgār Khan became news-reader *vice* Āshraf Khan, his own place of *bayutāt* being taken by 'Ināyet Khan. Bad'i-uz-zamān Mahābatkhāni whose skill helped him in the service of the Emperor, got the title of Rashid Khan and became *peshdast* of khālsa *vice* 'Ināyet Khan. On Sunday, the 30th January, 1681/20th Muharram, Mir Sayyid Muhammad Qanauji came from Delhi and had audience. One thousand rupees and two trays of fruits were sent to him.

On Tuesday, the 1st February/22nd Muharram, Shihābuddin Khan with the division under him, received robes, a dagger, and a *kalgi*. On Tuesday, the 1st March, Irij Khan was appointed Subahdār of Burhānpur *vice* Khan Jahān Bahādur; (on 1st March) Afrāsiāb Khan, son of Islām Khan, came from his faujdāri of Dhāmuni and had audience. Sayyid Āshraf [*var.* Sharif] was made a khān and *mir-i-sāmān* of Begam Sahib. On Sunday, the 20th March/10th Rabi. A., Faizullah Khan left for Morādābād, after receiving an elephant and a robe. 'Ināyet Khan became faujdār of Ajmir, and began to make strong exertions for punishing the Rāthors. [207] Khān Mirzā, envoy of the ruler of Urganj, had audience on Friday, the 25th March/15th Rabi. A., and received a robe and belt-dagger. On the 16th April when taking leave, he was presented with a jewelled *jigha,* 5,000 rupees, a *mohar* weighing fifty *mohars,* and a rupee weighing one hundred rupees. A jewelled sword worth 2,000 rupees was sent with him to Ānushā Khan, ruler of Urganj.

On Saturday, the 9th April/30th Rabi. A., Muhammadi Rāj, son of Jaswant Singh came to Court from Delhi, on the 23rd April/14th Rabi. A., Hāmid Khan, son of Dāud Khan, became faujdār of Bhojpur, Mirak Khan that of the Jalandhar Doab, Murid Khan qiladār of Kābul *vice* Shahāmat Khan, and Raja Māndhāta, thānadār of Ghorband. Saifullah Khan, mir bahar, who had joined the service of

Shah 'Alam Bahādur, and received no reward, was ordered to be paid 5,000 rupees on behalf of the Prince, which amount was to be deducted from the cash dues of the Prince. Āshraf Khan, Mir Bakhshi, and Itimād Khan, peshdast of the *daftar-i-tan,* received crystal ink-pots. On Sunday, the 8th May/30th Rabi. S., Qalich Khan having been released from the prison of punishment, had audience. On Thursday, the 23rd June/16th Jamad. S., he received for the second time the high post of Sadr, *vice* Razavi Khan deceased.

The Rānā had fled from his country and abode * * * and received severe chastisement from the imperial army. The thousand years' home of the desert-rat was overturned by the hoofs of the horses [208] of the imperialists. He fled as far as his frontier, and then, when his powers were exhausted and no resource was left save to beg for quarter, he begged Prince Muhammad 'Āzam to intercede for him, offered to cede the parganahs of Mandal-Pur and Badhnur as a substitute for *jazia* and to interview the Prince as the means of saving his country and property. The Prince, pitying him, reported his requests to His Majesty, who overlooked the Rānā's offences and resolved to gratify the Prince by acceding to his proposal. Accordingly on Tuesday, the 14th June, 1681/7th Jamad. S., the Rānā interviewed the Prince at the lake of Rajsamudra. Dilir Khan and Hasan 'Ali Khan advanced to conduct him to the Prince. He presented 500 *āshrafis* and eighteen horses with gold and silver *sāz.* The Prince graciously ordered him to sit on the left side and presented him with a robe, a jewelled sword, a dagger with *phulkatāra,* a horse with gold *sāz,* and an elephant with silver *sāz.* His title of Rānā was restored and he was created a 5-*hazāri* (same tr.) and then permitted to return. His followers received 100 robes, ten jewelled daggers and forty horses [209]. When the Rānā went to the house of Dilir Khan, the Khan on his part sent men to welcome him : nine *thāns* of cloth, one jewelled sword, a shield with jewelled *gul,* a spear carved in relief, nine horses and one elephant were presented to him; and three cloths, a jewelled dagger, a jewelled *arsi,* a jewelled armlet (*bāzuband*) and two horses to the son of the Rānā.

Multafat Khan after removal from the faujdāri of Ghāzipur Zamānia had become faujdār of the environs of Agra. He was wounded in attacking a village and died on Sunday, the 26th June/19th Jamad. S. On Friday, the 1st July, 1681/24th Jamad. S., Khān Zamān Khan, son of

'Āzam Khan and son-in-law of Āsaf Khan who had come with Shāh 'Alam from the Deccan and so long served under the Prince, became Subahdār of Burhānpur *vice* Irij Khan, and received a robe, a horse with gold trappings and an increment of 1,000 troopers, making him a 5-*hazāri* (2,000 tr.). On the 6th July/29th Jamad. S., Shāh 'Alam Bahādur who had hastened from Sojāt and Jitāran, interviewed the Emperor. Tarbiyat Khan was appointed faujdār of Jaunpur on the death of Iftikhār Khan who had been appointed to this post after his removal from the Subahdāri of Ajmir. Nizāmuddin Ahmad became faujdār of Sirhind *vice* Shukrullah Khan, Jānsipār Khan became qiladār of Bidar *vice* Mir Muhammad Khan deceased. Bahramand Khan [210] became dārogha of ghusalkhānah *vice* Lutfullah Khan, who became dārogha of *'arz-i-mukarrar vice* Shihābuddin Khan.

News came from Morādābād that Faizullah Khan, son of Zāhid Khan Kokah of Pādishāh Begam, had died. He had great intimacy with the Emperor, and the Begam Sahib. He lived like one of the free, and never bowed his head in supplication to any man. He was good, agreeable and charitable, indifferent to the affairs of this world. His only companions were all kinds of rare animals, beasts of prey, wild beasts, birds, grazing cattle, and serpents, that were procured for him from far-off countries and ports. In short, he had an odd nature. Eventually he got elephantiasis, and used to be carried about on an elephant. When he had to see His Majesty, he did not come to the darbār, but interviewed him while passing with his cortege. Afrāsiāb Khan became faujdār of Morādābād *vice* him.

On Sunday, the 10th July/4th Rajab, Prince Muhammad 'Āzam and Sultān Bidār Bakht returned from the war with the Rāṇā, and had audience in private.

On Tuesday, the 19th July/13th Rajab, Siddi Yahya brought to the harem Shahar Bānu, the daughter of 'Ādilshāh Bijāpuri. She was married to Muhammad 'Āzam on the 26th July/20th Rajab, The Emperor tied the *sahara*, Qāzi Shaikh-ul-Islām celebrated the marriage, in the mosque of *khās and 'ām* (Jām'a mosque). In accordance with the example of the Prophet (at his marriage with Khadija) the marriage portion was 500 *dirham*.

On Saturday, the 30th July/24th Muharram, [211] Muhammad Kām Bakhsh was married to Jamiat-unnisā *alias* Kalyān Kumāri, daughter of Amarchand, sister of

Jagat Singh, zamindār of Manoharpur. The Qāzi tied the knot in the mosque of *khās and 'ām.* The dowry was 50,000 rupees. Sher Muhammad Kohāti got the title of Sher Khan.

On Saturday, the 6th August/1st Shaban, a letter was received from Khan Jāhān Bahādur, to say that Akbar was living in the fort of Pāli, near fort Maspuli;* 200 cavalry and 800 infantry were with him; and Sambhā had assigned a pension to them.

ARMY SENT UNDER MUHAMMAD 'ĀZAM TO EXTIRPATE SAMBHĀ AND THE KINGS OF BIJĀPUR AND HAIDARABAD—THE CHASE OF MUHAMMAD ĀKBAR FROM AJMIR TO THE DECCAN—THE GRANTING OF THE TITLE OF SHĀH TO PRINCE 'ĀZAM.

On Sunday, the 31st July, 1681/25th Rajab, Prince Muhammad 'Āzam got the title of Shāh, and was appointed to the Deccan expedition. Khidmatgār Khan conveyed to his house a robe with a *bālāband* and a *sarpech*. The Prince made his salutation in the khawābgāh, and was there presented with a half-sleeve woven with pearls worth two lakhs fifty thousand and four hundred rupees, and with a sword, two Arab and 'Irāqi horses, a Gaj-mānik elephant and five hunting-leopards in the Audience Hall. Sultan Bidār Bakht, at the same time as his father, [212] received a robe of farewell, a horse, and a jewelled *latkan*. The Prince's followers were rewarded.

On Thursday, the 18th August/13th Shaban, order was issued to 'Umdat-ul-mulk Āsad Khan to conduct, under the escort of his own men, Hakim Muhasan Khan to Delhi and bring to the Emperor a receipt stamped with the seal of Fulād Khan. Raja Bhim Singh, brother of Rānā Jai Singh, came to Court in hope of service. Muhammad N'aim who had conveyed a robe of condolence for the death of Rānā Rāj Singh to his son Rānā Jāi Singh, returned and had audience. He had received (from the Rānā) 4,000 rupees in cash, two horses, 19 *thāns* of cloth, and four camels. He was permitted to retain them instead of surrendering them to the State.

---

* In *Ind. Atlas,* 25 S.E., there is a Pāli, 26 miles N.N.W. of Raygad, 6 miles E. of Nagothna. This was the place (as the Eng. F.R. say), about a day's journey from Nagothna (Orme. 268) at the foot of Paligarh. (269). *Maspuli* of the text is a copyist's error for *Bicholim* (in Portuguese territory), to which place Akbar removed, but later.

CHAPTER XXV

25TH YEAR OF THE REIGN. 1092 A. H.

4th September, 1681—23rd August, 1682.

* * * *

The Emperor's march from Ajmir to Burhanpur

On Monday, the 5th September/2nd Ramzan, the Emperor issued orders for his camp to be moved from Ajmir towards Burhānpur. On Thursday, the 8th/5th Ramzan, he started from that city and halted at the stage of Deorāi. On Friday, the 9th September/6th Ramzan, Shāhzāda Muhammad 'Azim was sent back to Ajmir, after being presented with a special robe, a pearl *smarani,* a jewelled dagger, a sword, a horse, and an elephant [213]. 'Umdat-ul-mulk Āsad Khan was appointed to accompany him, and received a special robe, a jewelled dagger, and a horse. 'Itiqād Khan, son of Āsad Khan, Kamāluddin Khan, son of Dilir Khan, Raja Bhim and his son, Dindār Khan, son of Nāmdār Khan (who became Marhamat Khan) and others, after being given robes, jewels, horses and elephants were appointed to this army. 'Ināyet Khan, faujdār of Ajmir, and Sayyid Yusuf Bukhāri, qila'dār of Garh Bithli, were sent back. On Saturday, the 10th September/7th Ramzan, news came from Delhi that Jahānārā Bānu Begam had died on Tuesday, the 6th September, 1681/3rd Ramzan. She was buried in the compound of the sepulchre of Shaikh Nizām-ud-din Āulia, where she had constructed her own tomb in her lifetime. The Emperor was very sorry to hear of the death of his loving eldest sister and forbade the beating of *naubat* for three days. This lady, now wrapped up in divine forgiveness, was endowed with the gracious quality of charity and the noble trait of benevolence. She always took care to be polite in her manners to her equals and bestowed her gifts and compassion on the general public. (With her death) the shade of bounty was withdrawn from the head of the world, and the store of liberality disappeared from the hand of the age. The Emperor ordered her title to be written as *Sāhibat-uz-zamāni.* * * * *

[214] He bestowed favours on her servants and dependants. Uzbak Khan Nazar Bey, who had been dismissed from rank and permitted to go to Mecca, died on Wednesday, the 21st September/18th Ramzan. On Monday, the 10th October/7th Shawwal, Mukhtār Khan had audience and the next day received an '*asa* with a jasper handle. On Saturday, the 22nd October/19th Shawwal, news came that Fulād Khan, faujdār of Delhi, had died. Shukrullah Khan succeeded him. On Thursday, the 27th October/24th Shawwal, Qalich Khan was sent on the Deccan expedition, and presented with a special robe, a horse, and kettledrums. Shihābuddin Khan was ordered to guard the rear of the imperial army till the arrival of the camp-followers. News came that Muhammad 'Āzam had left Burhānpur for Aurangābād on the 29th October/26th Shawwal, and reached the latter place, on Friday, the 11th November/10th Zil. Q.

On Sunday, the 13th November/12th Zil. Q., the Emperor reached Burhānpur. News came that on the 14th November, 'Itiqād Khan and other imperialists had attacked the Rāthors who had assembled in a body of nearly 3,000 troopers in Mertā; a severe battle was fought. Five hundred of the enemy [215] fell in the battle including Sonang, his brother 'Ajab Singh, Shyāmaldās, Bihāridās, Gokuldās and other chiefs, killed or wounded. The rest fled away. Many of the imperialists were slain. Sardār Tarin, Sher Afkan and others were wounded. 'Itiqād Khan received an increment of 500, and his followers too were rewarded. On Tuesday, the 22nd November/21st Zil. Q., Abdunnabi Beg Rozbhāni, got the title of Khan and the dāroghaship of the Deccan artillery. At midnight on the 23rd November, two chambers of gunpowder near the citadel of Burhānpur fort caught fire; many men were killed. That very night robbers attacked the camp (*dāira*) of Lutfullah Khan Kokah, near Lālbāgh, at Dacca; six men were slain, twenty wounded and the property was looted.

The news-writer of Junnar wrote that a son was born to a zamindār, having two branches or horns of the length of a finger on his head. The child died after two days. A woman delivered a daughter with a black head and face and a red and white nose; the child lived.

Hasan 'Ali Khan, coming from Islamābād (Mathura) interviewed, and, after being given a robe, a horse and an elephant, was sent on the Deccan war. Raziuddin Khan, who was by command superintending the imperial household and the force attached to it, was sent away. On Monday, the 21st November/20th Zil. Q., the Emperor [216] visited the tomb of Shaikh 'Abdul Latif. After reading the *fātiha,* he prayed to the saint's soul for help in crushing the enemy of the true faith. On the 22nd November/21st Zil. Q., Rahman Quli, envoy of Bukhārā, reached the Court. He presented two horses, ten pairs of *dāna-i-kesh,* and one camel. He was rewarded with a robe and 5,000 rupees and sent back. Ghaznafar Khan was sent to convey treasure to the army of Muhammad 'Āzam Shah. Shihābuddin Khan became Mir Bakhshi of āhadis. Salābat Khan was restored to his rank and made dārogha of artillery *vice* Bahramand Khan.

On Wednesday, the 30th November/29th Zil. Q., the zamindār of Chānda visited the Emperor and presented four elephants and nine horses. On Sunday, the 1st January, 1682/2nd Muharram he was sent home with a special robe, a horse with gold *sāz,* an elephant, and an emerald *sarpech.* A letter was received from Khan Jahān Bahādur stating that he had plundered Siwāpur. Muhammad Shāh, son of Muhammad Ali Khan Dārā Shukohi, was sent as envoy to Golkonda. Ruhullah Khan was sent to attack Bijāpur. Shihābuddin Khan and the servants of the retinue, and Fath M'amur, son of Dilir Khan, were ordered to accompany him. Lutfullah Khan became news-reader *vice* Kāmgār Khan.

On Sunday, the 5th February 1682/7th Safar 'Abdur Rahim Khan, the third bakhshi died and was buried in his father Islām Khan's tomb at Aurangābād. Kāmgār Khan succeeded him [217]. News came that the Rāthors had attacked the parganah of Mandal-Pur and carried off much property.

THE EMPEROR'S MARCH FROM BURHANPUR TO AURANGABAD

He started from Burhanpur on the 28th February, 1682/1st Rabi. A. On the 1st March, Muhammad Mu'izzuddin was sent away from Bahādurpur to stay at Burhanpur, after being presented with a robe, a sarpech, a sword, and an elephant. Khan Zamān, the *nāzim* was appointed to accompany him and received a special robe

Hāmid Khan was ill, interviewed the Emperor, and was kindly ordered to stay in Burhānpur till his perfect recovery; and the Emperor untying the *bālāband* from his own waist presented it to him. Shaikh Jahān, daughter's son of old Shaikh Ibrāhim, qiladār and faujdār, was sent back to Āsir.

On the 19th March, 1682/20th Muharram, Muhammad 'Āzam Shah, having come from Aurangābād to Kumāri, interviewed the Emperor. On Wednesday, the 22nd March/23rd Muharram, the Emperor reached the palace of Aurangābād. Yalangtosh Khan Bahādur became qurbegi *vice* Ābu Nasar Khan. The Emperor visited the *āb-pāsh-darah* (the watershed of the valley) and the garden of Farmān Bāri. The gardeners were all rewarded. Kumār Kishan Singh, son of Raja Rām Singh died on Monday, the 10th April/12th Rabi. S., of wounds received in a brawl. On the 13th April, his son Bishan Singh got his father's place with the *mansab* of a *hazāri* (400 tr.). On Sunday, the 16th April/18th Rabi. S., 'Ināyetullah, son of S'adullah Khan, got the title of Ikhlās Khan. Jāmshid Khan, son of [218] Dāud Khan who was lying ill in Burhanpur, died.

On Thursday, the 6th April/8th Rabi. A., Chimnāji, zamindār of Kharg-garh and servant of Sambhā, came to the Emperor and received a robe. Makarand Singh, son of Pratab Singh, zamindār of Kālibhit, was imprisoned by Khan Jahān Bahādur for non-payment of money dues. By order he was sent to Court. He was only seven years old. On Thursday, the 11th May/14th Jamad. A., he was released from prison and permitted to return home. On Saturday, the 13th May/16th Jamad. A., Yādgār 'Ali, the agent of Sikandar 'Ādil Khan, king of Bijapur, was given a robe and 2,000 rupees, and Shaikh Hasan, the agent of Siddi Mas'aud Bijapuri, a robe and 1,000 rupees and dismissed. The elephant and ring sent as *peshkash* by Sikandar were not accepted but returned with the agent. Muhammad M'asum, agent of Qutbulmulk, king of Golkonda, interviewed and received a robe. He presented as *peshkash* two lakhs and 44,000 rupees.

On Saturday, the 20th May/23rd Jamad. A., Sharif Khan went out to forage when the enemy appeared, and a severe fight was fought, many of the infidels being slain. Zāhid Khan Churāghāsi, and Saifullah and Āhasānullah, grandsons of S'aid Khan, were slain. Qamruddin Khan, qarāwwal begi, killed a nilgāu with three shots of his musket and presented it to the Emperor, its length was 3 *gaz* and 6½ *girah*, its height 2 *gaz* and 3 *girah*, and its tail 1 *gaz* and 3½ *girah*.

On Tuesday, the 23rd May/26th Jamad. A., Ruhullah Khan was sent to chastise the rebels near Ahmadnagar, and received a sword [219] damascened with gold. Hayāt Khan was appointed sazāwal for the assault on fort Rāmsij. On Wednesday, the 14th June/18th Jamad. S., Muhammad 'Āzam Shah was given leave to march towards Bijapur. A robe, two horses, an elephant, a *muttaka*, a *kalgi*, a *punchi* and an *arsi* were presented to him. Bidār Bakht was given a robe, a horse and an elephant, and sent with his father. Muhammad Panāh, adopted son of the Shah ('Āzam) got an emerald *parkhānah*. Shamsuddin Khan and other subordinates of the Prince were rewarded. Sharif Khan became Sadr of Hindustan *vice* Qalich Khan. Yaswant Rao Deccani was made a 4-*hazāri* (same tr.) and given a jewelled *arsi*. 'Abdullah, 'Abdul Hādi, and 'Abdul Bāqi, sons of Iftikhār Khan came to Court after their father's death and received mourning robes.

On Monday, the 26th June/1st Rajab, news reached the Emperor that on the 16th Hāfiz Muhammad Āmin Khan, Subahdār of Ahmadābād, had died. He was endowed with uprightness, greatness, goodness of speech, and devotion to the Emperor. He had a wonderful memory. During his Subahdāri of Ahmadābād he succeeded in memorising the Qurān, in a very short time. Mukhtār Khan replaced him as Subahdār [220] of Ahmadābād, Khān Zamān becoming that of Mālwa in his place. Mughal Khan was ordered to stay in Burhānpur in the place of Khān Zamān. Muftakhar Khan, son of Fakhar Khan became qarāwwal begi *vice* Qamruddin Khan, son of Mukhtār Khan, while the latter accompanied his father. Ātish Khan became Mir Tuzuk *vice* Silāh Khan. Kānhoji Deccani interviewed the Emperor and was made a 5-*hazāri* (same tr.). On Friday, the 18th August, 1682/24th Shaban, Khan Jahān Bahādur Zafar Jang Kokaltāsh came from Gulshanābād [Nāsik] and had audience. He received a special robe, a jewelled dagger, and fourteen trays of food from the royal table. Sayyid Munawwar Khan was sent to Burhānpur *vice* Mughal Khan. Mir 'Abdul Karim, son of Āmir Khan, *sarbāri* of khawāses, a favourite of the Emperor, became dārogha of the *ja-namāzkhānah vice* 'Abdul Qādir, son of Hāfiz Ibrāhim. Ikhlās-kesh, news-writer, one of the disciples of Mullā 'Abdullah Siālkoti, was given this special name on Sunday, when he was converted to Islām and made *mushrif* of the purchase department [221].

CHAPTER XXVI

26TH YEAR OF THE REIGN : 1093 A. H.

24th August, 1682—13th August, 1683

* * * *

On Friday, the 25th August/2nd Ramzan, Hamiduddin Khan, son of Mirzā Ābu S'aid, brother's son of Nur Jahān Begam, was sent as faujdār of Mungi-Pattan, *vice* Karamullah Khan deceased. The sons of the deceased received robes. On Monday, the 28th August/5th Ramzan, gracious robes for Yāqut Khan and Khairiyat Khan, faujdār of the country of Dandā Rājpuri, were entrusted to Bahramand Khan. On the 30th, Khan Jahān Bahādur Kokaltāsh was sent to Gulshanābād with a special robe, a *kamarband*, a horse, and an elephant. Jagdeo Rai, brother of Jādav Rāi Deccani, had audience and received a robe. On Saturday, the 2nd September/10th Ramzan, Muhammad Taqi, son of Dārāb Khan, was married to Bahramand Khan's daughter, and received a robe, a horse, and a pearl *sahra*. Sālih Khan, son of 'Āzam Khan deceased, became mir bakhshi of the *āhadis vice* Shihābuddin Khan. Sayyid Yusuf, one of the sons of Mir Sayyid Muhammad Gisudarāz [222], was given leave to go to Gulbarga, and presented with a female elephant. All the servants at the Court and the provinces received robes for the rains. On Monday, the 18th September/26th Ramzan, Muhammad Mu'izzuddin came from Burhānpur and had audience, receiving a robe. Ranmast Khan, brother of Khizir Khan Pani, Dāud Khan and his brother Sulaimān Khan interviewed and received robes. Sayyid Mubārak Khan, qiladār of Daulatābād, came to Court and later went back. Lutfullah Khan became darogha of the imperial retinue and *khās chauki*. On the 28th September/6th Shawwal, Prince Muhammad Mu'izzuddin was sent to punish the rebels near Ahmadnagar, after being given a robe, a pearl necklace, an emerald *muttaka*, a powerful horse, and an increment of a *hazār* troopers, making him a 8-*hazāri* (6,000 tr.). Ranmast Khan, Dāud Khan, Ghaznafar Khan and other subordinate officers and servants (of the Prince) were sent away with rewards.

Sharif Khan, Sadr died on Wednesday, the 4th October/12th Shawwal. His sons, Muhammad 'Ādil and Muhammad Sālih, received robes of mourning. Shaikh Makhdum munshi became chief Sadr, and Muhammad Sālih Kambuh *peshdast* of the Sadr *vice* Mir Husain. Sardār Tarin became faujdar of Shiwgāon. 'Azizullah Khan brother of Ruhullah Khan became Mir Tuzuk *vice* Muhammad Yār Khan. Ikhlās-kesh became mushrif of Jā-namāz-khānah. [223] Hedāyetullah, son-in-law of Khalifā Sultān, was sent as diwān of Delhi. Shukrullah Khan became faujdār of Sikandarābād and Kāmil Khan that of Sahāranpur. Muhammad Masih, son of Himmat Khan, became Mir Tuzuk *vice* Silāh Khan. On the 23rd October/2nd Zil. Q., the Emperor learnt that 'Ināyet Khan faujdār of Ajmir had died. On Thursday, the 2nd November/12th Zil. Q., Hamidā Bānu Begam, mother of Ruhullah Khan died. The Emperor graciously sent Muhammad Kām Bakhsh and Āshraf Khan, Mir Bakhshi, to Ruhullah's house to condole with him and bring him to Court. Robes were given to him and to his brothers. Zinatunnisā Begam visited his house by command.

On Tuesday, the 5th December/15th Zil. H., Kāmyāb Khan was appointed bakhshi of the Deccan and sent to the army of Khan Jahān Bahādur. Sayyid Muhammad, sister's son of Hāfiz Muhammad Āmin Khan deceased, came from Ahmadābād and had audience, receiving a robe, Subhān-wardi, son of Yalangtosh Khan Bahādur, from Delhi, had interview, and received a robe. On Tuesday, the 26th December/6th Muharram, Shihābuddin Khan was appointed in his absence dārogha of the macebearers *vice* Mukarram Khan. Sayyid Ughlān acted as his deputy. Muhammad 'Ali Khan, Khān-i-sāmān, owing to great weakness fell down from the kathra; the Emperor gave him a phial of rose-water, *bid-i-mishk* and a few pomegranates. The building of a fortified city-wall for Aurangabad had been entrusted to [224] Ihtamām Khan. 'Abdul Qādir, son of Āmānat Khan guaranteed that he would complete it in four months. On Saturday, the 20th January, 1683/1st Safar, Khan Jahān Bahādur came within three *kos* of Aurangābād for interview. A robe was sent with his son Nasrat Khan to convey to him the order that he should not come to have interview, but must proceed towards Bidar, and stay there

* On p. 518 Khizir Kh. Pani is mentioned as Batani.

so that he might go in pursuit in whatever direction he might hear of Akbar coming. On Tuesday, the 6th February/18th Safar, Khan Jahān Bahādur reported to the Emperor that the rebel Akbar, having come out of the territory of Sambhā, had fled away in a ship.

The Emperor ordered that mansabdārs below two *hazāris* must not wait to have the *fātiha* read when taking leave of the Emperor, the exception to it being those officers in whose case the Emperor would himself raise his hand to bless them by means of the *fātiha;* and that dismissed Qāzis should not be reappointed Qāzis.

On Thursday, the 22nd February/5th Rabi. A., Silāh Khan was entrusted with one hundred Arab, 'Iraqi, Turki and Kachhi horses, a hundred camels, twenty mules, a tall elephant, jewels worth 80,000 rupees, a robe worth 2,000 rupees and other dresses worth 14,000 rupees, for Muhammad 'Āzam Shah, robes for Bidār Bakht and Gaiti Ārā Begam, and robes for all their officers according to their ranks; and he was ordered to summon each of the commanders separately for *istiqbāl,* give him his robe; and after making bows for the Emperor they were to go to the Prince.

On Wednesday, the 28th February/11th Rabi. A., by command, Kām Bakhsh held audience in the old ghusalkhānah [225] and conferred favours on the officers of the Emperor and his own. Bahramand Khan was ordered to be present whenever the Prince held Court, and to remain standing. On Sunday, the 4th March, 1683/15th Rabi. A., Kām Bakhsh was married to Āzarm Bānu, daughter of Siādat Khan Safavi. Khidmatgār Khan conveyed to the Prince's house a special robe with half-sleeves woven with pearls, and Khidmat Khan jewels worth two lakhs and 26,000 rupees. Five lakhs of rupees in cash, two Arab and 'Irāqi horses, and an elephant were presented to the Emperor (as *salāmi*). The knot was tied in the mosque in the presence of the Qāzi Shaikh-ul-Islām. After one *prahar* of night was over, the Emperor himself placed a pearl *sahra* on the Prince's head; and, by order, all the grandees formed a lane on foot from the *deorhi* of the ghusalkhānah to the *deorhi* of the mahal of Zinatunnisā and conducted the bridegroom. A grand and joyous festivity marked the occasion.

On Sunday, the 11th March/22nd Rabi. A., Husain Miāna, one of the grandees of Bijapur, interviewed the Emperor, and was welcomed at the gate of the ghusalkhānah by Ātish Khan. At the time of interview Āshraf Khan from the platform (*chabutra*) said 'welcome'. He was granted the rank of 5-*hazāri* (same tr.), a banner, kettledrums, the title [226] of Fath Jang Khan, and 40,000 rupees as *in'ām*. His brothers and relatives got proper robes and ranks.

Mān Singh, son of Rup Singh, faujdār of Māndal-Pur, was given the faujdāri of Badhnaur in addition, *vice* Dalpat. Udwat Singh, son of Mahā Singh Bhadauriya, got the title of Raja on his father's death. Saif Khan, the dismissed Subahdār of Bihār, reached Court on the 8th March, 1683/19th Rabi. A. As he had taken out of the treasury of the province 56,000 rupees without the authorisation of the Emperor, he was refused audience. By order Mughal Khan kept him confined in the guard-room of Bahramand Khan, till the 3rd April/15th Rabi. S., when the money was made good. Mukarram Khan, after deprivation of the fortune of audience, was honoured with an interview on Saturday, the 31st March 12th Rabi. S.; Khusrau Beg the slave brought the property of Hāfiz Muhammad Āmin Khan deceased from Ahmadābād to the Court: seventy lakhs of rupees and one lakh and thirty-five thousand āshrafi and Ibrāhimi coins, seventy-six elephants, 432 horses, 117 camels, 114 mules, ten chests of Chinaware of all kinds, sixty carts (rahkala), one maund of shot, 54 maunds of gunpowder.

On Saturday, the 21st April/4th Jamad. A., the Emperor learnt that Durjan Singh Hādā had taken Bundi by siege. On the 25th Muhammad Sharif ambassador of the king of Bukhārā, had audience and received a robe. Bakhshi-ul-mulk [227] Ruhullah Khan reached the Court from the Konkan expedition and received a robe, a jewelled dagger, and an Arab horse. 'Azizullah Khan his brother, Nawāzish Khan Rumi, and Ākrām Khan Deccani, each received a robe and an elephant. Sayyid 'Abdullah of Bārha *alias* Sayyid Miān, one of Ruhullah's subordinates and a servant of Shāh 'Alam, a hazāri (600 tr.) received a *mansab* in the imperial service (*zābita*). Sayyid Nur Muhammad of Bārha got the title of Sayyid Khan and Sayyid Muzaffar, one of the grandees of Haidarābād whom Ābul Hasan Qutbulmulk had imprisoned through the prompting of his all-powerful minister Mādanna Brahman, and who had been released from prison by the imperial ambassador at the instance of the Emperor, arrived at the Court. On the day of interview he received a special robe and a jewelled dagger. His two sons got high mansabs and the titles of Āsālat Khan and Najābat Khan. On the 9th May/22nd Jamad, A., Hari Singh, brother of Chhatra Singh, zamindār of Garha, had audience, and received a robe; Sayyid Āhmad, brother of the ruler of Barbary (*maghrib-zamin*), came to the Emperor and was highly favoured, receiving a robe, a jewelled dagger, and 5,000 rupees. Mughal Khan was appointed to extirpate Durjan Singh. Anirudh Singh, grandson of Bhāo Singh Hādā, was sent to Bundi, after receiving a robe, a horse, an elephant and kettledrums. [228] Udwat Singh, son of Mahā Singh Bhadauriya, Sayyid Muhammad 'Ali, sister's son of Hāfiz Muhammad Āmin Khan deceased, Khwāja Bahā-uddin, son-in-law of Sulaimān Shukoh, and others, after being rewarded with robes, horses and elephants, were appointed to accompany the aforesaid Khan. On Monday, the 21st May/4th Jamad. S., Āyyub Beg, ambassador of Kāshghar, was dismissed after being presented with a robe, a dagger and 2,000 rupees.

Khwāja 'Abdur Rahim was appointed envoy to Bijapur and received a robe, a horse, and 1,000 rupees. Sayyid 'Abdullah was restored to his title of 'Izzat Khan and appointed diwān of the army of Muhammad 'Āzam Shah. Dilir Khan, Fath Jang Khan and others, who had been appointed to the Bijapur expedition, were ordered to stay at Court till the arrival of Muhammad 'Āzam Shah. Kishordās, son of Manohardās Gaur, became qiladār of Sholāpur. Shihābuddin Khan having come from the side of Junnar, interviewed.

On Friday, the 29rd June/14th Rajab, Princes Muhammad Mu'izzuddin from Zafarābād [Bidar] and Muhammad 'Azim from Burhānpur, arrived and had audience. Prince Muhammad Raf'i-ul-qadr showed a piece of *nastāliq* writing of his own, and received a *sarpech* of ruby. On Sunday, the 15th July/30th Rajab, when the 41st year of Shāh 'Alam Bahādur's life began, he was presented with a jewelled turban-end worth one lakh and 5,180 rupees. The Emperor learnt that the great scholar Mullā 'Abdullah, son of Mulla 'Abdul Hakim Siālkoti had died. The Emperor [229] favoured his four sons and widow with robes and increase of stipend. This prince of scholars, with all his learning was strongly inclined towards piety (*faqr*), and had secular learning united with spiritual knowledge. The Emperor, who recognised wisdom and sanctity, knew the true value of such men, and while he was staying at Ajmir, wrote him a letter with his own hand, offering the sadrship to him. And that intimate courtier, Bakhtāwar Khan, who on account of his friendship with scholars and hermits was the intermediary of their applications to the Emperor, was ordered to write to the Mullā on his own behalf giving him a hint of this matter. After the *farmān* and the letter had been received, the Mullā wrote in reply to the Khan "(The present) is the time of separation, (from the world) and not a time for acquiring fame in this world. In obedience to the Emperor's command, I am going to the Court and shall secure the blessing of visiting the tomb of Khwāja Mu'inuddin and interviewing the Emperor". The Emperor liked these words from this chief of wise men. As he had written, he came to Ajmir and stayed at Court for some days, constantly enjoying the Emperor's company. After performing the pilgrimage to the saint's tomb he returned home with the Emperor's consent, and died there (shortly) afterwards.

[230] The Emperor learnt that Prince Muhammad 'Āzam Shah, who had been summoned to the Presence from the bank of the Nirā, had arrived by forced marches, inspite of the excess of rains and abundance of mud, and that on account of the lack of porters he had brought only a small tent. The Emperor ordered one of his own tents to be pitched (for the Prince) near the mosque of the 'Idgāh. In the evening the Emperor learnt that on the way while the Prince was coming on horseback, the elephant of Fath Jang Khan turned mad, charged the troops, and approached the Shah. He shot an arrow at it; it came nearer. His horse shied; dismounting he faced the elephant and hit its trunk with his sword. By this time his retinue, who had been scattered, gathered together and slew the elephant with blows. Prince Muhammad Kām Bakhsh and Ruhullah Khan went (by order) immediately and presented (to the Prince) 4,000 rupees from the Emperor, 500 mohars from Kām Bakhsh and 100 mohars and 1,000 rupees on behalf of Ruhullah. The Prince Kām Bakhsh departed after one quarter of the day and four hours. Next day, when the interview with the Emperor was to take place, the Prince with all the grandees down to *hazāris,* advanced to meet 'Āzam. Every one made presents according to his rank. By command, the Shāh reached the citadel, playing joyous music from his own camp. Prince Bidār Bakht had also the honour of being received in audience. [231] As the Shah's mansion (*haveli*) was out of repair, he was permitted

to live in the apartments close to the old hall of audience till its repair. Muhammad Sālim Āslam, a servant of the Emperor wrote a long *masnavi* on this incident. [*omitted*] * * *

[234] Rashid Khan reported to the Emperor that His Majesty had ordered fifty-two lakhs of rupees spent in Gauhati to be recovered from the Āmir-ul-umarā; but the latter had written that in all seven lakhs of rupees only were spent; the balance of the amount was the price of the materials previously sanctioned as subsidy in aid of the Bengal administration. The Emperor ordered only that amount to be recovered from him. On Thursday, the 26th July, 1683, a *parastār* (servant-girl) bore a son to the Shāh ['Āzam], who presented 1,000 mohars to His Majesty; the child was named Wālā-jāh. Hāji Shaf'i Khan was sent to superintend and ascertain the revenue of the new territories conquered for the Emperor by Khan Jahān.

Qāzi Haidar, Shivāji's munshi, came to the Emperor for service; he was given a robe, ten thousand rupees, and the rank of 2-*hazāri*. Hakim Muhasan Khan by command came to the Court with the treasure convoy of Delhi, and was released from the imprisonment of punishment. Mirzā Sadruddin got the title of Khan and the faujdāri of Rāmgir. On the 27th July/12th Shaban, the Emperor was shown a jewelled necklace (hār), a pearl *arsi,* and two elephants, which Qutb-ul-mulk had sent to Khan Jahān and the latter to the Court. On the 5th August/21st Shaban [235] the Emperor visited the guard-room of Muhammad 'Āzam Shāh situated within the fort of Aurangābād. The Prince received as present a ring worth 275 rupees, Jahānzeb Bānu Begam a pearl necklace and ruby pendent worth 14,000 rupees, Gaiti-Ārā Begam, daughter of the Shāh, a pearl necklace worth 19,000 rupees, Bijāpuri Mahal a jewelled wristlet (*karah*) worth 2,200 rupees. The Shāh presented as *peshkash* two lakhs, 98,400 rupees, which the Emperor graciously accepted. Ranmast Khan got the title of Bahādur Khan. On Monday, the 13th August/29th Shaban, a letter was received from Mughal Khan stating that he had assaulted Bundi with lightning speed; arrows and bullets had been showered for three *prahars;* at last Durjan Singh had fled away under cover of the darkness of the night. Thereupon Anirudh Singh had entered Bundi with his own troops and other officers of the Emperor.

CHAPTER XXVII

27TH YEAR OF THE REIGN : 1094 A. H.

14th August, 1683—1st August, 1684

* * * *

[236] The Emperor spent the month of Ramzan in the mosque of the palace, in doing deeds of charity.

On Monday, the 20th August/7th Ramzan, Muhammad 'Āzam Shāh was sent on the Bijapur expedition, after being presented with a robe, a *sarpech,* a jewelled dagger, an elephant, 100 horses, and two lakhs of rupees. Bidār Bakht was presented with a robe, a *sarpech,* a *kalgi,* a dagger, and an elephant and sent with his father. Sayyid Sher Khan, Ikhlās Khan, Kamāluddin Khan and others appointed to the army of the Prince were variously favoured. On Friday, the 17th August, 1683/4th Ramzan, a letter was received from Ibrāhim Khan, Subahdār of Kashmir, stating that through the exertions of his son Fidāi Khan, the land of Tibet was conquered from its zamindār Dalāi and added to the Empire. The Emperor ordered his courtiers to make their bows for the conquest and the music of joy to be played. The Khan was rewarded for the victory with an increment of 2-*hazāri* tr., making him a 5-*hazāri* (same tr. 2,000 *do-āspa*) one *kror* of *dām* as *in'ām,* the despatch of a farmān full of praise and the presentation of a special robe, a jewelled *phul katāra* dagger with pearl *'ilāqa* worth 7,000 rupees, an Arab horse worth 200 mohars with gold *sāz* and an elephant from the Emperor's own stable worth 15,000 rupees. His duteous son [237] from a 7-*sadi* (400 tr.) became a *hazāri* (700 tr.) and was presented with a special robe, a sword wrought with gold, with enamelled *sāz,* an *'Irāqi* horse with gold *sāz,* worth 100 mohars, and an elephant worth 11,000 rupees.

Ātish Khan went by command to the army of Muhammad 'Āzam Shah and brought to Court Muhammad Hādi, son of Mir Khan. He was at first kept in the custody of Ruhullah Khan and then in that of Salābat Khan. On Friday, the 7th September/25th Ramzan, he was ordered to be imprisoned in the fort of Daulatābād.

On the 15th September/3rd Shawwal, as commanded by His Majesty, the advance-tents of Shāh 'Ālam Bahādur came out of Aurangābād, playing sweet music, with the object of extirpating the enemy in the direction of Konkan and Rāmdarah and other lands of the Marāthas.

Dilir Khan Afghān died of severe illness. He had fought well in many battles. He was a powerfully built man and of great strength. He had a wonderful appetite, control over his clansmen, and good luck all through his life.

I shall now give some description of the tombs of the saints of the Faith and the village of Ellorā. Eight *kos* from Aurangābād and three *kos* from the fort of Daulatābād are the blessed tombs of Shaikh Burhānuddin, Shaikh Zain-ul-Haq, Shaikh Muntakhabuddin Zar-bakhsh, Mir Hasan [238] of Delhi, Sayyid Rāju, father of Mir Sayyid Muhammad Gisudarāz and other knowers of God, many of whom were followers of Nizāmuddin Āulia. These are places of pilgrimage to the world. These holy men came to this country and repose here, through the exertions of Muhammad Shāh Malik Junā, son of Tughlaq, who considered the fort of Deogiri the centre of his kingdom, named it Daulatābād, wished to make it his capital, and removed the people of Delhi with their families to this place.

A short distance from here is a place named Ellorā where in ages long past, sappers possessed of magical skill excavated in the defiles of the mountain spacious houses for a length of one *kos*. On all their ceilings and walls many kinds of images with lifelike forms have been carved. The top of the hill looks level, so much so that no sign of the buildings within it is apparent (from outside). In ancient times when the sinful infidels had dominion over this country, certainly they and not demons (*jinn*)* were the builders of these caves, although tradition differs on the point; it was a place of worship of the tribe of false believers. At present it is a desolation in spite of its strong foundations; it rouses the sense of warning (of doom) to those who contemplate the future (end of things). In all seasons, and particularly in the monsoons, when this hill and the plain below resemble a garden in the luxuriance of its vegetation and the abundance of its water, people come to see the place.

* I form the three words *Sābqān bafarāwān ā'wām* into one phrase of time. I also put a period after *jinn* in the text, and accept *'ibrat* of the MS. for *ghairat* of the printed text.

A waterfall a hundred yards in width tumbles down from the hill. It is a marvellous place for strolling, charming to the eye. Unless one sees it, no written description can correctly picture it. How then can my pen adorn the page of my narrative? [239].

THE EMPEROR'S MARCH FROM AURANGABAD TO AHMADNAGAR

On Friday, the 12th October, 1683/1st Zil. Q., the Emperor reached Karnpurā. The sound of artillery struck the ears of the enemy. Muhammad 'Āzam Shah and Bidār Bakht who had come to the Emperor were sent to Gulshanābād [Nāsik] on Tuesday, the 30th October/19th Zil. Q., with robes, *sarpech,* elephant, and a short sword (*nimchah*). Pam Nayak, zamindār of Sagar, interviewed and received a robe, a sword and a dagger. The zamindāri of Chānda was transferred from Rām Singh to Kishan Singh.

On Tuesday, the 13th November/3rd Zil. H., the Emperor arrived at the earthen fort of Āhmadnagar, built by Dilir Khan. Qāzi Shaikh-ul-Islām, son of Qāzi 'Abdul Wahhāb, was seized by a longing for God, on account of his merit and natural godliness. He decided to renounce the world, and though the Emperor pressed him not to resign the Qāziship for which such men are pre-eminently fit, he did not recoil from his purpose. The Emperor had to assent. At the recommendation of that favoured holy man, he gave the Qāziship of the imperial camp to Sayyid Ābu S'aid, son-in-law of Qāzi 'Abdul Wahhāb. He came from Delhi, had his interview, and received a robe, a sword, and a dagger.

On Tuesday, the 20th November/10th Zil. H., Muhammad Khalil [240], envoy of the king of Shahr-nau, interviewed, receiving a robe and 1,000 rupees. The agents of the zamindār of Srirangpatan arrived with *peshkash* and received 200 rupees. Sayyid Ughlān was appointed tutor of Kām Bakhsh. Muhammad Sālih, Qāzi of Aurangābād, became Qāzi of Delhi, and Muhammad Ākrām, mufti of the Emperor's camp, took his place as Qāzi of Aurangābād. Mir 'Abdul Karim, became *āmin* of the seven *chaukis* in addition to the dāroghaship of the *jā-namāz-khānah.* Sarbuland Khan (originally Khwāja Y'āqub) was sent to chastise the rebels near Bahādurgarh. Kāmgār Khan became *akhta begi vice* Mughal Khan; Shujā'et

Khan, son of Qawāmuddin Khan, Mir Ātish; and Matlab Khan bakhshi of the *āhadis*. At midnight, on Tuesday, the 18th December/9th Muharram, Ruhullah Khan was sent to punish the enemy near the river Nirā and Bahramand Khan towards Āshti. M'amur Khan, who had got the title of Dilir Khan, attacked the enemy and gained a victory, being rewarded with a robe, *a farmān,* a *tugh,* and a banner. On Monday, the 24th December, 1683/15th Muharram, Shihābuddin Khan, who had repeatedly defeated the enemy in severe fights was created Muhammad Ghāziuddin Khan Bahādur. [241] His brother, Muhammad 'Ārif, got the title of Mujāhid Khan, and Muhammad Sādiq Khosti that of Sādiq Khan, while robes, elephants, horses and promotions were granted to Dalpat Bundela, Raja Udwat Singh and other subordinates of the Khan according to their respective ranks. Mir Hāshim, servant of 'Āzam Shāh, brought to the Emperor the Prince's letter announcing the birth of a son, and 1,000 mohars as *nazar*. The child was named *Zi*-jāh, and presented with a cap woven with pearls, a jewelled *chashmak,* and a pearl string (*lari*). The Mir got a robe and 500 rupees.

News came that the enemy had spread near Pattan. At midnight Bahramand Khan received a quiver and bow and (set off to) carry out the order (to beat them away). On Sunday, the 27th January, 1684/19th Safar, a letter was received from Khan Jahān Bahādur, stating that the enemy had gathered together on the bank of the Krishnā; he had hastened from a distance of thirty *kos,* and after a severe fight slain countless infidels, and captured their property and women. A *farmān* was sent to him in praise of his deed. Of his sons Muzaffar Khan got the title of Himmat Khan, Nasrat Khan that of Sipahdār Khan, Muhammad Som'i* that of Nasrat Khan, Muhammad Baqā that of Muzaffar Khan, and Jamāluddin Khan son-in-law of [Bahadur Khan] and the son of 'Āzam Khan Kokah that of Safdar Khan. 'Umdat-ul-Mulk Āsad Khan [242], who had been (left) at Ajmir, came to Court. On Saturday, the 2nd February/25th Safar, Bakhshi-ul-mulk Āshraf Khan advanced to the door of the ghusalkhānah to welcome him. On the 4th Muhammad 'Āzam Shah and Bidār Bakht had audience, and left for Bahādurgarh on Wednesday the 13th February/7th Rabi. A., after receiving robes and jewels. Salābat Khan

* Another text reads Shaf'i.

having come from Naulakhah-Audh received a robe at interview. Muluk Chand, diwān of 'Āzam Shāh, after receiving a robe was ordered to take with himself sixty elephants which had been presented to the Prince. Sufi Bahādur came from Kāshghar in search of service, had interview, and received a robe, a dagger band with gold *sāz*, a sword, and 1,000 rupees.

On Tuesday, the 11th March, 1684/4th Rabi. S., Randaula Khan died. On Sunday the 16th/9th Rabi. S., Shukrullah Najam-i-Sāni got the title of 'Askar Khan, Sayyid Āhsan, son of Khān-i-daurān, that of Āhsan Khan, Muhammad Murād, son of Murshid Quli Khan, that of Muhammad Murād Khan. On Monday, the 31st March/24th Rabi. S., Ghāziuddin Khan Bahādur was sent towards Punā and Garh-namunā, and presented with a quiver and bow, 10,000 rupees and two *maunds* of gold. Qamruddin, son of the daughter's son of S'adullah Khan deceased, got his first mansab of 4-*sadi* (100 tr.). On Saturday, the 5th April/29th Rabi. S., Muhammad N'aim became diwān of Delhi. On Sunday, the 20th April/15th Jamad. A., Bakhshi-ul-mulk Ruhullah Khan was appointed with a strong force to reinforce Shah 'Ālam Bahādur. [243] With him were sent 20,000 āshrafi, 100 horses, 500 camels, twenty-five mules, for the Prince, and robes jewels, elephants, and horses for the Prince's sons and officers. On the same day Muhammad 'Āzam Shah, Bidār Bakht, and Wālājāh were presented with robes, jewels, horses and elephants, and sent away. Safi Khan was appointed to guard the subah of Aurangābād. Bahramand Khan coming from Gulshanābād, interviewed and received an elephant. Shujā'et Khan got the title of Saf Shikan Khan, a special robe, a *jigha*, a banner and a *tugh*, and was sent towards Srirangpatan. One hundred and twelve servants of the rebel Sambhā, who were imprisoned in the *chabutra* of the *kotwāli*, were executed. Muhammad Yār, son of Dilir Khan M'amuri, got the title of M'amur Khan and was sent to his father. On Sunday, the 11th May/6th Jamad. S., a daily pension of eighty rupees was assigned to Sultān Wālājāh.

On Saturday, the 17th/12th Jamad. S., news was brought by Khwāja Yākut of the birth of a son to Kām Bakhsh; the Khwāja got a robe, and the Prince a robe with a *bālāband*, and a jewelled turban-end. Hāji Ism'ail khāsnawis, who hit upon the phrase "the son of Kām Bakhsh" as giving the date of his birth, got a robe. The child was named Ummed Bakhsh. Shujā'et Haidarābādi came to Court in hope of service, and received the rank of 5-*hazāri* (same tr.) and the title Shujā'et Khan. 'Itiqād Khan was sent with a strong force towards Zafarābād Bidār. [244] Mirak Khan, faujdār of Jālandhar doāb, became that of Gujrāt. On Sunday, the 18th May, 1684/13th Jamad. S., Shah 'Ālam Bahādur from the Konkan had audience, and received a robe and jewels worth three lakhs and 90,000 rupees. His sons got robes and jewels. Ruhullah Khan and Munawwar Khan interviewed, receiving robes. Mughal Khan, who had gone to back Anirudh Singh [of Bundi] and root out Durjan Singh, came back victorious and had audience, receiving a robe and praise. Hāji Māhtāb Haidarābādi made his bow of service to the Emperor. On Thursday, the 26th June/23rd Rajab, Muhammad J'afar, envoy of Qutb-ul-mulk, had audience. He was the son of the preceptor of Hāfiz Muhammad Āmin Khan. When Md. Amin went from Agra to Kabul, he requested Bakhtā-war Khan to present him to the Emperor for service. After presentation he was given a mansab under Muhammad Akbar. His ability made him rise to the post of dārogha of filkhānah under that Prince. After Akbar's revolt he went to Haidarābād. There he bragged of being a high person connected with great āmirs and thus influenced Ābul Hasan and his ministers, and got the title of 'Ain-ul-mulk. When Qutb-ul-mulk had occasion to send an envoy to the Emperor, J'afar was appointed to the office on account of his false pretensions. He had no help but to come on the embassy. At the audience Bakhtāwar Khan said to the Emperor, "This man [245] is so and so." The Emperor said, "See the mischievousness of Abul Hasan! He has sent Akbar's officer as envoy to me." J'afar knew me and sent a message asking me to see him. After beholding his splendour, wealth and prodigality in the market as a buyer, I sent to him to ask "Why did you come here?" He said, "The desire of seeing (old) friends brought me here." I replied, "You have acted very ill." After two days the kotwāl all of a sudden went to his house, brought him to the *chabutra*, and confiscated his household furniture and slaves, with much cash. After a time he was given the rank of a 3-*sadi* and was sent to Bengal.

On Monday, the 30th June/27th Rajab, Zinat-un-nisā Begam came from Aurangābād to the Court. Muhammad Kām Bakhsh, Siādat Khan and Kāmgār Khan advanced to welcome her and conducted her to the imperial harem. On Thursday, the 24th July/21st Shaban, 500 mohars were presented to the Emperor by Muhammad 'Āzam Shah as *nazar* for the birth of a son to the mother of Wālājāh. The courtiers bowed. The child was named Wālāshān. On Friday, the 1st August/29th Shaban, the Emperor learnt that Mirzā Muhammad and Bihāri Dās, jeweller, who had gone to Qutbulmulk, had received—the former 10,000 rupees, an elephant, and an *arsi,* and the latter 8,000 rupees and an elephant—and they had returned leaving the presents with the ambassador. The Emperor ordered them to be returned (to Qutbulmulk). An acknowledgment-receipt bearing the seal of 'Abdur Rahman qiladār of Bahādurgarh, for two wives, one daughter, and three slave-girls of the wretched Sambhā, was placed before the Emperor. Khan Jahān Bahādur Zafar Jang Kokaltāsh, Dilir Khan, Ghāziuddin Khan Bahādur, and other high grandees [246] and warriors had up to this time captured from the enemy and added to the Empire so many forts and mahals attached to them that it would require a volume to give details about them. * * *

CHAPTER XXVIII

28TH YEAR OF THE REIGN: 1095 A. H.

2nd August, 1684—21st July, 1685

* * * *

The Emperor passed the whole month of Ramzān in religious performances in the retreat of the mosque. On Sunday, the 3rd August/2nd Ramzan Mughal Khan became Subahdār of Mālwa *vice* Khan Zamān deceased, and received a robe, an elephant named Zulfiqār, and promotion to the rank of 3½-*hazāri* (3,000 tr.). On the 6th/5th Ramzan Siādat Khan was given the title of Mu'azzam Khan, and appointed *Qush begi vice* him. Hāji Shaf'i Khan became commandant of Aurangābād *vice* Safi Khan, who was made nāzim of Agra *vice* Muhatasham Khan, who [247] was made subahdār of Allahabad *vice* Saif Khan deceased. Muhammad Taqi, son of Dārāb Khan, Matlab Khan and other relatives of Mukhtār Khan, Subahdār of Ahmadābād, who were mourning his death were graciously presented with robes. The family of Bani-Mukhtār is well-known to the world for many excellent qualities. Mukhtār Khan was pre-eminent among them and renowned for goodness of every kind.

In the afternoon, on Tuesday, the 19th August/18th Ramzān, Qāzi Ābu S'aid united Prince Mu'izzuddin to Sayyidunnisā Begam, daughter of Mirzā Rustam son of Mukarram Khan in the presence of the Emperor and Shāh 'Ālam Bahādur; 1,000 rupees and a robe were presented by His Majesty to the Qāzi. News came of the death of Kifāyet Khan J'afar who was without *mansab*, at Delhi on Saturday, the 23rd August/22nd Ramzan, and of Saif Khan, Subahdār of Allahabad, on the 26th August.

On Monday, the 1st September/1st Shawwal, occurred the 'Id-ul-fitr. * * * On Thursday, the 4th September/4th Shawwal, Salābat Khan became *mutasaddi* of the port of Surat *vice* Kārtalb Khan Muhammad Beg, who was appointed faujdār of Ahmadābād. Khānahzād Khan, son of Himmat Khan, was made dārogha of the servants of the retinue, *vice* the former. Sālih Khan son of 'Āzam Khan

Kokah became faujdār and diwān of Bareli. [248] His son Nuruddin received a robe and accompanied him. Kāmyāb became bakhshi of the archers *vice* him. Yalangtosh Khan Bahādur who was enjoying an annual pension, received a *mansab* on the 2nd September, 1684/2nd Shawwal. Bahrām, brother of J'afar Khan, father of Bahramand Khan, died at Delhi. To Umdat-ul-mulk Āsad Khan, sister's son of the deceased, was presented a half-sleeve of silk embroidery, which the Emperor took off from his own person. Āshraf Khan condoled with Bakhshi-ul-mulk Bahramand Khan and brought him to Court, where he received a mourning robe.

On Monday, the 8th September/8th Shawwal, the marriage entertainment of Mu'izzuddin took place. He was presented with a *bālādast khil'at,* precious jewels worth one lakh and 50,000 rupees, a horse with gold *sāz,* and an elephant with silver *sāz.* To Sayyidunnisā Begam were presented jewels worth 67,000 rupees. After the *maghrib* prayer, Shāh 'Alam Bahādur and other Princes with great pomp conducted the bridegroom through a lane bordered by lighted lamps from his own mansion to the imperial palace. The Emperor placed a pearl *sahra* on the bridegroom's head with his own hands. The celebration was supervised by Zinat-un-nisā Begam. After two *pās* the bride reached the bridegroom's house. On Sunday, the 21st September/21st Shawwal, Ghāziuddin Khan Bahādur when sent to conquer fort Rāhiri, [249] received a special robe and five horses. His son Qamruddin received a sword, and other officers robes. On Wednesday, the 8th October/9th Zil. Q., 100 Turki and hill horses were sent to Muhammad 'Āzam Shāh as aid. Fakhruddin was sent as thānahdār of Supā, Ābdul Hādi Khan as faujdār of Chākan and Marhamat Khan, son of Nāmdār Khan thānahdār of Garh-Namunā. On Saturday, the 25th October/26th Zil. Q., Bakhshi-ul-mulk Ruhullah Khan, after being presented with a robe, a dagger and a horse was sent to punish the enemy. Qāsim Khān, Muhammad Bad'i of Balkh, Ilhāmullah Khan, and 'Abdur Rahman, officers of Shāh 'Alam Bahādur received an increment of 1,000 troopers; Hayāt Ābdāli, who had come to Court from Qandahār, and other officers of the force were favoured with promotion, robes, horses, elephants, swords and *jighas*. Padamji, Ekkoji, Malhār and Rao Subhānchand, sent by Ghāziuddin Khān Bahādur, each received robes. Shāhzāda Daulat-Āfzā was presented with a ruby *sarpech* with a pearl pendant. Kifāyet Khan Hātim Beg was appointed diwān of the subahs of the Deccan. 'Ināyetullah, mushrif of the jewellery department and *khil'atkhānah,* became news-writer and mustaufi of *āima.* Sultan Ummed Bakhsh, son of Kām Bakhsh, died on Sunday, the 2nd November/4th Zil. H., [250] The Emperor visited the Prince's house to console him.

News came that Rām Singh, zamindār of Chānda, had been defeated by the imperial army; on Sunday, 2nd November/4th Zil. H., he fled to the hills with 200 troopers, leaving his family behind; 'Itiqād Khan, Hamza Khan and Kishan Singh entered Chānda. On Wednesday, the 19th November/21st Zil. H., Rām Singh came to Chānda with three men and wanted to enter his mansion. Murād Beg, a servant of Kishan Singh, who was guarding the door, rose to oppose him. Rām Singh stabbed him with a *jamdhār,* but was himself attacked and slain by others. Murād Beg died the next day. On Wednesday, the 3rd December/6th Muharram, the Emperor sent a robe, a *farmān,* and an elephant to Kishan Singh. A robe was sent to Hari Singh, zamindār of Garha.

Bāltun Beg, sister's son of Qalich Khan, came from Bukhārā, and received a sword, a dagger with gold *sāz,* 2,000 rupees and the rank of 6-*sadi* (200 tr.). 'Abdul Qādir, son-in-law of Mukhlis Khan deceased, who had wrested fort Kondāna from the enemy and entrusted it to 'Abdul Karim, reached the Court on Sunday, the 14th December/17th Muharram. By receiving an increment of 100 (50 tr.) he became a 5-*sadi* (100 tr.). Ihtamām Khan Sardār Beg became dārogha of nawāra *vice* Saifullah Khan. The daughter of Sayyid Muzaffar Haidarābādi was married to Kāmgār Khan, who received a robe. 'Itiqād Khan, who had returned from Chānda to the Court, [251] became Qurbegi *vice* Yalangtosh Khan, receiving a robe, an elephant and the increment of 5-*sadi* (150 tr.) which made him a 2-*hazāri* (400 tr.). Hayāt Khan became āmin of the seven *chaukis vice* Mir 'Abdul Karim. Khidmatguzār Khan died; his son Muhammad Quli received a robe of mourning. His posts of dārogha of the slaves and of the halting-places (manāzil) were given to Fath Muhammad and Diw-āfkan. Qāzi Haidar munshi got the title of Khan. Shaikh Makhdum, munshi and sadr, got the title of Fāzil Khan; Hāji Ism'ail, the head of the khushnavises (calligraphists) of the age, who used to write the Emperor's own *farmāns*, got the title of Raushan-raqm.

On Sunday, the 28th December, 1684/1st Safar, Qāzi Shaikh-ul-Islām begged permission to visit Mecca and Medina. He was presented with a *doshāla* of *parm-narm* (soft downy wool) and the pamphlet *Ādāb-i-ziārat*. A casket full of supplicatory letters to the Prophet was entrusted to him, to be conveyed to the Prophet's tomb; the casket was to be opened before the door of the latticed enclosure of the sacred tomb, the pouch taken out and carried inside the enclosure for being deposited below the hallowed lintel.

Suhrāb Khan, son of Barqāndāz Khan, was sent to convey to the Bakhshi-ul-mulk Ruhullah Khan at Bijapur, a big gun taking one maund balls, and three other guns [252] taking 20 seer balls. 'Itiqād Khan was sent to punish the rebels scattered near Pārnir and Sangamnir. Rashid Khan, *peshdast* of the khālsa office, was sent to Indur for deciding the question of sowing the *chena* millet.*

The sons of Khān-i-Zamān after their father's death came to Court from Burhānpur, and received robes and promotions. Ātish Khan was sent towards Nawalgonda with a strong force and a company of 500 troopers of Kām Bakhsh. Hamiduddin, son of Ihtamām Khan became dārogha of the *khatam band-khānah vice* his father. On the 22nd January, 1685/26th Safar, news came that Ghāziuddin Khan Bahādur had set fire to the *petta* at the foot of fort Rāhiri, slain many of the infidel chiefs, plundered their money and things, taken possession of the women, seized their cattle, and gained a great victory. Sayyid Ughlān, who brought this joyous news, received an elephant. Shāh Muhammad, *chobdār* of Ghāziuddin Khan Bahādur, who had come from the Khan without change of dress, received a robe and two hundred rupees. The Khan was created Firuz Jang and presented with kettle-drums. More than one hundred and fifty robes were sent for his officers, high and low. On Thursday, the 29th January/4th Rabi. A., Khānahzād Khan went to Aurangābād to bring the Emperor's consort (parastār) Udipuri Mahal. [253] On Wednesday the 4th February/10th Rabi. A., winter robes were presented to all imperial servants at Court and the provinces.

---

* The printed text has been corrected from the MS. *Chena* is a kind of millet, panicum miliaceum. *Indur*, now named Nizamabad, is a district south of the junction of the Manjera and the Godavari.

DEATH OF BAKHTĀWAR KHAN

On Monday, the 9th February, 1685/15th Rabi. A., Bakhtāwar Khan dārogha of the khawāses died, after thirty years of service. His Majesty was very sorry to hear of the death of this confidential companion, wise minister, and highminded man. By his order the bier was brought near the *'adālat-gāh;* the Emperor himself acted as Imām, followed the bier a few steps, read the *fātiha,* distributed alms, and had the whole *Qurān* read, and the corpse sent to the tomb which the deceased had previously built at Delhi. He was a great friend of scholars, hermits, and poets and tried to further their desires. He was an expert in the classic style and knowledge of history, wrote the *Mirāt-ul-'ālam,* and was unrivalled in good breeding and benevolence to mankind. Yalangtosh Khan Bahādur succeeded him as dārogha of the khawases, Hakim Muhasan Khan as dārogha of the jewellery department and Mir Hedayetullah as that of the gold-ware. I, Muhammad Sāqi, the author of this history, was the diwān and munshi of Bakhtāwar Khan, and used to show to the Emperor for correction the drafts of secret orders written by him. [254] The Emperor kindly took me into his service and immediately made me news-writer of Thursdays. * * *

DEATH OF DARBĀR KHAN NĀZIR.

On Thursday, the 26th February, 1685/2nd Rabi. S., Darbār Khan superintendent (*nāzir*) of the harem (*mahal*) died. He was an old, high-minded, and benevolent officer, devoted to His Majesty, who similarly ordered his bier to be brought and himself acted as Imām at the funeral prayer. The corpse was sent to Delhi. (In succession to him) Khidmat Khan became *nāzir,* in addition to holding his post of (*dārogha* of) petitions, and Shaikh 'Abdullah, son of Shaikh Nizām, became superintendent of the medical stores. On Saturday, the 14th March/18th Rabi. S., Shujā'et Khan Haidarābādi died. His son Malik Miran received a robe and a *mansab.*

On Monday the 16th/20th Rabi. S., Ruhullah Khan was sent to punish the enemy near Bijapur and presented with a special robe, a jewelled *kalgi,* and silver kettle-drums. With him were sent two and a half lakhs of rupees, a *jigha* with diamond *parkhānah,* and a diamond *sarpech* for ('Āzam) Shah, a necklace of two strings of pearls for

Jahānzeb Bānu Begam, a jewelled *muttaka* for Bidār Bakht, a *smarani* for Wālājāh, a pearl necklace *do-lari* for Wālāshān and [255] thirty-two robes for Sarāfrāz Khan, Fath Jang Khan, Kānhoji, Basant Rao, and others. On Saturday, the 21st March, 1685/25th Rabi. S., Wafādār Khan grandson of S'aid Khan Bahādur, was given the title of Zabardast Khan and sent as envoy to Balkh, with the reward of a robe, a dagger, a sword, a shield with jewelled *sāz,* a jewelled *jigha,* a quiver, a bow, a horse, an elephant, 10,000 rupees, and an increment of 5-*sadi* (100 tr.). An elephant valued at 18,000 rupees and other presents and precious things were sent to Subhān Quli Khan along with him. Shafqatullah, who had the title of Sazāwar Khan, was given pardon for his fault, and made the second mir-tuzuk.

Khujistah Ākhtar coming from Aurangābād, had audience on Monday, the 23rd March/27th Rabi. S., receiving a robe and a jewelled bracelet (*bāzuband*). Khwāja 'Abdur Rahim returned from the embassy to Bijapur, and received a robe, an elephant, and 5,000 rupees. Mir 'Abdul Karim in addition to his post at the *jā-namāz-khānah,* got the dārogha-ship of *naqqāsh-khānah.* I became mushrif of this department. On Thursday the 26th March/1st Jamad. A., Firuz Jang Bahādur had audience and received a special robe, a jewelled dagger, five horses and seven *tolahs* of rose-*'attar.*

The Emperor learnt that on Friday, the 27th March/2nd Jamad. S., the siege of Bijapur had begun.* Khan Jahān Bahādur Zafar Jang had begun to dig entrenchments [256] from the side of Zuhrapur, at a distance of half a *kos,* and Ruhullah Khan and Qāsim Khan at a distance of a quarter *kos* from the fort walls.

A courier brought the message that on Tuesday, the 14th April, 1685/20th Jamad. A., the Rāthors had captured fort Siwānah. Purdil, son of Firuz Khan Miwāti, was slain with many men. Sharza Bijāpuri boldly advanced towards the army of Muhammad 'Āzam Shāh on the bank of the Tungābhadrā river. After a severe fight and losing many men, he fled. On Sunday the 12th April/18th Jamad. A., a slave came from Muhammad Ākbar to the Emperor with two horses as *peshkash.* He was refused audience but

* Actually four days later than this date, on 1st April, as the *Ākhbārāt* show.

commanded to go to the *deorhi* of the Lady Nawwāb (Zinat-un-nisā). On Thursday, the 23rd April/29th Jamād. A., Sarbuland Khan (Khwāja Y'aqub) died.

DESCRIPTION OF THE CITY AND FORT OF ĀHMADNAGAR

The fort of Āhmadnagar is situated on a plain; for giving it firmness and strength, the foundation of this hill-like fort has been sunk to the lowest stratum of the earth. It would not be wrong to say that this nail of the hill had been inserted to prevent earthquakes. Around the fort is a champaign. Within the fort are buildings and fresh gardens, under which cellars of great rarity have been built. Around the fort is a deep ditch ever full of water. Two canals come into the fort from outside. [257] The city of Āhmadnagar is situated a quarter *kos* from the fort; it has no defensive wall. Formerly it was without an equal for its buildings, the abundance of canal water in every house, and the extent of habitation. The late Dānishmand Khan, who had passed some time here when he was a merchant, used to say that Āhmadnagar excels Kashmir in many points. In the environs of the city are the gardens of Farah-bakhsh and Bihisht-bāgh, which present a wonderful spectacle. They were built by Salābat Khan during the period of the insanity of Murtaza Nizāmulmulk, in his name. In order to preserve their memory I shall give the length and breadth of these two gardens and a description of their buildings which are rare.

The garden of Farah-bakhsh is 2000 *zir'a* in length and breadth (alike) which makes (the area) 278 *bighas*. In the middle of it is a reservoir 528 *zira* (square), which makes the area 19 *bighas*. An underground channel brings water to it from the foot of the hill. In the centre of the reservoir is a lofty and wonderful building in two storeys, having 160 *hujra* (rooms) and a high cupola. Archers practise shooting at its summit. Bihisht-bāgh is 312 *zir'a* in length and breadth alike which makes the area 100 *bighas*. In the middle is an octagonal reservoir, which is also fed with canal water. In the centre is a building now in ruins. On the bank of the reservoir are a charming building and a neat Turkish bath, fit for the residence of elegant people.

Five *kos* from the fort is a halting place (*manzil*), known as Manjar Samba or Manzil Sabā. It is said that a high building has been constructed in the waist of the hill. The fountain of the garden leaps up of itself incessantly to a height of 100 yards, through the force of the water that comes from a spring in the hill. The Emperor [258] visited this "flower of the earth" and ordered the ruined houses to be repaired. The tomb of Salābat Khan situated on the top of the hill, is a wonderful building. The climate of this tract is not very hot; at night one has to use coverlets.

THE EMPEROR'S MARCH FROM ĀHMADNAGAR TO SHOLĀPUR

On Sunday, the 26th April, 1685/2nd Jamad. S., the imperial camp moved from Āhmadnagar, on an auspicious day and hour, and was pitched near the Farah-bakhsh garden. On Wednesday the 29th April/5th Jamad. S., the Emperor went there.

On the 30th Sayyid Ughlān got the title of Siādat Khan. This noble-minded Sayyid, the tutor of Firuz Jang Khan, had come to Hindustān from Persia (*vilāyat*) with him, and had the fortune of being enrolled in the Emperor's service, and rose to honour and high position through the Emperor's favour.

Qāzi Sayyid Ābu Sa'id, owing to some ailments, begged hard to resign his high office, [*added from ms.*]. Arjunji, uncle's son of Sambhā was made a 2-*hazāri* (1000 tr.) and presented with a robe and a horse. 'Izzatullah Khan was appointed qiladār of Āhmadnagar. On Friday, the 1st May/2nd Jamad. S., Firuz Jang Bahādur was sent to stay at Āhmadnagar and presented with an amulet containing the *Qurān,* a special robe, and 20,000 rupees. His companions were rewarded with robes and daggers. Khwāja 'Abdullah [259] son of Muhammad Sharif, who had been the Qāzi of the Emperor's army before his accession, became Qāzi of the Court. On Saturday, the 23rd May/29th Jamad. S., Qamruddin, son of Firuz Jang, got the title of Khan. On Sunday, the 24th May/1st Rajab, the Emperor reached Sholāpur. 'Itiqād Khan was sent towards Zafarābād [Bidar], receiving a special robe, a quiver, and a bow; his followers got robes, swords, and horses. Bahramand Khan was ordered to hasten toward Haidarābād. On Saturday, the 30th May/7th Rajab, when Shah 'Alam Bahādur was coming to Court on horseback, a man ran towards him with an uplifted sword; he was seized and made over to the Prince's kotwāl, by imperial command.

ARMY SENT UNDER SHAH 'ĀLAM BAHADUR AGAINST ĀBUL HASAN.

As the Emperor had ordered that Muhammad M'asum and Muhammad J'afar, servants of Haidarābād, who were staying in the imperial camp as envoys, should lodge in the quarters of Ihtamām Khan, kotwāl, and that the letters they wrote to Haidarābād and received from that place, should be first shown to the Khan, and [260] that he should report to the Emperor if he found anything worth reporting, spies worked hard to get news (of the enemy). As the time for the destruction of the Haidarābādi ruler had come near, a letter from Ābul Hasan reached his servants, saying "His Majesty is a great man, and has acted like the great up to this time. But now that finding Sikandar ('Ādil Shah) an orphan and powerless, he has besieged Bijapur and pressed him hard, it is proper that, besides the large army of Bijapur, Raja Sambhā should exert himself with a countless host to aid this helpless king from one side, and I should appoint 40,000 tr. under the command of Khalilullah Khan Palang-hamla to conduct the war, and see on which side the Emperor can encounter and resist his many enemies. You, who have been detained near the kotwāli *chabutra,* should not be alarmed at the news, as your release would come about soon". The Khan sent this letter to the Emperor. Therefore on Sunday, the 28th June, 1685/6th Shaban, the Prince was sent against Haidarābād, receiving a special robe, a jewelled dagger, a *muttaka,* and twenty horses. His sons and high officers were favoured with robes, jewels, horses, elephants, and promotion. On the 15th July/23rd Shaban Ruhullah Khan, coming from Bijapur was sent to Āhmadnagar in the place of Firuz Jang Bahādur. Kāmgār Khan became dārogha of the retinue *vice* Khānahzād Khan, and Mukhtār Khan dārogha of the stable *vice* the first-named and was sent on Sunday, the 19th July/27th Shaban, to convey a dagger having a jasper hilt with 'ilāqa, [261] and *phul katāra* to 'Āzam Shah and a *smarani* of pearl, a *punchhi,* and rain-coat (*farghal*) for Prince Bidār Bakht. Mughal Khan, *nāzim* of Mālwa, died on Tuesday, the 14th July/22nd

Shaban, and Tarbiyat Khan, faujdār of Jaunpur on the 19th/27th Shaban. Mir 'Abdul Karim was punished for an offence by being removed from the dārogha-ship of *jā-namāz-khānah,* Muhammad Sharif *khawās* of the touring camp (*cor.*) taking his place.

The Emperor said, "I had at first put off the chastisement of this vendor of China-ware, this ape-like buffoon and this drummer [Qutb Shah]. Now that this hen has come forward crowing, I can't wait any longer." Inspite of the delay and hitch which it would cause to the Bijapur expedition the Prince was ordered to extirpate the wretch. Khan Jahān Bahādur Zafar Jang, who was staying at the thānah of Indi for conveying provisions to the army of Shāh 'Alijāh ['Āzam], was ordered to join the army of the Prince and exert himself much in rendering good service.

CHAPTER XXIX.

29TH YEAR OF THE REIGN : 1096 A.H.

22nd July, 1685—11th July, 1686.

* * * *

[262] Sikandar Bey, who had come from Persia (*vilāyat*) to Court, received a robe, a jewelled dagger and 10,000 rupees. Āmānullah Khan, son of Ālahwardi Khan and Fath M'amur Khan son of Dilir Khan died fighting heroically in the trenches of Bijapur. Kamāluddin Khan, son of Dilir Khan and Fath Jang Khan Miāna were wounded. A mourning robe for Āmānulla Khan was sent to Hasan 'Ali Khan Bahādur 'Alamgirshāhi. The powder magazine of the army of Muhammad 'Āzam Shāh caught fire; nearly 500 *bahalias* (hill-climbing infantry) and musketeers were killed.

On Thursday, the 13th August/23rd Ramzan, Irij Khan Subahdār of Berār and Sayyid Sher Khan, an officer of the army under 'Āzam Shāh, died. Firuz Jang Bahādur, coming from Āhmadnagar, had audience; the Emperor presented to him a dagger adorned with a sher-māhi handle taken out of his own belt and received in his own hand the *nazar* presented by the Khan Bahādur. Mir Khan, diwān of Muhammad 'Āzam Shāh, was sent as deputy (*nāib*) Subahdār of Burhānpur. On Monday the 24th August/4th Shawwal, Sikandar Bey received the title of Khan and the rank of 3-*hazāri* (same tr.). Husain 'Ali Khan became Subahdār of Berār *vice* Irij Khan deceased, and Raziuddin became his *nāib*. Lutfullah Khan was sent to convey to Shah 'Ālam Bahādur certain orders of the Emperor. [263] Siādat Khan became dārogha of '*arz-i-mukarrar vice* him. Khwāja Hāmid, son of Qalich Khan got the title of Khan and a female elephant, and was ordered to convey treasure to 'Azam Shāh's army. On Thursday the 1st October/13th Zil. Q., Qalich Khan went as Subahdār to Zafarābād, receiving a robe, a *zarah* (steel armour), and an elephant. Āsālat Khan and Najābat Khan, sons of Sayyid Muzaffar Haidarābādi, Ākrām Khan, Nāsir Khan and Sayyid Hasan Khan were sent with him.

The Emperor learnt of a famine in the army of Muhammad 'Āzam Shāh; it was so severe that a grain of wheat laid the snare of seduction for a hundred Adams, and in the fear that the lack of gram would render them weak, all the soldiers felt themselves helpless. Every day severe fighting took place, in the trenches and also with the out-lying troops. The soldiers had no sleep and food, the two sustainers of life. Death rode rampant. There came no food from any side. A letter "By order" was written to the Prince saying, "As you have come to such a pass, return to the Court with your army." The Prince after receiving the letter held a council of consultation with his chief officers. First he turned to Hasan 'Ali Khan Bahādur 'Alamgir-shāhi and said, "The carrying out of the expedition depends on the co-operation of the officers. I have received such a letter from the Emperor. Your advice is important in these matters of peace and war, haste and delay. [264] You have seen and undergone many difficulties and hardships of this kind. What is your view of this case?" The Khan replied, "In view of the good of the army and happiness of the people at large, I think a retreat is advisable. When in the Balkh campaign, Prince Murād Bakhsh owing to the rigour of winter could not stay there, he had to give up sieges and battles by order of Shāh Jahān and return to Court. What our men are undergoing is known; and your Highness has received the order to retreat." After this the Prince turned to the others; they all supported the Khan. The Prince then said, "You have spoken for yourselves. Now hear from me! Muhammad 'Āzam with his two sons and Begam will not retreat from this dangerous place so long as he has life. After my death, His Majesty may come and order the removal of my corpse for funeral. My companions may stay or go away as they like." Then they all said in concert, "Our opinion is the same as your Highness's." When the Emperor learnt of this determination of the Prince to stay, he ordered Firuz Jang Bahādur on Monday, the 4th October, 1685/16th Zil. Q., to set out with a large army and provisions beyond calculation [265] to reinforce and supply the Prince's army. The Emperor excused the branding of the horses of the 3rd and 4th fractions of their contingents in the case of the *sadi* and 4-*sadi* in attendance on the Emperor and mansabdars out on expedition. The imperial officers were ordered to buy for the State horses after taking them out of *dāgh* and send them to the Prince, for distribution to the men who had lost their horses in action. Firuz Jang, on the day of taking leave, was presented with a robe, the *māhi,* and an elephant for carrying it, four banners (*nishān*) and four hairy (two-humped) camels for carrying them, and was permitted to kiss the feet of the Emperor, who stroked him on the back with his hand. His officers were favoured with robes, horses, elephants, and promotion. Firuz Jang reached the Prince with the speed of lightning, and the famished army gained the hope of life. The Shāh appointed his revived troops to punish the enemy who used to sally out of the fort for fight.

It happened by chance that when Firuz Jang was staying at Rasulpur in the environs of Bijapur, six thousand infantry, sent by the wretched Pam Naik with provisions carried on the head in aid of Bijapur, were advancing by stealth at night, and arrived at this place at midnight, thinking that a Bijapuri force must be staying so near the fort. Firuz Jang, who had been informed of it by spies, seized the opportunity; [266] and fell upon them before dawn; no living creature escaped from the Mughal swords with his life; a crushing defeat was inflicted on the enemy. Sixty-two mansabdars sent by Firuz Jang to convey the heads of the enemy received a reward of 2,000 rupees. A mohar weighing 1,000 mohars was sent to Firuz Jang.

On Saturday, the 10th October, 1685/22nd Zil. Q., 'Itiqād Khan was sent as thānahdār of Indi up to the bank of the Bhimā. Of his comrades Sayyid Nur-ul-bahar of Bārha got the title of Saif Khan and others robes, horses and elephants, at the time of their departure.

Marhamat Khan was sent as thānahdār of Mudgal between Zafarābād [Bidar] and Haidarābād; his followers were rewarded with robes, horses, elephants and cash. Pahār Singh Gaur, who had caused disturbances near Ujjain attacked with a large force Muluk Chand, naib and officer of 'Āzam Shah, who had ridden out to punish him. After a stiff fight an arrow hit the rebel, and he died. Muluk Chand's letter reporting this victory was shown to the Emperor. The courtiers bowed and invoked blessings. Robes were presented to Fazāil Khan, who had previously learnt of the matter from the letter of a secret-writer and reported it to the Emperor, to 'Ināyetullah, agent, who presented Muluk Chand's letter to the Emperor, and 'Abdul Hakim, a servant of the Prince, who brought the rebel's head to the Emperor. [267] His Majesty ordered the head to be sent to the Prince. Muluk Chand was rewarded with the title of Rāi-i-Rāiān, a robe, and promotion making him in all a 7-*sadi.*

CONQUEST OF HAIDARABAD BY SHĀH 'ĀLAM BAHĀDUR

On Sunday, the 18th October, 1685/30th Zil. Q., despatches from Shāh 'Alam Bahādur and Khan Jahān Bahādur announcing the capture of the city of Haidarābād, the shutting up of Ābul Hasan in the fort of Golkonda, the interview of Ibrāhim, the enemy's commander-in-chief (who had been created Khalilullah Khan), Muhammad Taqi the courier, Sharif-ul-mulk, Ābul Hasan's sister's husband, and others with the prince, the recommendation of mansab for each of them, and the arrival of Ābul Hasan's supplicatory letter, were brought to the Emperor by Mir Hāshim, an officer of the Prince. The courtiers made their bow of thanks-giving for the victory; joyous music was played. The Emperor ordered Ābul Hasan's letter to be shown to him. Mirzā Muhammad Shirāzi,* son of Hakim Fathuddin, and uncle of Hakim Muhasan Khan, presented to the Emperor the following verse as embodying the date of the victory. [268] * * * He received a robe. Prince Shāh 'Alam Bahādur got an increment of 10,000 making him a 40-*hazāri* (30,000 tr.). Mir 'Abdul Karim, the ex-dārogha of of the *jā-namāz-khānah,* was ordered to carry robes and jewels to the Prince, his sons, Khan Jahān, Ibrāhim, sar-i-lashkar, and the high grandees serving under the Prince. Muhammad Shaf'i, mushrif of deorhi, Ālah Yār, mushrif of the qarāwwals, Mir Hāshim, servant of the Prince, Sayyid Abu Muhammad son of Munawwar Khan, and Kalyān, son of Hirā mason were travelling together on the way to their work. When they arrived at Mangal, four *kos* from Haidarābad, Shaikh Nizām Haidarābādi with a numberless force appeared like a flood coming on to sweep away houses. Though these men had not such a force with them as to be able to resist, yet they fought valiantly, and excepting Mir 'Abdul Karim who fell down wounded [269] and was afterwards carried off as a prisoner, all the others perished.

---

* Surnamed Ni'āmat Khan 'Ali, and finally Dānishmand Khan. He wrote a well-known account of the siege of Golkonda and an incomplete official history of Shah 'Alam I, entitled *Bahādur-Shāh-nāmah.*

Najābat Khan and Āsālat Khan, sons of Sayyid Muzaffar, who had been sent with an escort from Zafarābād supplied by Qalich Khan, fled after some fighting, on account of their previous understanding with the enemy, and joined Shaikh Nizām. Many men who had joined them like a caravan and not for any other reason, were slain. The enemy captured the jewels and robes sent by the Emperor and other articles, including the property of the merchants and travellers. After four days Mir 'Abdul Karim was conveyed by the men of Ābul Hasan from Golkonda to the camp of the Prince on the border of the city of Haidarābād and then they disappeared. Muhammad Murād Khan envoy (*hājib*), getting news of it, carried him to his own house. In a few days his wounds healed; he interviewed the Prince, reported to him the orders verbally sent to the Prince through him, and then took his leave. He reached the Court with Khan Jahān Bahādur, who had been summoned by the Emperor. On Thursday, the 29th October/11th Zil. H., Muhammad Ibrāhim, sar-i-lashkar was on the Prince's recommendation made a 6-*hazāri* (same tr.) with the title of Mahābat Khan, Sharif-ul-mulk a 3-*hazāri* (300 tr.), Muhammad Taqi the running courier,* a 2-*hazāri* (300 tr.) with the title of 'Itibār Khan. On Monday, the 2nd November/15th Zil. H., Sazāwār (*cor.*) Khan died. His son Rahmatullah was given a mourning robe.

The Emperor received a letter from Firuz Jang announcing the capture of the raised battery of Bijapur. An emerald ring was made over to Siādat Khan for being sent to Firuz Jang. [270] On Wednesday, the 9th December 1685/22nd Muharram, a mourning robe was sent to 'Umdat-ul-mulk Āsad Khan for the death of his mother at Delhi. Rahim Bey arrived from Turān and Hāji Muhammad Raf'i, son-in-law of Saf Shikan Khan deceased, from Irān; they received robes. Mirzā Muhammad, son of Hāji Qāsim, naskh-navis, who had gone to Mungi-Patan to copy the *Qurān,* and returned to Court after completing it, received a reward of 1000 rupees. Bahramand Khan was sent towards Patan. Sikandar Khan and others were appointed to accompany him. Ink-pots of jasper stone were presented to Siādat Khan, dārogha of *'arz-i-mukarrar,* and Fāzil Khan, sadr. Mukhtār Khan was given a quiver

---

* The printed text reads *Taqi wa Dāud.* The MS. reads *Taqi dawādu,* or running courier, which I have accepted.

and bow and sent to the thānah of Hālsangi. On Thursday, the 24th December/7th Safar, Khan Jahān Bahādur came from Haidarābād, had audience and received a robe. Robes were also given to Subhānji and eight other Deccanis brought by the aforesaid Khan Bahādur. On Thursday the 31st December/14th Safar, Rashid Khan was commanded to go to Hindustan in order to regulate certain mahals. The *haveli* of Bakhtāwar Khan deceased, situated in Delhi, was presented to Siādat Khan. A gracious *farmān* was sent to Āmir Khan, Subahdār of Kabul, announcing the grant of a special robe and an increment of a *hazār zāt*. Hātim, who had been formerly a servant of the Rānā, became faujdār of Tuda-Bhim.

Braj-bhushan Qawāmuddin-khāni, a convert to Islam under the name of Dindār, became mushrif of the *jā-namāz-khānah, vice* Ikhlās-kesh, who became mushrif of petitions *vice* Raushan-raqm. [271] Qamruddin Khan who had come to Court, was sent (back) to his father with the gift of an elephant. With him were sent a robe and a sword for his father. Āhmad Āqā, ambassador of the Sharif of Mecca, had audience, and received a robe and 2,000 rupees. On Sunday, the 31st January, 1686/16th Rabi. A., Mahābat Khan and Sharif-ul-mulk had audience. The Khan received a special robe, a sword with gold *sāz,* forty-one horses, an elephant, 50,000 rupees and nine *tolahs* of *'attar,* while the latter received a robe, a dagger with a crystal handle, 10,000 rupees and seven *tolahs* of *'attar*. His sons, Hedāyetullah and 'Ināyetullah got robes. 'Abdul Qādir Deccani got the rank of 2-*hazāri* (1,000 tr.) and an elephant. Achlāji the son-in-law of Shivāji, received the rank of 5-*hazāri,* (2,000 tr.) and kettledrums, a banner, a jewelled *punchhi* and an elephant on the day of interview. Saf Shikan Khan dārogha of the artillery, had come from Bijapur; after being given a dagger and an elephant, he was immediately ordered to return. Yalangtosh Khan Bahādur was punished by removal from his post and rank. In his place Silāh Khan, son of Wazir Khan Shāhjahāni, became dārogha of the khawāses, an officer close to the Emperor, with the title of Ānwār Khan. Suhrāb Khan became Mir Tuzuk *vice* Silāh Khan. On Saturday the 6th March, 1686/20th Rabi. S., Khan Jahān Bahādur [272] was sent to Burhānpur to bring the Emperor's consort (*paraṣtār*) Aurangabadi Mahal; the Emperor with his own hands presented him with a jewelled dagger with a *phul katāra* and pearl *'ilāqa*. An emerald *smarani* was made over to him for the *parastār*.

The sons of Khan Jahān and Ruhullah Khan saluted each other by raising the hand to the head. The Emperor ordered that in future nobody at Court should raise his hand to the head to salute another; and if anybody disobeyed the order, he should not enter the ghusalkhānah.

Mir Jalāluddin, one of the servants of 'Abdul 'Aziz Khan, king of Bukhārā, who after a pilgrimage to Mecca wished to return to Court but had died at that place, came to the Court, and received a robe, a dagger with a gold handle, and 1,000 rupees. Hedāyetullah, son of Tarbiyat Khan, came to Court after his father's death and received a mourning robe. On Tuesday, the 16th March/1st Jamad. A., Zain-ul-'ābidin a relative of Ābul Hasan, had audience and received a robe. Ābul Hasan cut off and sent to Shāh 'Ālam the head of Mādanna Brahman as a proof of his own obedience and submission. The Prince sent it to the Emperor with Bahādur 'Ali Khan. Hamiduddin Khan, faujdār of Patan, was made qiladār of Qandahār. The dismissed Rustam Beg came to Court. The late Hāfiz Muhammad Āmin Khan's *haveli* at Delhi was presented to Mahābat Khan. Sayyid Zain-ul-'ābidin became qiladār and faujdār of Sholāpur *vice* Sayyid Ānwār Khan deceased. Mukhtār Khan, after receiving a jewelled dagger, [273] was sent to Bijapur.

Bakht-buland was given the zamindāri of Deogarh *alias* (*cor.*) Islāmgarh, and a robe, an *arsi*, and a horse. Buland Afghān, a servant of Prince Muhammad 'Āzam Shāh, brought to the Court the heads of the sons of Pahār Singh Gaur sent by Rāi-i-Rāiān Mulukchand, and got a robe. The heads were ordered to be taken to the Prince. Imāji and Tukoji, brought by Fazāil Khan, each got a robe and an elephant. Rāi-i-Rāiān Mulukchand died; Bahrawar Khan became deputy Subahdār of Mālwa *vice* him. On Wednesday, the 21st April/7th Jamad. S., Aurangābādi Mahal reached the Emperor's camp from Delhi. Prince Muhammad Kām Bakhsh advanced to the door of the fort near the *deorhi* to welcome her. Khan Jahān Bahādur on interviewing received a robe, so also did his sons and officer Sayyid Munawwar Khan. His eldest son Himmat Khan after receiving a robe, a sword, and an elephant, was sent to Bijapur. Jaswant Singh Bundela received a robe, an elephant, and kettledrums; Fāzil Beg, brother of Pādishāh Quli Khan the rebel, got the title of Tahawwar Khan and was appointed under Himmat Khan. Sayyid Mubārak Khan, qiladār of Daulatābād, got the title of Murtaza Khan. Marhamat Khan was ordered to convey treasure to Bijapur.

At midnight Khwāja 'Abdur Rahim Khan conducted to the Emperor the two sons of Vindhāchal, who was brother of Rām Rāi munshi of Fāzil Khan 'Ala-ul-mulk. [274] They accepted Islām and were named S'ādatullah and S'adullah. At the end of next day, the Khwāja, by command, placed both on elephants and carried them through the city, with flags flying and music playing.

On Monday, the 3rd May, 1686/19th Jamad. S., Khan Jahān Bahādur was sent towards Agra in order to punish the rebels of Hindustan, and was presented with a special robe, a jewelled sword, a horse with gold *sāz*, an elephant, and two krors of *dām*. His sons other than Himmat Khan and Munawwar Khan received robes when sent along with him. 'Abdul 'Aziz Khan, qiladār of Junnar, died. His son Ābul Khair Khan gained his place. Jān Sipār Khan, faujdār of Zafarābād, who had come to Court, was sent away. Fāzil Khan, mir munshi and sadr, got in addition the dārogha-ship of petitions, *vice* Khidmat Khan. Mir Hasan, son of Ruhullah Khan, was married to the daughter of Āmir Khan and received the title of Khānahzād Khan and a horse with gold *sāz*. Ihtamām Khan became *nāzir* of the imperial harem *vice* Khidmat Khan. Bahramand Khan was sent to the *thānah* of Indi. Muhammad Matlab, his deputy, laid his head on the ground of service. On Monday, the 7th June, Shāh 'Ālam Bahādur had audience, receiving a robe with a *gosh-pech* and a jewelled *punchhi*. [275] All the Shāhzādahs and sultāns got robes. On his birthday, Friday, the 12th June/30th Rajab, the Prince received an *arsi* with a ruby stone worth 40,000 rupees. Mumin Khan, the Prince's servant, brought to the Emperor 100 elephants from Ābul Hasan. Muhammad M'asum, envoy of Ābul Hasan, got a robe at interview. Qalich Khan from Zafarabād had audience. Muhammad Matlab became Mir Tuzuk *vice* Saifullah Khan deceased. Muhakam Singh Chandrāwat came to Court from home and got a robe,

THE EMPEROR'S MARCH FROM SHOLAPUR TO CAPTURE THE FORT OF BIJAPUR

* * * *

As Sikandar ('Ādil Shah) was not befriended by the happy arrival of Khizir,* he could not reach the *elixir vitæ* of dominion. The sharers of his power, [276] appointed Siddi Mas'aud, 'Abdur Rauf, and Sharza the general, to exercise control over him and they treated him as of no account. Persisting in self-will and haughtiness, they even quarrelled among themselves; the king could not leave the city, but oppressed the citizens. Having come under the influence of the infidel Sambhā, he used to be his co-sharer in harming the Muslims. He considered the strong fort of Bijapur as his refuge in evil days.

One day Shaikh Muhammad Naqshbandi of Sirhind had audience. In course of conversation he said, "I have heard that Your Majesty wants to march against Bijapur". The Emperor replied, "The only benefit which we kings derive from our position in the world is the gaining of fame. I had wished that one of my sons would gain it; but it is not to be. I therefore, wish to go (in person) and see what sort of barrier this wall is that it is not being removed from before us." On Monday, the 14th June, 1686/2nd Shaban, the imperial standards moved from Sholapur in that direction. On Saturday, the 26th June/14th Shaban, Prince Muhammad 'Āzam and Bidār Bakht [277] had audience, and received robes. Bahādur Khan and Rāo Anup Singh, son of Rāo Karn, got robes on interview. On Saturday, the 3rd July/21st Shaban, when the imperial camp reached Rasulpur, three *kos* from Bijapur, Firuz Jang Bahādur had audience, and after receiving 30,000 rupees, ten horses worth 9,500 rupees, an elephant with silver *sāz,* and a special robe, was sent to the post of Bidār Bakht. His son Qamruddin Khan received a jewelled dagger with pearl *'ilāqa.* On Sunday, the 4th July/22nd Shaban the Emperor ordered the trenches to be advanced, the towers to be overthrown by cannonade, and the moat to be filled up.

---

* A play upon the name *Sikandar*=Alexander the Great, who, guided by the prophet Khizir, traversed the dark wilderness (*zulmat*) and reached the spring of the water of life, by tasting which he became a world-conqueror.

CHAPTER XXX.

30TH YEAR OF THE REIGN : 1097 A.H.

12th July, 1686—30th June, 1687.

* * * *

[278] Nawāzish Khan was made faujdār and qiladār of Mandasor, receiving a robe. Suhrāb Khan was given a jewelled *jigha*. Sarāfrāz Khan and Dāud Khan got robes at interview. Ābul Khair, son of Shaikh Nizām, became dārogha of *jā-namāz-khānah vice* Muhammad Sharif, and I (the author) became mushrif (of that department) *vice* Dindār. Muhammad Mumin, son-in-law of Irij Khan, was appointed nāib subahdār of Berār *vice* Raziuddin Khan deceased, who had been administering the province as the deputy of Hasan 'Ali Khan and had fallen down dead while talking with his soldiers. On Saturday, the 21st August, 1686/11th Shawwal, Qalich Khan was appointed to the trenches after receiving a bow and a quiver. Kamāluddin Khan, son of Dilir Khan, recovered from his wounds, interviewed and received a robe, a sword, and a mace (*'asā*) set with *jasper*. 'Itiqād Khan coming from Āhmadnagar, had audience. Raja Bhim Singh came from Ajmir by command and had audience.

On Saturday, the 4th September/25th Shawwal, the Emperor rode to the edge of the moat, in order to inspect the battery which had been raised opposite the turret (*kangurah*) of the fort, and to learn the reason why the conquest was still delayed. Great noise was made by the cortege, and rockets and muskets began to be fired with great noise from the fort. [279] Flaming cannon-balls passed over His Majesty's head. Mir 'Abdul Karim, through his ingenuity, composed an extempore hemistich embodying the date, "Bijapur will be soon conquered", which he showed to the Emperor after scrawling it on a bit of paper with a lead pencil. The Emperor took it as a good omen and said, "God grant it be so!" Thank God, the capture of the fort was accomplished that very week. On Saturday, the 11th September, 1686/3rd Zil. Q., the slave Jalāl was rewarded with the title of Sarbarāh Khan for his excellent work in trenching. As the imperial warriors had collected in two months and twelve days all the materials necessary for destroying the enemy, Sikandar and his companions, seeing death near, begged pardon for their faults and cried for quarters. On Sunday, the 12th September, 1686/4th. Zil. Q., the fort was captured by 'Ālamgir, and all the people of the country, high and low alike, were glorified by coming under the Emperor's rule. The banners of Islam, which had been turned upside down in this country for a long time, again uplifted their heads. From every side of the earth the cry "Truth came and falsehood vanished" rose to the vault of the sky.

The Emperor graciously [280] accepted the prayer of Sikandar, who thus escaped the imperial wrath (for his misdeeds.) He was granted an interview in the Public Audience-hall, and presented with a special robe, a jewelled dagger with pearl *'ilāqa* and *phul katāra* worth 700 rupees, a pearl necklace with emerald pendant worth 13,000 rupees, a jewelled *kalgi,* and a jewelled *'asā.* He was given the title of Sikandar Khan and an annual pension of one lakh of rupees. A tent was fitted up for his residence within the *gulālbār,* and supplied with all necessary articles. Sikandar Bey, who held the title of Sikandar Khan, had the letter *alif* added to his name (*i.e.,* became Iskandar Khan). 'Abdur Rauf and Sharza came to interview, each receiving a robe, a sword, a jewelled dagger with pearl *'ilāqa,* a horse with gold *sāz,* an elephant with silver *sāz,* and the rank of 6-*hazāri* (same tr.). The first was entitled Dilir Khan, the second Rustam Khan. To Mahābat Khan, Sharif-ul-mulk, Mukhtār Khan and Sarāfrāz Khan elephants were presented, to Qalich Khan a dagger and a horse, to Lutfullah Khan and Ghaznafar Khan banner and *tugh,* to Saf Shikan Khan kettledrums, to Himmat Khan a sword with jewelled *sāz,* to Qamruddin Khan a jewelled dagger. [281] The Emperor in his presence graciously permitted Umdat-ul-mulk Āsad Khan to sit cross-legged on a cushion. Khwāja Wafā, dārogha of the *sukh-sajyā-khānah* (cosy bed) carried to him a *masnad,* a gold-woven sofa, (*takia-gāh*) and a *suzani* ornamented with gold-embroidered figures, and received (from the Khan) a robe and 1,000 rupees. The Emperor permitted him to keep the money.

Hasan 'Ali Khan Bahādur 'Alamgirshāhi died of severe illness. He was a matchless hero and commander, unique in benevolence to all, truthfulness of speech, and goodness of action. His sons, Muhammad Muqim and Khairullah, received robes. Mahābat Khan became Subahdār of Berār *vice* the deceased, and was presented with a robe, a steel coat of armour (*zarah*), a helmet, *rāk shalwār* (trousers) and *du-balgha*. Muhammad Sādiq became his deputy.

On Sunday the 19th September/11th Zil. Q., the Emperor's tent was moved from Rasulpur to the tank half a *kos* from the fort and opposite the gate of Ālapur. That day he rode out to view the citadel, the buildings and outer breastwork of the city-wall. On Friday the 17th Sept./9th Zil. Q., Āshraf Khan, Mir Bakhshi, died; with him withered the rose in the garden of correct understanding and rapid writing. Ruhullah Khan became First Bakhshi *vice* him, and Bahramand Khan Second Bakhshi *vice* Ruhullah, while Bahramand was succeeded by Kāmgār Khan as dārogha of ghusalkhānah; Kāmgār's place of First Mir Tuzuk was taken by Qāsim Khan. [282] Mourning robes were conferred on Muhammad Husain and Muhammad Bāqr, brother's sons of Āshraf Khan. In the night of 25th September/17th Zil.Q., the Emperor summoned Sikandar to his presence, kindly requested him to sit down, and presented him with a diamond *sarpech* and three packets of betel-leaf. * * * Ruhullah Khan was appointed nāzim of Bijapur, which was now named *Dār-ul-Zafar,* and he was made a 5-*hazāri* (4,000 tr.) by an increment of a *hazāri zāt* and troopers. 'Azizullah Khan became qiladār, Muhammad Raf'i diwān, S'ādat Khan bakhshi and news-writer, Siddi Ibrāhim kotwāl and faujdār, Hāji Muqim darogha of artillery, Zain-ul-'Ābidin and Muhammad J'afar dārogha and āmin of *dāgh and tashīh,* Ābul Barkāt Qāzi, Muhammad Āfzal censor (of the newly conquered province). On Thursday, the 14th October/6th Zil. H. Sikandar Khan got a present of 10,000 rupees. Khānahzād Khan was sent towards Miraj. Himmat Khan Bahādur son of Khan Jahān Bahādur was made Subahdār of Allahabad; he was a 2½-*hazāri* (2,200 tr.) and received eighty lakhs of *dām* as in'ām. Kifāyet Khan Hātim was sent towards Sagar for settling the new territory, his son-in-law J'afar accompanying him as the diwān of that mahal. [283] The Khan got an elephant. Ikhlāskesh became *pesh-dast* of the Mir Bakhshi *vice* Yār 'Ali Beg, who became *peshdast* of the second bakhshi. Raja Anup Singh became faujdār and qiladār of Sagar. 'Abdul Wāhid Khan was sent to the new territory; Qādirdād Khan became qiladār of Miraj; Qāsim Khan was sent towards Bāsavapatan, and Shaikh Chānd was sent as qiladār of that place. On Saturday, the 23rd October/15th Zil. H., 150 mohars were presented to sixteen men of the family of Sikandar Khan, the fingers of whose left hand had been cut off and who had thus been excluded from the succession according to the agreement of their grandfathers; these men were ordered to stay at Sholāpur with their children and families, stipends being granted to each. Sipahdār Khan, son of Khan Jahān Bahādur became Subahdār of Lahore *vice* Mukarram Khan. 'Itiqād Khan was detached to punish the force sent by Sambhā, which had spread near Mangalbedā and was presented with a jewelled crest (*kalgi*) with *par-khānah* of heron's feather.

RETURN OF THE EMPEROR FROM BIJAPUR TO SHOLĀPUR

On Saturday, the 30th October, 1686/22nd Zil. H., the Emperor left Bijapur [284] and reached Sholapur, on Tuesday, the 2nd November/25th Zil. H. He ordered Sikandar Khan to be brought with the cortege of the ladies of the imperial harem, and his māhi-marātib, umbrella and other insignia of kingship to be deposited in the store-room. That day Firuz Jang was sent to capture fort Ibrāhimgarh in Haidarābād, and presented with a special robe and an elephant. The officers appointed to the army of Firuz Jang, Dilir Khan, Sharza Khan, Jamshid Khan, Māluji, Gopāl Rao, Kamāluddin Khan, Rāo Dalpat, Saf Shikan Khan, Āqā 'Ali Khan, 'Abdul Qādir Khan, Jahāngir Quli Khan, Safi Khan, Udwat Singh Bhadauriya, Sarbarāh Khan (slave) and other officers, high and low, were rewarded with robes, jewels, horses, elephants, promotions, titles, etc. On Saturday, the 6th November, 1686/29th Zil. H., the Emperor visited the fort of Sholāpur. On Sunday, the 21st November/15th Muharram, Bidār Bakht was married to the daughter of Mukhtār Khan, Qāzi 'Abdullah pronounced the *nikāh*. The settlement on the bride was two lakhs of rupees. The Shāhzādah was presented by his grandfather with a robe, a ruby *sarpech,* an *arsi,* a pearl necklace, an *ek-lari,* eight rings, one lakh of rupees, two horses and an elephant. [285] The bride received a ring, a pearl necklace, and a jewelled bracelet (*anant*). On Monday, the 22nd November/16th Muharram, 'Ali Āqa,* envoy of the Sharif

* Named Ahmad Āqā on p. 271.

of Mecca, after being given a robe, a dagger, a horse and 3000 rupees, was permitted to depart. 'Aisha, daughter of Sikandar Khan was presented with a cap with pearls attached. Mir 'Abdul Karim became āmin of the seven *chaukis* for the second time.

THE EMPEROR MARCHES FROM SHOLAPUR TOWARDS HAIDARĀBĀD

Ābul Hasan, the ruler of Haidarābād, was stupid and sunk in sinful lust; misled by his evil fortune, he shut his eyes to the sins punishable in the next world, and made the vagabond Hindus the managers and administrators of the affairs of his State, and gave currency to the rites of that accursed race. And, those travellers in the wrong path of futile wandering and ignorance, those carrion-eating demons (*ghul*) of the wilderness, (namely) the Persians (*i.e.*, Shias) with the support of that worthless sect (the Hindus) began to practise there publicly all kinds of shameful sins. No respect was left for Islam and its adherents; mosques were without splendour, while idol-temples flourished; the requisites of canonical practice remained closed under bolts, while the gates of irreligious practices (*bida't*) were flung open. In the excess of his intoxication with the wine of negligence, Ābul Hasan did not distinguish the night from the day; thanks to his addiction to evil company and his badness of aims, he refused to prefer Faith to Infidelity. In the many kinds of injury that the hellish Sambhā had inflicted on worshippers of the True God, Ābul Hasan became his helper and ally. On seeing a single (really) unsubstantial frown and on hearing one vain threat (from that Marātha king), what vast sums did he not send to that enemy, and simply through his meanness of spirit and cowardice kept himself safe from plunder by that man? [286]

This Emperor of Emperors is the asylum of Muslims. He honours none but the people of the true Faith; he injures none but the infidels and heretics (*āhal-i-bid'at*); the sharpness of his sword has cleansed the face of the earth from the filth of the blood of disturbers; although he has conquered with his bright sword strong forts, the spring-breeze alone can* open the buds in the garden. Our Emperor's zeal

---

* I have omitted the negative particle of the text, in order to make sense of the passage.

for the Faith and his delicate sense of honour as a master of the world, persuaded him that, inspite of his wielding a world-conquering sword, he ought first of all, by following the generous policy of admonition and direction, try to remove the cotton-wool of heedlessness stuffing the ears of Ābul Hasan, and open the gates of entrance into the Islamic land of right guidance before the face of that unlucky man. His Majesty repeatedly sent messages full of advice and good counsel to that wretched fellow urging him to abandon his alliance with the infernal infidel enemies (of Aurangzib and Islam), his vicious attachment to practitioners of irreligious acts (heresy, *bid'a*), and the sins of appointing Brahmans as his ministers (*peshkār*), in giving help (in the form of money and troops) to the hostile misbelievers (*kāfirs*), the promotion of various degrees of prohibited practices [such as drinking wine] and treading the open path of cherishing vain ideas (of independence). The result (of listening to this advice) would be that his innocent subjects would not be helplessly trodden under the feet of the imperial cavalry and he himself would personally remain safe from the tempest of overthrow and humiliation. But as Fortune had deserted him, Ruin instigated him (to refuse). He gave his house up to plunder (at Haidarābād) by the army of Prince Muhammad Mu'azzam, who had been appointed to guide him to the right path of submission. At that time, Ābul Hasan by procrastination, *i.e.*, by deceiving the Prince with promises and flattery and clouding his intellect with many kinds of fraud and spells, secured his release from the grasp of the Prince, and made the increase of his treasure [287] and troops and the strengthening of the four walls of his fort (Golkonda) the veil over the eyes of his knowledge and the lock on his pardon-begging tongue.

Therefore the Emperor had no help but to act according to the verses :—

> You should fondle the heads of asses with the stick in your hand,
> When they set their refractory steps outside the right path.

On Sunday, the 5th December, 1686/29th Muharram, the Emperor started from Sholāpur to visit the tomb of Mir Sayyid Muhammad Gisudarāz at Āhsanābād Gulbargā,

He repeatedly visited the holy place. Twenty thousand rupees were presented to the representatives of the holy saint and the residents including the hermits and beggars. After passing a week there, the camp moved towards Zafarābād Bidar, where it stayed for twenty days, in the vain hope that Ābul Hasan would come to his senses. But the latter was not guided by Providence to such good fortune. Therefore at last on Friday, the 14th January, 1687/10th Rabi. A., the Emperor mounted his horse to punish that luckless man. When Ābul Hasan heard of it, he in terror of the imperial army, could think of no place of refuge save his fort. So he shut himself up in it and remained bewildered with his face to the wall, like a picture, lips despairing of laughter, eyes full of tears, head vacant of sense, tongue speechless. At this time, [288] when the day of his destruction had drawn near, he wished to submit and make a new protestation of fidelity * * *. The Emperor did not assent to his prayers : the only reply given to him was the sword. The Emperor advanced and then halted two stages from Haidarābād. Firuz Jang who had been sent from Bijapur to conquer Ibrāhimgarh, hastened to the Court by way of Haidarābād after accomplishing his task. Despatches from him were now received announcing that he had arrived at and taken possession of the city of Haidarābād, for His Majesty. But thanks to the power of the fortune of 'Ālamgir, the enemy, inspite of their countless number and incalculable wealth were struck with such terror that during the advance of the imperial army, no human being appeared either before the Emperor's own force or the army of Firuz Jang.

On Friday, the 28th January 1687/24th Rabi. A., the Emperor ordered the enemy's army which had assembled at the foot of the fort [289] like swarms of ants and flies around a carrion or on a lump of sugar, to be driven away. The imperialists made great efforts, in carrying out the command. As they say, "The wind came and the gnats fled", the enemy fled, leaving their property, children and families in the hands of the imperialists. Qalich Khan galloped up to the fort and wanted to enter it immediately. But God had willed it otherwise. * * * A *zamburak* ball hit him on the shoulder-blade and save Lutfullah Khan who had heroically accompanied him in this bold enterprise, none advanced to aid him. So the Khan had to return on horse-back from that terrible place of slaughter, and reached his own camp (*dāira*). By the Emperor's command 'Umdat-ul-mulk went to visit him in his sickness. At that time the surgeons were extracting the splinters of bones from his shoulder-blade, and he was sitting composedly and talking with the persons present without any contraction of the muscles of his forehead, and was sipping coffee with the other hand. He remarked, "I have got an admirable stitcher! "Although the surgeons and physicians, by command, employed all sorts of remedies [290], he died after three days. The Emperor bestowed robes and other favours on Firuz Jang Bahādur and other sons of the deceased and on Siādat Khan.

On Monday, the 7th February, 1687/4th Rabi. S., orders were issued for digging trenches. Although guns, muskets, and rockets were fired incessantly day and night from the fort, which seemed as if made of fire, the heroes of the imperial army under the leadership of Saf Shikan Khan recked not being burnt or slain, but carried the trenches to the foot of the ditch in the space of one month. This work, which usually takes years, was finished in a twinkle of the eye. Heavy guns were mounted opposite the fort, the pillars of which were demolished by the fire of their guns, but success remained distant. Saf Shikan Khan, having constructed a lofty gun-platform raised it up to the height of the turret of the fort and mounted guns on it, yet owing to his spite and enmity with Firuz Jang, he withdrew his hand from the work and resigned. Salābat Khan became Mir Ātish *vice* him. [291] He too could not discharge the duty as it should have been and resigned. Sayyid Ghairat ('Izzat) Khan succeeded him. At midnight owing to the neglect and self-will of the chiefs, the enemy fell upon the raised battery, spoiled the gun, bound and carried off ('Izzat) Ghairat Khan, Sarbarāh Khan (a slave), and a party that had fallen into their hands. Saf Shikan Khan was punished with removal from mansab and imprisonment. Salābat Khan was again appointed Mir Ātish. Lutfullah Khan and the party of the khās chauki and other eager soldiers were appointed to guard the raised battery. The Khan stayed for three days in the middle of the river which flows at the foot of the fort, when another force arrived and expelled the enemy and firmly established the battery. After two days Ābul Hasan sent back 'Izzat Khan and others with robes. They came by the way of the battery. But owing to the severity of the rains and this unseasonable delay, much of the battery was ruined. Saf Shikan Khan guaranteed that in a short time he would construct batteries up to the turret by the side of another bastion; he was released and did what he had promised.

At this time owing to excess of rain the river Manjerā raged in flood. No provision could come from the neighbourhood. Famine prevailed; wheat, pulse and rice disappeared. [292] Cries of grief at the disappearance of grain rose from the famished on all sides of the camp. Of the men of Haidarābād, not a soul remained alive; houses, river and plain became filled with the dead. The same was the condition of the camp. At night piles of the dead were formed round the Emperor's quarters. Daily sweepers dragged them and flung them on the bank of the river from sunrise to sunset. The same thing happened every day and night. The survivors did not hesitate to eat the carrion of men and animals. *Kos* after *kos* the eye fell only on mounds of corpses. The incessant rain melted away the flesh and the skin; otherwise the putrid air would have finished the business of the survivors. After some months when the rains ceased, the white ridges of bones looked from a distance like hillocks of snow. Through the grace of God to the survivors, the rains abated, the violence of the river ceased, and provisions came from the surrounding country. In the place of Sardār Khan, *karori-ganj*, Sayyid Sharif Khan, son of Mir Sayyid Muhammad Qanauji, the spiritual guide of Shāh Jahān, and an honest, able and accomplished man, was appointed. Thanks to the gracious aim of the Emperor, the custodian of the livelihood of the people, the scarcity was removed, and cheapness restored.

IMPRISONMENT OF PRINCE MUHAMMAD MU'AZZAM

* * * [293] The Prince, in spite of his excellent understanding, reason and imagination, was so misled by his bad companions and evil counsellors that the Emperor apprehended from him mischief and disloyalty, which was likely to cause affliction to the Prince himself and disgust to the Emperor's mind. For some time he overlooked the Prince's conduct, not wishing such a scandal to be made public. But when the Bijapur undertaking was thrown into confusion, some men who used to convey secretly messages to Sikandar in the fort, were captured and executed. On Saturday, the 28th August 1686/18th Shawwal, others

of his disloyal servants *viz.,* Mumin Khan dārogha of artillery, 'Aziz Afghān, Multafat Khan the second bakhshi, and Brindāban Purfan (the cunning) were ordered to be expelled from the camp. The lamp of wisdom and far-sightedness had been extinguished in the Prince's council by all this darkness of evil fortune (*i.e.,* evil counsellors). And in conducting the war against Haidarābād, he was overcome by the fraudulent seductions of the foolish Ābul Hasan. [294] Gradually the letters which used to be sent into the fort of Golkonda through the medium of the secret-writer of the trenches, fell into Firuz Jang's hands. And other signs of disloyalty bore witness to the truth of the matter. One night the Khan went from his lodgings to the Emperor and showed the letters, and convinced the Emperor of the Prince's self-will, and various acts of disobedience and disloyalty. The Emperor summoned Hayāt Khan, younger brother of Ihtamām Khan, who was the dārogha of the Prince's diwān-i-khās, and said, "Carry this order to the Prince, Shaikh Nizām Haidarābādi wants to make a night-attack on the army to-night; send your men to bar the way of the enemy. As your men will go there, Ihtamām Khan will remain round your tent (as a guard)." The necessary order was issued to Ihtamām Khan. It was done. Next day the Prince with his sons Muhammad Mu'izzuddin and Muhammad 'Azim was brought to the Emperor, who was sitting in the Hall of Audience. After the Prince had come and sat down for some time, the Emperor said, "I have spoken to Āsad Khan and Bahramand Khan about certain matters. Hold conference with them in the prayer-room." The three princes went, willy nilly. They were stripped of their arms, and detained there while a tent was being pitched (for them), and then they were taken to the tent. The Emperor rose from the Court and went to the harem by way of the *deorhi* of the *khās parastār.* Crying "alas! alas!" he struck his hands on the two knees and continued saying, "I have razed to the ground the work of forty years!" [295] In short, through the exertions of Ihtamām Khan guards were posted round (the Prince's camp.) The imperial clerks confiscated the goods and slaves of the Prince's household, in one twinkle of the eye, and as it were carried a drop of water to the ocean. Ihtamām Khan was a *hazāri;* he now got the title of Sardār Khan and the increment of 500. His son Hamiduddin, who was a 2-*sadi,* received an increment of 2-*sadi* (50 tr.).

In the course of a long period, mines were run by Jamshid Khan, treasure (*māl*) was brought by 'Abul Wāhid Khan; the Emperor went to the quarters of Firuz Jang Khan by way of the old raised battery; high officers were appointed to make the assault; they worked hard all day. Firuz Jang Khān Bahādur and Rustam Khan were wounded, many of the bold fighters were slain at the end of the day. Kām Bakhsh was sent with 'Umdat-ul-mulk Āsad Khan (as reinforcement); the men could not advance one inch, owing to the shower of musket bullets, rockets, *chādar* and *huqqa* (bombs) without being slain or wounded. But still the object was not gained. After spending the night in the quarters of Firuz Jang, the Emperor returned to the camp at early dawn without ceremony. Various other plans were tried; immense wealth was spent. The godless atheists, in greed of gain, co-operated with the enemy and played their juggling tricks. Some avaricious traitors joined him and after at first getting hopes from him, (at last) went to hell through his deception. Some by sending in grain [296] caused their own perdition and met with the fate of ungrateful persons. The siege was protracted. The Emperor decided that a fort of wood and mud should be built round the fort of Golkonda. In a short time it was completed, and guards were placed at the gates, ingress and egress being forbidden except on producing pass-ports. By this time Firuz Jang Khan recovered from his wound and had audience, receiving a robe, a *zarah*, a special *jahalam*, and a jewelled mace. A robe was presented to the wounded Rustam Khan; Bahrām Khan, son of Mahābat Khan deceased, was killed by a cannon-ball. A mourning robe was given to his brother Farjām. Jān Nisār Khan's brother was slain, and for this reason favours were conferred on the Khan. Shujā'et Khan, brother of Saf Shikan Khan, Mir Ābul-mu'ala, bakhshi of the army of Firuz Jang Khan, Ekkatāz Khan, Suhrāb Khan, Muhammad Hākim and other wounded and scorched soldiers recovered through the Emperor's gifts.

On Saturday, the 28th May, 1687/26th Rajab, Shaikh Nizām, the best servant of Ābul Hasan, who commanded the force outside the fort-wall, came to interview the Emperor, presented 500 mohars and 1,000 rupees, and received the title of Muqarrab Khan, the rank of 6-*hazāri* (5,000 tr.) a special robe, a sword, a dagger with pearl *'ilāqa*, a jewelled shield, a banner, kettledrums, 100,000 rupees in cash, twenty Arab [297] 'Irāqi, Turki and Cutchi horses, and two elephants. Malik Munawwar, Shaikh Lād, Shaikh 'Abdullah and his sons, and some of his relatives got high titles, ranks,—none less than 4-*hazāri*,—robes, banners, kettledrums, horses, and elephants.

Āsuji Deccani, who was Sambhā's qiladār of Sālhir, had audience, receiving a robe, a standard, a *tugh*, kettledrums, a horse, an elephant, and 20,000 rupees. Sarbuland Khan brother of Sarfarāz Khan was given a standard, a *tugh*, and kettledrums. Mānkoji, Sambhā's qiladār of Sāngola had audience after the capture of this fort and received a robe and the rank of 2-*hazāri* (1000 tr.).

On Friday, the 20th May/18th Rajab, Muhammad 'Ali Khan, Khān-i-sāmān, died. He was noble-minded and generous; everybody who went to him had his wish fulfilled. He had rectitude, piety, honesty, truthfulness, and sagacity. Kāmgār Khan got his post, and was succeeded by 'Itiqād Khan as dārogha of the ghusalkhānah, near the Emperor's person. Iftikhār Khan, son of Sharif-ul-mulk Haidarābādi, sister's son of Ābul Hasan, had audience, receiving a robe and the rank of 3-*hazāri* (1000 tr.). Sharif Khan, who was appointed karori-ganj of the camp and collector of jazia for the four subahs of the Deccan, was ordered to tour in the subahs, in order to see that the jazia was collected according to the rules of the Holy Law. [298] Mir 'Abdul Karim, in addition to his own duties, became deputy of the Khan, in the post of karori-ganj. Sharif-ul-mulk died on Saturday, the 25th June, 1687/24th Shaban. Robes were presented to his sons.

CHAPTER XXXI.

31st year of the reign (1098 A.H.)

1st July, 1687—19th June, 1688.

* * * *

On Thursday, the 7th July/7th Ramzan, the Emperor rode out to inspect the trenches and the raised battery of Saf Shikan Khan which had been carried in a short space of time up to the height of the turret of the fort a second time. For two hours the Emperor viewed the condition of the fort on foot. Muhammad 'Āzam Shāh, who had started to punish the rebels of Hindustan before the Emperor set out from Sholāpur, and had reached Burhānpur, and [299] Bakhshi-ul-mulk Ruhullah Khan, who had been engaged in administering the disordered subah of Bijapur, both reached the Presence by command on Sunday the 10th July/10th Ramzan. The Prince was placed in command of the operations against the fort.

CAPTURE OF GOLKONDA FORT.

At midnight, on Wednesday, the 21st September/24th Zil. Q., the Bakhshi-ul-mulk with a party of heroes including Bahādur Khan, and others on the look-out for an opportunity, was walking round the fort, when through the treachery of Sarāndāz Khān Batni Bijāpuri, who had deserted to the imperial service before the capture of Bijapur, and afterwards joined Ābul Hasan and become his trusted officer, they entered the fort through a back door (*khirki*) close to the old entrenchment. The Prince who was staying at the river that flows at the foot of the fort in order to support this corps, now reached the entrenchment and struck up the music of victory. The Bakhshi-ul-mulk reached the haveli of Ābul Hasan, and in spite of the frantic opposition of him and his companions, captured and brought him away to the presence of the Prince. 'Abdul Wali, son of Shaikh 'Abdus-samad J'afar Khani, munshi of the [300] Emperor presented a quatrain embodying the date. * * * Out of his innate graciousness 'Āzam Shāh refrained from ordering this doomed man to be given the due meed of his acts, but, with the Emperor's permission brought him to his (the Prince's) own tent. At the end of the same day, he took him to the Emperor's quarters. That captive in the prison of error, after being freed from the terror which filled his heart, was lodged in a tent pitched for him; he fell under the Emperor's gracious indifference instead of wrath. * * *

Thank God that such a strong fort was captured in the space of eight months and a few days. What a marvel that after one year's interval, in the same month two forts whose fall had not been previously imagined as possible were captured. Mir 'Abdul Karim found out the date of this wonderful conquest in the words "Conquest of the fort of Golkonda, God bless it!" and was praised for it.

I shall now describe the strength of this fort, the charms of this city, and the climate of this country. In former times Golkonda [301] was called Mangal; its Raja was named Dev Rai. After him it was captured by the Bahmanis. After the fall of the Bahmani dynasty, the fort was taken possession of by 'Ali Naqi Qutbul-mulk, a *ghulām* of Sultān Mahmud Bahmani, who was in charge of it. The fort is situated on a hill, the summit of which pierces the armour of the sky like the blade of a sword. The celestials meet the terrestrials here. None but 'Ālamgir ever conquered this fort. On no side has it any ledge that might supply a handle for the noose of the fancy of capturing it to raise itself. But it had a hillock which might have helped a very great general to attack it successfully. Before his accession to the throne when Aurangzib invaded this country but afterwards graciously paradoned 'Abdullah Qutb-ul-mulk, he, in the thought that Aurangzib might return, built a strong fort round this hillock and included it within the fort of Golkonda, and thus gained security. * * *

The city of Haidarābād is situated two *kos* from the fort of Golkonda; it was founded by Muhammad Quli Qutb-ul-mulk, [302] who was infatuated by the courtezan Bhāgmati and named the city Bhāgnagar after her. Afterwards it got its present name. Now that it has been annexed to the Empire, turned into an additional subah of the Deccan, it has been named *Dār-ul-jihād* Haidarābād. It is a very pleasant place, delightful to the body and the mind.

The cultivated area is more extensive than fancy can picture, the houses higher than one can imagine; the air is so moist, the fountains so pure and flowing, and the verdure so fresh that you may think that the flowers and herbs of the land have the colour of emerald and ruby. * * *

It would verily require another volume to describe in detail the coming of the Haidarābādis to the imperial Court, their gaining of mansabs from seven *hazāri* to 5-*sadi*, and the admission into the imperial service of professional men, men of skill, and artisans of every kind.

On Monday the 26th September/29th Zil. Q., Muhammad Kām Bakhsh was made subahdār of Berār. He had been a 10-*hazāri* (5,000 tr.), and now received an increment of 5,000 tr. 'Umdat-ul-mulk Āsad Khan and Firuz Khan each received an increment of a *hazār* tr. and became a 7-*hazāri* (same tr.). Mahābat Khan was promoted by the addition of a *hazār zāt* (1000 tr.). His grandson [303] Muhammad Mansur, newly come from Persia (*vilāyet*), had audience and received the title of Mukarramat Khan and the rank of 1½-*hazāri* (1000 tr.). 'Abdullah, adopted son (*khānda*) of Ābul Hasan got the rank of 4-*hazāri* (same tr.). Lutfullah Khan was a 2-*hazāri* (1000 tr.) and now got an increment of 200 troopers. Muhammad Yār Khan got an increment of 5-*sadi* and became a 2-*hazāri* (300 tr.). Mir Muhammad Āmin son of Mir Bahāuddin, brother's son to Qalich Khan deceased, came to the imperial Court after his father had been slain in Turān on the suspicion of being in league with Ānusha Khan, the king of Urganj, who was at war with his own father-in-law 'Abdul 'Aziz Khan, king of Bukhārā, and was graciously favoured with the title of Khan and the rank of 2-*hazāri* (1,000 tr.). Mukhlis Khan, son of Saf Shikan Khan, who was acting as his father's deputy in the dāroghaship of artillery, got the post for himself with an increment of 200 tr. making him a *hazāri* (300 tr.). 'Ināyetullah, mushrif of the jewellery department, a 4-*sadi* (50 tr.), got an increment of 10 troopers. Yār 'Ali Beg, a 4-*sadi* (40 tr.) got an increment of 15 troopers. Shukrullah Khan, son-in-law of 'Āqil Khan, was appointed faujdār of the environs of Haidarābād *vice* Siddi Yahya. [304] He was a 5-*sadi* (same tr.), and now got an increment of a *hazār* troopers. Mir 'Abdul Karim was appointed dārogha of fines. Lutfullah Khan became dārogha of the servants of Muhammad Mu'azzam, each of whom now got a mansab, according to his position and rank, in the

Emperor's establishment. The depressed Khidmat Khan was appointed nāzir *vice* Sardār Khan, who became dārogha of filkhānah *vice* Mu'ataqad Khan. Muhammad Matlab became a Khan.

CONQUEST OF THE LAND OF SAGAR.

When the Emperor's mind was freed from the tasks of occupying the spacious kingdom of Haidarābād, taking possession of all its forts, sending administrators and regulators on all sides and granting interviews and posts to the Haidarābādi officers, he sent a large army under Khānahzād Khan, son of Ruhullah Khan, against the land of Sagar. This country is situated between Bijapur and Haidarābād; and Pam* Nāyak of tribe of Dheḍh is its infamous ruler. Fortune likes to favour the mean and the servile; and so this utterly worthless infidel, lower than the meanest of tribes in every generation from grandfather to father, uplifted his [305] arrogant head in authority over this country. By reason of his commanding 12,000 tr. and one lakh of infantry and his possessing some strong forts, especially the place of his residence, which was one of the famous strongholds of the time, he held up his head as the equal of the kings of Bijapur and Haidarābād. None could extirpate him. Nay more, Muslims adoring him as a leader considered him as their mediator and defender in evil days, so that at the siege of Bijapur he had the audacity to send 6,000 fighting footmen, with provisions carried on the head, who were slain by Firuz Jang, as has been already narrated. And also at the siege of Golkonda he had repeatedly aided the Ḥaidarābādis and thereby made his own downfall sure.

Khānahzād Khan was instructed that if this misguided man agreed to visit the Emperor he should not take steps to desolate his country or slay and imprison his subjects, otherwise he should serve him right. The Khan hastened to the country and wakened him from the sleep of pride, by sending the imperial order to him. As the people of his country were not destined for ruin, nor were his wealth and household effects doomed to destruction, in spite of his not

* The text writes the name variously on different pages—Padam, p. 239, Pid, pp. 264, 304 and 305. The correct name is Pam (*vide* my *History of Aurangzib*, Vol. V, Ch. 56, § 2).

believing in a Day of Judgment, he on receiving the imperial message and anticipating a vast army, sent word to say that he would surrender his kingdom to the King of Kings and submit to the Emperor. And so his effects were saved from destruction [306], and none of his men was killed. According to the Emperor's instructions, the Khan guarded his family and did not permit a blade of grass to be destroyed. He came out of the fort and met the Khan; and on Monday, the 28th November, 1687/2nd Safar, the fort bowed to the Muslim leaders. In a place where since the far-off foundation of the world none had been able to utter the cry of prayer (*namāz*), the Musalmāni drum was so loudly beaten that it deafened the ears of false believers. The cry "Islam is true, infidelity is false" rolled up to the dome of the sky, and strengthened the spirits of the Islamites. The Khan after appointing a defender of the fort and regulating and taking possession of the neighbourhood, came to the Court with the Nāyak, and was properly rewarded. His father had served well at the siege of Golkonda, and now the son, too, showed no less ability in capturing Sagar. Pām Nāyak was a strange creature, of an uncouth shape. * * * [*Verses*]:

> Night has gone into mourning at being taken for his emblem.
> The day has turned into night on account of the bulk of this black cloud.
> Bears and pigs would have felt deeply disgraced if likened to him.
> Even the washer of the dead was disgusted at the sight of him.

[307] I do not know how in the dark recess of his heart this light flashed that he should acquire the fortune of seeing the Emperor. On Tuesday, the 27th December, 1687/2nd Rabi. A., the Emperor granted him an interview and honoured him by giving him a place to stand far above his condition. After attending the Court for five or six days he suddenly set off to visit hell. Verse:—

"It is better that such a bad-liver should be dead."

His sons and relatives were given proper mansabs. His Majesty ordered the country of Sagar to be called *Nasratābād*. The land is delightful, fresh, and fertile. * * *

THE EMPEROR'S RETURN FROM HAIDARĀBĀD TO BIJAPUR

As the only work agreeable to the Emperor was to regulate the world and train mankind, and he never desired to seek bodily repose from this task of conquering countries, therefore, inspite of the agreeableness of the climate of Haidarābād, [308] he decided to march to those cities his stay at which would lead to the most satisfactory conclusion of the affairs of the empire, especially to inflict proper punishment on the militant and unclean infidel Sambhā, who had formed a protective alliance with those two lost travellers in the wrong path, namely Sikandar and Ābul Hasan, and who by the assertion of this false claim left these two rulers in the enjoyment of no trust or respect of the public.

On Wednesday, the 25th January, 1688/1st Rabi. S., the Emperor started for Bijapur. At an auspicious hour Khān Bahādur Firuz Jang was appointed to capture the fort of Ādoni from Mas'aud Habshi, a slave (*ghulām*) of the father of Sikandar, who during the confusion in the government of this dynasty became the supreme head of affairs, and ungratefully left to his master's son nothing save the name of king and carried off and stored in that strong fort the chief treasures, buried hoards, choice articles, and precious jewels. 25,000 tr. were appointed to accompany the Khan Bahādur. Muhammad 'Āzam, after being variously favoured, was sent to extirpate Sambhā; 40,000 experienced tr. followed him. On Tuesday, the 7th February/14th Rabi. S., the Emperor reached [309] Zafarābād Bidar, and lodged on the bank of the tank of Kamthānah. Here Ābul Hasan, who had never during his fifteen years of reign travelled farther than from the city of Haidarābād to Muhammadnagar, one *kos* distant, and to whom this daily riding (with the Emperor) was very painful, begged permission to take to a life of retirement. The Emperor ordered Jān-sipār Khan to convey him to Daulatābād, and the officers to get ready for him such articles of bed and board as are indispensable to pampered worldlings of weak faith. Fifty thousand rupees a year was fixed for his needs. What marvellous kindness was it on the part of His Majesty to nurse such a felon in the cradle of ease and comfort and pardon his sins!

It would be no exaggeration to call that tank the Tigris. Whosoever sits on the embankment on its northern side, gives repose to his own life. Nowhere are the air and water better than here. The sown fields about this blessed water are green; the cultivators are not beholden to the rain-clouds. They scatter the seeds one year, and reap the harvest for some years after. Here the great saint Khwāja Muhammad Y'aqub Joibāri left the caravanserai of life. The Emperor [310] had great kindness for the deceased. He conferred favours on his relatives and sent his corpse to his 'home' to be buried in the vault of his forefathers.

After three days' halt here the army again marched. On Saturday, the 25th February/3rd Jamad. A., the Emperor reached the outskirts of Gulbarga, and made a pilgrimage to the tomb of Mir Sayyid Muhammad Gisudarāz, removing the veil of poverty from the heads of the residents of that blessed place. After seven days' halt the army resumed the march towards Bijapur. On Thursday, the 15th March, 1688/22nd Jamad. A., the Emperor reached that city. All kinds of inhabitants, faqirs, and hermits, who had fallen into want through the ruin of the city and its environs, were relieved by the Emperor's charity. * * * [311]

CHAPTER XXXII

32ND YEAR OF THE REIGN:

20th June, 1688—8th June, 1689

* * * *

I have no space to mention the numberless strong forts which were conquered by the imperial officers during this time. As the conclusion of the affair of the rebel Rajarām Jāt under the command of Muhammad Bidār Bakht and the supervision of Khan Jahān Bahādur Zafar Jang and other heroes, was a grand event, and as great feats were performed, much activity displayed and large sums spent in it, I ought to narrate a little of it. On Saturday, the 11th August/3rd Shawwal, the Emperor learnt from the news-writers of this army that the infernal dog had gone to hell through a gun-shot, on Wednesday the 4th July/15th Ramzan; the neighbourhood had been cleared of the rebel infidels, and vast multitudes of people were praising and blessing the Emperor for giving them peace. [312] On the 5th September, 1688/19th Zil. Q., the rebel's head was brought to the Emperor.

Kāmgār Khan was married to the daughter of Sayyid Muzaffar Haidarabadi, and received from the Emperor a robe, a horse, and a *sahra* worth 10,000 rupees. I'timād Khan, brother's son of 'Alā-ul-mulk Fāzil Khan received the post of Khān-i-sāmān of the Emperor's household *vice* Kāmgār Khan, and an increment of 500 *zāt* (100 tr.) making him a 2-*hazāri* (400 tr.), a *kalgi* and *'asā* of jasper. Mirzā Mu'izz got the title of Musavi Khan and the post of daftar-dār-i-tan *vice* him. Khwāja 'Abdur Rahim Khan became bayutāt *vice* Muhasan Khan, Mu'atamad Khan succeeded him as darogha of dāgh and tashihā. I'tiqād Khan on the death of his wife (the daughter of Āmir-ul-umāra Shāista Khan) received a special robe and a dagger. Ābul Hasan Haidarabadi had three daughters: by the imperial command the first was married to Sikandar Bijapuri, the second to Muhammad 'Umar son of Shaikh Muhammad Naqshband of Sirhind, the third, to 'Umdat-ul-mulk Āsad Khan's [313] son 'Ināyet Khan who received a robe, a horse, an elephant, and a *sahra*. Mukhlis Khan, Mir Ātish, was sent to bring the water of the river Krishnā to the city of Bijapur, by an aqueduct and was presented with a dagger.

Fazl 'Ali, son of that Murshid Quli Khan who was a servant of the days of prince-hood, became a Khan and news-writer of the *kachari* of the High Diwān. When conferring the title the Emperor said "Ask him if he wants to have 'Khan' added to his name or his father's title." The man for certain reasons (of his own) chose the title of Fazl 'Ali Khan. The Emperor said "My parents and I are the sacrifice of 'Āli (*Qurbān-i-'Ali*). Tell this fool, 'Ali is gone, you will be Quli'. Fazl Quli Khan is better." I remember other remarks of His Majesty suited to this subject. A courtier of Indian origin made suit that two house-hold slaves had finished memorizing the *Qurān* and hoped to be permitted to recite it to His Majesty. The Emperor ordered them to be brought to him at night. When they appeared and the courtier said "The sons of so and so are present," His Majesty remarked, "Don't utter the name of a heretic (Shi'a)." The courtier was surprised and said, "I was speaking of so and so." The Emperor replied, "Well, if you don't believe me, ask the names of both." He went out, asked, and reported, "They are called Hasan 'Ali and Husain 'Ali." The Emperor retorted "My parents and I are the sacrifice of 'Ali. What connection have Hindustānis with this name? Through evil desires they are afflicted with friendship for the heretical Shi'as, leave the right path and go astray. May God awaken us from the drowsiness of the negligent!" [314]

Mihrunnisā Begam received permission to go to Delhi. Lutfullah Khan was ordered to escort her. Sardār Khan dārogha of fil-khānah, on getting a robe and an increment of 100 tr., became a 1½-*hazāri* (500 tr.). Sayyid Ābu S'aid, the dismissed qāzi of the camp, died. Mourning robes were presented to his sons Nizāmuddin and Faiyāz-ud-din. * * Saf Shikan Khan became dārogha of 'arz-i-mukarrar *vice* Siādat Khan. Prince Daulat-āfzā died, and by command was buried in the tomb of 'Ali 'Adil Khan Bijapuri. 'Ināyetullah, mushrif of the jewellery-department, became Khān-i-sāmān of the household of Zinat-un-nisā Begam. Lashkar Khan, son of Khan Jahān Shāhjahāni, who had the title of Munawwar Khan was appointed defender of Bijapur. Hamiduddin Khan son of Sardār

Khan, became dārogha of fil-khānah *vice* his father; he was a 5-*sadi*, and now received an increment of 100 troopers.

I shall now write about the victories of Prince 'Āzam Shah and Firuz Jang. The Prince after taking leave of the Emperor for punishing Sambhā turned [315] his attention to the conquest of the fort of Belgaum which was one of the strong forts belonging to Bijapur. In a short time he put the garrison to hard straits by running trenches and bombardment. Those foolish men had set up as their chief a boy, whose father had been governor on behalf of Bijapur but had died a short time before this. When they found their efforts unavailing, and the imperialists firmly determined, they capitulated, and the fort with its dependencies was conquered and named '*Āzam-nagar*.* Through the kind mediation of the Prince, the boy made his bow at Court and received a suitable *mansab*. The Prince returned to Court as it was the season for going into quarters (*chhauni*). Firuz Jang Bahādur who had been engaged in besieging the fort of Ādoni, first invited the [Adilshahi] slave Mas'aud to visit the Emperor, but at last on seeing that the old fool chose the wrong path, he plundered and occupied the prosperous districts of the country, burnt the *wādi*, slew the men who had boldly come out of the fort, ran trenches, fired guns and muskets, and so pressed the besieged hard. [316] At last he came out of the fort with all humility, stating his demands, on the 6th August, 1688/8th Shawwal. The fort was renamed *Imtiāzgarh*.

When Khan Firuz Jang's despatch announcing the conquest arrived, the bearer and Siādat Khan were rewarded with robes; the band played joyous notes; the courtiers made their bow of invoking blessings. The Emperor in his infinite mercy gave the wretch Mas'aud the title of Khan the rank of 7-*hazāri* (same tr.) and the faujdāri and jāgirdāri of Morādābād, and ordered that he should accompany the army of Firuz Jang Khan till he left the Deccan. His sons and relatives were highly favoured. Firuz Jang Khan after taking possession of the materials in the fort and the regulation and occupation of the neighbourhood, reached the court on Monday, the 19th November/5th Safar, and was rewarded for his excellent services. [317] 'Itimād Khan, Khān-i-sāmān, got the title of Fāzil Khan and Mir Husain, son of Āmānat Khan got his father's title.

---

* Printed text reads '*Āzamābād*, but the O.P.L. Ms. reads '*Āzamnagar*.

THE GREAT PLAGUE—MARCH OF THE EMPEROR FROM BIJAPUR TO THE COUNTRY OF SAMBHĀ

Khan Firuz Jang, on his return from the capture of Imtiāzgarh, stayed at Court for a few days and was then sent to extirpate the infidel. The Emperor resolved to march in aid of the Prince. Friday, the 14th December/1st Rabi. A., was chosen as the day for starting, and porters who had gone to distant parganahs were summoned back to the Court.

In the middle of the month of Muharram (16th October —14th November, 1688) a terrible plague broke out and carried off men. The health of the people became impaired and ruined, by declining from their normal condition. Joyous practices ceased. All sat down in mourning. Death wanted to remove the seed of human kind altogether from the world. I cannot say that the great Day of Judgment had come; but this was a day of doom at the power of which great and small alike lost their lives. * * * [318]

A bubo appeared in the armpit or the corner of the thigh; high fever and unconsciousness raged; the treatment of physicians produced no effect. Few men lived through two days; but most died within two or three days. Even those who lived and had lost no dependant, on seeing the prevailing state of things, considered themselves as dead. How fine would it have been if this thought had remained in the mind in times of prosperity! In short, none looked after anybody else; everywhere the cry rose "My own self! my own self!" The half-dead people abstained from all worldly works and affairs and lay in expectation of death every hour. Among the victims were, the Emperor's *parastār,* the old and devoted hand-maid, Aurangābādi-Mahal, Muhammadi Raj, the son of Maharaja Jaswant Singh, who had been brought up in the imperial harem and attained to the age of thirteen years and a high *mansab,* Fāzil Khan Sadr, and many other grandees. The middle class men and the common people, Muslims and infidels, who died cannot be numbered, but are conjectured to have been not less than a lakh. Many were afflicted by disorder of the brain or lost the use of their eyes, tongues and ears. Among the highest, Firuz Jang Bahādur received injury in his eyes. Who spoke or heard anything of the plight of the common people? Historians have not recorded any such havoc in any former age. The oldest man living has not seen or heard of such an epidemic, which lasted for two months. * * * [319]

In the midst of such a destruction the Emperor, relying on the help of God, came out of Bijapur on the above-mentioned date with strength of heart and firmness of purpose. Praised be God that after one week of violence the epidemic began to abate. Through the grace of God, the Emperor marched to Ākluj. As according to the physicians the eye of Firuz Jang Khan was not likely to be healed soon, the Prince alone was sent off with the army to the country of the enemy [Sambhā].

CAPTURE AND EXECUTION OF SAMBHĀ :

* * * *

While the Emperor [320] was staying at the aforesaid place for transacting certain affairs, the ears of the world were gladdened by a happy news from the invisible world. The merry music of victory, which the ears of the Muslims had been expecting, resounded through the sky. Peace and safety were restored through the blessings of the justice and virtues of the Emperor. Disturbance sank down. Satan was chained. To speak more plainly, through the power of the Emperor's fortune, the infernal infidel Sambhā was made prisoner by the army.

Shaikh Nizām Haidarābādi, surnamed Muqarrab Khan, a brave general who with his sons and relatives enjoyed among themselves the ranks of 25-*hazāri* (21,000 tr.) in recognition of his military capacity, had been appointed from Bijapur before this to capture fort Parnālā, which was in the enemy's possession. Like a prudent and watchful man, he had sent spies to bring in news of the infidel. Suddenly they brought to him the true news that Sambhā, on account of his feud with the family of the Shirkés, who were connected with him by kinship, had gone from Rāiri to fort Khelnā, and after making a settlement with that family, and gaining composure of mind about provisioning this fort, he had gone to Sangameswar [321] where his minister Kavi-kalas had constructed gardens and lofty buildings, and was there engaged in merriment and pleasure. Attended by a party of honour-seeking devoted followers, the Khan out of devotion to the Emperor, in utter disregard of his life started from Kolhāpur, from which the above place was forty-five *kos* distant, and the path full of hill-tops and passes so difficult and dangerous that travellers have not seen the like of them on earth. He made forced marches. Although the spies of Sambhā informed him that the Mughal army was coming, that man intoxicated with the wine of folly and pride had them beheaded by giving the signal of a frown and saying, "You heedless men, you are mad. Can a Mughal force arrive here?" The Khan after patiently enduring much fatigue, suddenly came upon Sambhā with the speed of lightning or the wind; that cursed wretch charged him with the support of four or five thousand Deccani spearmen; Kavi-kalas was accidentally hit by an arrow and fled. After a little fight Sambhā concealed himself in a hole in the mansion of Kavi-kalas in the hope that none had noticed him. Spies gave correct information to the Khan as to his hiding-place. The Khan without pursuing the fugitives, surrounded the *haveli*. His son Ikhlās Khan entered by the steps with a company of heroes and dragged that low fellow and Kavi-kalas by the hair to the elephant ridden by the Khan. [322]

* * * *

Twenty-five of his chief followers with their wives and daughters were made prisoners. This news reached the Emperor at Ākluj, which was henceforth named *Ās'ad-nagar*. He ordered Hamiduddin Khan, son of Sardār Khan, the provost-marshal (*shahna*) of the camp, to hasten to Muqarrab Khan and bring the captive chained and manacled. The victorious Khan came out of the country (in safety) by prudent management, and through the good luck of 'Ālamgir none of the infidel chiefs made any effort (to rescue the prisoner). On Friday, the 15th February, 1689/5th Jamad. A., when the imperial army after marching from Ās'adnagar had encamped at Bahādurgarh, Sambhā was brought to the court. The Emperor out of his devotion to Islām ordered that from two *kos* before the camp the disgraced and unlucky Sambhā should be made to wear a wooden cap* (the badge of a condemned criminal) and his comrades should be clad in the dress of buffoons, punished in various ways, mounted on camels, and brought to the

* Kulah-i-Zangula—a ridiculously shaped cap, from which are suspended many little bells and foxes' tails, and in which any person detected in selling short weight is exposed to public view.

encampment and the darbār with drums beating and trumpets pealing,—so that the Muslims might be heartened and the infidels disheartened by seeing it. The night preceding the morning on which he was brought to the Court, was without exaggeration the *shab-i-barāt* because nobody slept till morning for the pleasure of seeing the spectacle; and the day was like the day of 'Id because all men old and young went out to see such a scene of joy and happiness. In short, this man, who deserved a degrading parade and execution, was taken round the whole camp, and then [323] brought to the Emperor, who was sitting in the Hall of Public Audience. He ordered him to be removed to the prison of retribution. That very moment the Emperor descended from the throne, and kneeling on the carpet of prayer bowed his head to the ground in thanking God and raised his hands in prayer to the Judge of Actions and Promoter of Hopes. The cloud of the Manifestation of the handiwork of Providence was dissolved and drops of Marvel (at God's power) fell from his far-sighted eyes. (*Verse*)

The peak of his cap is in high heaven, [and yet]
His head is ever bowed down to the earth in reverence.

As Sambhā had previously ignored the value of imperial mercy, and fled first from the Emperor's court in the company of his father, and the second time from the late Dilir Khan, therefore that very night his eyes were deprived of the power of seeing, and the next day the tongue of the deceitful speaker Kavi-kalas (was cut out). * * * [324]

Where was Sambhā in his heaven-facing stronghold of Rāiri! and where was his present disgrace and captivity in retribution for his ingratitude! Of the various verses embodying the date composed by rhetoricians, that of 'Ināyetullah, the agent of 'Āzam Shah, *viz.*,

"Sambhā became a prisoner with wife and son", [best] expresses the event, and it was accepted by all. His captor was rewarded for this splendid service with the title of Khan-i-Zamān Fath Jang, a reward of 50,000 rupees, a special and resplendent robe, a horse with jewelled saddle and *sāz,* a dagger, a *dhup,* with jewelled *purdalah,* and promotion raising him to the rank of 7-*hazāri* (same tr.). Of his sons, Ikhlās Khan got the title of Khān-i-'Ālam, a robe, and promotion making him a 5-*hazāri* (same tr.), Shaikh Mirān the title of Munawwar Khan and Shaikh

'Abdullah that of Ikhtisās Khan. Ihtarām Khan and other relatives and companions of the Khan each got a robe and a *mansab*. In consideration of the harshness and insult that he had practised by slaying and imprisoning Muslims and plundering the cities of Islam, the destruction of this wicked infidel preponderated over the reasons for keeping him alive, [325] and the decision of the masters of the Holy Law and Faith and the counsel of the dignitaries of the Church and State were in favour of despatching this hellish robber. Therefore, after the arrival of the Emperor at Koregāon on Sunday the 3rd March/21st Jamad. A., he was executed along with Kavi-kalas with the sword on Monday, the 11th March, 1689/29th Jamad. A.

I shall finish the account of this matter by narrating an event which was the preface to the Emperor's success. Before this, when the capture of Sambhā never came on the tongues of the people and was regarded as an impossibility, Sayyid Fath Muhammad, one of the sons of Mir Sayyid Muhammad Gisudarāz, who after spending his long life in the military profession had taken to retirement in his home at Āhsanābād Gulbarga, and whose son Sayyid Badi'-ullah (whose forehead indicated his asceticism and goodness and fitness to be the successor of a saint) had been appointed successor at the saint's own tomb by the Emperor on account of his devotion to the saints of olden times and kindness to the members of this family, and who had been granted the *sairghul* (rent-free land) of some fertile villages, besides [326] lavish *inā'ms*,—came to the camp, interviewed the Emperor who loved hermits, and narrated, "I have often sat in prayer face to face with the illuminated tomb, with a view to [fore-] seeing the end of this infidel's career. One night I dreamt that I was travelling in order to visit holy places, and was passing over a hill difficult to traverse. A party was setting up poles. They asked me "Where are you going?" I made my wish known. They said "A hog has established himself in this hill for a long time past. You, too, should exert yourself with us to catch him." After dawn it struck me that I should soon come to the army, and take part in this holy war till the completion of the affair of the wicked infidel." The Emperor was greatly delighted to hear these words, and showed respect to and conferred favours on the Sayyid. In less than ten days the wish of the people was gratified. The very day that the news of Sambhā's capture reached the Emperor he summoned the Sayyid and after giving him good wishes and pecuniary aid permitted him to depart. By way of showing gratitude for this wonderful victory, ten thousand rupees were sent to the blessed tomb for the poor and the attendants.

On Tuesday, the 2nd April/21st Jamad. S., the Emperor left Koregāon to see the fort of Islāmābād or Chākna. Prince Muhammad 'Āzam, who was encamped five *kos* in front of it, came there and had interview. That day after bidding farewell to the Prince [327] His Majesty returned to his mansion.

One of the events of this auspicious year was the capture of the chiefs who had accompanied Rāmā [Rajaram] in his adversity. This infidel, the younger brother of Sambhā, had been kept in prison by the latter. After Sambhā's death he became chief and gained some authority in Rāiri. Before the capture of Rāiri, while Zulfiqār Khan was pressing the besieged very hard, he disguised himself as a *yogi* and fled from the fort. (*Verses*)

Behold this coward, who will never
See the face of good fortune.
He sought his own personal ease,
He left his wife and son in distress.

When this news was confirmed by the letters of spies, the Emperor issued orders to 'Abdullah Khan Bārha,—who after he had acted for some time as the deputy of Bakhshi-ul-mulk Ruhullah Khan when the latter was summoned to Haidarabad, and had become himself Subahdār of Bijāpur, and had then by the Emperor's command gone to capture two strong forts in the dependencies of Bijāpur,—now to capture Rāmā if he wandered on that side. Spies brought to him the true news that Rāmā [Rajaram] lay concealed for some time, but had now gathered about 300 followers of the rank of chiefs, [328] and after passing within a few *kos* of that place had entered within the frontiers of the Rāni of Bidnur. The Khan deferring to another time the capture of the forts, first sent his eldest son Hasan 'Ali quickly in that direction, and himself making forced marches for three days and nights reached the enemy at night within the border of the zamindāri of this she-bear, near the fort of Subhāngarh and Jarā, belonging to her and situated on the bank of the Tungabhadrā, in the island of which the enemy had taken refuge. He reddened his sword in their blood. Many died and went to hell. Other men, more than a hundred, including chiefs like Hindu Rao, and Vyankoji, the brother of Santā, and Baharji and Māniā Ghorparé,* were taken prisoners. In the midst of this tumult of lamentation, Rāmā [Rajaram], leaving his turban, coat and shoes, not to speak of his weapons behind, fled in such a manner that nobody got information of it. Although the Khan had performed such a grand feat, yet his ill-luck made him show negligence in the affair of the escape of Rāmā. And the she-bear too was suspected of having concealed Rāmā and afterwards let him go. At the first news that Rāmā had been captured, the Emperor ordered Hamiduddin Khan to bring him to Court. On the arrival of the second news, he ordered the prisoners to be confined in the citadel of Bijapur. Jān Nisār Khan was appointed with a large party [329] to invade the zamindāri of the she-bear. The Satanic Santā at this time triumphantly resisted the Khan, Matlab Khan and Sharzā Khan. At last the affair of the Rāni ended in her paying a small money-tribute under the name of fine. As he (Santā) was destined to live some time more, he escaped being caught by the imperialists. It was a wonder that Hindu Rao, Baharji and some others of the prisoners escaped from this strong prison, —escape from which is incredible except in concert with the guards. On the matter being reported to the Emperor the remaining eighty prisoners were executed. Lashkar Khan became nāzim *vice* 'Abdullah Khan. His son Wajih-ud-din the qiladār of the citadel and Faujdār Khan the kotwāl were punished by diminution of *mansab*.

---

* The MS. reads—Hindu Rāo, Yekoji the brother of Santā, Baharji, and Māniā Ghorparé.

CHAPTER XXXIII.

33RD YEAR OF THE REIGN : 1100 A.H.

9th June, 1689—28th May, 1690 [330]

* * * *

Haji Shaf'i Khan became daftar-dār of tan *vice* Musavi Khan, who got the former's post of diwān of the Deccan. Robes for the rains were presented to all the imperial servants at the Court and the provinces. Abul Khair Khan, son of 'Abdul 'Aziz Khan, became qiladār of Rājgarh; Mukhtār Khan Mir-Ātish *vice* Mukhlis Khan, who became (dārogha of) 'arz-i-mukarrar *vice* Muhammad Yār Khan. Mir 'Abdul Karim, a favourite of the Emperor was rewarded with the title of Multafat Khan for his good services as karori-ganj, when he made abundance and cheapness to appear in stead of scarcity and famine at Haidarabad, and thus deserved the Emperor's recognition. Hamiduddin Khan, son of Sardār Khan, worthy of upbringing, got the title of Khan and was sent to bring Muhammad Khujista Ākhtar, the son of Prince Muhammad Mu'azzam, from Aurangabad to the Court. Kāmgār Khan with a party was appointed to escort the servants of the harem of Mu'azzam to Shahjahanabad. Mubārakullah, son of Irādat Khan and grandson of 'Āzam Khan became faujdār of [331] Islāmābad Chākna and Kamāluddin Khan son of Islām Khan Wālā-shāhi, qiladār of that place. Ikhlās-kesh became news-writer of the kachari of Khān-i-sāmān, *vice* Sharfuddin. When Salābat Khan applied to come to Court, 'Itimād Khan became diwān and faujdār of the blessed port of Surat *vice* him. Jān Nisār Khan Ābul Mukāram, receiving a dagger with a jasper handle and *sāz,* was sent to punish the enemy. On Wednesday, the 10th July 1689/2nd Shawwal, Bakhshi-ul-mulk Ruhullah Khan was appointed to wrest the fort of Raichur from the infidels. Mukhtār Khan became his deputy. Before the capture of Sambhā 'Itiqād Khan had been sent to conquer fort Rāiri, the home and treasure-house of this villain; on Saturday, the 19th October/15th Muharram he captured the fort and made the mothers, wives, daughters, and sons of Sambhā and of Rāmā [Rajaram] prisoners. 'Umdat-ul-mulk presented to the Emperor his son's despatch announcing the conquest and received a special robe, and a jewelled *jigha* adorned with a heron's feather (*par-i-kaling*). The band played joyous tunes. The courtiers made their bows and presented *peshkash*. 'Abdur Rahim Khan bayutāt was ordered to go to Rāiri and confiscate Sambhā's property. [332] 'Itiqād Khan had audience on Saturday the 23rd November, 1689/20th Safar and was rewarded by promotion to the rank of 3-*hazāri* (2,000 tr.), and presented with a robe, a horse, a jewelled quiver, a bow, 30,000 rupees in cash, and the title of Zulfiqār Khan Bahādur. The Emperor graciously ordered that tents fit for holding Sambhā's mother (Shivāji's wife) and other relatives of the deceased should be set up in the *gulālbār* and they should be made to alight there with all respect and privacy. Close to the *misl* of 'Umdat-ul-mulk, the *misl* of the Rāni's bāzār was located for her servants and dependants to live in. Annual pensions were fixed on all of them according to their position. Shāhu, the nine year old elder son of Sambhā, was given the *mansab* of 7-*hazāri* (same tr.), the title of Raja, and a robe, a jewelled dagger, *ārsi,* horse, elephant, kettledrums, and standard. Madan Singh and Ādhu (Mādhav) Singh, his younger brothers, were given *mansabs* and gifts and ordered to live with their mother and grandmother. Imperial clerks were appointed to the establishment (*sarkār*) of each, to manage their household affairs. Qamruddin Khan son of Firuz Jang Khan, had come to Court; he got leave to depart after being given a robe, a jewelled dagger, and an increment of 5-*sadi* (200 tr.) making him a $2\frac{1}{2}$-*hazāri* (2,000 tr.).

CONQUEST OF RAICHUR

On Friday the 29th November, 1689/26th Safar, Bakhshi-ul-mulk Ruhullah Khan [333] captured the fort of Raichur, which was now named Firuznagar. A robe and a *farmān* of praise were sent to him. His son Khānahzād Khan was promoted to $1\frac{1}{2}$-*hazāri* (600 tr.). On Wednesday the 18th December/16th Rabi. A., the imperial camp started on the return journey from Koregāon towards Bijapur. On Friday the 3rd January, 1690/2nd Rabi. S., the army arrived at this city for passing some time. After passing fifteen days, on the 9th February, 1690/10th Jamad. A., the camp reached the village of Badri. Bakhshi-ul-mulk

Bahramand Khan chose a neat place on the bank of the Krishnā for the imperial quarters. The Emperor liked it, and presented the Khan with a diamond ring. Here His Majesty stayed for two months.

One day while the Emperor was holding the high Court of Justice, Salābat Khan, the first Mir Tuzuk, presented a man who said, "I have come from the far-off land of Bengal to become your majesty's disciple. I hope that I may gain my desire." The Emperor smiled, took out of his pocket and gave the Khan about 100 rupees and bits (*churn*) of gold and silver to be presented to the man and said, "Tell him that the favour he expects from me is this!" The Khan gave him the money, but he flung it away and [334] jumped into the river. The Khan raised a cry lest he should be drowned. By command some people swam and rescued him from the river. His Majesty turning his face towards his inner circle, said to Sardār Khan, "A man has come from Bengal with the silly notion of becoming my disciple. (*Hindi verses*)*

Tupi lende bāwri dende, gahare nilaj,
Chuhā khadan māwli tu kal bandhe chhaj!

"Take him to Miān Muhammad Nāf'i Sirhindi and request him to admit him as a disciple and to lay the cap of Sirhind on his head." God be my witness that there is (not) in this age any Shaikh or faqir except this Emperor, who reveals the ascetic behind the veil of the king and exalts asceticism by this type of kingship, who has reached such a degree of holiness as to train a disciple and lead him up to the rank (of a perfect hermit). But in spite of his possessing power that stretches up to the heavens, his nature is marked by humility, and in spite of his possessing riches and the materials of pomp, he is a man of prayer. (*Verse*)

I am the servant of that king of kings under whose sovereignty
Are combined the externals of the lord and the soul of the ascetic.

---

* I offer the following forced interpretation of this couplet, for what it may be worth: "O deeply shameless man! You talk of putting on a peaked cap and digging a large well with steps (*bāori*); rats are eating away the foundations [of your house] while you propose to construct its gallery to-morrow!" For *lende* read *lenge*, for *dende* read *denge*, for *gahar gaharā*, for *māwli mul*, and for *chhaj chhajja*. [Translator.]

On Saturday, the 15th February 1690/16th Jamad. A., the Emperor learnt from the letters of the news-writers that fort Sansani had been wrested from the infidels by Muhammad Bidār Bakht, [335] and the vanquished had been sent to hell. On Sunday the 18th May/19th Shaban, the imperial camp marched from Badri to Galgala. Āmānat Khan diwān of Bijapur, became daftardār of tan *vice* Hāji Shaf'i Khan; Ābul Mukāram succeeded him. Khwāja 'Abdur Rahim Khan became dārogha of dāgh and tashiha *vice* Mu'atamad Khan deceased. A robe, and a *sarpech* were sent to Muhammad 'Āzam, and a robe, a jewelled quiver and bow, a horse, an elephant, a *sarpech,* a gracious *farmān,* and the title of Bahādur to Bidār Bakht. Muhammad Mu'azzam was presented with five maunds of rose-water and two maunds of the essence of *bid-i-mishk.* Udwat Sing, who had come from home and had audience, received a robe and the title of Raja. Khan Jahān Bahādur Zafar Jang Kokaltāsh was made Subahdār of Allahabad, and his son Himmat Khan that of Oudh and faujdār of Gorakhpur. 'Abdullah Khan became faujdār of Nānder *vice* Sazāwār Khan and Sardār Khān that of (the circuit of) twelve *kos* round the camp, receiving a promotion of 400. The Emperor learnt that Safdar Khan, son of 'Āzam Khan Kokah, faujdār of Gwalior, had attacked a *garhi,* and been killed by musket shot. Prince [336] Khujista Ākhtar was brought from Aurangabad to the Court by Hamiduddin Khan dārogha of the fil-khānah. The Prince had audience and was ordered to stay with his father. As Hamiduddin Khan paraded the elephants in a stout condition, he received an increment of thirty troopers. It was learnt from the letters of news-givers that Rustam Khan Sharzā, who had been appointed to patrol on the side of fort Sātārā, had been attacked by the enemy in that district, defeated after a long contest, and made prisoner with his family and children.

CHAPTER XXXIV.

34TH YEAR OF THE REIGN: 1101 A.H.

29th May, 1690—18th May, 1691.

Khwāja Khidmatgār Khan became nāzir and dārogha of the jewel department *vice* Khwāja Khidmat Khan, who became caretaker (*wali*) of the tomb of Shah Jahān, thus taking to a life of retirement. The Emperor ordered the officers (governors) [337] of every province to send 2,000 rupees to the Khan (latter) as a standing practice. Lutfullah Khan was sent to the thānah of Khatāv. Shaikh Ābul Mukāram, was appointed thānahdār of Budā Panchgāon. Ahmad Āqā, ambassador of the Kaisar of Roum, Nazar Bey, envoy of the king of Bukhārā, and 'Abdur Rahim Beg, envoy of the king of Kāshghar, had audience, presented the letters and gifts of their masters, and were rewarded, with their followings at the first interview, during the period of their stay, and at the farewell audience, with all kinds of gifts and presents, consisting of robes, precious jewels, horses, elephants, and some cash. In return for the friendly presents of these kings, rare objects and woven stuffs of Hindustan and jewels and precious and substantial articles were sent to them. Hamiduddin Khan was ordered to convey treasure to the army of Muhammad 'Āzam Shah. Mir Nuruddin became qiladār of Murtazābād Miraj. Jān Nisār Khan was presented with a robe and an elephant (and sent) to punish the enemy. Diānat Khan, son of Āmānat Khan, became diwān of the subahs of the Deccan *vice* Musavi Khan deceased. The late Khan was one of the pure breed of Irān, unique by reason of his greatness of character, his patronage of scholars and artists, [338] his knowledge of the rational branches of learning, and his skill in poetry. He was a son-in-law of Shāh Nawāz Khan and thus senior to His Majesty (by marriage).

ĀSAD KHAN GOES BEYOND THE KRISHNĀ

On Wednesday, the 12th November, 1690/19th Safar 'Umdat-ul-mulk Āsad Khan set out by command to punish the enemy roving on the further side of the river Krishnā. He was presented with an amulet containing the *Qurān* in a diamond-ornamented *khānah* (cover), a special robe, and a horse worth 500 mohars. His chief subordinates were favoured with robes, jewels, swords, horses, and elephants. All others got robes according to their positions. Multafat Khan dārogha of jā-namāz-khānah, got the post of the head of ābdār khānah (close to the Emperor) in addition to his own duties, *vice* Khwāja Hayāt Khan Wafā. Muhammad Mun'im got the āminship of the 7-chauki *vice* him. On Monday, the 23rd February, 1691/4th Jamad. S., the Emperor marched from Galgala, newly named Qutbābād, and alighted outside the fort of Bijapur opposite the gate of Rasulpur, this being his fourth visit to the environs of Bijapur. On Saturday, the 11th April/22nd Rajab, Khan Jahān Bahādur was appointed nāzim of the Panjāb *vice* Alijah. Himmat Khan, his son, succeeded him as the subahdār of Allahabad. [339] On Monday the 18th May, 29th Shaban, Bakhshi-ul-mulk Bahramand Khan, who had gone to beat the enemy, had audience, receiving an increment of 5-*sadi,* which made him a 3½-*hazāri* (2-*hazār* tr.). Mukhtār Khan was sent to punish the enemy. Muftakhar Khan, one of his subordinates, was appointed to go to Sholāpur, and then return escorting Shaikh-ul-Islām, who was coming to court by command.

CHAPTER XXXV

35TH YEAR OF THE REIGN.

19th May, 1691—6th May, 1692.

On Wednersay, the 27th May, 1691, 9th Ramzan, Muhammad Kām Bakhsh was sent to put down the rebels of the country of Jinji and to root out the enemy who ruled there. By an increment of 5-*hazāri* (3-*hazār* tr.) he became a 20-*hazāri* (15-*hazār* tr.). [340] He was presented with a robe, a *sarpech* and half-sleeves, a jewelled dagger, sword, shield, *kalgi,* inkpot and *mānik,* twenty horses with *sāz* of enamel and gold, a horse with silver *sāz* and two lakhs of rupees in cash. Among his companions, Bakhshi-ul-mulk Bahramand Khan and other chiefs, and his clerks, were presented with jewels, robes, horses, and elephants. Dindār, zamindār of Islāmgarh [Deogarh in Gondwana], was given the rank of a *hazāri* (same tr.) a robe, a horse, an elephant, the title of Raja, and permission to go 'home'.

From Raja Bishan Sing, (faujdār of Mathurā) came a letter with a gold key announcing that Garhi Soghar had been wrested from the infidels on the 21st May/3rd Ramzan and that the baffled enemy had fled ruined to nooks and corners. On Friday, the 19th June/2nd Shawwal, Hamiduddin Khan was sent to punish the enemy towards Sakkhar,* receiving a jewelled *jigha.* Mukhtār Khan Mir Ātish, was appointed to punish the rebels near Rāibāgh and Hukri, receiving a robe and an elephant. Ghāziuddin Khan Bahādur Firuz Jang and his son Chin Qalich Khan were favoured by female elephants being presented to them. Lutfullah Khan became dārogha of the khās chauki *vice* Salābat Khan. Mukhlis Khan Qurbegi, Khānahzād Khān, son of [341] Ruhullah Khan and Jān Nisār Khan were each promoted to be a 2-*hazāri* (700 tr.). Salābat Khan became a 2½-*hazāri* (1200 tr.), Sayyid Saif Khan Nur-ul-dahar, a 1½-*hazāri* (700 tr.), Muhammad Yār Khan, a 1½-*hazāri* (400 tr.) and Khidmatgār Khan, a *hazāri* (200 tr.). Lutfullah Khan was removed from his *mansab* of 2½-*hazāri* (1000 tr.) for some offence.

---

* *Sakkhar*, near Shorapur in the country of the Berads.

RELEASE OF PRINCE MUHAMMAD MUʿAZZAM FROM CAPTIVITY

At the beginning of the Emperor's displeasure, the Prince and his sons were not allowed even to cut the hair of their heads. Six months passed in this way. Khidmat Khan nazir who had been *nāib* of Shah Jahan, and could speak boldly in consideration of his old services, urged this matter before the Emperor beyond limit. At that time the Emperor only ordered the Prince to be reformed [by punishment.] After a time, when the violence of his anger gradually abated, and the natural kindness of His Majesty returned, transcripts of Quranic prayers were repeatedly entrusted to Sardār Khan, *muhāfiz,* with the order "Convey these to this second Joseph and captive Jonah and tell him to be engaged in reciting them, so that the kindness of God may incline my heart to release [342] him, and cause him to be freed from the pain of separation from me." A fine idea was contained in this rare expression, so that the aforesaid Khan submitted to the Emperor, "It is in your Majesty's discretion to release him." The Emperor replied, "Yes, but the King of kings—supreme is His wisdom—has made me ruler of the habitable globe; so that wherever oppression is practised by anybody on another, the victim may hope that he will complain to me and will thus secure justice. Owing to certain earthly considerations, I have inflicted hardship upon him. But the time has not yet come for releasing him. He has no asylum except the Court of God. Then, he ought to be kept in hope that he may not despair of me and complain to God; for, if he complains to God where shall I have refuge?" As it was destined that this Prince would one day become sovereign, the Emperor's heart was inclined to this that the Prince would come out of his sufferings and troubles into the sunshine of royal favour. He began to give gradual and systematic relief to the Prince, with every caution and care so that even a fly might not trouble this soul-sick patient. * * * *

On the day when His Majesty marched away from Badri, he ordered the said muhāfiz, [343] that whenever the Emperor would ride away from his halting-place, the imperial tent should be kept standing with its carpets and decorations uncharged, and the Prince be brought from his quarters to it, shown all the places and made to sit everywhere for some time, so that all his senses and limbs might acquire a proper change of relish from the delight and exhilaration. It was done. The Prince said to the muhāfiz, "I ought to have an interview. How can the thirst for an interview be slaked by a mere view of the house?" This went on till the news of the death of the Prince's mother Nawwāb Bāi came from Delhi. Pavilions were spread from the courtyard of the Private Audience Hall to the Prince's quarters, and a screened lane formed, and the Emperor with Zinat-un-nisā Begam visited the Prince and condoled with him. After this, on Monday, the 20th July, 1691/4th Zil.Q., the Prince was granted an interview. He was ordered to perform the *zuhar namāz* in company of the Emperor and to come and perform the Friday prayer in the mosque of the palace (Bijapur), whenever the Emperor went to the Jām'a mosque to say his Friday prayer. And similarly, the Prince sometimes came by command to the baths situated in the fort for washing and purifying his body, and sometimes in order to enjoy delights he visited the garden and tank of Shāhābād, founded by the Emperor. In short, the veil was gradually removed.

Khwāja Daulát *Mahalli* (eunuch) was ordered to bring the Prince's family from Delhi to the court. [344] Muhammad Mu'izzuddin and Muhammad 'Azim each received the rank of 9-*hazāri* (2000 tr.), Muhammad Raf'i-ul-qadr that of 7-*hazāri* (1000 tr.), and Muhammad Khujista Ākhtar received a robe. They made their bows for these favours in the Hall of Public Audience. Hamiduddin Khan received an elephant and a robe. On Monday, the 20th July, 1691, Bakhshi-ul-mulk Ruhullah Khan was sent towards Nasratābād Sakkhar, his followers being rewarded. Tahawwar Khan, son of Salābat Khan, became *sazāwal* of the army of Kām Bakhsh; he was a 8-*sadi* (300 tr.), and now received an increment of 100 (50 tr.). Lutfullah Khan after dismissal, was reinstated. Saf Shikan Khan brought to the Court the harem ladies and dependants of Muhammad Mu'azzam who had arrived from Delhi at Aurangabad. News came that on Sunday, the 4th October/21st Muharram, 'Umdat-ul-mulk Āsam Khan had interviewed Kām Bakhsh at Kadāpā, and that the two had reached Jinji, on Wednesday, the 16th December, 1691/5th Rabi.S.

On Friday, the 18th December/7th Rabi.S., a mad pauper unsheathed a sword in the Jām'a mosque and ran towards the Emperor. The bodyguard captured him. He was made over to Salābat Khan. On Thursday, the 24th

December/13th Rabi.S., while the Emperor was riding out to hunt, Muhammad 'Āzam and Bidār Bakht interviewed him, and accompanied him during the whole journey [345] and on the spot received their leave to set out for Nasratābād Sakkhar. Bakhshi-ul-mulk Bahramand Khan, who had come by command from Kām Bakhsh's army to the Court, had his interview on Thursday, the 31st December, 1691/20th Rabi. S. On Saturday, the 16th January, 1692/7th Jamad. A., Zulfiqār Khan Bahādur was rewarded for the capture of fort Trinomali by being promoted to the rank of 4-*hazāri* (2,500 tr.). On Tuesday, the 26th April, 1692/19th Shaban, Sultāns 'Azzuddin and 'Izzuddin, sons of Prince Mu'izzuddin, and Muhammad Karim and Farrukh Siyar, sons of Muhammad 'Azim, had audience, receiving increase of their daily stipend, favours, robes and jewels.

On Tuesday, the 3rd May/26th Shaban, the Emperor started from Bijapur, and halted at Qutbābād for the second time. During his stay he used to visit the city for the purposes of offering his (daily) prayers, Friday prayers, and 'Id (prayers). Rashid Khan daftar-dār of khālsa was appointed to collect the money and ascertain the revenue of some khālsa (*mahals*) of Haidarabad. The Emperor's favourite and pupil, 'Ināyetullah, *mustaufi* of *āima* and news-writer of the kachari of Khān-i-sāmān, became the deputy of the Khan and got the title of Khan and an increment of 100 making him 800 [*cor.* 600] (60 tr.). Sardār Khan [346] an old and trusted household slave, died. He was devoted to the Emperor's good and the service of the people inwardly and outwardly alike. He loved faqirs. His son Hamiduddin Khan who deserved the Emperor's favour for giving indications of fidelity, got the kotwālship and other posts *vice* his deceased father. The Emperor visited the mosque which was being built close to the private Audience Hall, for saying his five daily [*cor.*] prayers and performing his constant devotional exercises, and laid a few stones with his own hands in order to accumulate spiritual merit.

CHAPTER XXXVI.

36TH YEAR OF THE REIGN : 1103 A.H.

7th May, 1692—25th April, 1693.

* * * *

On Sunday, the 8th May/2nd Ramzan, Muhammad Mu'izzuddin was sent to punish the enemy, spread near Āsa'dnagar (Ākluj), being given a robe with *bālāband* and *sarpech,* twenty-one horses, an elephant, and an increase of a *hazār zāt* (same tr.), making him a 10-*hazāri* (3,000 tr.). [347] Prince Raf'i-ul-qadr got an increment of a *hazāri zāt,* becoming a 8-*hazāri* (*cor.* 1,000 tr.) Muhammad Khujista Ākhtar received his first *mansab,* 7-*hazāri zāt.* Āmānat Khan became defender of Aurangabad *vice* M'amur Khan, who become faujdār of the country of Bir; the former was a 1½-*hazāri* (600 tr.) and now received an increment of 300 troopers, the latter was a 1½-*hazāri* (400 tr.) and now received an addition of 400 tr. Muhāmid Khan son of Sayyid Murtaza Khan deceased, who had been previously known as Hāmid Khan,—became faujdār of Miwāt and was made a 3-*hazāri* (2,500 tr.) by an increment of 500 tr. 'Abdur Razzāq Khan Lāri, of Haidarabad, became faujdār of Konkan and the environs of Rāiri, receiving an increment of a *hazār* troopers, making him a 4-*hazāri zāt* and 4-*hazār* tr., a horse, an elephant and kettledrums.

MARRIAGE OF PRINCE MUHAMMAD 'AZIM.

On Sunday, the 26th June 1692/21st Shawwal, Muhammad 'Azim [-ud-din] was married to the daughter of Ruhullah Khan, son of Khalilullah Khan. The bridegroom received a *sarpech* worth 17,000 rupees, a *bāzuband* worth 8,000 rupees, a horse with jewelled *sāz,* an elephant, and an increase of a *hazār zāt* making him a 10-*hazāri* (2-*hazār* tr.). Sayyid Muhammad and Sayyid Muhammad

J'afar Gujrāti, successors at the tombs of Qutb-ul-'Ālam [348] and Shah 'Ālam, came from Ahmadabad to interview the Emperor, and according to the fixed custom each received a robe, an elephant and a certain pecuniary aid when going back. On Tuesday, the 5th July 1692/1st Zil. Q., the Emperor issued an order to Himmat Khan son of Khan Jahān Bahādur Zafar Jang, Subahdār of Allahabad, to come to Court. Buzurg Ummed Khan, son of Āmir-ul-umāra, Subahdār of Bihār, succeeded him at Allahabad, and Muzaffar Khan, another son of Āmir-ul-umāra, became faujdār of the sarkār of Jaunpur *vice* him.

Ruhullah Khan died. In lineage he was like the Sun; in acquirements foremost in all points; of all good manners he was the master and he set his heart on bestowing favours on the people. As he was the son of the Emperor's maternal aunt's son (*cor.*) and was adorned with many noble qualities, his departure grieved His Majesty. God pardon him! One of the signs of his being most probably pardoned was the fact that the Emperor visited him in his last moments and prayed to God for pardon on his behalf. At the time of his death he recited the verse:

> With what pride is (thy) servant leaving the world, [349]
> That you have come to his (bed) head at the time of his giving up life!

Khānahzad Khan, his worthy and favourite son, got an increment of 500 *zāt* (300 tr.) making him a 2-*hazāri* (1,000 tr.), and became Qurbegi *vice* Mukhlis Khan. Bahramand Khan became Mir Bakhshi *vice* the deceased, and received an increment of 500 (same tr.) making him a 4-*hazāri* (2,000 tr.). Mukhlis Khan succeeded him as second bakhshi, receiving an increment of 500 *zāt* which made him a 2½-*hazāri* (700 tr.). 'Azizullah Khan, brother of the deceased, became 1½-*hazāri* (600 tr.). Khwāja 'Abdur Rahim Khan died. Mir Husain Āmānat Khan became bayutāt *vice* him. 'Ināyetullah Khan became diwān-i-tān *vice* the last, receiving an increment of 100 (20 tr.) making him a 7-*sadi* (80 tr.). The diwānship of *sarf-i-khās* too was entrusted to him, and he received a further promotion by twenty troopers. Salābat Khan, begged permission to go to Delhi on account of severe illness, but died after passing a few stages. At this time he used frequently to recite (*verse*) :

> I have myself come and betaken myself to the corner of the sepulchre,
> That my bones may not burden any body's shoulders.

[350] He was honest and skilful in conducting business, and quick and expert in pleasing his master. Muhammad Bad'i of Balkh, after dismissal was reappointed 3-*hazāri* (700 tr.). On Friday, the 22nd July, 1692/18th Zil. Q., the Emperor ordered that Muhammad Mu'azzam should come to the Court-house (*'adālat-gāh*) and have the honour of an interview and kissing the ground. On Friday, the 2nd September/1st Muharram Khidmatgār Khan, nāzir got an increment of 500 (150 tr.), Muhammad Yār Khan that of 500, making him a 2-*hazāri* (400 tr.). Kākar Khan, an officer of the army of Kām Bakhsh, was appointed thānadar of Jinji, and received an increment of 500 (300 tr.) becoming a 1½-*hazāri* (700 tr.). Mir Husain, mushrif of macebearers, was sent to Delhi to bring the servants (ladies) of the harem of Muhammad Mu'izzuddin to Court. Muhammad Jamil, envoy of the ruler of Hadramaut, got leave to return, a robe, and 2,000 rupees. On Monday, the 24th October/23rd Safar Raf'iulqadr and Khujista Ākhtar were ordered to come to the mosque for the *zuhar* prayer in company with their father. Lutfullah Khan and Āsālat Khan were sent to the thānah of Ās'adnagar. Two thousand troopers who had been reduced from Raf'i-ul-qadr's *mansab* were restored to him. Khwāja Mubārak was appointed *nāib* of Khidmatgār Khan in the post of *nāzir* of the establishment of Prince Muhammad Mu'azzam. Raja Udwat Singh, zamindār of Urchha, serving in the army of Firuz Jang Khan was made faujdār of [351] Irij with an increment of 500 *zāt* (same tr.), making him a 2-*hazāri* (1,500 tr.) 'Abdul Hai, mushrif of farrāshkhānah, reported to the Emperor that according to his command the residence-tent of the Prince had been charmingly furnished. The Emperor ordered Khidmatgār Khan and (other) servants to join the Prince's cortege and convey him to this mansion. On Wednesday, the 30th November 1692/1st Rabi. S., Kamāl-uddin Khan, faujdār of Hindaun-Bāyāna, was promoted by 500 *zāt* (same tr.) to the rank of 2-*hazāri* (1,000 tr.) in reward for his having extirpated the rebels of that quarter.

'Itiqād Khan, son of the Āmir-ul-umārā deceased, became Subahdār of Agra and faujdār of its environs, receiving an increment of 200 tr. which made him a 1½-*hazāri* (1,200 tr.) Zulfiqār Khan Bahādur was made a 4-*hazāri* (3,000 tr.). Khudābanda Khan son of the late Āmir-ul-umārā,* became faujdār of Bahrāich; he was a 9-*sadi* (400 tr.) and now got a hundred more. Ābul Muhammad Khan Bijapuri, was a 3-*hazāri* (1,000 tr.), and now got an increment of 500 troopers. Mukhtār Khan a 3-*hazāri* (1,500 tr.), was now given back the 500 *zāt* (100 tr.) which had been reduced from his *mansab*. Hamiduddin Khan passed in review the elephants in a robust condition; 200 troopers were added to his rank of *hazāri* (600 tr.). On Thursday, the 12th January, 1693/15th Jamad. S., Muhammad 'Azim was presented with sixty pieces of cloth, coats, *sarpech, fota*, half-sleeves, and [352] *bālāband*. Ānwār Khan dārogha of khawāses, son of Hakim 'Alimuddin entitled Wazir Khan in Shah Jahan's reign, died, leaving nothing on earth. On Wednesday, the 1st March/14th Rajab, Multafat Khan, dārogha of ābdār-khānah, received the above post *vice* the deceased, and was promoted by a hundred *zāt* (50 tr.) to the rank of a *hazāri* (150 tr.). His office brought him close to the Emperor's person.

Letters of spies informed the Emperor that owing to the scarcity of grain which prevented the army from standing firmly, Zulfiqār Khan Bahādur had retired twelve *kos* abandoning the trenches at Jinji. Some time before this, letters had been received stating that the enemy had crowded round Zulfiqār Khan at the siege of Jinji, that no provision was coming to him, and that if any reinforcement arrived, he would be relieved from distress. An urgent order was issued to 'Umdat-ul-mulk Āsad Khan, who was staying at Nandiyāl, to hasten to his son's aid. As he delayed in going, the Emperor wrote another *farmān* with his own hand in open court, when I happened to be present and overheard the Emperor saying to Fazāil Khan Mir Munshi, "Āsad Khan represents himself as eager to see his son. Now that the latter is hard pressed, he delays and neglects in hastening to him. He might well say (*verse*):

> 'O Angel of Death! I am not heavy,
> I am (only) an unfortunate old man.' [353]

---

* Shāista Khan died in April, 1694. (P. 368.)

"It is easy to make a boast but quite another matter to prove it true." As, before going to that side 'Umdat-ul-mulk had openly said in his own circle, "The Emperor has not yet assigned any task to me. If I were to be commissioned, he would see what a Turk can do" and this speech had been reported to the Emperor, His Majesty now addressed the aforesaid Fazāil Khan and Qābil Khan, the dārogha of the library, "His Turkship is over. How runs the proverb?" Both of them recited it, as they had heard it,

'Digar ba-khud manāz ke Turki tamām shud,
'Don't brag again; as your Turkship has ended,
(*i.e.*, your boast has failed).'

This verse was embodied in the *farmān*.

CHAPTER XXXVII.

37TH YEAR OF THE REIGN :

26th April, 1693—15th April, 1694.

* * * At the gracious arrival of the blessed month of Ramzan, exhilarating to the Muslims, the bud of 'Id blossomed in the garden of fasting, and the thorn and bramble of the oppression and injury done by the infidels were totally swept away from the flower-bed of the age. * * *

A glazed *pālki* was sent by the Emperor to Prince 'Āzam Shah, who was attacked by dropsy, [354] so that when journeying he might travel in care and safety. The Emperor ordered that excepting those who had been granted *pālkis* by him, none of the Princes, shāhzādas and āmirs should come in a *pālki* within the *gulālbār*. After a time permission was given to 'Umdat-ul-mulk Āsad Khan and the intimate servant Multafat Khan to come [in their *pālkis*] so far. The āgent of the Rāni of Bidnur presented her letter and tribute, consisting of 300 *hun*.

THE SAD CONDUCT OF KĀM BAKHSH

* * * *

'Umdat-ul-mulk, after conquering the fort of Nandiyāl in Kadāpā district, which is the frontier of Karnātak Haidarabadi, had encamped. The Prince was sent from the Court to capture fort Wāgingerā in company with Bakhshi-ul-mulk Bahramand Khan [355] and engaged in the work. When Bakhshi-ul-mulk Ruhullah Khan was appointed to this task, the Prince by command turned to reinforce 'Umdat-ul-mulk. When he arrived at Kadapa, an imperial order was received directing him and 'Umdat-ul-mulk to go to the aid of Zulfiqār Khan Bahādur Nasrat Jang, who was besieging Jinji and who had been put to hard straits by the assembling of the enemy and the failure to get provisions. The Prince, in his pride of youth and under the influence of the evil counsels of flatterers and his disinclination to listen to the words of experienced and far-seeing men, travelled all the long way from beginning to end, stage by stage on horseback, the journey including hunting and visiting (noted) places. Bahramand Khan utilising his opportunities, pleased the Prince by his smoothness (of tongue) and gentleness, and left for the Court. 'Umdat-ul-mulk, inspite of his great weakness and the infirmities of age, had to undergo trouble and hardship in observing proper etiquette, and travelled all the way on horseback in constant sadness. But as the kernel of complaint turns into the grain of vexation in the soil of friendship, and the result of mutual opposition is calamity and disgrace, the ill-feeling between the partisans of the two chiefs grew stronger. The displeasure and bitterness on the two sides increased through the intervention of bad men. When the army came near Jinji, Nasrat Jang Khan advanced to welcome the Prince, and had audience. The Prince sat in the audience-hall. [356] 'Umdat-ul-mulk, Nasrat Jang, and Sarfarāz Khan got permission to sit down; Lashkar Khan, son of Sayyid Khan Jahān of Bārha had expected equality of treatment with Nasrat Jang, but on being disappointed in that hope, left the audience-hall in anger, and never again went to interview the Prince. The servants of the Prince alleged to Lashkar Khan that this incident was due to the machination of the father and the son, while these [two] generals made him believe that it was owing to the Prince's disfavour. All the materials for ill-feeling and malignity were thus assembled, and these things increased the irritability and disturbance in the mind of the Prince. Meantime, through the agency of some reckless fools, the Prince opened a secret correspondence with Rāmā [Rajaram] in the fort. The enemy were greatly encouraged by this occurrence and practised mischief-creating and deception and misled the Prince. Nasrat Jang who watched every direction and paid one thousand rupees daily to his spies in the fort, learnt the truth about this secret affair, and the father and the son wrote to the Emperor about the state of affairs and were permitted, at their request, to station Rao Dalpat Bundela in constant attendance at the Prince's residence, and to forbid the Prince's riding, holding court, and the ingress and egress of strangers without the permission of 'Umdat-ul-mulk. The quarrel became public. The spies within the fort repeatedly sent news that the Prince in concert with his wicked servants [357] wanted to enter the fort on a dark night, by reason of his difference with 'Umdat-ul-mulk and Nasrat Jang. The father and the son being shaken by their fear of the king of men, held a consultation with the chiefs of the army and with the consent of them strengthened the *chauki* (sentry) and strictness (in examining visitors) at the door of the Prince, and by common consent called in the thānahdārs from around the fort. As soon as the army withdrew from around the fort, the enemy getting news of it came out in a strong body to fight, and a battle raged on every side. 'Umdat-ul-mulk was busy at the base-camp (*bungāh*) in guarding the Prince, Nasrat Jang was engaged in the trenches in planning to remove the large guns and other siege materials. They could not help the thānahdārs; everyone who could come away safely by his own exertions did so; the rest were destroyed. Isma'il Khan Makhā, a great commander, who held the thānah in the rear of the fort, stood up to fight; but the enemy were too many and he was wounded and carried off through the exertions and reinforcement of Santā. A great confusion occurred. Nasrat Jang hastened the work of withdrawal from the trenches; the large guns were (*mekh zadah*) damaged by hammering nails into their touch-holes, and having arranged his men he carried off all the property to the camp. At this time the enemy in great confidence, joy, and vigour surrounded Nasrat Jang in a body of one lakh of horsemen and infantry. The (Prince's) camp was two *kos* and the fort-wall only a quarter *kos* from the place. The audacity of the infidels was beyond measure, and death faced the Muslims. At this time the Khan Bahādur and all the other commanders had not with them more than [358] 2,000 troopers. The Khan relying on God's help and keeping the Emperor in his remembrance, joined the battle with a loud cry. The heroes made brave charges, a great give and take battle was fought. About three thousand infantry of the enemy were slain by the Islamic ghāzis, and three hundred cavalry too. The Khan Bahādur, on an elephant drove them back to the door of the fort, the garrison shut the gate. In this conflict one thousand infantry of the enemy perished. The imperialists gained the victory and the enemy took to flight. The Muslims captured one thousand mares which the enemy had left behind when fleeing to the fort. About four hundred horses and four elephants of the victorious warriors were slain by cannonball and *zamburak* fire. And the same number of eager fighters from among the *mansabdārs* of the retinue and other corps became martyrs. Few were unwounded. After such a great victory the Khan Bahādur arrived at the camp at the end of the day, and met 'Umdat-ul-mulk. As they had learnt that the Prince and his advisers had formed the plan of imprisoning the father and the son when they would come to visit him, the two rode out and unceremoniously entered the Prince's house and in fidelity to their master, took their master's son [359] into their custody. Next day the Khan Bahādur reassured and cheered all the members, great and small, of the army, and made them happy by the presentation of elephants, horses, robes and cash rewards. He gained victories (several) times over the enemy. As grain was exhausted and the troops had not the strength to stand up, he made some sort of truce with the enemy, marched away to the imperial dominions, and halted. At this time orders were received from the Emperor commanding that the Prince should be sent to Court with Muharram Khan. 'Umdat-ul-mulk set out for the Court. The Khan Bahādur [Nasrat Jang] returned after four months, again laid siege to the fort, and pressed the garrison hard. I shall narrate in its place the capture of the fort and the escape of Rāmā [Rajaram] and Santā.

On Wednesday, the 14th June 1693/20th Shawwal, Kām Bakhsh arrived at the Court, and through the mediation of Zinatunnisā Begam had an interview with the Emperor in the harem. He presented one thousand mohars as *nazar* and the same number of rupees as *nisār*.

An imperial order was issued that no āmir to whom a *sarpech* of jewellery was granted should wear it except on Sunday; they should be content with it and should not make another (*sarpech*) themselves and should not wrap their head [with any such unauthorised *sarpech*]. [360]

On Sunday, the 13th August, 1693/21st Zil. H., Khan Jahān Bahādur Zafar Jang Kokaltāsh Khan, the dismissed nāzim of Lahore, had audience. His son Himmat Khan Bahādur the dismissed Subahdār of Allahabad, prayed for an audience, but was ordered to convey the family of Muhammad Mu'izzuddin to him at Parnālā. Hamiduddin Khan, who had gone to punish the enemy returned and had audience on Saturday the 7th October/16th Safar. Formerly he had to stand outside the barrier (*katra*) railing; the Emperor now graciously gave him the honour of standing within it. 'Ināyetullah Khan on the occasion of the death of his maternal uncle Mullā Muhammad Tāhir, received a shawl *bālāband*. On Thursday, the 9th November,

1693/20th Rabi. A., 'Umdat-ul-mulk Khan Jahān Bahādur informed the Emperor that Himmat Khan had had a three days' fight with Santā, and had defeated the infidel after great exertions. Raja Anup Singh became faujdār of Nasratābād Sakkhar, R'adāndāz Khan, qiladār of Imtiazgarh Ādoni, Sardār Khan that of Muhammadābād Bidar, and M'amur Khan, faujdār of Bir and Shiwgāon, receiving promotions and rewards.

ARRIVAL OF 'ALIJĀH 'ĀZAM AT COURT.

Prince 'Alijāh, who had been summoned to Court on account of his illness, (arrived) with Muhammad [361] Bidār Bakht Bahādur and Shāhzāda Muhammad Wālajāh on the 22nd October/2nd Rabi. A., and had audience. As he had not yet fully recovered, the Emperor wished to be himself his physician and nurse. (The Prince) resided in the tent which had been set up for his residence in the middle of the *gulālbār* close to the Hall of Private Audience, and in which a hall and two rooms had been built for sheltering him. On Sunday the 5th November, 1693/16th Rabi. A., Muhammad Wālājāh became a 7-*hazāri* (2,000 tr.) and was given a standard and kettledrums. Khan Zamān Fath jang, an officer of the Prince's army, had audience. Hakim-ul-mulk and Fazāil Khan Mir Hādi, Mir Munshi, who had been sent by the Emperor to the Prince for treating and soothing him respectively, returned with him and had audience. The Emperor went once every day to see the Prince, and partook of the Prince's sick-diet with him and Zinat-un-nisā Begam. And that was the only food which the two took till the Prince recovered. Thank God, through the blessed efforts of the Emperor, the Prince recovered from such a fatal illness. Muhammad Sālim Āslam a servant of the Prince found the date of recovery in the verse :

> "The Prince's medicine was only the Emperor's prayer." [362]

The Emperor heard it and praised the poet.

On Saturday, the 23rd December, 1693/5th Jamad. A., the Prince (on recovery) came to the Private Audience Hall, sat down before the Emperor, and so gladdened him. Hakim-ul-mulk, who had shown marvellous skill in the treatment, was rewarded with promotion of a *hazār zāt* making him 4-*hazāri*. Shāh 'Ali Jāh narrated the history of his own illness thus: "Three years before this dropsy appeared, Hakim M'asum Khan used to say indirectly in my presence but plainly by messengers that he had observed the symptom of dropsy in me and was trying as far as possible to guard my health and check the disease, and that he would feel satisfied if I took medicine, followed a strict regimen, and abstained from the things that caused the disease. I did not listen to the words of the deceased. Two years after his death I reached the brink; when I was about to go towards Jinji, this disease appeared. Although Hakim Muhammad Shaf'i, Hakim Muhammad Razā, and Hakim Muhammad Āmin Sāwji, worked hard, the disease became severer, till it came to this that the girth of my sleeve was increased to 14 *gira* and yet I felt it as too tight. The girth of the cloth of my drawers (*pāijāma*) was one yard and six *gira*. I abstained from whatever was fit to be given up. Instead of water I drank essence of white succory and night-shade. The doctors, as they were of good intention, used to say "the Prince does not abstain". [363] At night all gave up hopes of recovery and expected my skin to crack. The Begam, Muhammad Bidār Bakht, Gaiti Ārā, Bakht-un-nisā, and some other inmates of my harem, who surrounded my couch, and I were half dosing and half awake, when a luminous man with beard and moustaches, yellow like wheat and barley, appeared at the foot of the bed facing me, and standing near he said, 'Up to this time no part of the disease has gone away. Make sincere and unrelapsing penitence, and God will give you quick recovery.' I said, 'I shall repent in any form of words that you command, and God willing, shall not relapse into the sin.' And so I repented at the direction of that internally and externally great being, and felt ease of body. He vanished. I informed the Begam and other people and gave them the glad news of my recovery. That instant I felt inclination to pass water, passed two large ewer-fuls in one discharge, and felt the traces of lightness and relief. Up to dawn this sort of urination occurred five times, and seven parts of my swelling disappeared. Men asked me, 'Could you recognise the great person who appeared at the bidding of the Great Healer?' I answered 'I do not know him or his name.' But on the second day, Shaikh 'Abdur Rahman Darvish wrote from Ādoni forty *kos* from that place. 'Today when three *gharis* of night remained, His Holiness the Commander of the Faithful 'Ali, the son of Ābu Tālib, said to me, 'To night I have given him dust, and begged his recovery of God; he will speedily recover. Don't doubt at all.' After my recovery, my servants, such as [364] Mustafa Kāshi and others distributed their own household property with a certain amount of cash to faqirs and poor men. Mir Zain-ul-'Ābidin gave away 12,000 rupees. After my bath of recovery Hedāit Khan held feasts for a week and entertained (all) people, at an expenditure of 15,000 rupees. The Begam sent 60,000 rupees as present to the blessed Najaf and the exalted Karbalā. One lakh and twenty thousand rupees were sent to the poor of Mecca and Medina and other sacred places from (my) own purse. The Begams and Shāhzādas gave away some amount of gold to the poor. When Hakim-ul-mulk and Fazāil Khan arrived from the Emperor, only a little swelling on the face and hands was left. The Hakim prescribed electuary of gold; on taking it a [new] swelling appeared. He said 'There is no fear, it will now totally disappear' Then I started for the Court. I gave 2,000 āshrafis to the Hakim, with a robe and an elephant. Favours were conferred on Fazāil Khan too."

Munawwar Khan son of Fath Jang, (by an increment of 5-*sadi*) became a 3½-*hazāri* (2,000 tr.). 'Ali Mardān Khan Haidarabadi had been captured by the enemy; on being released he was made a 5-*hazāri* (same tr.). 'Umdat-ul-mulk, who had retired from Jinji, and by command stayed at Nasratābād Sakkhar, arrived at Court on Monday, the 8th January, 1694/21st Jamad. A., at the Emperor's invitation. On account of the affair of Kām Bakhsh, he had anticipated the severe anger of the Emperor. On the day of interview, when he arrived [365] at the place of making salām, Multafat Khan who was standing close to the throne by virtue of his office of dārogha of the khawāses, recited in a low tone :—(*verse*) 'Forgiveness has a sweetness which vengeance lacks.' The kind Emperor said, "You have recited it at the right time". Looking kindly at the chief of ministers he ordered him to kiss his toes, and raised his head from the dust of distress. Sipahdār Khan son of Kokaltāsh Khan Zafar Jang, who had become Subahdār of Allahabad *vice* Buzurg Ummed Khan deceased,* got in addition the faujdāri of Jaunpur, and the increment of 500 tr. to his

* On p. 369, he is said to have died on 12th May, 1695.

rank of 3-*hazari* (2,500 tr.) and one *kror dām* as *in'ām*. Khānahzād Khan, who had gone towards Garh-namunā to guard the way, arrived at Court on Thursday, the 8th February, 1694/22nd Jamad. S. Bidār Bakht was sent to chastise the enemy, receiving a dagger with a fish (*māhi*) handle and pearl *'ilāqa* worth 10,000 rupees. Khan Fath Jang, (his) sons and relatives, and others appointed to the Prince's army were rewarded with robes, promotion, jewels, horses, and elephants. On Thursday, the 8th March/21st Rajab* Muhammad Mu'izzuddin, giving up the siege of Parnālā, came to Court; he was granted an interview in company with his son 'Izzuddin in the private chamber. Mukhtār Khan became Mir Ātish. Nawāzish Khan Rumi became defender of chakla Morādābād.

A Sayyid of Bārha, who was a mansabdār and officer of the imperial service and Āmānullah, a trusted servant of Shāh 'Alijāh, were friends. [366] One day as they were going together to the same place, they had words, their friendship was broken up, and a quarrel followed. Āmānullah fatally stabbed the Sayyid with a cutlass (*jamdhār*). The other Sayyids in a body went to the residence of Āmānullah, situated in the camp of the Prince, on whose side too, a large party appeared; a great tumult occurred. The Emperor on being informed sent Mukhtār Khan Mir Ātish, to the place to try his best to bring about a reconciliation. The Khan tried to carry out the command and put down the tumult, but the Sayyids could not be pacified. He reported the matter. The Emperor wrote on the sheet of the letter the Qurānic verse :—

"If two parties of the faithful quarrel, reconcile them, and if either of them rebel against the other, you may fight against the party that has rebelled until it inclines to the commandment of God". That day passed. Next day the Sayyids in a body sat down outside the Court of Justice. The Emperor ordered them to go to the Qāzi-ul-quzāt, whose decision according to the Holy Law would be carried out. These fools cried out, "We wo'nt go to the Qāzi. We shall settle the matter with our enemies."

The Emperor became angry on hearing these words; he rolled up his sleeves and cried out, "A group of men who have often been beaten by me and felt my anger, dare give such a reply when asked to conform to the Holy Law! Let

* *Akhbarat* shows that Mu'izzuddin had audience on the 28th or 29th March : so the 8th March was the date on which he started from Parnālā.

as many of them as may be here, come on in a body." He ordered all the Sayyids serving in the *khās chauki* and the old retinue to be dismissed, and to be expelled from the tent in front of the door of the ghusalkhānah where they used to sit. [367] No man durst now speak a word. Saif Khan and Sayyid Khan and other chiefs of the Sayyids like them, took refuge in the houses of influential grandees and protested a thousand times, "We were not in it". They remained under disfavour and removal from service for some time, and were then reinstated through petitioning and mediation. They restrained their breath in their throats and sat down on the knees of good manners. On one of these days some twenty of the servants of Mu'izzuddin became rude to his diwān Fazl 'Ali Khan and like ruffians acted so violently that every one who tried to reason with them met with abuse only. When it was reported to the Emperor, he ordered Hamiduddin Khan to go and punish these men, as the recent affair of the Sayyids had disgusted his mind. When the Khan went there they did not withdraw but rushed into the burning fire. The capacity of moths is well-known; if a thousand of them collect together, they cannot fill a closed fist. But when those few desperate men charged these thousand men, all of the latter were shaken and they fled away uncontrollably. At this time the elephant of the Khan Bahādur frightened by the crowd and tumult, stampeded out of the field and ran for one *kos* towards the Bādshāhi ganj. The Khan saw before him a large thatched house in which grain was heaped up. The instant the elephant came beside it, he coolly jumped down on it from his *howda* [368]. People pursued and brought back the elephant. The Khan returned to the battle on another remount. Ultimately the men were destroyed by the fire of their own kindling.

CHAPTER XXXVIII.

38TH YEAR OF THE REIGN : 1105 A. H.

16th April, 1694—4th April, 1695.

* * * *

News came that Āmir-ul-umārā Shāista Khan, Subahdār of Agra, had died. The excellent qualities and praiseworthy virtues of this noble āmir were such that the fame of his liberality and charity enveloped the sky. His memorials are the many caravan-serais and bridges which he built at the cost of lakhs all over Hindustan. Sālih Khan, son of 'Āzam Khan Kokah, got his father's first title Fidāi Khan and leaving the faujdāri of Gwalior, became Subahdār [369] of Agra *vice* the deceased. Bakhshi-ul-mulk Bahramand Khan, a 4-*hazāri* (2,500 tr.) got an increment of a *hazāri*, on Tuesday, the 31st July/1694/18th Zil. H., Zulfiqār Khan Bahādur a 4-*hazāri* (3,000 tr.) got an increment of a *hazāri zāt*. Bakhshi-ul-mulk Mukhlis Khan a 2,500 *zāt* (600 tr.) got a promotion of 500 (100 tr.). By an increment of 500 Fāzil Khan Khān-i-sāmān was made a 2½-*hazāri* (500 tr.). On Sunday the 7th October/27th Shabān, Ism'ail Khan Makhā came to Court on being released by the enemy, and was made guard of the road from Indi up to Murtazābād, receiving an addition of a *hazār* to his rank of 5-*hazāri* (same tr.). Khānahzād Khan became dārogha of the servants of the khās chauki. 'Askar Khan* Haidarābādi was made Subahdār of Oudh. Raja Bhim Singh 5-*hazāri,* died. 'Itiqād Khan and Ābul Mu'āla, sons of the Āmir-ul-umārā, and Murlidhar, diwān of the same deceased, reached the Court on Friday, the 14th December, 1694/7th Jamad. A., and got mourning robes. Ikhlāskesh, after transacting certain business for which he had been sent by the Emperor to Ujjain, returned to Court. On Tuesday, the 12th February, 1695/8th Rajab, Buzurg Ummed Khan, Subahdār of Bihār, died. His brothers 'Itiqād Khan and Ābul Mu'āla, received mourning robes. Fidāi Khan became

* 'Askar Khan, evidently Muhammad Ali Beg of Golkonda service, created 'Askar 'Ali Khan by Aurangzeb. Often mentioned in the Fort St. George Diary of 1688-90.

Subahdār of Bihār *vice* Buzurg Ummed, being [370] succeeded at Agra by Mukhtār Khan, who was succeeded as Mir Ātish by Khānahzād Khan, who received an addition of 500 to his rank of 2½-*hazāri*. The Emperor ordered the high bakhshis to enter in the records the mansab of Muhammad Mu'azzam as 40-*hazāri* (same tr.).

Orders were issued at Court and in the provinces that no Hindu except Rajputs should bear arms, or ride elephants, *pālkis*, or Arab and 'Irāqi horses. On Monday, the 1st April, 1695/26th Shaban, the Emperor marched from Qutbābād, and on the 3rd April/28th Shaban arrived at Bijapur for the fifth time. His camp was set up near Nauraspur and Āfzalpur.

CHAPTER XXXIX.

39TH YEAR OF THE REIGN : 1106 A. H.

5th April, 1695—24th March, 1696.

* * * *

The Emperor passed the month of Ramzan here, as Brahmapuri was not fit for his residence (as yet). One day Khan Jahān Bahādur Zafar Jang presented to the Emperor a small circular China ewer in the Court house (*'adālatgāh*), [371] saying that it was the cup of Moses. The Emperor glancing at it, gave it to Princes Muhammad Mu'izzuddin and Muhammad 'Azim. On its neck were inscribed two lines of drawings resembling writing. The Shāhzādas said, "Then this writing must be Hebrew." The Khan Bahādur looking at the characters said, "I don't know Hebrew or Mebrew. The man who sold it gave this information". The Emperor said "These are letters, and the workmanship is not bad". Many wonderful and fantastic anecdotes are current among the people about this merry and virtuous Khan. But as the above incident happened in my presence, I write it as his memorial.

The Emperor ordered Nāzir Khidmatgār Khan with Khwāja, Manzur to take a special robe to Muhammad Mu'azzam's house, and bring him to the prayer-room to make his bow for it. He then came with the Emperor to the diwān-i-'adālat, offered two-fold prayers and was permitted to kiss the feet . The Emperor kissed his forehead. After being presented with a diamond *sarpech* worth one lakh of rupees, a sword, two horses with enamel and gold *sāz,* and an elephant with silver *sāz* and *talāir,* he was sent back to his mansion. Khudābanda Khan son of Āmir-ul-umārā, after his father's death came to Court from the faujdāri of Bahrāich, and got a mourning robe. Hamiduddin Khan on receiving an increment of 100 tr. became a $1\frac{1}{2}$-*hazāri* (500 tr.).

As the [372] eldest son of the Emperor always sat on His Majesty's right hand and during Shah 'Alam's 'retreat' (disgrace), Shah Alijah had been given that honour, the eldest prince asked the Emperor, "What is your Majesty's order about my right on the day of 'Id?" He replied, "Go to the 'Idgāh before my cortege and you will sit on my right side" He did so. When the cortege reached the steps, Mu'azzam advanced, interviewed, and kissed the feet of the Emperor, who, after shaking hands with him took his left hand in his own right hand and went to the mosque, and so it happened that the eldest son sat on the right, touching the Emperor. Shāh 'Alijāh who came behind and had a special sword in his hand, deposited it before the Emperor, and touched the arm of his brother wishing him to make room for him and let him sit down on the right side of the Emperor. His Majesty's glance fell on that side; with his right hand he grasped the skirt of 'Alijāh and brought him to the left side. Who else had the audacity to advance or hang back? After the prayers had been said and the khātib had ascended the pulpit (*mimbar*), as soon as the Emperor's name was uttered (by the Khātib), His Majesty rose up holding the hand of 'Alijāh, and made a sign to the eldest Prince to depart. Shah 'Alam went out with his sons by the third door and the Emperor by the second.

Zakiat-un-nisā and Safiyyat-un-nisā, daughters of Muhammad Ākbar, who had come to Court by command, were ordered to be married to Raf'i-ul-qadr and Muhammad Khujistah Ākhtar. On Thursday, the 9th May, 1695/5th Shawwal Prince Muhammad Mu'azzam [373] came to the prayer-room and made his bow for the robe of farewell to [act as Subahdār of] Agra, which had been sent to his mansion with Khwāja Manzur. He then went with His Majesty to the diwān-i-'adālat, and kissed his feet, the Emperor kissing his forehead, and dismissing him after reciting the *fātiha*. Of his sons Muhammad Raf'i-ul-qadr and Khujistah Ākhtar were sent with him, and Muhammad Mu'izzuddin and Muhammad 'Āzim were left with the Emperor; (they) were ordered to accompany the Prince to his camp (*dāira*).

THE EMPEROR'S MARCH FROM BIJAPUR TO BRAHMAPURI RENAMED ISLĀMPURI. (1695).

On Saturday, the 11th May/7th Shawwal the imperial army moved from Nauraspur and Afzalpur, and reached Brahmapuri on the bank of the Bhimā on Tuesday, the 21st/17th Shawwal. By order, all the Emperor's sons, shāhzādas, and nobles made their "bow of blessing", on the occasion of arrival here. On the way to his mansion the Emperor passed by the tent of Shāh 'Alijāh; the circuit of the *dāira* appeared to him to be too large. The surveyor was ordered to measure the area, and restrict it to the area of Aurangzib's own *dāira* before his accession. A son was born to Muhammad 'Azim and the daughter of Ruhullah Khan [374], the father presented 500 mohars as *nazar*; the son was named Ruh-ul-quds. On Friday, the 23rd August/22nd Muharram a son was born to Bidār Bakht and Mukhtār Khan's daughter. Shāh 'Alijāh made his bow at Court and presented 500 mohars; the newly-born child was named Firuz Bakht. On Sunday, the 22nd September/22nd Safar, Muhammad Mu'izzuddin and 'Azim, when getting leave to go to Agra, went to visit Shāh 'Alijāh and each received a robe with *bālāband*, half-sleeves, turban-end and necklace of pearls, and an elephant. Khudābanda Khan was married to 'Umdat-ul-mulk's daughter, and got a robe. Zulfiqār Khan Bahādur was promoted to a 5-*hazāri* (4,000 tr.), Bakhshi-ul-mulk Bahramand Khan a 5-*hazāri* (3,000 tr.), Bakhshi-ul-mulk Mukhlis Khan a 3-*hazāri* (1,000 tr.) and Hamid-ud-din Khan a 2-*hazāri*.

A SHORT ACCOUNT OF THE DISASTER THAT BEFELL KHĀNAHZĀD KHAN AND QĀSIM KHAN BAHĀDUR.

When the Emperor learnt that Santā after robbing the imperial dominions was hastening with heavy loads to his own country, [375] and would pass within eighteen *kos* of the imperial camp, he ordered Qāsim Khan, an active and able officer who was commander of the country of Serā and had arrived near Serā, to go with his army to the path of the enemy and to punish him severely in company with Khānahzād Khan, Saf Shikan Khan, Sayyid Āsālat Khan, Muhammad Murād Khan and others who had been sent by the Emperor with forces composed of the mansabdārs of the khās chauki, the khās retinue and a large party from the 7-chauki and artillery.

On Sunday, the 19th January/23rd Jamad. S.,* the two

* The date given here is wrong by two months. *Akhbarat* 3972 shows that Qāsim Khan had been killed more than a month before 19th January 1696, and that 19th January, 1696 was the date on which mace-bearers sent to succour Khānhzād after the disaster and urge Hamiduddin on, returned to the Emperor's side. *Fort St. George Diary*, 5th December, 1695 records "A credible report that a Maratha army of about 15,000 men are coming into these parts and have already defeated Qāsim Khan Nawāb of Sirā."

forces united six *kos* from the track of the enemy. As Qāsim Khan's household property was at Ādoni and he wished to entertain Khwāja Khānahzād Khan and others to his heart's content, he brought out of the fort showy articles, like Karnātaki tents not yet used, gold, silver, copper and china vessels of all kinds, and sent them the next day with his own advance-tents and those of other āmirs to a distance of three *kos* (in advance). The enemy learning of the arrival of the advance-tents, divided his army into three bodies, of which one went to plunder the camp, the second to encounter the army, and the third was kept ready (in reserve). At four *gharis* after dawn the first body fell upon the advance-tents, slew and wounded many, and carried off everything. All of a sudden the news reached Qāsim Khan, who without rousing Khānahzād Khan from his sleep, hastened to the battle. [376] Before he had gone one *kos*, the second body of the enemy told off for the battle appeared and began to fight. Khānahzād Khan, on waking, heard of it and leaving the baggage camp, porters, burdens, and tents there, advanced quickly. As the enemy had a numberless force of "black infantry" musketeers and a very large body of cavalry too, a great battle was fought, and many were slain on both sides. In spite of the firmness of the imperial generals and men, and the loss of the enemy, the latter did not yield one foot of ground or show the least shaking. At this time the third or reserve division of the enemy fell upon the camp and baggage left behind and plundered everything. When this news reached Khānahzād Khan and Qāsim Khan in the very heat of the battle, their firmness was shaken, they held a consultation and resolved to go to the place where the advance tents had been sent, where there was a small fort (*qilacha*) named Dodderi and a tank before it. Fighting for a *kos* they arrived at the tank in the evening. The enemy now left this party at peace, and formed their *dāira* on one side. The imperial men who were in the small fort shut the gates upon them. The two Khans shared the food they had brought with the others; and the common soldiers had nothing to eat except the water of the tank, not to speak of grass and gram for the horses and elephants. As the night closed, the enemy surrounded [377] the imperialists who stood ready to fight. But for three days the enemy only appeared in view without fighting; till some thousand infantry from the zamindār of Chitaldurg, who had been humiliated by Qāsim Khan, came out to fight on getting an opportunity. On the fourth day, before it was dawn, ten times the former number of (black) infantry darkened the plain and began to fight. As the artillery ammunitions had been plundered, and what had been brought with the soldiers had been exhausted, the troops sat down in helplessness, after running about and groaning and sighing for some hours. As the enemy continued to hail musketballs, many men were destroyed here also. The survivors, seeing the path of egress closed to them, forced their way into the small fort. Trustworthy reporters who were present at the catastrophe and fought boldly said, "One-third of our soldiers were slain by the infidels in the two advance-tents (*pesh-khānahs*), on the way, and on the bank of the tank. The enemy besieged the fort on all sides and felt sure that the garrison would die of hunger. On the day of entering the fort, all the soldiers, high and low, were given bread of *jawār* and *bājra* out of the provisions of the place, and the straw of old and new thatches to the cattle. On the second day neither was bread left for men nor barley for the horses. In this irremediable distress, if life departs let it depart; Qāsim Khan was an inveterate opium-eater, his life depended on it, the lack of opium [378] became the cause of his death. He died on the third day, and thus escaped the enemy, who became bolder on hearing the news. The garrison were correspondingly depressed. Though the enthusiasts said, "How long should we bear hunger and die in this miserable way? Let us once fling ourselves on the infidels, and gain either martyrdom or victory. In either case, we shall escape from distress and gain merit," the chiefs did not assent to it. And while many died of hunger and the horses chewed each other's tails mistaking them for straw, the enemy overthrew one tower and raised tumult on all sides. Khānahzād Khan begged for safety, and a truce was made on condition that he would surrender to Santā the cash, articles, jewels, horses, and elephants of Qāsim Khan, besides twenty lakhs of rupees, and that the son of Balkishan, his trusted munshi and chief officer of his household, would be hostage. It was agreed. Santā sent word that the men might come out of the fort without any misgiving and stay two nights in front of the gate; those who had anything need fear no molestation; they might buy from his soldiers what they needed. The imperial soldiers left the fort after three days. From one side the enemy gave them bread and from the other water. They stayed two nights at the gate of the fort. On the third day, Khānahzād Khan started for the Court with an escort of the enemy. Hamiduddin Khan Bahādur who had been sent from the Court and Rustamdil Khan from Haidarabad to aid the besieged, united near Ādoni. [379] They gave necessary help to the defeated nobles in the form of tents, dress, and cash. R'adāndāz Khan, qiladār, exerted himself in helping beyond his means, and articles more than they needed were collected from the houses of all (the citizens) and from all sides. The enemy, who after gaining such booty had started for their homes, wished to fight Himmat Khan Bahādur, who on account of the smallness of his force, was staying at Basvāpatan inspite of his having received an order to punish the enemy.

DEATH OF HIMMAT KHAN.

The Khan Bahādur who had not more than a thousand soldiers with him, reached the enemy, and seemed likely to defeat them, when suddenly a musket-shot struck his breast, and he died instantly. The elephant-driver wanted to turn back, but Bāqi Beg, commander of the Khan's contingent, arrived there and told him, "The Khan is alive; drive the elephant forward. I shall drive away the enemy". He encountered the enemy and stood his ground well. But how long can a headless (army) make a stand? There was a small fort at hand, and he entered it. The enemy plundered his baggage, and besieged the fort for some days. Then finding it fruitless, they withdrew; Bāqi Beg seized the opportunity and came to Court. The Emperor ordered Khānahzād Khan to go to Zafarābād (Bidar) as Subahdār, Saf Shikan Khan to Dhāmuni as faujdār, Sayyid Āsālat Khan to Ranthambor as qiladār, and Muhammad Murād Khan to Dohad and Godrā as faujdār. The other soldiers joined the imperial camp. [380] The Emperor gave to Khan Jahān Bahādur and other sons of the deceased General mourning robes, for the death of Himmat Khan, and consoled them with his gracious words. With his own hands he presented to that high grandee (Khan Jahān) some *khardali* and said, "For a long time I have been eating these instead of betel-leaf". Bāqi Beg got a mansab of 5-*sadi*. Lutfullah Khan became ākhta-begi *vice* Saf Shikan Khan and dārogha of khās-chauki *vice* Khānahzād Khan, while Ikhlās-kesh, āmin of *jazia* for the province of Bidar became āmin and faujdār of the parganah of Indur *vice* Muhammad Kāzim. He was a 4-*sadi* (50 tr.) and now got 100 tr. more. Shāh 'Alijāh went towards Bahādurgarh, receiving a robe with half-sleeves, a *balaband,* and a *muttaka* of emerald with a ruby set in it : Prince Wālājāh got a robe and *arsi,* and Jahānzeb Bānu Begam a neck-pendant of ruby. Multafat Khan dārogha of khawāses, was promoted to be a $1\frac{1}{2}$-*hazāri* (200 tr.).

CHAPTER XL.

40TH YEAR OF THE REIGN : 1107 A. H.

25th March, 1696—13th March, 1697.

*   *   *   *

[381] On Wednesday, the 25th March/1st Ramzan he started from Islāmpur for Sholāpur, in order to observe the fast, say the Friday prayers, attend constantly at the mosque, and perform the prayer of I'd.

Sultan Muhi-us-sunnat, son of Prince Muhammad Kām Bakhsh, had interview; a daily allowance was assigned to him. Sher-āfkan Khan son of Shāhwardi Khan became faujdār of Narwar and was promoted to be a 1½-*hazāri* (1,700 tr.). Ārslān Khan a *hazāri,* got an increment of 500. Tarbiyat Khan getting an increment of 200 tr., became a 2-*hazāri* (1,200 tr.). Sayyid 'Azmatullah Khan by receiving an increment of 500, became a 2-*hazāri* (900 tr.). Bakhshi-ul-mulk Mukhlis Khan presented to the Emperor a poetical work (*diwān*) of Sāib in Sāib's own handwriting containing one lakh of couplets. As most of his poems are considered the choicest in the world and as they deal with moral advice and spiritual improvement, the Emperor accepted it. And for a long time the following ghazal was recited in the Emperor's Court, and men of wit used to imitate it, [omitted]. [382] Tarbiyat Khan, who had gone to punish the enemy towards the hill of Mahadeo, had audience on return and got a robe. 'Itiqād Khan son of Āmir-ul-umārā deceased, became faujdār of Islāmābād *vice* Raja Bishan Singh. On Monday, the 2nd August, 1696/13th Muharram, promotion of a *hazār* troopers was awarded to each of Raf'i-ul-qadr and Khujistah Ākhtar. Ramchand, thānahdār of Khatāv, was promoted to be a 2-*hazāri* (1,500 tr. *do āspā*), Dhundi Rao, brought by Tarbiyat Khan got the mansab of 1½-*hazāri* and the thānadāri of the hill of Mahadeo. Raja Kaliān Singh, zamindār of Bhadāwar, who had come to court, was given leave to depart. He was a 7-*sadi* (400 tr.), and now got an increment of 200 *zāt* (same tr.), Khudābanda Khan became first mirbakhshi of the āhadis *vice* Murid Khan. The Emperor learnt that Prince Muḥammad Mu'azzam had on Friday, the 2nd July/22nd Zil. H., started for Multān, by order of the Emperor. [383] Irādat Khan II named Mubarākullah, son of Irādat Khan I, son of 'Āzam Khan became faujdār of the environs of Aurangābād and was promoted to be a 7-*sadi* (1,000 tr.). Hamiduddin Khan who had gone to punish Santā and to raise the siege of Garh Dodderi reached Court and received praise and the title of Bahādur. At his request Rustamdil Khan and other subordinates received proper promotions. Shujā'et Khan Muhammad Beg, nāzim of Āhmadābād, became a 4-*hazāri* (same tr.). The Emperor learnt that 'Āqil Khan Subahdār of Delhi, had died. He was endowed with asceticism, freedom of spirit, independence (of worldly possessions), and control of mind. He served with vigilance and treated his peers with haughtiness. Mahābat Khan Ibrāhim, who was made Subahdār of Lahore, applied to the Emperor for permission to view the fort and palace-buildings of Delhi. A 'by order' granting the prayer was written to the Khan ('Āqil Khan). He wrote to the Emperor in reply, "I shall not invite him (to the fort) for certain objections : First, he is a Haidarābādi and not a man of such position that he should be allowed to view an imperial palace for his diversion. Secondly, the doors of all the rooms have been closed, lest (the things within) should be handled; the chambers are without carpets, and the sightseer is not such (an important person) that for his sake the palace should be cleaned and spread with carpets. [384] Then, again, at interview he will not behave in the manner I expect. Therefore there are preponderating reasons for not admitting him." When he arrived at Delhi and sent a message about this desire, 'Āqil Khan did not invite him, but gave a sharp and rough reply, and he had to leave for his destination. The Emperor shut his eyes to the Khan's selfwill and haughtiness on account of his long service, honesty, and devotion, and entrusted the discharge of important tasks to him. He was not without external accomplishments. Rāzi was his pen-name, and he has left a poetical work and *masnavis* behind. He considered himself peerless in solving the difficult minute points of the *masnavi* of Maulānā Rumi. He was liberal and charitable by nature.

Muhammad Yār Khan, who after going from the Court to Delhi, was without employment, became Subahdār of Delhi *vice* the deceased. He was a 2½-*hazāri* (1,500 tr.) and now got an increment of 5-*sadi* (same tr.). Sadruddin Khan a 1½-*hazāzi* got 500 *zāt* more, besides a position of honour. Ekkātāz Khan, son of Ekkātāz Khan became faujdār of Āhmadābād [*corr.* Jahānābād] Korah, a dependency of the province of Allahabad, *vice* 'Abdus Samad Khan. Tahawwar Khan, son of Salābat Khan, went to Sahāranpur as faujdār. Chhatra Sāl, an officer of the force of Lutfullah Khan, became a qiladār and faujdār of Nasratābād. Sakkhar, *vice* Sarfārāz Khan. Khan-i-'Ālam, son of Khan Zamān Fath Jang, a 6-*hazāri* (4,000 tr.), got an increment of a *hazār* tr. Munawwar Khan, his brother, a 4-*hazāri* (2,000 tr.), got 500 tr. more. Fathulla Khan a 2-*hazāri* (500 tr.), got an increment of 200 tr. Khānahzād Khan, who had been appointed [385] Subahdār of Zafarābād, had audience.

CHAPTER XLI.

41ST YEAR OF THE REIGN: 1108 A. H.

14th March 1697—2nd March 1698.

* * * *

The Emperor went from Islāmpuri to Sholāpur to perform the religious duties of Ramzān. After performing the two-fold prayers of 'Id-ul-fitr (13th April) he returned to Islāmpuri. Prince Muhammad Kām Bakhsh, 'Umdat-ul-mulk and others, great and small, who were in the base camp (*bungāh*), had audience and presented *peshkash*. Bakhshi-ul-mulk Mukhlis Khan, had a son born to him, for which he presented *nazar* to the Emperor, who named the child Muhammad Hasan. 'Abdur Rahim, son of Fāzil Khan Khān-i-sāmān, came to the Court from Delhi: his father presented some beautifully-woven pieces of China cloth (*khatāi*) and was praised. Kifāyet Khan Mir Āhmad, the dismissed diwān of Bengal, became peshdast of the Khālsa office *vice* Rashid Khan deceased. Hedāyetullah, son of 'Ināyetullah Khan, peshdast of the diwān-i-tan, became mir-i-sāmān of Zinat-un-nisā Begam *vice* his father. Subhān-wardi, son of Yalangtosh Khan [386] Bahādur offered presents on the birth of a son; the child was named Rahman-wardi. Fāzil Khan resigned the post of Khān-i-sāmān, and became Subahdār of Kashmir *vice* Ābu Nasar Khan. Khānahzād Khan got the post of Khān-i-sāmān with the title of Ruhullah Khan. Ābu Nasar Khan became Subahdār of Lahore *vice* Mukarram Khan who was summoned to Court. Khudābanda Khan became bayutāt of the Emperor. Sarup Singh, son of Raja Anup (*cor.*) Singh, was sent to his father. He was a 7-*sadi* (500 tr.) and now got 300 more. Matlab Khan and (*cor.*) Wajihuddin Khan were sent towards Indāpur to punish the enemy. Chin Qalich Khan Bahādur son of Khan Firuz Jang, being displeased with his father, came to Court. On coming near the imperial camp, he was granted an interview after a month's waiting. Ikhlāskesh became peshdast of Ruhullah Khan, Khān-i-sāmān. Bidār Bakht Bahādur was ordered to go to Shāh 'Ālijāh at Bahādurgarh, receiving a robe and an 'Irāqi horse with gold *sāz*. Matlab Khan, a *hazāri* (400 tr.), got an increment of 500 (100 tr.). Ihtamām Khan, by name Ālah Yār, became ākhta begi *vice* Lutfullah Khan. Tahawwar Khan, son of Salābat Khan, [387] came to Court, on being removed from the faujdāri of Sahāranpur, and got the post of dārogha of qurkhānah. Prince Muhammad 'Azim (Shāhzāda) became Subahdār of Bengal and faujdār of Kuch Bihar, *vice* Ibrāhim Khan who became Subahdār of Allahabad *vice* Sipahdār Khan, and whose son Zabardast (*cor.*) Khan became faujdār of Jaunpur. According to the Emperor's custom every year, rain-robes were presented to the princes, the Sultāns, the high amirs, and high and low among the officers at Court and the provinces. Mu'ataqad Khan, grandson of Lashkar Khan Shāhjahāni, was appointed defender of the Subah of Burhānpur *vice* 'Ināyet Khan son of S'adullah Khan deceased. Zulfiqār Beg, son of Dārāb Beg macebearer, showed the fruits of good training; he was promoted from the mushrifi of the stables to that of the diwān-i-Khās. Multafat Khan and 'Ināyetullah Khan were given rings set with ruby stones. Ism'ail Khan Makha was appointed faujdār of Islāmgarh *alias* Rāiri *vice* 'Abdur Razzāq Khan Lāri, who became faujdār of 'Ādil-Khāni Konkan.

FLOOD OF THE BHIMA

One of the marvellous occurrences of this mirage-like deceptive world, which is a testing ground (for true manhood) was the raging up in billows, of the waterless calamity-breeding ocean and the whirling of the fire-showering circle (the heavens), in a tempest of clouds. It took the form of the outbreak of a second Noah's flood, on the morning of Monday, the 19th July, 1697/10th Muharram, in the river Bhimā. Owing to heavy rains at a distance, [388] a terrible flood swept down, the very sight of which robbed people of their lives; none had the courage to look at it. Every moment the current, violence and wildness increased.

* * * *

At a distance of thirty *kos* from Bahādurgarh was the camp of Shah 'Ālijāh; the stores of fodder and fuel (*panthi* wood) which the merchants had collected, came down the river without being scattered. Many of the villages were totally destroyed by the force of the flood. The men and cattle seated on thatches were carried helplessly down, by the swift flowing water. Natural enemies like cats and mice, dogs and hares, looking at each other trembled for their own lives and drifted down peacefully together. After the water had extended and covered the plain, the *misls* of 'Umdat-ul-mulk Āsad Khan, Mukhlis Khan and others—many of (these) rich men having built charming houses on the bank of the river at great expense—were destroyed by the flood. The rich men got into boats and reached the bank of safety after being tossed about. Others lost both life and property in the river. * *

[389] The hillock on which stood the mansion of Wālā Shukoh, the tents of Shah 'Ālijāh, of Kām Bakhsh and other great and poor men, was forty yards high, more or less. In three days only four yards of it remained above water. Through God's grace, the water began to subside, in the middle of the third night, and the people were released from the captivity of water. * * * *

As the illness of Khan Jahān Bahādur Zafar Jang grew severer, the Emperor while returning from Sholāpur visited him at his house on Saturday, the 20th November, 1697/16th Jamad. A. The Khan was confined to his bed and could not rise; the Emperor sat on the *masnad,* and the Khan continued to lament that he could not kiss the imperial feet. He said, "I had wished to die in battle and thus be of service to Your Majesty." The Emperor replied, [390] "You have been devoting yourself to my service all through your life, and yet your desire for it is not satisfied!" Behold a servant's devotion and a master's favour! On Tuesday, the 23rd November, 1697/19th Jamad. A., the Khan died. He was a grand āmir, full of piety and virtues, and a great commander. His assembly (*muhafil*) was of great splendour, in which few persons spoke except he alone; he himself said what he desired; others had nothing to say except "Yes, it is so!" He did not like much talk. In his assemblies, the topics of conversation were mostly verse, prose, sword, jewel, horse, elephant, and aphrodisiacs. He did so many well-executed tasks and acts of bravery that even a few of them can not be recorded here.

On Friday, the 24th December, 1697/20th Jamad. S., Kām Bakhsh was made Subahdār of Berār. He was a 20-*hazāri* (7,000 tr.), and now got 3,000 tr. more. Mirak

Husain, his diwān, went as his deputy. As 'Umdat-ul-mulk's illness made it difficult for him to sign his name, the Emperor in order to expedite business ordered 'Ināyet-ullah Khan to sign. 'Umdat-ul-mulk Āsad Khan placed before His Majesty Zulfiqār Khan Bahādur Nasrat Jang's despatch, announcing that the Islamic heroes, with God's help, [391] had captured Jinji which was situated on a high hill and enjoyed the greatest fame and pre-eminence among the forts and strong places of Karnātak in respect of height and abundance of materials of war and defence, and that he had slain large numbers of the infidels; and that the wretch Rāma [Rajaram] who had taken refuge in this stronghold, being frightened at seeing the valour and hearing of the assault of the ever-victorious army, had fled away from the fort, leaving his family, property and things behind. On Monday, the 7th February, 1698/16th Shaban, this strong fortress, consisting of seven forts, was forcibly captured and annexed to the Empire. Four wives, three sons and two daughters of the luckless infidel, his dependants, friends, and assistants were made prisoners. And the hundred other forts which make up the kingdom of Karnātak with some ports of the Europeans, were annexed to the empire. The powerful and rich zamindārs (of the country) submitted and sent suitable tributes to the Emperor through the Khan Bahādur. 'Umdat-ul-mulk in reward for the excellent work, [392] got an increment of a *hazār* tr. making him a 7-*hazāri* (same tr.); Nasrat Jang by an increment of a *hazār* tr. became a 5-*hazāri* (same tr.), Rao Dalpat, an officer of Nasrat Jang, who had endured great labour and hardship in this war, was a 2½-*hazāri* (1,300 tr.), and got an increment of 5-*sad* (200 tr.). The conquered fort was named Nasrat-garh. 'Itiqād Khan who was appointed Subahdār of Agra, *vice* Mukhtār Khan, had his 500 conditional tr. made unconditional, and was given kettledrums. Siādat Khan died of pestilence. His son got his title, and with his other relatives received mourning robes and promotions. The post of dārogha of the diwān-i-khās, vacated by his death was given to Ruhullah Khan as an addition to his own post of Khān-i-sāmān; Qāzi 'Abdullah became Sadr.

CHAPTER XLII.

42ND YEAR OF THE REIGN : 1109 A. H.

3rd March, 1698—20th February, 1699.

* * * *

As in the last year, this year too, the Emperor went to Sholāpur to pass the month of Ramzān in religious observances. On the 2nd April occurred the 'Id-ul-fitr. Shāhzāda Bidār Bakht Bahādur who had been summoned from Bahādurgarh to Court, halted at Deogāon. Bakhshi-ul-mulk Bahramand Khan and Mansur Khan, Mir Tuzuk, advanced to welcome him and conducted him to the Emperor. Before coming to the Audience Hall, the interview took place in the mosque. He was sent towards Parnālā and presented with a robe with *sarpech* of ruby and emerald, a jewelled *punchhi,* a horse, and an elephant. The officers of his force all got suitable favours. Bhāgu Banjārah, who on his first coming to the Emperor had got the rank of a 5-*hazāri* (4,000 tr.) and had afterwards joined the enemy, again came over to the Emperor and was restored to his former rank, and given a robe, a horse, and an elephant. (*Verse*) :—

> This my court is not a court of despair; Even if you have broken your repentence hundred times, come (unto me) again.

Qāzi 'Abdullah died of (lateral) paralysis. Muhammad Ākram, one of the hereditary muftis of Delhi, who had been serving as qāzi of Aurangābād was summoned to court to act as qāzi of the imperial camp. 'Ināyetullah Khan was ordered that, as the department of the Sadr was a part of the department of the diwān, he should discharge the former work as deputy, till the appointment of another Sadr. He was a 9-*sadi* (70 tr.), and now got a *sadi* (30 tr.) more. The Emperor sent with Nur-ul-Haq a gracious *farmān,* eagerly inviting his brother Shaikh-ul-Islām [394] to come to the Court, as he had not come once to the Court after his resignation of the qāziship and return from the Holy Land, but was staying at Ahmadābad. The Emperor's desire was to appoint him Sadr, if he consented after reaching Court. The holy man was planning to go to the Court, when a severe illness overtook him and he hastened to the world for which he had been feeling a great desire. The Emperor sent orders to Muhammad Āmin Khan, to hasten to the Court from the army of Firuz Jang Khan, in order to take up this post (of Sadr). Ārshad Khan Ābul 'Ala, son-in-law of Āmānat Khan, had reached court after service in Kabul, and was now appointed diwān of Khālsa *vice* Kifāyet Khan deceased.

News came to the Court that Āmir Khan Subahdār of Kabul had died on Thursday, the 28th April, 1698/27th Shawwal. He was a perfectly beneficent āmir, of high dignity, one of the chief servants of the Crown, and a loyal expert officer. Among his great feats was the regulation and settlement of the disordered administration of the province of Kabul. The Emperor greatly trusted him. As he was the son of the Emperor's maternal aunt and had done excellent services and had thus displayed his greatness of character in the period of prince-ship, His Majesty was very sorry for his death. He sent an order to Mu'azzam to start for taking charge of Kabul, with [395] a *sarpech* worth 50,000 rupees.

On Friday, the 20th May, 1698/20th Zil. Q., Durgādās Rāthor, through the intercession of Shujā'et Khan Subahdār of Āhmadābād, brought to Court, as the instrument of his pardon, Buland Ākhtar, son of Muhammad Ākbar, who was born during that Prince's wanderings in the land of the Rāthors, left there on his flight from the country, and brought up by the Rājputs with a view to causing tumult and confusion. At his interview Durgādās came with his wrists tied together. The Emperor ordered him to be unbound, and gave him a robe, a jewelled dagger and the rank of 3-*hazāri* (2,500 tr.). Buland Ākhtar had audience in the private-chamber and got a robe and a *sarpech;* his residence (*dāira*) was placed within the *gulālbār*. Ābul Fath Khan, son of Khan Jahān (Bahadur) deceased, got a robe and a horse and permission to go to Delhi, in order to be married there. Neknām Khan, son of Himmat Khan, and grandson of Islām Khan, became bakhshi and news-writer of the force of Bidār Bakht Bahādur and was made a *hazāri* (300 tr.) by an increment of a *sad,* (200 tr.). Chin Qalich Khan Bahādur after punishing the enemy near Bijapur, came to Court. Satvā Daflé, had audience, through the mediation of Mun'im Khan, and got the rank of a 6-*hazāri* (5,000 tr.) and kettledrums. Bakhshi-ul-mulk Mukhlis Khan became a 3-*hazāri* (200 tr.). Tarbiyat Khan [396] Mir Ātish, who was sent towards Berār to break up the enemy's *chhauni*, became a 2½-*hazāri* (1,200 tr.). Ruhullah Khan, Khān-i-sāmān, got the same mansab. Muhtasham Khan, son of Shaikh Mir deceased, was reinstated after dismissal, as a 2-*hazāri* (1,000 tr.). Chin Qalich Khan Bahādur was sent against the enemy near Kotā, and presented with a belt dagger.

Hedāit-kesh Bholānāth, a convert to Islam, son of Chhattar Mal, became the head (*kul*) news-reporter after his father's entry into hell. Fazl 'Ali Khan (son of) Murshid Quli Khan became diwān of Multan. Mullā Ābul Qāsim had been enjoying a daily stipend of one rupee, on condition of chanting the Quran at the tomb of Shah 'Ālijāh's mother in Āurangābād. He was admitted as one of the new Deccani mansabdārs, and on account of his accomplishments he become a high officer and the first bakhshi of Kām Bakhsh and diwān of Bijapur, and got the title of Darāit Khan. He used to say, "I have a taste for poetry (*taba'-i-mauzani*) too". He took the pen-name of *Tez-hush* on account of his acuteness. Hamiduddin Khan Bahādur who had gone to demolish a temple and build a mosque (in its place) in Bijapur, having excellently carried out his orders, came to Court and gained praise and the post of dārogha of ghusalkhānah, which brought him near the Emperor's person. 'Askar 'Ali Khan Haidarabadi, was appointed Subahdār of Berār *vice* Kām Bakhsh. Muhammad Āmin Khan on coming to Court, got [397] the post of Sadr of all Hindustan, and three emerald rings with silver enamel. Muhammad Ākram came to Court from Aurangābād and became Qāzi of the imperial camp. Haibatullah 'Arab, having brought from Haidarabad things worthy of Emperors, presented them. Among them was a copy of the *Nehāiya* written by Mullā 'Abdullah, (the cook); the Emperor had got the first volume and had been longing for the second. He rewarded the man with an elephant, an increment of fifty troopers, a mansab of *hazāri*, and 1,000 rupees. Qutbuddin, envoy of Bukhārā, had audience. On the day of interview he was given a robe, 10,000 rupees, a mohar weighing 200 mohars, a rupee weighing 200 rupees, and on the day of farewell, a female elephant and 15,000 rupees. Zabardast Khan, subahdār of Oudh, was promoted to be a 3-*hazāri* (2,500 tr.). Fathullah

Khan was appointed to patrol round Parendā, and presented with a robe and an enamelled dagger.

YĀQUT, EUNUCH, WOUNDED WITH AN ARROW:

Khwāja Yāqut, *nāzir* of Kām Bakhsh, owing to his sincere fidelity and devotion to his master's interests, sometimes spoke to him true but harsh words [398], which offended some ruffians who had access to the Prince and stuck in his service. The villains wished to pierce him with an arrow. On Monday, the 12th December, 1698/18th Jamad S., when he was returning at night from the Prince's palace to his own house, a rascal, who was waiting on the way for an opportunity, shot a two-forked lance-like arrow at him. As he had some life still left in him, the Defender of Life prevented the arrow from entering into the membrane of his stomach, and made his arm serve as a shield. Otherwise he would have been killed.

(*Verse*) If the enemy is strong, the Protector is stronger still.

When the Emperor learnt of it, * * * he decided to inquire into the matter in order to protect his servants and ordered the chief of police of the camp to imprison five of the chief jam'ādars of the Prince's service, and to exert himself in finding out the archer. The kotwāl, after getting hold of four men who loyally surrendered themselves, reported that the *Kokah* (foster-brother) of the Prince was refractory. The Emperor ordered that Khwāja Muhammad, the Prince's bakhshi, [399] should bring the man to His Majesty. The bakhshi, after softening him with flattering words brought him in his company near the imperial palace, when he turned back at the instigation of some wicked men. What could he do? Fate was adverse to him. Khwāja Muhammad reported to the Emperor, "He will not come, and is making preparations for disobedience." The Emperor ordered that the Prince should expel him from the camp. The Prince summoned him, gave him two hundred *āshrafis,* a tent, and porters, and sent him away, and was displeased at his expulsion. He had not yet crossed the river, when the Emperor sent a message to the Prince, ordering him to bring this man with himself to His Majesty's Court and to intercede for the pardon of his insolence. The Prince summoning him back, took him to the Court. On being informed of it, the Emperor ordered the Prince to come to the Presence, leaving the Kokah in the diwān-i-khās. The Prince replied, "This man and I must have audience at the same place," and after taking off his own *bālāband,* he tied the Kokah to his person firmly round the waist. When these unpleasant acts were reported, the Emperor ordered him to remain in the Court-house (*'adālatgāh*). Then according to command, Bakhshi-ul-mulk Mukhlis Khan conveyed good advice to him. As fate was then hostile to the Prince, he did not listen to the good counsel. Hamiduddin Khan Bahādur was ordered to separate this bad companion from the Prince. The Prince drew his dagger (*katār*), the Khan grasped his hand to wrest it. The Khan received a cut, but through God's mercy the Prince remained safe; and what happened happened to that wretch. [400] The Emperor on learning of it, ordered that a tent should be set up near the jewel-room and the Prince confined in it by way of punishment, and the Kokah should be sent to prison for punishment. The Prince was dismissed from his mansab, and all his wealth, furniture, and insignia of dignity were confiscated. By order, the Prince's chief officers were brought before the Emperor, presented with robes. and taken into His Majesty's service.

At this time the head of Santā, sent by Ghāziuddin Khan Firuz Jang, reached the Court, and was ordered to be paraded through the chief parts of the Deccan. In many places of this book something has been already narrated about the villain; the rest of his history is this:—After the affair of Dodderi and the martyrdom of Himmat Khan Bahādur, Santā wanted to go towards Jinji. An imperial order to pursue him reached Hamiduddin Khan Bahādur who left the company of Ruhullah Khan to carry out the order, arrived quickly, fought with him, and recovered some of the elephants of Qāsim Khan. Then an order reached the Khan that Bidār Bakht had been ordered to chase him, and that he should come to Court leaving some of his officers who had been appointed to accompany the Prince behind. The Shāhzāda too had severe fights with the wretch, who escaped in safety every time. On the way to Jinji [401] the villain had had a fight with Dhanā Jādav, who was conveying Raja Rāma to Jinji, on account of an old quarrel. Santā triumphed, and capturing Amrit Rao, brother-in-law of Nāgoji, the companion and assistant of Dhanā, had him trampled down by an elephant. He also captured Raja Rāma, but Dhanā escaped. The next day Santā appeared with his hands tied together before Raja Rāma and said, "I am the same servant (as before). My rudeness was due to this that you wanted to make Dhanā my equal, and to reach Jinji, through his help. I shall now do any service that you may command". He released and conducted Raja Rāma to Jinji. In fighting with Zulfiqār Khan Bahādur, intriguing to instigate Kām Bakhsh, throwing the siege into confusion, and in capturing Ism'ail Khan Makhā, he took a leading part. When the fort was captured, he fled with Raja Rāma, and went towards Satārā to fight with Dhanā, who was there. In this battle with Dhanā fortune deserted Santā, he was severely defeated and fled from the field with only a few men to the zamindāri of Nāgoji, with whom he sought refuge. Nāgoji politely gave him shelter in his house; but his wife, whose brother had been slain by Santā, urged her husband and another brother not to let him go away alive. Nāgoji dismissed him with friendliness but his wife's brother went in pursuit, seeking for an opportunity of wreaking vengeance. At this time an imperial order to pursue Santā [402] reached Firuz Jang, and in addition to his own troops, the troops of Shāhzāda (Bidār Bakht) and Hamiduddin Khan were placed under his command. Matlab Khan, who was appointed *sazāwal,* on hearing this news came upon Santā. The stories vary, but he was either seized by the Khan and sent to hell, or was slain by the same claimant of blood (Mané's brother-in-law); his head fell into the hands of the soldiers of Firuz Khan and was sent to the Emperor. * * * * In return for this splendid service, the Khan was rewarded with a turban (*'āmat*), in addition to praise; and Matlab Khan got an increment of 500.

CHAPTER XLIII

43RD YEAR OF THE REIGN : 1110 A. H.

21st February, 1699—9th February, 1700.

* * * *

The Emperor went to Sholāpur to pass the month of Ramzān and to celebrate the 'Id. Mansur Khan was ordered to bring the harem of Kām Bakhsh from the base (*bungāh*). M'amur Khan became faujdār of Karnātak *vice* Ātish Khan deceased. Hamiduddin Khan Bahādur [403] became dārogha of the second jewellery department *vice* Muharram Khan (Khwāja Muharram 'Ali-Mardān Khāni) deceased. Rustam Beg Khan Circassian, one of the relatives of Rustam Khan Bahādur Shah-Jahāni, who had newly come to India and got into service, became qiladār of Mangalbidā *vice* Yahyā Khan. The Emperor ordered that Kām Bakhsh should perform the *zuhar* prayer in the mosque of the palace of Hasan-bāri and the *'asar* prayer in company with the Emperor. Muhammad Āmin, deputy of Sarbarāh Khan Kotwāl, was ordered that, as Mirak Husain the dismissed diwān and nāib of the Prince had misappropriated large amounts of imperial money, he should confine him in the *chabutra* and realise what the diwāni officers would report as due from him.

I knew this noble; he had many praiseworthy qualities but had no genius for conducting business. One of the many mistaken acts which are notorious through the world is this : like two or three other grandees whose names need not be mentioned here, and who delighted in the praise of mean people and their own servants for their alleged practical ability and honesty,—he too remained satisfied with such a [false] reputation. At last the whole thing was exposed. During his nāibship of the subah, his wicked sons, ruinous hereditary acquaintances, roguish faqirs, nimble-handed and glib, who enjoyed the confidence of this grandee, on seeing him so negligent and inexperienced, misappropriated the money of the Emperor and the Prince, and at last landed him in the police lock-up (*chabutra-i-kotwāli*), and then they themselves quickly fled to their homes, leaving him to suffer. [404] In short, some virtuous nobles, like Mukhlis Khan, Multafat Khan and 'Ināyetullah Khan, finally took pity on him, came to his aid, and together spoke well of him to the Emperor, so that he was released from confinement, but did not look up again, till death came to him.

By order Khudābanda Khan went to guard the base, and 'Umdat-ul-mulk came to Court to perform the prayer of 'Id. On the day of 'Id Kām Bakhsh rode on horseback in the cortege of the Emperor. Peshkash was presented to His Majesty (by many). Rewards and favours were conferred (for the 'Id). Buland Ākhtar came to make the bow of blessing for the 'Id. Ruhullah Khan after transfer from the dārogha-ship of the diwān-i-khās, got an increment of 5-*sad* to his former rank of 2½-*hazāri*. Hedāitullah Khan presented nazar on the birth of a son. Mansur Khan dārogha of artillery of the Deccan, reported that his brother Muhammad Yusuf Khan qiladār of Qamrangar (Karnul) had sent as prisoner, a man who had given himself out in that neighbourhood as the rebel Ākbar. He was ordered to be made over to Hamiduddin Khan.

On Thursday, the 20th April, 1699/29th Shawwal, Kām Bakhsh went to a tent, pitched one chain (*jarib*) outside the *gulālbār*. On Tuesday, the 16th May/26th Zil. Q., the messengers of Rānā Amar Singh had audience: they brought one elephant, two horses, nine swords, and nine drawers of leather as peshkash. [405] Kāmgār Khan and Raja Mān Singh son of Rup Singh (Rāthor) were 2½-*hazāris*, each got 500 more. 'Abdur Rahim Khan, brother of Khan Firuz Jang, a *hazāri*, got 500 more. On Tuesday, the 30th May, 1699/10th Zil. H., Kām Bakhsh went to and returned from the 'Idgāh before the arrival and return of the imperial cortege. On Sunday, the 18th June/29th Zil. H., he made his bow for being restored to his rank of 20-*hazāri*. On Saturday, the 24th June/16th Muharram, Chin Qalich Khan Bahādur returned to Court after chastising the enemy near Kotā. The Emperor ordered Bakhshi-ul-mulk Mukhlis Khan to advance to the gate of the fort of Islāmpuri to welcome him and to conduct him to his presence. By an increment of 500 (200 tr.) he was made 3½-*hazāri* (3,000 tr.). On Monday, the 10th July/22nd Muharram, Muhammad Ibrāhim, son of Najābat Khan deceased, who had the title of Khan-i-'Ālam, after being released from prison, was restored to the rank of 3-*hazāri* (2-*hazār* tr.) and appointed faujdār of Jaunpur. Indra Singh and Bahādur Singh, sons of Rānā Rāj Singh, were made 2-*hazāri* (1,000 tr.) and a *hazāri* (500 tr.) respectively. Muhammad Āmin Khan reported to the Emperor from the letter of Firuz Jang Khan that the zamindār of Islāmgarh, on being defeated by the imperial forces had fled and that Islāmgarh had been captured. A bogus Buland Ākhtar, the son of Shujā' who had appeared near Allahabad, was captured and conveyed to Gwalior by a mace-bearer, who brought a receipt under the seal of the qiladār. A cup of *mariyam* stone* [406] sent by Shujā'et Khan to Multafat Khan was shown to the Emperor. As it was dappled, the Emperor liked it. The Khan was ordered to write to Shujā'et Khan to make vessels like the cup and tray and send them to the Emperor. The Khan made and sent extremely nice vessels with some additional things, *viz.*, throne, cistern and bedstead of one piece and many carpet-stones of exquisite fashion and size. They were accepted by the Emperor. Wahid Khan, grandson of the famous Chagtāi, became thānadār of Ghorband; he was a 3-*sadi* (same tr.). Satvā Daflé,† who had come to Court, fled from the army through the deception of the dragon of ill-luck. Tarbiyat Khan Mir Ātish, Sayyid Khan, Shukrullah Khan Kashghari and others were sent to pursue and punish him. Hāji Khānam, sister of Khan Jahān Bahādur, came from Delhi to Court after her brother's death and received jewels worth 5,000 rupees, a half-sleeve, a *do-shāla* and 2,000 rupees in cash. Nasrat Khan son of Khan Jahān Bahādur, a 9-*sadi* (500 tr.) got 100 more, while his youngest son Ābul Fath Khan, a 7-*sadi* (300 tr.) got 3-*sadi* (100 tr.) more. Ziāullah, son of 'Ināyetullah Khan presented suitable peshkash on the birth of a son. Mukhlis Khan conducted to the Presence Muhammad Taqi, the chief of the merchants of Persia; he presented a *Qurān*, a Ghori *langar*, 27 tāqa of gold-embroidered cloth, and *'atr* of *fitna*. Ruhullah Khan became dārogha of the imperial retinue *vice* Zulfiqār Khan Bahādur [407] and Siādat Khan that of 'arz-i-mukarrar *vice* 'Abdur Rahman Khan. He was a *hazāri* (200 tr.), and now got 500 more. Saf Shikan Khan became agent of the Crown Prince. The Emperor ordered

* Stones used as weights to keep carpets stretched; usually placed on the corners.

† Satvā Dāflé—He was Satvāji Rāo Dāflé, the father of Bāji Rāo Chāvan Dāfle. The latter was mortally wounded in trying to storm the breach at the siege of Satārā, and the jāgir of Jath, W. of Bajapur, was given to the family in reward. The father was the jāgirdār. The family entered Bijapur service about 1672. (Letter from the present chief of Jath to me, 6-8-1916.) Satvā Dāflé is frequently mentioned in *Akhbārāt*, ann. 43, 48.

that Sarup Singh, son of Anup Singh, should bring the dependants of Raja Rāma from Zulfiqār Khan Bahādur to the Court; and that the dependants of Shivā who were in the *misl* of the 'Umdat-ul-mulk, should be brought by Hamiduddin Khan from that place and kept near Raja Shāhu in the *gulālbār*. Hifzullah Khan, son of S'adullah Khan, Subahdār of Tatta and faujdār of Siwistān, got an increment of 300 to his rank of 2-*hazāri* (700 tr.), at the request of Muizzuddin. Hamiduddin Khan Bahādur a 2-*hazāri* (1,400 tr.), got 100 tr. in addition. Shaikh S'adullah was removed from the mushrifi of the khawāses. I got that post in addition to my former one. Nasrat Jang Khan had audience, and received a robe, a horse, an elephant, and a jewelled dagger.

EMPEROR'S MARCH TO CAPTURE THE FORTS OF THE INFIDELS:

Conquest of Vasantgarh *alias* Kilid-i-fath :

[408] The Emperor after four years' stay at Islāmpuri, * * * wished to set out on expedition in person and to trample under the hoofs of his horse the land and forts of the infernal infidels. He ordered that a cutcha wall (lit. fort) with a circuit of two and a half *kos* should be built around the small fortalice of stone and plaster which had been constructed a year earlier to enclose the Emperor's quarters. This work was finished in fifteen days. Zinat-un-nisā Begam, the mother of the Prince, (*i.e.*, Udipuri), and other ladies of the harem, and the families of all (common) people were left in this safe base under the care of 'Umdat-ul-mulk Madār-ul-mahām Āsad Khan with a suitable force.

On Thursday, the 19th October, 1699/5th Jamad. A., the Emperor started at an auspicious moment. [409] I cannot record the marches and places of alighting at all the stages (of his journey). In short, he reached the outskirts of Murtazābād Miraj in twenty days. Prince Muhammad 'Āzam, who had been summoned to the Emperor from Pedgāon, had audience here, and received various favours, a special robe, a jewelled *dhakdhaki,* and a horse with enamelled *sāz*. As true news was received that Raja Rāma had gone towards Berār, Bidār Bakht was ordered to leave his camp at Murtazābād and hasten in pursuit of him.

Ruhullah Khan was given a robe and a sword and Hamid-uddin Khan Bahādur a robe and a *katār* and ordered to ravage the tract between Parnālagarh and Satārāgarh, leaving not the name or vestige of habitation. On the way, when the imperial camp reached the neighbourhood of the parganah of Karād the Emperor learnt that an imperial out-post (*thānah*) once stood here, but the enemy had ruined it, and that a mosque built here in former times was without a lamp. The Emperor marched two *kos* in that direction and [410] said two-fold prayers in the mosque and issued an order to populate the place and restore the *thānah*. The runaway ryots being reassured with promises of safety and reward, resumed their residence there. A party was appointed to guard them. From this place the Emperor went to a *thānah* named Masur, where a body of Islamic troops were staying. Opposite it, at a distance of three *kos* on the top of a strongly fortified hill was a firmly-built fort named Vasantgarh, belonging to the enemy and famous for its strength. * * *

The Emperor ordered Tarbiyat Khan Mir Ātish to ascend the hill and fight the devils. The Khan did in two days the work of two years, carried the artillery-men under the gate of the fort, and placing guns opposite to it, got ready for destroying the enemy, who did not abstain from cannonade and showering fire. On learning of it the Emperor ordered his tent to be pitched on the bank of the Krishnā, which flows at the foot of the fort at a distance of one *kos,* and said, "My object in this journey is nothing except holy war (*ghazā*), so please God and His Prophet. Next morning I shall mount my horse to conduct the assault, and raise my banner to slay the infidels". [411] On seeing the tent set up so near and hearing of the Emperor's determination, the enemy lost heart. * * * They cried quarters that very day, and wanted only to escape with their honour (family). As the Emperor is the protector of the weak, he graciously ordered that the garrison should be allowed to go out without their arms, instead of being put to the sword. At night the enemy got their opportunity of evacuating the fort, and next morning, Saturday, the 25th November, 1699/12th Jamad. S., the fort was conquered and renamed *Kilid-i-fath.* Much buried treasure, provisions, and weapons were seized by the imperialists in the fort.

On Friday, the 17th November/4th Jamad. S., the Emperor learnt that Bidār Bakht had had a severe fight with

Rāmā on the further side of the Nirā. Khan-i-'Ālam and Sarāfrāz Khan had distinguished themselves and the enemy had fled leaving his camp and baggage behind. The Shāhzāda and other [412] good warriors had rewards sent to them. Khan Bahādur Nasrat Jang was ordered to serve under the Shāhzāda and punish the vanquished Rāmā [Rajaram] wherever he might raise his head.

Two servants of Muhammad Ākbar from Qandahār brought to the Court a letter begging forgiveness and a casket of 'attar. A robe and a *farmān*,—stating that so long as he did not come within the frontiers of India he would not be pardoned, but that on his entering the imperial dominions a gracious order appointing him Subahdār of Bengal and conferring other favours would be issued to him,—were sent to Ākbar with these men.

Āmānat Khan *mutasaddi* of the port of Sūrat, died; his elder brother Diānat Khan succeeded him. Saifuddin Khan Safavi became qiladār of Sholāpur. Lutfullah Khan became Subahdār of Bijapur; he was a 2½-*hazāri* (1,400 tr.) and now got 500 *zāt* (600 tr.) more.

CAPTURE OF SATĀRĀ.

[413] * * * On Friday, the 8th December, 1699/25th Jamad. S., the imperial tent was pitched at the foot of the fort, at a distance of half a *kos*. On the other side was placed the camp of 'Āzam Shah. The army surrounded the environs of the fort. By order, Tarbiyat Khan Mir Ātish began to run trenches. In a few days the heroes reached the waist (of the hill) and carried heavy guns [414] up. A terrible fire was directed upon the fort. But what looked like the wall of the fort was entirely rock, thirty yards high, and above it had been placed sixty yards of *muzawwar* and *sangchin* (loose stones); there was no wall which could be shaken (by bombardment). As Satārā was the refuge and abode of the hellish infidel Rāmā [Rajaram], it was full of all the materials of strength, such as artillery, provisions, abundance of water from fountains which flowed even in summer, and soldiers of skill and desperate courage. Day and night, rockets, muskets, *huqqa, chādar, mashk* and *matwāla* were fired incessantly (from the fort). The countless force of the enemy outside the fort fell on the provisions and burnt the grass, the means of life of the cattle, for twenty miles round. On some occasions they boldly approached

the camp but were put to flight. Scarcity of grain and fodder reached the extreme point. Those who looked at the external aspect of things thought the conquest of the fort an impossibility. The Emperor relying on the Helper of *jihad*-fighters in the path of Allah, remained as firm and courageous as ever to vanquish the infidels, till at last, 13 *zir'a* from the door of the fort a raised battery was erected opposite the tower; in procuring materials for it not a tree was left within thirty or forty *kos*. From the side of the Prince, too, all the trenches were run to the foot of the fort. It was ordered that miners should run mines under the foundations of the fort. [415] Within a few days twenty-four yards of hard stony soil were excavated from the neighbourhood of the same raised battery. With these men (the miners) were present, according to command, two thousand Māvlé infantry who were very expert in capturing forts. One lakh and thirty thousand rupees, the salary of three years, was paid in advance to these men. And materials for scaling the fort, such as, ladders with steps, rope-ladders (*māl*), and leather covers (*jāmah*) were provided. * * *

And as in the opinion of the chiefs the mere assembling of these materials was not likely to result in the capture of the fort, Tarbiyat Khan made a portable ladder from the foot of the same raised battery, which (battery) was twenty four yards in height. For the materials of this ladder he used up a thousand camel-litters and bags of sack-cloth and (even) fine linen—the last of which was so scarce that less than four yards of it could be had for a rupee—and all the firewood of the plain around. After making a glacis, he carried the mine to the foot of the fort, and planted the wooden ladders above it. But the business did not prosper beyond this that the Khan had mounted rahkalas (small cannon) on the former raised platform (damdama) and the garrison could not show their heads above the fort-wall or fire muskets but had to sit down in hiding behind the wall and throw stones. The plan of storming the walls was not likely to succeed. The Emperor ordered that under the leadership of Ruhullah Khan, Fathullah Khan should run another trench from the side of the gate of the fort. On Friday, the 15th March, 1700/5th Shawwal, the Khan boldly following the right plans (416) carried the trench under the rewni (fausse-braye) of the fort in one month. Tarbiyat Khan, in order to remedy the weakness in planning he had shown in the work of forming ladders, excavated a recess in the sangchin of the fort, and made a cavity four yards on one side and ten yards on the other in the length of the wall. There was only a thin screen between the garrison and the heroes who kept watch in this recess. But from neither side did any body dare to cross this zir'a of land. It was decided to fill the whole cavity with gunpowder and overthrow the wall, in order to open a path for the easy entrance of the storming party. The Emperor ordered that in addition to the cavalry, infantry, artillery, khaschauki, Afghan and Ghakkar clansmen, other troops, and Karnatakis, who were present there day and night, Bakhshi-ul-mulk Mukhlis Khan and Hamiduddin Khan Bahadur should go with some thousand troopers and wait for the opportunity so that, when after the explosion of the mine, the forlorn hope* would enter the fort, they might reinforce them. On Saturday, the morning of 13th April, 1700/5th Zil. Q., at first a fuse was fired, the fort-wall fell inside and a large body of the garrison were burnt. In the expectation that this wall too would be thrown down inside, no warning was sent to the storming party to run back, but the (second) match was fired. The wall fell on the Mughal side, hills of stone and clay were showered on the thousands of men ready for the movement; those who had hidden themselves in mud-holes in wait for the opportunity (to storm), found ready graves there. [417] Many were flung into the nadir which resembled the coffin of (their) destruction, and their limbs were scattered. In short, nearly two thousand brave soldiers perished. Although a wide path for men opened of itself (in the wall) and some infantry ran to the top of the wall and cried "Come on! there is none here", yet so overcome were the men of the trenches by fear that none advanced. The plan was upset. What was done produced no better result than if it had not been done; so that, when after a few hours, the opportunity passed away and the enemy saw that none appeared on that side, they mounted the wall and made the hot place hotter still, occupied it firmly, and began to fire their muskets. As the damdama too had been thrown down, the rahkalas had fallen down, and the soldiers withdrew their hands from their work, who could encounter the enemy? At this time the Emperor boldly supported them from behind, so that they began to enter the fort over heaps of the slain. Yes, without the leader works fall into

* This was Bāji Chāvan Dāflé, ancestor of the chief of Jath (in the Bijapur district).

confusion; without the commander the hearts of heroes become as limbs without the head; even if the soldiers are one lakh, in the absence of that single individual (the leader), they do not amount to one, and if he alone enters the field he does not need the aid of this lakh of men. There is no doubt about it. (Verse) * * *

[418] This was the reason: the Emperor had in his foresight ordered a tent to be pitched in the waist of the hill, in order to go there personally with the Prince and himself conduct the operations. As Providence wished to further His own design, all the ministers joined together in dissuading His Majesty by entreaty. This day, too, the imperial cortege was kept ready to start, but after the work had been thrown into confusion what would be the good of his going there? The Emperor * * * repeatedly said, "How excellent would it have been if I had been with them and had thus accomplished a great success!" He sent cheering messages to the demoralised troops urging them to be firm, "Why are you overcome by mere imagination and agitation of mind? The enemy have not triumphed over you. Only your plan has miscarried. Well, if a roof falls down, do not a body of men perish in the sleep of negligence?" That very day Sarfarāz Khan, Manāji, and the troops of Bakhshi-ul-mulk Bahramand Khan were ordered to go and hold the trenches in company with Tarbiyat Khan. The relatives of some of the buried persons, who could make their way to the places where they were trapped, extracted the dead and the wounded and carried them to their quarters. What was more strange was that the *bahlia* infantry, saddened by the sinking down of their brothers, sons and friends, and angry with the Mir Atish, [419] on seeing that it was impossible to extract the dead from under the hill of stone and clay—and as it was the rule of their bad religion to burn the dead, secretly set fire that night to the entrenchments, which were entirely of wood. The fire burnt for seven days and nights. Where was the water to quench this wilderness of fire? Many Hindus and some Muslims that could not be brought out, were burnt together.

This nobleman (Tarbiyat Khan), in the hope of bread and fear of life, which all slaves of the Emperor have, had made such exertions in conquering the fort as the imagination cannot picture. But "Men plan, God alone performs". Holy God! the fortune of the Emperor was such as in these eighty-five years of his life wherever he turned his face, many remote objects and many high designs hastened to welcome him. On Tuesday, the 5th March 1700/25th Ramzan, news came that Rāmā, [Rajaram] who had made a dash towards Berar, had returned disappointed to his home and gone to hell there. On Wednesday, the 20th March/10th Shawwal, news came that his 5-year old son, whom his chiefs had set up as their king, [420] had died too. On seeing these divine aids and fearing extirpation, Parsuram, the chief officer of the infidel's household, came out of the fort (Parli) seven *kos* from Satara, and got the Emperor's pardon through the mediation of Ruhullah Khan. Subhān, the commandant of Satara, a prudent and lucky man, on seeing that other (Maratha leaders) were going to outstrip him in offering submission, and serving their own ends, that the fort wall on the side of the trenches of Tarbiyat Khan had fallen down for seventy yards up to half the tower, that many men had been destroyed by artillery fire, especially the gun 'Mulk-zabt', which had been mounted on a hillock behind the trenches of the Prince and commanded the fort, was demolishing the houses in the fort, that 400 men had been destroyed at the explosion of the mine, that Fathullah Khan had run lofty entrenchments to the gate of the fort, and was wishing to break the gate and demolish the wall at one blow,—found no refuge left to him except begging the Emperor's forgiveness, and sent an envoy (*miānji*) to Prince 'Āzam Shah to beg for quarters. He, taking pity on the lives of the thousands of men and women in the fort, interceded with the Emperor who granted his request. [421] The order of pardon was issued : the garrison were allowed to go in safety out of the fort. On Sunday, the 21st April, 1700/13th Zil. Q., our banners mounted the towers and parapets of that fort of infidelity. * * *

As the fort was captured through the mediation of the Prince, it was named 'Āzamtārā. The next day, the Prince brought Subhān with his hands and neck tied together to the Emperor who ordered him to be unbound and enrolled in the imperial service. He was given a mansab of 5-*hazāri* (2,000 tr.) a robe, a *katār,* a horse, an elephant, a *tugh,* a standard, kettledrums, and 20,000 rupees. * * *

[422] The siege of the fort from its commencement on 8th December, 1699/25th Jamad. S., to its conclusion on 21st April 1700/13th Zil. Q., occupied four months and eighteen days. I shall now narrate briefly the other events that happened during this period.

On Wednesday, the 6th December, 1699/23rd Jamad. S., four hundred *āshrafis* sent by 'Umdat-ul-mulk from the base as peshkash for the conquest of Kilid-i-fath, were presented to the Emperor. Bakhshi-ul-mulk Mukhlis Khan by command conveyed Kām Bakhsh to Shāh 'Alijāh; and at the Shāh's request it was ordered that at the time of holding Court Kām Bakhsh too should come. Shaikh Farid, son of Hamid Khan got the title of Khan. On Tuesday, the 26th December/14th Rajab, Bidār Bakht, returning from the punishment of Rāmā, [Rajaram] had audience. Nasrat Jang had audience and received many favours. On Saturday, the 6th January, 1700/25th Rajab, Ikhlās Khan, who had the title of Ihtamām Khan went out for patrolling, when the enemy appeared one mile from the imperial camp; a severe battle was fought; he was slain with his son and a son of Najābat Khan deceased, and many soldiers were slain or wounded. The post of the deceased [423] was given to Hamiduddin Khan, who got a special robe with a jewelled waist-*muttaka*. The Emperor learnt that Muhammad Āmin Khan was having an encounter with the enemy one and a half kos from the camp, and that if he got reinforcement he might vanquish the rebels. Hamiduddin Khan Bahadur was ordered to go to his aid. Bakhshi-ul-mulk Bahramand Khan and Hamiduddin Khan Bahadur who had gone towards Khatāv to bring in provisions, beat and drove away the enemy wherever he appeared, and conveyed large supplies to the imperial camp. After interview they were praised. Bahramand Khan got an emerald *muttaka* and Hamiduddin Khan a *sarpech*. Ramchand, thanadar of Khatāv, was promoted to be a 2-hazāri (3,000 tr.). On Wednesday, the 31st January, 1700/20th Shabān, the Crown Prince was made Subahdar of Lahore *vice* Ibrāhim Khan; a sword, a dagger, a shield, a quiver and a bow-case were presented to Buland Ākhtar. He made his bow in the private chamber.

CHAPTER XLIV.

44TH YEAR OF THE REIGN : 1111 A. H.

10th February, 1700—28th January, 1701.

* * * *

[424] Fāzil Khan, Subahdār of Kashmir, was ordered to administer the Panjab as the deputy of the Crown Prince. He was a $2\frac{1}{2}$-*hazāri* (1,200 tr.) and now got an increment of 500 (200 tr.). Vijay Singh, zamindār (*bumi*) of Amber, got the title of Raja Jai Singh on the death of his father, and his brother (Jamunā) got the title of Vijay Singh: He was a hazāri (800 tr.) and now got an increment of 500 (1,200 tr.). Chin Qalich Khan Bahādur was restored the 500 *zāt* deducted from his rank, and became a 4-*hazāri* (3-*hazār* tr.). Chhatra Sāl Bundela [*cor.* Rathor] became qiladār of 'Āzamtārā. On Monday, the 22nd April, 1700/ 14th Zil. Q., the Emperor visited the fort, and performed the two-fold prayer of thanks in the old mosque, built by the Bahamani kings, which was white-washed at His Majesty's command.

CAPTURE OF FORT PARLI :

When the Emperor [425] had finished the conquest of Āzamtārā and had appointed its qiladar and faujdar, he wanted to conquer Parli-garh. He ordered Fathullah Khan to go in advance and besiege the fort. The Khan reached the fort that very day and decided to run trenches directed towards the tower under which was a small door of the fort. The imperial officers quickly conveyed the siege materials collected at Satara to the foot of Parli. On Tuesday, the 30th April/22nd Zil. Q., the Emperor having traversed the intervening space in three days, encamped on the plain in front of the fort-gate. The Prince's camp was located before the imperial mansion. Ruhullah Khan became mir murchal. Chin Qalich Khan Bahadur and the soldiers of the Prince, and other forces of the army surrounded the hill of the fort on all sides forming a circuit of a few kos. Parli is even stronger than Satara. In short, the Khan without heeding its strength, worked hard to run trenches and to mount guns on a hillock commanding the fort, doing the work of years in as many days. But what shall I write about the excess [426] of rain and scarcity of grain and fodder? * * * The dark clouds showered day and night like the eyes of orphans. Houses were submerged. * * * In short, owing to the flood of the rivers and the non-arrival of provisions from all sides, famine became severe. I wonder at the firmness and strength of the Emperor who, without being alarmed by it, encouraged and consoled the soldiers. At last the Khan carried the trench under a very broad and long sloping rock, which on one side fifteen yards high and on another ten yards high, was situated opposite the small door. It was very difficult to mount this rock, but if it could be captured the conquest of the fort would be easy. On Tuesday, the 4th June, 1700/27th Zil. H., a few ladders were placed on the side which was ten yards high, and the heroes were ordered to escalade so that the enemy would assemble to oppose them. Then the Khan mounted the rock by means of another ladder secretly planted [elsewhere], with a body of heroes, and brought under their swords the enemy in the plain which extended up to the small door of the fort, and afforded ground for horse-riding. The infidels unable to resist ran to the door and the Mughals arrived there speedily. As it was not [427] the Khan's intention to enter the fort, he wished to mount the rock, station his men on it, and mounting a gun on it break the door. At this time he himself went down to send up bundles of wood and straw to make a refuge for the soldiers (on the rock). In the course of the fight three or four Mughals and one Bahalia entered the small door pell-mell with the infidels; others too wanted to do the same, when suddenly a Mughal was shot down, and the Bahalia losing heart, fled away in such a way as to mingle himself with others in flight. Seizing the opportunity the enemy closed the door, and began to fire muskets and throw huqqas from the top of the wall, and set fire to the gunpowder which, in anticipation of such a day they had hidden underground on the way leading to the fort. Faqirullah Khan, grandson of Fathullah Khan and sixty or seventy other men were killed, and many were wounded. The rest who could not maintain their stand on the top of the rock for its lack of shelter as it was exposed to deadly attack on all three sides, descended and took up their old position. But this feat struck terror into the hearts of the infidels. Next morning they permitted the two men who had entered the fort with them to go out by the gate towards the imperial army, and crying quarters besought the Prince for safety. As the Emperor had based the work of conquest on the counsel of the Prince and he always accepted the Prince's suggestions, according to the Emperor's order the Prince's men sent the garrison out of the fort on Sunday, the 9th June/3rd Muharram, [428] without their weapons, property and wealth. This seat of Islam, which through the tricks of the hellish Shiva had gone out of the possession of the Bijapuris and been turned into a seat of war (dar-ul-harb) verified the verse "Truth came and falsehood disappeared". The old mosque was filled again and the new temple was destroyed; this fort had been built by Ibrāhim 'Ādil Khan in 1625 A.D./1035 A.H. and as he used to give the name of Nauras to all newly-made things, (such as the title of the book of Mullā Zahuri, the name of the city of Nauras-i-Ibrāhim, and the name of the *dam* or coin Nauras,) it was now named Nauras-tārā. * * *

MARCH OF THE IMPERIAL ARMY TOWARDS BHUSANGARH :

After the capture of Nauras-tārā, the Emperor wished to march towards Bhusangarh. Although getting out of such a bad place was regarded by high and low in the army as a great boon, yet owing to material and celestial calamities there was no beast of burden left in the wide camp. * * * The soldiers considered it a great comfort to stay there, [429] and could not march under the load of fatigue. But the Emperor is the custodian of the comfort of his people and if he had not wished it, none could have come out of that dangerous place.

The return march commenced on Friday, the 21st June, 1700/15th Muharram. The gypsies willy nilly, had to load their household goods on cocks. One march was followed by two halts, in order to enable the men mounted on pack-saddles devoid of baggage to arrive by any means they could find. Many of the army passed over five kos in three stages, and reached the Krishnā which was in such a high flood that the banks could not be seen. The army finished the crossing in a few days, and with great difficulty reached Sābitgarh and the neighbouring villages. On Thursday, the 25th July/19th Safar the camp arrived near

Bhusangarh. The rains went back to their houses. The army regained peace of mind. The violence of the rivers and nullahs ceased. The people got safety and comfort. The Prince was ordered to go to Khāndesh, the land of repose and stay at Burhanpur, in order to refresh his troops. And the war-worn soldiers were sent to various flourishing places in the old dominion. Orders were sent to the provincial governors to send fresh troops to the Emperor. Prince Bidār Bakht, who with his own troops, [430] had been guarding the base, was summoned to the Presence. After interview he was deputed to conquer fort Parnāla. In addition to his own troops, Zulfiqār Khan Bahādur Nasrat Jang was appointed to serve under him; and after some time Tarbiyat Khan, Mir Atish, too. As the Emperor's sole wish was to give ease to the people, he decided to make Khawāspur, which was about one day's journey, his base, so that the soldiers accompanying him might enjoy repose during his stay there. On Friday, the 30th August, 1700/26th Rabi. A., the army started for the place, and on the arrival there the soldiers really gained ease through the comparative abundance of grain, fodder and most other necessaries. * * *

In a waterless river, the name of whose bed (*qalb*) is "the mirage of abundant water", and on both banks and middle of which many commanders and soldiers of the right and front (divisions) [431] had pitched their tents, never dreaming that up to the day of Resurrection, a drop of water would descend on it except in the rainy season, the verse "The oven spouted forth water" at Noah's deluge came to be proved true. On the night of Tuesday, the 1st October, 1700/28th Rabi'. S., there was rain in the heights, the hill streams set their faces towards it. While the men were fast asleep in their tents, all on a sudden the water came down raging from both banks and spread over the plain, turning the land into water. The tents were ruined. Vast numbers of men and animals were drowned. The rest became prisoners of water. If the remaining period had been night and the flood had continued longer than four or five gharis of day, no one would have remained alive. By the grace of God the dawn appeared; the men saved their lives. They sought for the traces of their houses and found none. Giving up all hopes of their property they went crying in all directions. In some *misls* which had been located on distant and high hillocks, no news arrived of what happened (in the river). Praised be God that no harm befell the imperial tent which was pitched very high. * * *

As I have not yet recorded certain incidents from the beginning of the 44th year [432], I shall now narrate them to the end of the Sh'abān (last month) of that year, it being necessary for the historian of events to preserve the chain of narrative.

Zulfiqār Khan Bahadur Nasrat Jang, who had been ordered to punish Dhanā Jādav returned to Court, after crushing him. He and his companions Dāud Khan, Dalpat, Rām Singh, and others, got praise, robes, jewels, and promotion. Prince Muhammad Mu'izzuddin, Subahdar of Multān, was rewarded for having wrested the fort of Dhaohar from the possession of the zamindar of Dogra, with an increment of 2-*hazar* tr. making him a 12-*hazari* (6,000 tr. doāspa). Prince Muhammad 'Azim, Subahdār of Bengal, got the hazār tr. that had been reduced from his rank. Hifzullah Khan Subahdār of Tatta, a 2-*hazāri*, (same tr.) got 500 more at the Shāhzāda's request. Fāzil Khan Subahdār of Kashmir, who had declined to act as deputy Subahdār of Lahore, and applied for permission to come to Court, had the 200 tr. which had been given him on condition of being deputy, taken away from his mansab, and his application was granted. On the way, he died at Burhānpur. He was an upright, honoured, and faithful man. 'Ināyetullah Khan was ordered to give jagir for 3,000 tr. to Kām Bakhsh in *tankhwā* and not to insist on a new memorandum (*yād-dāsht*). Khudābanda Khan bayutāt, became Subahdār of Muhammadābād *vice* 'Askar Khan, with an increment of 500 (same tr.); Fazāil Khan, mir munshi, dārogha of the library, [433] became bayutāt *vice* him. 'Ināyetullah Khan became diwān of Bidār Bakht Bahadur. The Emperor learnt that Hindus did not take (cooked) food during imprisonment, and hence Raja Shāhu, son of Sambhā, used to eat sweet-meats, fruits, and *pakwān*, instead of (cooked) food. Hamiduddin Khan conveyed to him this message, "You are not a prisoner; you are living in your own house. You should eat cooked food." Zinat-un-nisā Begam who had been summoned from the base, arrived on Saturday, the 12th October, 1700/10th Jamad. A., mounted on a chaudol. Kām Bakhsh and Buland Ākhtar welcomed her by advancing. Fidāi Khan, Subahdar of Bihar, got the faujdāri of Tirhut and Dārbhanga. He was a 2½-hazāri (same tr.) and now got an increment of 500 *zāt* unconditionally. When the affairs of the country fell into confusion on the death of Bulbāris Khan, king of Kāshghar, the Emperor ordered Ārslān Khan, son of Shāh Khan and grand-son of the late king's uncle, who was in the imperial service, to go home and take possession of the kingdom. Sardār Khan of the Crown Prince's army, was permitted to help him. Sadruddin Muhammad Khan became Subahdār of Khāndesh *vice* Mu'ataqad Khan, and was made a 2-hazāri (same tr.) by an increment of 500 troopers [434].

EMPEROR'S MARCH TO CAPTURE PARNĀLĀ

On Monday, the 16th December, 1700/16th Rajab, His Majesty marched towards Murtazābād Miraj, arriving there on Wednesday, the 1st January, 1701/2nd Shabān. Bakhshī-ul-mulk Mukhlis Khan, son of Saf Shikan Khan, grandson of that Qawāmuddin Khan who had been Ṣadr of Persia, and brother's son of the renowned Khalifā Sultān, died of severe illness on Saturday, the 3rd January, 1701/4th Sh'abān and was buried in the tomb-garden (*rauza*) of the saint Sayyid Shamsuddin, situated in the new city (Miraj). He combined nobility of birth with perfection in the discharge of his profession. Independence of earthly needs and freedom of spirit were natural to him. The Emperor used often to say about him, "I have a young Khalifā Sultān with me". Ruhullah Khan became second bakhshi *vice* the deceased, and was succeeded by Saf Shikan Khan in the posts of Qurbegi and bakhshi of the āhadis.

CHAPTER XLV.

45TH YEAR OF THE REIGN :

29th January, 1701—18th January, 1702.

The Emperor stayed at Miraj during the month of Ramzān. When it was over, on Sunday, the 2nd March, 1701/3rd Shawwāl, he started for the conquest of Parnālā and Pawangarh, close to it, a very lofty fort nowise inferior to Parnālā in strength. On Saturday, the 9th March/10th Shawwāl, the imperial camp was pitched in the environs of the fort, at a place (facing) the door of the fort, on the bank of the river that flows under the fort within gunshot. [435] That day I took omens in the poetical works of His Holiness Hāfiz concerning the conquest of the fort, and my eyes fell on the following couplet :

> The heart which has the invisible world in sight
> possesses the cup of Jamshid,
> Why be anxious about a ring which gets lost for a
> moment ?

In truth, this ring of auspicious inscription (*i.e.*, Parnālā) had often been taken possession of by Muhammadan kings. Shivā wrested it from the 'Ādil-khani kings. Afterwards, when the whole country of the Deccan was cleansed of the filth of infidel dominion, it was captured by the imperialists through the exertions of Muhammad 'Āzam. Then Sambhā recovered possession of it through some of its defenders conducting themselves like infidels and the negligence and cowardice of its qiladār. Thank God, it now again came into the hands of the Muslims. In short, Nasrat Jang Khan, was sent to punish the rebel 'thieves' on whichever side they might raise their heads. Shāhzāda Wālā-tabār and other forces having come, some of the troops accompanying the Emperor were ordered to pitch their tents on the other side of the fort. The army surrounded the circuit of both the forts, seven kos in extent. Under the supervision of Tarbiyat Khan trenches were run, and guns [436] began to play on the enemy. In a short time five towers of the fort were demolished down to more than half their height. This commander exerted himself marvellously in breaking the stony soil and running up lanes (tunnels) into the hilly region. Having excavated a distance of some *jarib* (land-measuring rope) under the ground, he made a path, through which three fully armed men could walk abreast at their full height. At a distance of some paces a chamber was made large enough to seat twenty soldiers. On all sides of it windows were made for the wind to blow and the sun to shine in. He stationed his artillerymen in this house to prevent with their muskets the enemy from showing their heads above the wall. This lane was carried under the tower on which the guns were playing, and its base was hollowed out so much that a party of heroes kept watch in it without being touched by the *huqqa* and *matwala* of the enemy. And at last he led this lane inside the fort by carrying it under the outer breast-work of the gate. But as delay occurred in the progress of the work, the rainy season was close at hand, and this country on account of its bad weather in the rains, the intervention of some rivers difficult to cross, and the difficulty of bringing in supplies, was not fit for the encampment (chhauni) of the imperial army, the Emperor ordered Fathullah Khan, who had gone to Aurangābād to refresh his broken troops and had recently returned to the Presence, [437] to run a second trench from the side of the troops of the Emperor's son, under the command of that Prince [Kām Bakhsh] and with the co-operation of Mun'im Khan. The Khan, in one month, cut away the stony soil of the high hill and carried the lane to the foot of the gate. The garrison of both the forts fought (for a long time). But when they saw the running of lanes, and the skill of the musketeers, and apprehended that Tarbiyat Khan from one side and Fathullah Khan from the other would destroy the impregnability of their fort, that Muhammad Murād Khan with his followers and Khwāja Muhammad, bakhshi of the army of Kām Bakhsh wished to overthrow the towers and battlements of Pawangarh, that the besieging army had left to the garrison little chance of flight, and that it was the Emperor 'Ālamgir who never gave up his purpose on account of rain or other accidents and these were troops who never left their work undone, * * they saw no recourse left to them but to submit and sent men through the mediation of Tarbiyat Khan [438] to the Emperor's son and the Shahzada to beg for quarters. These two gracious ones taking pity on the multitude of likely victims recommended the prayer for mercy, which the Emperor granted. Trimbak, the qiladār was permitted to depart with his life and property. On the 28th May, 1701/1st Muharram, the conquest was accomplished, and the two forts annexed to the Empire. Parnālā was so high that Āzamtārā could not lift its head above the wall of the former. * * * [439] Parnālā was renamed Nabishah Durg.

I shall now narrate certain former and synchronous events of this year. Sher Zamān Khan, qiladār of Kabul, became nāib Subahdār *vice* Nāsir Khan, who was punished by reduction of his rank by 500 *zāt* (600 tr.); Sadruddin Muhammad Khan Safavi, got the tittle of Mirzā. The Emperor learnt that Ghāziuddin Khan Bahadur Firuz Jang had arrived by command to guard the base. Chin Qalich Khan Bahadur, son of Firuz Jang, having left his father on account of ill-feeling, by command went to Aurangābād. Jān Sipār Khan, son of Mukhtār Khan, nāzim of Haidarabad died; the subadārship was entrusted to the agents of Kām Bakhsh. Rustam-dil Khan, son of the deceased, (Jān Sipār Khan) became nāib (Subahdār) and received an addition of 500 *zāt* (same tr.) to his rank of hazāri (500 tr.). Bulbāris Khan became guardian of the base at Murtazābād, and received an addition of 500 *zāt* (100 tr.) to his rank of 1½-hazāri (500 tr.). Dāud Khan became faujdar of Karnātak Haidarābādi (Bijapuri) as deputy of Nasrat Jang.

As the Emperor could not ride out to perform the two prayers of 'Id-ul-fitr (28th February, 1701) owing to the violence of his catarrh (*nazlah*), [440] Kām Bakhsh with his sons and Buland Ākhtar, made the bows of congratulation (for the 'Id) to the Emperor, who ordered that instead of the name of *nazar* that of *niāz* should be applied to the presents made by the Princes, and that of *nisār* to those of the āmirs. Qutbuddin, envoy of Turān, who had received his *congee,* begged the Crown Prince on reaching Kābul to admit him into the imperial service; he was given the rank of a hazāri (200 tr.).

On Friday, the 18th April, 1701/21st Zil. Q., the lightning struck the courtyard of the diwān-i-khās; a *kahār* of the *ābdār-khāna* was hit by it and killed but the other men remained safe. The Princes, Sultans, and āmirs of the Court and the provinces sent money for *tasadduq* to the Emperor. Hifzullah Khan, son of the late S'adullah Khan, Subahdār of Tatta, died. Among the sons of the Khan he was not without ability. Khānahzād Khan, son of S'aid Khan Bahādur Shāh-Jahāni, was appointed Subahdār of Tatta and faujdar of Siwistān, at the request of Mu'izzuddin. He was a 2-hazāri (100 tr.) and now got an increment of 500 (700 tr.) and the title of S'aid Khan. Multafat Khan got the title of Khānahzād Khan. Ism'ail Khan Makha became faujdar of Nabishāhdurg. He was a 5-hazāri (4000 tr.) and now got 1000 tr. more. Muhatsham Khan son of Shaikh Mir, had been appointed a 2-hazari *zāt*, he got back a hazār tr. which had been reduced. Hamidudddin Khān Bahadur got [441] a robe and waist-*muttaka*, Tarbiyat Khan Mir Atish a robe and *sarpech*. Khairāndesh Khan Kambuh faujdār of Etāwah, got seven lakhs of *dām* as *in'ām* and the faujdāri of Dhāmuni also. Chin Qalich Khan Bahādur became faujdār of Karnātak Bijapuri *vice* M'amur Khan; a 4-hazāri (3,000 tr.) before, he now got an increment of 600 tr.

News came to the Emperor from the subah of Ahmadābād that Shujā'et Khan Muhammad Beg, the nāzim, had died on the 16th June, 1701/20th Muharram. He was a wonderfully fortunate man, as he rose from a low position to the dignity of an āmir. He was an upright and efficient officer, an able general and administrator, never committing any blunder, and possessing many noble qualities.* Ārshad Khan, diwān of Khālsa, died.

'INĀYETULLAH KHAN BECAME DIWĀN OF TAN AND KHALSA.

'Ināyetullah Khan, in addition to his post of diwān of *tan*, got the post of diwān of *Khālsa vice* the deceased. He was a 1½-hazāri (150 tr.), and now got 100 tr. more. 'Umdat-ul-mulk Āsad Khan, who had been summoned from the base to the imperial army, had audience on Thursday, the 28th August/4th Rabi. S., Lutfullah Khan was transferred from the subahdāri of Bijapur to that of Aurangābād and by an increment of 500 tr. became a 3-hazāri (2,500 tr.)

---

* The MS. here adds the following words which have been omitted in the printed text :—"The people of the subah acknowledge his miracle-working power and read the *fātiha* on his tomb." For an account of this officer's able administration, see Sarkar's *History of Aurangzib*, V. Ch. 58, Sec. 3-7.

Ābu Nasar Khan [442] son of Shāista Khan was restored to his rank of 2½-hazāri (1000 tr.) and got the subahdarship of Mālwa *vice* Mukhtār Khan and an increment of 500 (1,500 tr.). The Emperor issued a farmān on Shāh 'Alijāh, who by command had formed his *chhauni* at Dhār in Mālwa, to march to Āhmadābād as Subahdār. As I have finished briefly narrating the events of the whole year, I shall turn to the account of the Emperor's march from Nabishāhdurg towards Khatāv.

Account of the conquest of Sādiqgarh, Nāmgir, Miftāh and Maftuh: * * * * * The Emperor who had stayed for some time in the environs of Parnālā in order to capture it, started for Khatāv for the benefit of the people, as the abundance of provision in that place would give comfort to the creatures of God, and also the report of the march of the imperial army would lead to the recovery of forts Wardhangarh, Nāmgir, and Chandan and Wandan, from the hands of the infidels. [443] With this view, the army started on Thursday, the 29th May, 1701/2nd Muharram.

Fathullah Khan, who had been created a Bahadur in reward of his splendid services, was ordered to go with an advanced detachment and put down the rebellious infidels. The Khan hastening, struck at the waist of the hill-garrison of all the four forts, and slew a number of the enemy, and seized innumerable cattle and prisoners. On seeing this feat and the arrival of the army, the garrison of Wardangarh saved their lives by flight, leaving the fort empty, on the 6th June/10th Muharram. As the Khan Bahadur's name was Muhammad Sādiq, the fort was renamed Sādiqgarh. On Monday, the 23rd June/27th Muharram, the Emperor ordered his tents to be pitched in the environs of the fort, which is two kos from Khatāv, for the purpose of *chhauni*. From this place he sent the Khan Bahadur with a large force under the command of Bakhshi-ul-mulk Bahramand Khan to conquer Nandgir. In ten or twelve days, the qiladar of Nandgir in fear of his life interviewed that great minister, and surrendered the key to the Khan Bahadur [444] and the fort was renamed Nāmgir, on account of the renowned (chiefs) having turned to its conquest. From this place the Muslim army started for the conquest of Chandan and Wandan, which were renamed Miftāh and Maftuh. First Chandan was besieged, and in a short time the garrison begged for quarters. Next, fort

Wandan, a first-rate fort, was encircled by the army. The garrison had no recourse except to beg for safety. On Monday, the 6th October, 1701 they evacuated the fort. * * *

These four strong forts were conquered not in four months [445] but in four days * * * *

In the course of this time, Umdat-ul-mulk Āsad Khan came by command from the base to the Court and had audience. Ghāziuddin Khan Firuz Jang arrived from Berar and was appointed to guard the base. Mukarram Khan, who had taken to a life of retirement on a pension, came from Delhi to see the Emperor, and after a few days was given leave to return to his place of pious retreat.

Capture of Khelnā and other events : [pp. 446-447] * *

The Emperor turned to the conquest of this (Khelna) fort. For this purpose the army started from the neighbourhood of the fort of Sādiqgarh on the 7th November, 1701/16th Jamad. S., and reached the environs of Malkāpur in twelve stages. On account of the roads from this place to the Āmbā-ghāt being difficult to traverse and for the purpose of removing obstacles and intricacies, there was a halt of seven days (here). Bidār Bakht, who at the time of returning from Nabishāhdurg [448] had been given leave to pass the rainy season near Hukri, and Gokak and the neighbouring tract, and had conquered many of the forts of the infidels in a short time, was now ordered to come to 'see' fort Khelna with his troops by way of Borgaon, and having burnt many villages and wadis on the way, met the Emperor at this stage. Owing to unseasonable rain, all sorts of hardship were borne at this unpleasant place. At last through the agency of Fathullah Khan Bahadur, came the joyful news of the roads being cleared and this distance of four kos which was extremely hard to pass, was traversed by the army with its abundant baggage with the greatest ease.

On Saturday, the 6th December, 1701/16th Rajab, the skirt of a hill, which on account of the spaciousness of its open space and the elevation of the ground was suitable for the residence of the army, was fixed upon as the quarters of the troops. As Khelnā is three and a half kos from it, and the imperial army had not passed through this region

* Hukeri and Gokak, in the Belgaon district (Bom. Gaz. xii. 567 and 500).

more than two or three times in such large numbers and with such materials (before?), the haughty heads of the inhabitants of that quarter were trampled by the chargers of the imperial army. In all the paths of this hilly tract are impregnable forests and dense thorny jungle, at which even the sun dares not look. [449] Lofty and stout trees abound on all sides like the wretched infidels. The branches were so intertwined that even an ant could hardly pass through them. The path that there was, was difficult even for footmen. The defiles and pits were deeply sunk. The hills were firmly rooted in the soil. The Khan Bahadur was ordered to remove these difficulties and hindrances from the path. Under his supervision and efforts, sappers (men with spades and axes) and stone-cutters in one week wonderfully accomplished the work. Hills were removed; ups and downs levelled, and trees cut down. Thus a level road was made broad enough for a hundred horsemen to march abreast easily.

On the 23rd December, 1701/3rd Sh'abān, the Khan Bahadur was presented with a special quiver and sent to guide the imperial army under the command of Umdat-ul-mulk Madār-ul-mahām Āsad Khan and with the co-operation of Hamiduddin Khan [450] Bahadur, Mu'nim Khan, Ikhlās Khan, and Raja Jai Singh, and begin the siege of the fort. On the 26th December/6th Shaban, Umdat-ul-mulk was given the title of Amir-ul-umara, a jewelled dagger, 4000 ashrafi as reward and the honour of kissing the Emperor's feet, and sent (to the siege). On that day the Khan Bahadur with Hamiduddin Khan Bahadur, Mu'nim Khan and some other brave warriors entered the pass before dawn. As the enemy had strengthened the walls of the towers on it and occupied before-hand the hillock overlooking the fort which the Khan Bahādur had kept in view for mounting guns on, the Khan turned to them. Having posted Hamiduddin Khan Bahādur to guard the ambuscade on the left, Fathulla Khan Bahādur himself went to the right side. Having extinguished with the wind of valour their first day's fuse, he with 13 or 14 men suddenly fell upon the devils without number, and doubled the height of the hillock with the heaps of the slain. The enemy saw no recourse save in flight. They flung themselves down in bewilderment from the hillock and wanted to run to the fort. The Khan Bahādur [451] before he started had sent (some) men armed with *jazirahs* (long matchlocks fired from rest) to punish the enemy, and these were staying in the road leading to the fort. The enemy finding this road closed by this measure, fled to the jungle and hid themselves under the trees. At this time another division of the imperialists had arrived close behind (the first), and spreading out captured many of the enemy. The Khan Bahādur sent them into the pit of destruction by tying rocks to their waists. After this victory, he thought it good generalship to take a firm stand on the hillock. Tents were pitched there. In the evening the news reached the Emperor. The Khan Bahādur was rewarded with an increment of 200 tr., a standard and a jewelled dagger, Hamiduddin Khan Bahādur with a *katār,* Mu'nim Khan with an Arab horse with gold coated *sāz* (as his horse had been killed) and the Emperor's own food. Promotions were given to all the followers (*barādari*) of the Khan Bahādur. The night was spent in entrenching. Next day another hillock was captured from which arrows and guns could be shot into the fort. Guns were mounted on the hillock so as to burn and demolish the houses of the garrison. A covered lane was commenced. [452]

On Sunday, the 11th January, 1702/22nd Shabān, the Emperor went to view the work done and inspect the fort, and ordered the trenches to be pushed on. And on Friday, the 16th January/27th Shabān, he removed his camp from its former position to the plain half a *kos* from the fort in order to back the front division and expedite the work.

CHAPTER XLVI.

46TH YEAR OF THE REIGN:

19th January, 1702—7th January, 1703.

* * * *

On Monday, the 19th January, Bidār Bakht, who had been sent to patrol round the base camp and that region, was ordered to turn back and station himself near Nabishāh-durg. Muhammad Āmin Khan, Sadr-us-sadur, was given a promotion of 200 tr. and a standard, and sent to descend through the pass (*kotal*) of Āmbā ghāt into Tal Kokan, and devastate the enemy's land up to the gate on the further side of Khelnā, and close the path of ingress and egress to the garrison of the fort. Tarbiyat Khan by command, sat down at the entrance (mouth) of Āmbā ghāt. Muhammad Āmin Khan, [453] plundered the parganahs and villages of that tract, seized many captives and cattle, and engaged in closing the Kokani gate of the fort.

I shall now record the deeds of Khan Bahādur Fathullah Khan. Having planted guns and *jazirahs* he boldly carried the (covered) lane up to the ditch situated before the *rewni* of the fort. The garrison, on their part incessantly fired guns and muskets, day and night, and carried away the lives of men of all kinds working in the covered gallery (lane of safety). The Khan Bahādur firmly pursued his work. The lives of friends and foes alike were not worth purchasing at half a grain of barley. The enemy who had run a concealed lane from the gate of the fort, and sat in the *rewni* for offering opposition, on seeing that the Khan Bahādur had made planks (*dhābs*), arrived in front and wished to mount the ladders,—lost their senses and stood perplexed with their faces to the walls. * * * They destroyed the ladders, which had been raised from the midst of the pit to the level ground under the gate. The Khan Bahādur having made ladders out of *kajāwahs* (camel-litter) and fastened *dhābs* above them, advanced in front of the advancing party.

I shall now briefly narrate the deeds of Muhammad Āmin Khan. He had been sent to close the Kokani gate.

Having bravely traversed the sky-high hill of Māchāl, [454] he arrived at a hillock opposite the gate overlooking the *rewni* of Khelnā. The enemy had built stone-walls on it and deep ditches before it. * * In short, for a time the veil of difficulty covered the face of the progress of the undertaking. On Wednesday, the 4th March, 1702/15th Shawwāl, in utter disregard of life, he climbed the hillock with honour-seeking heroes, expelled the enemy from the redoubt and drove them back to the *rewni*. Heaps were formed by the slain. The road was closed to the garrison and victory was gained. The Emperor on hearing of it gave the title of Bahādur to the Khan and sent him a *dhup* (Deccani sword), a robe, and a *farmān*. His comrades got suitable promotion, swords, waist-daggers, horses, elephants, and robes.

The Emperor in his foresight summoned Bidār Bakht from Nabishāhdurg, and ordered him [455] to attempt the conquest of the fort from the side of the Kokani gate, with his own troops and those of Raja Jai Singh, the defender of the trenches of Fathullah Khan Bahādur, and a few thousand infantry sent by Yāqut Khan, collector (*mutasaddi*) of Dandā Rājpuri. He began to run trenches and overthrow towers and battlements by cannonade. Muhammad Āmin Khan Bahādur was recalled to the Emperor on account of illness. Although Fathullah Khan Bahādur with great exertion fastened *dhābs* to the extremely hard rock and reached the waist of the tower, and ran lanes from all sides, * * * yet the success of the work did not come in sight at all. Inspite of the severe bombardment by the shots of the guns, *Sher-dahan* and *Kark-bijli,* which could split hills, only a few stones were loosened from the tower. The enemy ceased not to shower incessently *matwālahs* weighing 100 maunds and 200 maunds. Some nights they made sorties and fell on the trenches. The Khan Bahādur personally fought to resist them. One day he was himself helping the labourers in binding the *dhābs,* when a stone fell from above on a plank 16 fingers' breadth in width, and broke it to pieces. The Khan being hit on the head by it rolled down a long distance and at last reached the edge of the *Kajāwah,* which arrested his descent and saved his life. His waist and (some) other limbs were severely bruised. After a month he was able to leave his bed, had audience, received a special *sarpech,* and returned to his work. He was [456] planning to make a feint and assault the fort from the side of another tower, when through the exertions of Bidār Bakht the *rewni* of the fort was captured on the 27th April, 1702/10th Zil. H., which meant in effect that the fort of Khelnā was conquered. In this assault Raja Jai Singh and his men did splendid service. At the breaking down of this barrier the enemy lost their composure of mind, even though they were as numerous as (the armies of) Gog and Magog. * * *. The Shāhzāda was rewarded with a jewelled *sarpech*, the Raja with the increment of 500 *zāt* (2-*hazār* tr.), and other heroes with promotion and favours. Āsadullah, son of Saifullah Khan, who used to travel on the roads with great speed and bring intelligence, was given his father's title. The Shāhzāda (was) ordered to carry the guns forward and batter down the gate of the fort—which was not so very strong, high and hard to open as the gate on Fathullah Khan Bahādur's side. But what shall I write of the severity of the rain, which fell incessantly and fast, gallopping like a two-horsed* trooper without let or hindrance, and ran for 10 and even 20 days at a time without opening the eyes or raising the head? But inspite of all this, the warriors of both the [457] trenches moved with the speed of the wind *sarsar*: as they had no fear of the enemy, so they paid no heed to this cruel calamity. Fathullah Khan in spite of the road for assault not being prepared, the *dhābs* (planks) having fallen down, and confusion having overtaken the work, determined, that if he had to make an assault he should at once climb the wall with the speed of wind and thunder. Parashurām, on seeing all these preparations for his ruin, sent to the Prince some Brahmans to make certain requests and to offer to surrender the fort. A few days were spent in carrying messages to and fro, through the mediation of Bakhshi-ul-mulk Ruhullah Khan and Fazāil Khan bayutāt, who had been deputed by the Emperor. At last, His Majesty granted no prayer except this that he and the garrison would go out with their lives. On Thursday, the 4th June/19th Muharram, Parashurām planted with his own hands the flags of the Shāhzāda and the Bakhshi-ul-mulk; and on Sunday, the 7th June, 1702/22nd Muharram, he came out under the veil of the darkness of night. By the Emperor's command none hindered him. * * *

[458] The Emperor renamed Khelnā as *Sakhkharlanā* (=God made hell subject to us). The hills and soil of this

* *Du-āspa*—a trooper who carries a spare horse with him and can therefore always travel very fast,

tract are wonderful : there is (as it were) no trace of hill or land, you see only herbs and flowers. Those who want to behold God's skill will find nothing so appropriate for their purpose as this garden-like hill and plain. There is not a tree that does not confer some benefit. It has no flower that does not charm the brain with its smell. Every grain of this wide plain can supply the revenue of countries from its fruits and aromatic roots; every particle of its dust attracts the heart. * * *

On Wednesday, the 10th June, 1702/25th Muharram, the Emperor visited the fort by way of the trenches of Fathullah Khan Bahādur; Zābit Khan with sufficient materials was made its qiladār. Its face is very strong. * * * But inside it has no buildings, gardens or reservoirs that excel those of other forts or can please the mind. As it is a frontier fort and the vast kingdoms of Bālāghāt and Pāinghāt (Talkokan) were annexed to the Empire through its conquest, and as Emperors have a thousand secret political reasons for every affair, therefore its conquest [459] was regarded as a great victory. Next day the Shāhzada was rewarded with one lakh of rupees as *in'ām*, by the Emperor in greatness of joy, and sent towards Hukri and Rāibāgh to form his encampment. Fathullah Khan Bahādur was rewarded with a jewelled *jigha* and the addition of *'Ālamgirshāhi* to his title. Ruhullah Khan and Hamiduddin Khan Bahādur each received an increment of 200 tr. Khānahzād Khan, a 2-*hazāri* (400 tr.), close to the Emperor's person, got an increment of 500 tr. and an elephant. Mu'nim Khan became *dārogha* of *filkhāna* and was promoted to be a *hazāri* (300 tr.). 'Abdullah Khan, (*cor.*) brother of Khwāja Lutfullah (an old servant of the days of Princeship), the dismissed *qiladār of* Agra, was removed from his rank of 2-*hazāri* (1,000 tr.), for some reasons. Mir Ābul Wafā, grandson of Ziāuddin Khan deceased, elder brother of Khānahzād Khan, was made *dārogha* of *jā-namāz-khāna* in addition to his former post, *vice* Fath Muhammad Qul, the deceased old servant. The fineness of understanding and ingenuity of intellect which was innate in his fertile genius, displayed itself in the Emperor's Court in a short time. One instance of the brilliance of his genius was this : A letter was received by the Emperor from Muhammad Mu'azzam Bahādur Shāh written in cypher (*khatt-i-ramz*). As it could not be deciphered, the Emperor handed his private memorandum-book over to the Mir saying [460] "I have left (undeciphered) two or three obscure hints (*ramz*) of this letter. Compare them with these and extract the meaning." The Mir, guided by his penetrating sight and quick-moving brain, brought that puzzling *ramz* out of the veil of obscurity into the light of deciphering, and, writing out the purport of the Prince's letter in full, showed it to the Emperor. The Emperor praised him and formed a high opinion of his capacity. He was rewarded for this with a mohar weighing 50 mohars, 500 rupees, and an addition of 20 tr., to his rank by which he became a 4-*sadi* (30 tr.).

On the 18th February, 1702/1st Shawwāl, the 'Id-ul-fitr was celebrated as usual. As the Āmir-ul-umarā was ill, the Emperor graciously ordered that he would issue from the inner side of the hall of justice which was henceforth ordered to be designated "the hall of the oppressed", enter the passage and sit down in the *kathra* at a distance of one *zir'a* from the steps of the *hujra* (cell). For three days he sat there and afterwards stood as before. 'Ināyetullah Khan was presented with an elephant. Mukhtār Khan, nāzim of Agra, a 2½-*hazāri* got an increment of 500. Tarbiyat Khan Mir Atish, a 3-*hazāri* (500 tr.), got 500 more. Diānat Khan *mutasaddi* of the port of Surat, by an increment of 500 became a 2-*hazāri* (150 tr.). On the 27th April, 1702, occurred the 'Id-uz-zuha. On Tuesday, the 25th August/12th Rabi. S.,* screens were set up round a tent containing the prophet's relics. [461] The Emperor acquired blessing by making a pilgrimage (*ziārat*) and keeping vigil there. Incidentally he learnt that a person had come within the *gulāl-bār* in a *pālki*. An order was issued that none should come in a *pālki* except the Āmir-ul-umarā, Bahramand Khan, Ruhullah Khan, Khānahzād Khan and Hamiduudin Khan Bahādur. 'Azizullah Khan Qurbegi was made qiladār of Qandahār (within the Deccan) *vice* Sazāwar Khan. A 1½-*hazāri* (800 tr.), he got an increment of 200 tr. Bidār Bakht was ordered to guard Aurangābād. Lutfullah Khan, nāzim of that place was sent as Subahdār of Berār as deputy (*nāib*) of Khan Firuz Jang. But before reaching the place he died. He was endowed with learning and great bravery, and repeatedly did excellent service, and spent most of his life in high offices at the Court or in commanding troops outside. On Thursday, the 5th November/25th Jamad. S., Bahramand Khan Mir Bakhshi, brother's son of Ja'far Khan,

* On the 11th Rabi. S. Shaikh 'Abdul Qādir Gilāni died; on the 12th Rabi. A. the Prophet passed away.

son-in-law of the Āmir-ul-umarā died of paralysis. By command Kām Bakhsh condoled with the Āmir-ul-umarā and brought him to Court. The Emperor soothed his wounded heart with consolatory words, and presented him with a special robe and a jewelled *sarpech*. The deceased Khan was a noble possessed of dignity, modesty, grandeur, purity of nature, gracious looks and amiability. Zulfiqār Khan Bahādur Nasrat Jang became Mir Bakhshi *vice* the deceased. [462] Khudābanda Khan became faujdār of Karnatak-Bijapuri *vice* Chin Qalich Khan being restored to his former post. Muhammad Yar Khan *nāzim* of Delhi, became faujdār of Morādābād, and by an increment of 500 (same tr.) was raised to the rank of 3½-*hazāri* (300 tr.), and presented with kettledrums. As Mun'im Khan had shown delay in going to reinforce Muhammad Āmin Khan, he was punished with decrease of 200 *zāt* (50 tr.) and removal from the post of (dārogha of) *filkhānah*, Hamiduddin Khan Bahādur getting that post and an increment of 500 *zāt* (250 tr.) to his rank of 2½-*hazāri* (850 tr.). Although I had numerous offices and was appointed to write urgent secret orders, yet the post of munshi of the *nazārat* was added to them. The post of newswriter was conferred on my son Hāfiz Muhammad Muhasan *vice* myself.

News came to the Emperor from Delhi that Zebunnisā Begam had died. The Emperor was so saddened by the news as to shed tears, but had to resign himself to God's will. Order was sent to Sayyid Āmjad Khan, Shaikh 'Atāullah, and Hāfiz Khan (Nur Muhammad) to give alms (for the benefit of her soul) and build her tomb in the appointed place, namely the Garden of Thirty-thousand (*Tis Hazāri*), which was a legacy from Jahānārā.

* * * *

[463] Return of the Emperor from Sakhkharlanā to Bahādurgarh and some other events.

On Wednesday, the 10th June, 1702/25th Muharram, the imperial army set out towards Bahādurgarh. One can imagine how very long a time the army took to cross, in the midst of this heavy and incessant rain, the pass (*kotal*) which it had traversed in many days even in dry weather. Of the baggage-animals, * * * * the camels refused to set foot on this path; the elephants began to carry the loads of the camp in a dazed condition, but through the inclemency of the weather sank into the mud like donkeys. * * * * What was (to be) undergone was undergone. Porters carried on their heads the property and baggage of all the men (of the army). * * * * [464] Rich men, reposing in the paradise of comfort, somehow or other arrived at the foot of the *kotal* which was the first halting-place. Owing to the non-arrival of the stores (*kārkhānazāt*), the imperial army had to delay. The Emperor ordered the things to be entrusted to the commandant of Sakhkharlanā. After seven days the forward march was resumed. The *nullah* in the way permitted the imperial cortege to pass, and then opened its mouth to devour the people. For some time a halt had to be made here. Whosoever was drowned was drowned, and he whom fate saved was saved. As the march for the next stage was renewed, the same *nullah* was encountered. It was a strange fraud of the deceitful (*nullah*) that it first cunningly allowed the passage of the advance-tents of the Emperor and other owners of advance-tents, and afterwards ran like a rash horse, making all people utterly helpless. The owners of elephants with much persuasion and coaxing rescued from the *nullah* their usurped property. Others could only cry *Alas*! and strike their foreheads. At last at a distance of one *kos* the Emperor took the left side road to Malkāpur. In this stage a *nullah* obstructed the path without heeding the lamentations of the people. * * * In this evil time grain sold at a rupee a *seer;* fodder and firewood appeared only by mistake. The helpless people died from the heavy rain. Having trodden their property underfoot, the men passed their time in peace of mind, [465] and wondered at the hardness of their lives.

One day Muzaffar, a mansabdār of the Emperor's own retinue, interviewed His Majesty during his journey. After alighting at the mansion the Emperor addressed Hamid-uddin Khan Bahādur, saying "Dilarām was a slave-girl (*parastār*) of long service; after bringing up (her) daughter she had married her to Muzaffar, who to-day came under my notice during the journey as a whitebearded man. Have the couplet

> "Fix your heart on the Heart's Delight (Dilārām) that you have,
> Withdraw your eyes from the rest of the world,"

and this hemistich, "You will be unique if you be devoted to one", written in a large hand and carving them on a stone-slab, bring them to me". The Khan carried out the order in a few days and presented the piece to the Emperor who said "Give this stone-slab to Muzaffar to carry it to Delhi and fix it on the tomb of the deceased Dilārām." Five hundred rupees were presented to him. An order was issued to the clerks of Delhi to give a *tankhwa* (assignment) on the revenue of the province for one year's salary to the man. After two years when he returned to the Emperor he got his full and standard (*kamāl*) salary and an increment of 50 *zāt*. * * * *

[466] On Saturday, the 4th July, 1702/19th Safar, the Emperor crossed the *nullah* on an elephant and pitched his tent at a distance of one *kos* from it. He got a place to sit down in the *hujra* (small room or recess) of the *'adalat*. The Prince and other grandees had not even the power to stand in their tents. His Majesty, patient as a mountain, spacious as the ocean, used frequently to say, "A little cloud is showering rain, a little wind is blowing. Why then have the people been seized with despair?" He encouraged them by repeating the (Qurānic) verses, "O ye who believe! seek help with the patients and with prayer, for God is with the patient. But ye understand not. With a little fear and hunger, and loss of wealth and lives and fruits, will we surely prove you! but bear good tidings to the patient, who when a misfortune happens to them say, 'Verily, we are God's and to Him shall we return".*

Ah! After a few days of darkness, the sun broke forth again and cheered the people.

On Sunday, the 26th July, 1702/12th Rabi. A., when the labouring army after traversing fourteen *kos* [467] in one month and 17 days, reached the foot of fort Nabishāh-durg (*Panhālā*), the sun again shone in the former manner. The men in need of food began to stir, and appetite and avarice again prevailed. The chill passed away from the mind. Porters ran on all sides. A load descended from the heads and necks of the people. * * *

The men lagging behind, in a condition which may no man ever see! came up limping. On Wednesday, the 29th July/15th Rabi. A., the imperial camp reached Vadgāon.†

---

* *Qurān*, ii 150-151. A warning to the faint-hearted in the Prophet's army, uttered before the battle of Bedr or that of Ohod.

† Vadgāon, 13 miles east of Panhālā, and 4 miles south of the right bank of the Varnā.

After a stay of one month and eight days, it set out for Bahādurgarh. On Sunday, the 6th September/24th Rabi. S., although the rain did not cease, and news came of the flood in the Krishnā river, these difficulties could not deflect the Emperor from his purpose. Covering nine *kos* in sixteen days of march and halt, the whole army reached the river bank. The river was violent and wavy. The army began to cross in boats. [468] In this state of hardship half the army crossed over in ten days. The Emperor embarked to cross to the other bank. The imperial camp stayed for twenty days more on the opposite bank, till the whole army had crossed in safety. * * *

Hence he marched by stages to Ās'adnagar, where he halted a few days, and then encamped at Bahādurgarh. In travelling through these (last) stages, the Emperor gazed on a road four *kos* from beginning to end in length, bordered on both sides by the paraphernalia of the army of Ghāzi-uddin Khan Bahādur Firuz Jang. The Khan had sent from the base of Islāmpur his *mahalla* (troops for review) with splendid equipment and decorations and material exceeding the means of a high grandee, and guns above the allowance of a general, and abundant *peshkash* of every kind. Among them a short sword was accepted by the Emperor and named "the Young Ghāzi". Much of the artillery was confiscated to the State. The Emperor issued an order that the *āmirs* should not keep more guns than those allowed. It is proper to give here a copy of the sentences written by the Emperor himself, according to which a 'By order' letter [469] was written to Bidār Bakht, "The *mahalla* which Khan Firuz Jang, a 7-*hazāri*, showed in his quarters, contained guns, *gajnāl, shutarnāl, ghornāl,* and all (other) things, as many as he ought to maintain according to his *mansab,* nay, more than what ought to be kept by a general, in addition to what had been placed under him by the Government. Why do you, who are getting double his salary, waste your money, and spend it without any use (in return for it)? The doing of what is required of us as a duty, is in itself an evidence of perfection. Verse :—Only a little of life is left, and yet the master of the house is senseless with pride!" * * *

CHAPTER XLVII.

47TH YEAR OF THE REIGN : 1114 A. H.

8th January, 1703—27th December, 1704.

* * * *

Conquest of fort Kondānā : On Thursday, the 3rd December, 1702/24th Rajab, the army set out for the conquest of Kondānā and on Sunday, the 27th Dec./18th Shabān arrived at the foot of the fort.

[470] Muhammad 'Azim, the Subahdār or Bengal, got in addition the Subahdāri of Bihār, *vice* Shamshir Khan, who became Subahdār of Mu'azzamābād Oudh. A promotion of 500 *zāt* unconditionally in each case was given to Najābat Khan, Subahdār of Burhānpur and faujdār of Baglāna, a 2-*hazāri* (1500 tr.), Shiv Singh qiladār of Rāiri, a *hazāri* (same tr.) and Sarāndāz Khan, *nāib* of the subah of Berār on behalf of Khan Firuz Jang, a 1½-*hazāri* (500 tr.). Muhtasham Khan became qiladār of Naldurg *vice* Qāsim Khan, Bidār Bakht the nāzim of the subah of Aurangābād became Subahdār of Khāndesh (in addition?). A 15-*hazāri* (10-*hazār* tr.), he got an increment of 2-*hazār* tr. Nasrat Jang Khan was sent to punish the enemy near Burhānpur, and rewarded with a jewelled *muttakā* and four elephants. Sultan Muhi-us-sunnat, son of Kām Bakhsh, got the rank of 7-*hazāri* (2,000 tr.), a standard and kettle-drums. Mu'izzuddin, Subahdār of Multan and Tatta was rewarded for his exertions in extirpating the turbulent Bakhtiār, by the sending of a royal letter, a robe, a jewelled dagger, and praise. He was a 12-*hazāri* (8-*hazār* tr.) and now received an increment of 2-*hazār* tr. and a reward of ten lakhs of *dām*. [471] Chin Qalich Khan Bahadur got the Subahdāri of Bijapur, a *sarpech,* and a horse, and his son an elephant and a horse as reward. Kām Bakhsh was sent with a robe and a jewelled *sarpech* to bring Zinat-un-nisā Begam from Islāmpuri to Bahādurgarh. Sadr-us-sadur Muhammad Āmin Khan was appointed under him. On Saturday, the 13th March, 1703/6th Zil. Q., the retired

Fazāil Khan,* son of Wazir Khan, (Mir Hāji), Mir Munshi, Bayutāt and deputy Khān-i-sāmān, died. Virtues and accomplishments were the upper garment of this expert one of our times. He used to say about himself, "The man is present. Where is the work?" The Emperor said about him, "He used to discharge the duties of deputy Khān-i-sāmān in such a way as almost to illuminate my house". 'Abdur Rahim, son of Fāzil Khan deceased, who came to Court from Delhi after his father's death, got the post of bayutāt, the title of Khan and increase of rank. The Emperor said, "Fāzil Khan 'Ala-ul-mulk and Fāzil Khan (Burhānuddin) have great claims on me for their services. I shall cherish and bring up this house-hold servant". And he too had great capacity and worth. But he died in a few days in the bloom of youth. And as none was left of this family except Ziāuddin, brother's son and (own) son-in-law of Fāzil Khan Burhānuddin, he was summoned to Court from the diwāni of the country of Chināpatan [472], given an increment of rank, the title of Khan and the post of bayutāt. The good services and ability of Fathullah Khan Bahādur in conquering forts and punishing the enemy are so much in circulation in the mouths of people that there is no need to record them here. He had set his heart on being appointed to Kabul and had often requested the Emperor about it; on Friday, the 28th May, 1703/23rd Muharram, his desire was granted. He got an increment of 500 to his rank of 2½-*hazāri* (1,000 tr.) and started for Kabul in great joy; Muhammad Quli, newly arrived from Persia (*vilāyet*), got a *hazāri* (100 tr.), the title of Khan,

---

* Mullā 'Ala-ul-mulk Tuni, Fāzil Khan I, (life in *M.U.* iii. 524), one of the most learned Persian emigrants to India, died in June 1663 only sixteen days after being appointed High Diwan. His brother's son named Burhān-ud-din came to India about this time and was enrolled in the Delhi Government service, being created Qābil Khan, 'Itimād Khan (Dec. 1674), and finally Fāzil Khan III (in Nov. 1688). He held the posts of Khān-i-Sāmān (1688-1697) and Subahdār of Kashmir (1697-Oct. 1700), dying on the way at Burhānpur when coming to Court. (His life in *M.U.* iii. 34-38). In 1703, his son Abdur Rahim was appointed bayutāt, *vice* Fazāil Khan deceased, (below).

Fazāil Khan, was originally Mir Hādi, the son of Wazir Khan Mir Hāji, the diwān of Prince Muhammad 'Āzam, and a disciple of the scholar-saint Shaikh 'Abdul 'Aziz of Agra. (His life in *M.U.* iii. 38-40). Enrolled in the service of Prince Muhammad 'Āzam, over whom he acquired very great influence, after his Shaikh's death in April 1678. After having been detained at Agra without employment or liberty for many years from 1683 (probably because the Emperor suspected him of inclining the Prince towards the Shia creed), he was called to the Emperor's Court, appointed Chief-Secretary (*Mir Munshi*), keeper of the imperial library, deputy Khān-i-Sāmān and bayutāt, with the title of Fazāil Khan. He died on 13 March 1703. There was no connection between this Fazāil Khan and the two Fāzil Khans above.

a robe, and 2,000 rupees. Khwāja Muhammad, who had got the title of Āmānat Khan got the faujdāri of Sangamner in addition to his faujdāri of Bijapur, and an elephant. To the wife of 'Abdul Khāliq Arab, Imām of the Court, five jewels were presented. Irādat Khan, qil'adār of Gulbargā, a *hazāri* (700 tr.), got an increment of 300 troopers. Bakhshi-ul-mulk Ruhullah Khan got a jasper inkpot. Ziāullah Khan, son of 'Ināyetullah Khan, became diwān of Agra. Bakhshi-ul-mulk Mirzā Sadruddin Muhammad Khan, was presented with an elephant, a horse, and a robe, and sent to guard the base at Bahādurgarh. A 2½-*hazāri* (800 tr.), he got an increment of 500 (250 tr.). Raja Shāhu, son of Sambhā, was presented with an *arsi* having a ruby set in it, a gold *punchhi* set with diamond, five jewelled rings [473], a jewelled dagger, and a horse with gold *sāz*. Fath Daulat Qul conveyed Shāhu to Kām Bakhsh, by command. The Prince gave him a robe and an *ārsi* as reward. By order, the tent of Raja Shāhu was pitched near the mansion of Kām Bakhsh. Hamiduddin Khan Bahādur, dārogha of the diwān-i-khās, presented a wooden *bangla* fit for sitting on in the "Court of the oppressed". An increment of 500 (300 tr.) was made to his rank of 3-*hazāri* (1,700 tr.). Mir Khan, son of Āmir Khan deceased, had gone to Aurangābād for marrying the daughter of Bahramand Khan ; he interviewed and presented costly articles set with gems (*murass'a*). A robe was given him. Madan Singh, brother of Raja Shāhu, came from the base and had audience, according to command. Prince 'Ālijāh got the subahdāri of Ajmir in addition to that of Ahmadabad. A 40-*hazāri* (30,000 tr.), he got an increment of 10-*hazār* tr. Udwat Singh, qiladār of Sakhkharlanā, a 3-*hazāri* (1,200 tr.), got an increment of conditional and unconditional 500 (300 tr.). Siādat Khan, son of Siādat Khan Ughlān, a 2-*hazāri* (200 tr.), got an increment of 500 (same tr.). Ghālib Khan son of Rustam Khan Sharzā Bijapuri, a 3½-*hazāri* (3,000 tr.), got promoted by 500 (same tr.). Alahdad Khan Khweshgi became faujdār of Mandla (?) *vice* Rahmāndād Khan. A *hazāri* [474] (500 tr.) he was promoted by 500 (same tr.). Chin Qalich Khan Bahādur, Subahdār of Bijapur, was appointed faujdār of Talkokan Adilkhāni, 'Āzamnagar Belgāon, and thānadār of Sānpgāon, *vice* Saif Khan. A 4-*hazāri* (3,000 tr.), he got an increment of a *hazār* tr. and a *kror* of *dām* as reward. Niāz Khan was appointed his deputy, getting an increment of 500 tr. to his rank of 500

(300 tr.). Khānahzād Khan, close to the Emperor's person, was given the title of Mir.

After having done the recording of certain events of this year, I shall now narrate the conquest of Kondānā and other events. The Emperor ordered his soldiers to mount the hill under the command of Tarbiyat Khan, Mir Atish, and fire on the besieged. The Khan mounted (big) guns on a hillock opposite the tower of this tall fort, and for some time engaged in burning the enemy and demolishing their towers and battlements, so that the beastly enemy were driven out of their grazing ground. On Thursday, the 8th April, 1703/2nd Zil. H., this and other forts capitulated. It was renamed *Bakhshenda Bakhsh*. Truly it is so strong a fort that no amount of exertion but only the Giver's gift could have led to its conquest. As the rainy season was impending and the difficulty of the road extreme, [475] in view of the fact that the Emperor's aim was restricted to the conquest of fort Rājgarh, it was decided to pass the rainy season at Muhiābād Punā, and afterwards pursue the object. On Saturday, the 24th April, 1703/18th Zil. H., the return march to that place was ordered, and it was reached on Saturday, the 1st May/25th Zil. H.

I shall narrate an incident of this period which shows the Emperor's regard for his servants, recognition of merit, and attention to the rules governing men and perfect justice.

At the time of the imperial camp alighting at Punā, by chance the quarters of the Āmir-ul-umarā were located on a low land and those of 'Ināyetullah Khan, nāzim of Khālsa and tan on a higher tract. After some time when the Khan had enclosed the land adjoining the quarters of his harem, Vasant, eunuch of the Āmir-ul-umarā, sent a man to say "Get out of this place, the nawwāb's tent will be pitched here". The Khan sent reply "Very well; please wait till I have found some other spot in this *misl,* in which I have to take up (my) quarters". The eunuch gave a rude answer. The Khan removed his tent to another place in the same neighbourhood, and the Āmir -ul-umarā's tent was set up there. From the news-sheet of Ikhlāskesh, news-writer of the *kachari* [476] of the diwān, this matter came to the Emperor's knowledge. He immediately ordered Hamidud-din Khan Bahādur to go and tell the Āmir-ul-umarā, "It was not done well. You should go to your former place or some other spot. The man who had set up his tent before, should remain in his own place". The Khan conveyed the order. The Āmir-ul-umarā delayed in consenting to it. The Khan Bahādur leaving him there went in a friendly manner to 'Ināyetullah Khan's house and narrated the occurrence, saying "It is better that you should go to Āmir-ul-umarā and say that you have got another place and that you don't wish him to change his quarters." 'Ināyetullah Khan said "You went to the Āmir-ul-umarā by command. How can I go to him without order?" The Khan Bahādur on coming to the Emperor reported the whole affair. Next day when the Āmir-ul-umarā came to His Majesty at the time of holding Court, the Emperor ordered Ihtamām Khan Qul to take the Āmir-ul-umarā to 'Ināyetullah Khan and make him beg pardon for what had occurred. Āsad Khan had not so many lives that he could disobey the order now. He submitted and carried out the order. Āmir Khan sent me to convey this message to 'Ināyetullah Khan. "Such an order has been issued. But it is advisable that you should quickly petition the Emperor to postpone the visit of the Āmir-ul-umarā." My going at mid-day and the visit of the Āmir-ul-umarā to the Khan's house happened at the same time. My message remained undelivered. By chance 'Ināyetullah Khan was at his bath. The Āmir-ul-umarā came and sat down in the diwān-khānah in which the carpet had not been yet spread. The Khan quickly came out, the Āmir-ul-umarā took his hand, rose, and riding brought him to his own house. [477] He presented one *thān* of cloth by way of welcoming to the Khan and never to the end of the period of their being together did he in any way express complaint or displeasure (against the Khan) but increased his favours and attempts to please. Such men have lived under the sky and passed the stages of their lives in this excellent manner!

After a stay of six months and eighteen days, inspite of famine on account of drought, death of the poor, lamentation of the weak, the disappearance of wheat, vetch and rice, the filling of Shāhganj (royal market) to the brim with the groans of the stricken beggars, the Emperor's resolution would not turn back, let the celestial firmament turn back if it will! So, on Wednesday, the 10th November, 1703/12th Rajab, the army marched out for the conquest of Rājgarh. Four *kos* from this fort* is a *kotal* reaching

* Puna? according to Khafi Khan.

up to the sky. Although for two months labourers had been working hard to level the ups and downs, yet when can the looks of earthly men rise to the sky, and where can the hand of the celestials be equalled by that of the terrestrials? * * * In seven days the army crossed the pass, and after [478] passing one more stage, arrived on Sunday, the 28th November/30th Rajab, at the narrow plain at the foot of the fort.

Fort Rājgarh is a hill second only to the fort of the towered sky.

* * * *

Its circuit is twelve *kos*. Imagination cannot estimate its height. Its thorny jungles and spectre-haunted chasms can be traversed only by the wind. Nothing can descend on it except rain! In former days, the 'Adilkhani kings possessed it. The infernal Shivā after gaining possession [of Rājgarh], made terraces on three sides around it on a lower level [*māchi*] and there built three strong forts, namely *Suvelā* and *Padmāvati* situated towards Kokan uplands, and *Sanjivani* on the side of Kokan lowlands; he thus made its capture by any enemy impossible. On Thursday, the 2nd December, 1703/4th Shabān, the Emperor issued orders that under the supervision of Hamid-uddin Khan Bahādur and management of Tarbiyat Khan, Mir Atish, the army should begin the attack on the fort.

[479] The infidel now in hell (namely Shivāji) had formed a triangular enclosure, which is called a *sund* (? elephant's trunk) in the language of military fortification, by erecting two thick walls from the postern-gate (wicket) of the fort of Padmāwat to the end of the hillock, and making these two walls meet at a point. Below both of these (walls) the path declines so sharply and is so full of slippery holes that no one can pass there on foot. At the junction of the two walls, Shivā had built an even stronger tower, which opened upon the back of the hillock opposite to it. Here he had collected war materials.

As the apex of this tower is thirty yards in height, straight as a stretched rope, the two active generals told off by the Emperor for the attack, working from the side of Padmāwat, built a raised battery, lofty as a hill, opposite this tower and carried the work up to the *sang-chin* (protective bulwark of loose stones round the raised platform). While this work was being pushed on, although the garrison erected batteries of their own, they did not succeed (in stopping the imperialists). Our thundering guns, which were planted at certain points to demolish the fort-towers and walls, did havoc to them in many places.

CHAPTER XLVIII.

48TH YEAR OF THE REIGN : 1115 A.H.

28th December, 1703—16th December, 1704.

A marriage was settled between Hedāyetullah Khan, son of 'Ināyetullah Khan and the daughter of Muhammad Āfzal, son of Faizullah Khan deceased. [480] The Emperor presented him with a robe and a horse. Shamshir Beg, grandson of Āghar Khan was married to the daughter of (Rājā) Rām. The bridegroom was presented with three jewelled rings and a robe. Taqi Khan, grandson of Bahramand Khan, was married to a daughter of Shāista Khan, he was presented with ornaments worth 5,000 rupees. Shaistā Khan became faujdār and qiladār of Mandu *vice* Nawāzish Khan, son of Islām Khān Rumi. Mir Āhmad Khan, diwān of the establishment of Bidār Bakht Bahādur was appointed deputy Subahdār of Khāndesh. Rustam Khan Sharzā Bijapuri, who was nāib-Subahdār of Berār on behalf of Khan Firuz Jang, and had been captured in battle with Nimā [Sindhiā], secured his release and returned to the Khan; from his rank of 7-*hazāri* (same tr.) a *hazār* (same tr.) was reduced. 'Id-ul-fitr occurred on the 27th January, 1704/1st Shawwāl, 1115. Raja Neknām was married to the daughter of (Rājā) Rām and presented with a robe. Padāji, thānadār of Buddha Panchgaon, son of Shivāji's uncle, was a 2½-*hazāri* (1500 tr.); he now got an increment of 500 *zāt*. Sarfarāz Khan had been removed from his rank for an offence; at Kām Bakhsh's request he was restored to the *mansab* of 6-*hazāri* (5-*hazār* tr.). Saif Khan, son of Saif Khan Faqirullah, the dismissed qiladār of Belgāon, became nāib-Subahdār of Bijapur on behalf of Chin Qalich Khan Bahādur. [481] Mukhlis Khan who was formerly Mut'aqad Khan was sent to Agra as qiladār. Firuz Jang Khan was rewarded for his punishment of Nimā, with the title of Sipahsālār, an increment of 2-*hazār* tr. which made him a 7-*hazāri* (10-*hazār* tr.) and a *kror* of *dām* as *in'ām*. Muhammad Āmin Khan Bahādur a 3-*hazāri* (1000 tr.) got an increment of 500 *zāt* (200 tr.). Dilir Khan an officer under Firuz Jang Khan, a 7-*hazāri* (same tr.), got 500 tr. added to his rank. Sipahdār Khan nāzim of Allahabad, a

4-*hazāri* (3,000 tr.), was rewarded for the chastisement of Mahābat, zamindār of Jaunpur, with an increment of 500 tr. Hāmid Khan Bahadur, brother of Khan Firuz Jang, a 2½-*hazāri* (1500 tr.), got an increment of 500 *zāt* (200 tr.). Raja Indra Singh, a 3-*hazāri* (2-*hazār* tr.) got an increment of 500 *zāt*, Rahimuddin Khan brother of Khan Firuz Jang, a *hazāri* (250 tr.) got 500 *zāt* (100 tr.) more. Sayyid Husain, successor at the tomb of Mir Sayyid Muhammad Gisudarāz, was presented with a jewelled dagger and a horse with gold *sāz*. Khidmatgār Khan Khwāja Tālib, nāzir of the Emperor's harem, died at the base after a period of illness from paralysis. The Emperor had received him from Shāh Nawāz Khan as part of his wife's dowry; he was an old good-natured servant. Murhamat Khan son of Āmir Khan deceased, [482] a *hazāri* (250 tr.), got an increment of 150 troopers.

Kamgār Khan, dismissed Subahdār of Orissā, came to Court. Hamiduddin Khan Bahadur who received the blessed cap of Miān 'Abdul Latif, and Tarbiyat Khan a dagger, were sent to chastise the enemy spread near the river Ghod nadi. Mun'im Khan who had become diwān of the establishment of the Crown Prince *vice* Muhammad Āslam Khan, became diwān of the Panjab *vice* Sayyid Mirak Khan. Kām Bakhsh had been reinstated as a 20-*hazāri* (10,000 tr.); 5,000 tr. of his former reduction was now restored. 'Ali Naqi, daughter's son of Shāh 'Abbās, king of Irān, was led by fortune to visit the Emperor. Five thousand rupees were given from the treasury of the port of Surat for his travelling expenses. On coming to court, he got the rank of 3-*hazāri* (1,000 tr.) a robe, a horse, an elephant, and a jewelled *jigha*. Muhammad Muhiuddin, son of Sikandar Khan Bijapuri, was married to the daughter of Sambhā. The Emperor presented a dowry worth 7,000 rupees. The marriage of Rāja Shāhu, the son of Sambhā, was settled with the daughter of Bahādurji. He was presented with a jewelled belt, an enamelled *sarpech,* and a jewelled *jigha,* worth 10,000 rupees. The Emperor received a present sent by Muhammad 'Azim on the occasion of the birth of a daughter to Sultan Farrukh Siyar [483].

Qazi Ākrām Khan got an elephant. Robes for the rains were sent to all the imperial servants at the Court and in the provinces. Rustamdil Khan was appointed faujdār of Karnātak-Bijapuri *vice* Salābat Khan. A 1½-*hazāri* (1,000 tr.), he got 500 *zāt* (1,000 tr.) more and a *kror* of *dām* as *in'ām*. Khwāja Zāhid, ambassador of Balkh, received on the day of interview a gold coin weighing 100 mohars and a rupee weighing 100 rupees. On the day of taking congee he received a robe, a jewelled dagger, and 5,000 rupees in cash. A *farmān* with robe was sent to Bidār Bakht appointing him Subahdār of Mālwā in addition to Aurangābād. Dāud Khan, nāib of Nasrat Jang, became Kām Bakhsh's deputy in governing the subah of Bijapur, *vice* Muzaffar Khan. A 5-*hazāri* (same tr.), he got a *hazāri* (same tr.) in addition. Murshid Quli Khan, defender* of the province of Orissā and diwān of (the establishment of) Muhammad 'Azim and of the province of Bengal, was a 1½-*hazāri* (1,000 tr.) and now got an increment of 500 *zāt* (100 tr.). Hamiduddin Khan Bahādur and Tarbiyat Khan who had gone to chastise the enemy, returned to Court according to command. On the 21st November, 1704/4th Shabān,† the Emperor learnt that Firuz Jang Khan had started from Berār towards Hindustan to chastise Nimā Sindhiā and Chatrasāl Bundelā. News came from informants on the frontier of Persia that Prince Muhammad Ākbar, who had fled into the wilderness of disappointment and whose affairs have been described in previous years [484] had died. The Emperor consoled himself by reading the verse of *tarji'a* and said, "The great disturber of Hindustan has subsided." He sent the news to Zinat-un-nisā Begam, and presented a mourning turban-end to Ākbar's son Buland Ākhtar. Condolatory turban-ends were sent to his eldest son Nekusiyar in the fort of Agra, to Raziyyat-un-nisā‡ Begam, wife of Raf'i-ul-qadr and Zakiyyat-un-nisā Begam, wife of Khujistah Ākhtar, the daughters of the deceased.

I shall now turn to the narration of the history of the remaining portion of the siege of Rājgarh.

On Sunday, the 6th February, 1704/11th Shawwāl, our heroes mounted the tower and penetrated inside the wall, driving the enemy, who had come up to oppose them, back to confinement in the fort. They firmly established themselves here. Although these prisoners closed the door of submission on themselves and for a time did not slacken in discharging guns, muskets, rockets and stones, and

---

* *Hāris* (in text); *Akhbārāt* says that he was faujdār of Orissā; (evidently the subahdarship of Orissa was then kept in abeyance).

† The year wrong. According to *Akhbārāt*, 2nd December, 1703.

‡ On pp. 203 and 372 her name is given as *Safiat*.

through the lack of shelters many of the holy warriors met with martyrdom, yet the sight of their valour and sacrifice of life, shook the resolution of the enemy; [485] their generals Firangaji and Dāmāji* sent an envoy to the house of Bakhshi-ul-mulk Ruhullah Khan to beg for quarters. At the Khan's intercession the Emperor ordered that the garrison might go out without arms or armour. On Wednesday, the 16th February/21st Shawwāl, they with their own hands planted the imperial banner on the top of the fort, and themselves retired to the pit of ruin. That very day Bakhshi-ul-mulk Hamiduddin Khan Bahādur with other grandees entered the fort by the door, and raising to the sky the loud shout of conquering four such forts, expelled the infidels as he had been commanded. * * *

Hamiduddin Khan Bahādur, who a few days before had received the increment of 500 *zāt* (300 tr.), making him a 3½-*hazāri* (2-*hazār* tr.) was now rewarded for his heroism with the permission to beat the *naubat*. Tarbiyat Khan was rewarded for the conquest of the fort with an increment of 500 *zāt* (200 tr.) which made him a 3½-*hazāri* (1,800 tr.). [486] The Bakhshi-ul-mulk, who had been promoted to be a 3½-*hazāri* (1500 tr.) was presented with a costly jewelled *sarpech*. The fort was renamed Nabishāhgarh.

Capture of Tornā fort: Tornā was situated four *kos* from Rājgarh. On Wednesday, the 23rd February, 1704/28th Shawwāl, the imperial tent was pitched in its neighbourhood, and the heroes, as usual, were sent to attempt the capture of the fort. * * * In spite of the strength of the fort, Tarbiyat Khan engaged himself in running trenches on the side of its gate. Muhammad Āmin Khan Bahādur closed the path of egress to the garrison on the other side. Other guards enclosed it around. * * * [487].

Āmānullah Khan, grandson of Alahwardi Khan J'afar, who was famous for his reckless valour in this family of brave men, in the night of Friday, the 10th March, 1704/15th Zil. Q., when the 89th lunar year of the Emperor's life began, inspired some Mavlé infantry, from his own side, so that first one of them in disregard of life went up to the *sangchin* of the fort and fastened a rope ladder

---

* The printed text of *M.A.* gives the names as *Far'āunji* and *Hāmānji* (which I correct as *Firangaji* and *Dāmāji*. Khafi Kh. (ii. 513) names only *Hāmāji*. The Marathi annals and the *akhbarats* are silent as to the names. The Ms. reads *Far'aunji* and *Hāhānji*.

(*māl*) strongly to a rock, and then twenty-five others of the same party ascended the hill by means of the noose (rope-ladder), entered the fort, and raised the din of fighting. The Khan, his brother 'Atāullah Khan and some others in disregard of their lives followed them quickly on hearing of it. Hamiduddin Khan Bahādur, who was walking on every side in search of an opportunity, tied a rope to his waist like the first party and entered close behind. The infidels who offered resistance were slain. The rest fled to the citadel and shut the door. Although this hard enterprise in this simplified form was one of no small (danger), yet where could cowards resist the charge of heroes, and [488] the enemy became helpless and begged for quarters. The Emperor permitted them to leave the fort without their arms. The fort was renamed *Fatuh-ul-ghaib*. The Khan Bahādur Hamiduddin was rewarded with a robe, a *fathpech* and *doshāla* from the Emperor's own wardrobe. Āmānullah Khan by an increment of 500 *zāt* (200 *do āspā* tr.) became a 1½-*hazāri* (700 tr.). Others were properly rewarded. As through the blessedness of the aims of the Emperor, the people escaped the hardships and dangers of passing the rainy season in this fatal region, the Emperor set out on the return march towards the old dominions for making *chhauni* in the neighbourhood of Junnar. [489] On Wednesday, the 15th March, 1704/20th Zil. Q., Mir Khan, close to the Emperor's person, got his father's hereditary title of Āmir Khan. The Emperor said, "When your father Mir Khan became Āmir Khan he presented to the Emperor Shāh Jahan one lakh of rupees in return for the granting of *alif* (to his name). What will you present?" He replied, "May a thousand thousand lives be sacrificed to Your Majesty! My life and property are all propitiatory alms (*tasadduq*) for the sake of Your Majesty!" Next day he presented to the Emperor, a *Qurān* in the handwriting of Yāqut. The Emperor remarked, "You have made a present which exceeds the world and its contents in price," and gave him an elephant. On Tuesday, the 9th May, 1704/15th Muharram, Bakhshi-ul-mulk Ruhullah Khan died in the fulness of his youth and prosperity. Mourning robes were sent to the houses of his sons Khalilullah Khan and 'Itiqād Khan (who afterwards got the title of Ruhullah Khan). They came to bow to the Emperor who consoled them. The daughter of the deceased came to Court; she was consoled with the present of jewels worth 5,000 rupees,

Mirzā Sadruddin Muhammad Khan became second Bakhshi, *vice* the deceased. Mir Khānahzād Khan was ordered to act as his deputy pending his arrival from the base. Khudā-banda Khan became Khan-i-sāmān *vice* the deceased. On Monday the 17th April, 1704/23rd Zil. H., the Emperor fixed his camp at [490] the village of Khed, which was renamed Mas'audābād. After staying here for seven and a half months, the army started for Wāgin-gerā. * * *

MARCH FOR THE CONQUEST OF WĀGIN-GERĀ

I have already narrated some of the incidents of the capture of Nasratābād Sagar from Pām Nāik, his coming to the imperial Court at Haidarabad through the mediation of Khānahzād Khan, son of Ruhullah Khan, and his flight to hell shortly afterwards. [491] Afterwards when Ruhullah Khan, son of Khalilullah Khan, was ordered in the 32nd year of the reign (to go) from Fathābād Koragāon to conquer Rāichur, Pidiā, brother's son and adopted son of Pām Nāik, who, in the 28th [corr. 27th] year at the time of the Emperor's dismounting at Ahmadnagar, had come to Court and received a *mansab,* was taken by the Khan with himself, as likely to render help in the work. This trickster informed the Khan, after the conquest of Rāichur that if he could get permission he would like to go to Wāgingerā for a week, replenish his materials and equipment, and come back. This place was a village within the jurisdiction of Sagar. Its habitations are situated on a hill. After Sagar had been wrested from Pām Nāik, it developed into the home and refuge of the infidel (rebels). The Khan being deceived gave the permission. The wretch after reaching his shelter violated his promise, took up an attitude of opposition, and tried to strengthen this place, *i.e.,* to make a *qamargha* with twelve or thirteen thousand musketeers. * * *

When the Khan employed force against him, he kept himself safe partly by force and partly by money. The Khan was summoned to Court; and he outwardly conducted himself as a tenant, continued to pay revenue, but gradually gathered together wealth, built a wall on one side of the hill, and assembled [492] fighting footmen, and thus constituted Wāgin-gerā. By increasing the buildings of the town and the cultivation in its neighbourhood, he acquired power and authority, and became the leading partner of the

Marathas in raising disturbances and rebellion, and dispossessed Jagiā, the legitimate son of Pām Nāik, the heir to the estate. The latter betook himself to the Court and took service there. After learning of Pidiā's robberies on all sides and his devastation (of the property) of high and low, the Emperor sent 'Āzam Shah to extirpate him. Then he interviewed the Prince and saved himself from destruction by paying seven lakhs of rupees (as tribute). And during the governorship (lit., domination) of Ghāziuddin Khan Bahādur Firuz Jang, he followed the same policy, and by paying in all a tribute of nine lakhs of rupees saved himself.

When the Emperor's attention was absorbed in conquering the country of Bijapur, this short-sighted man again provoked his own ruin. Till at last, the Emperor being free from the conquest of those great forts and the opening of so many difficult passes leading to Junnar, the time of retribution on the infidel arrived. On Sunday, the 22nd October, 1704/4th Rajab, the Emperor set out towards it.

CHAPTER XLIX.

49TH YEAR OF THE REIGN. 1116 A.H.

17th December, 1704—5th December, 1705.

[493] * * * 'Azizullah Khan uncle of Ruhullah Khan deceased, who had been summoned from Aurangābād after the latter's death, had audience. At Firuz Jang's request, the *hazāri zāt* (same tr.) deducted from the rank of Rustam Khan, nāib-Subahdār of Berār, was restored; Mir Khan, son of Āmir Khan deceased, a *hazāri* (500 tr.) got an increment of a 100 tr. Tahawwar Khan, son of Salābat Khan deceased, dārogha of Qurkhānah, got the title of Fidāi Khan. The 'Id-ul-fitr occurred on the 16th January, 1705/1st Shawwal, 1116.

Buland Ākhtar's tent was a *sarācha* with *āsbak*. On account of some offence, the Emperor ordered that it should be a tent (*tambu*) with *qalandari* and an enclosure of cloth screens (*qanāt*.) Hāfiz Nur Muhammad, Mir-i-sāmān of the establishment of Gauharārā Begam, having written and corrected selections from the *Āhiā-ul-ùlum*, sent it as a present to the Emperor and was rewarded with an elephant, 1000 rupees in cash, and the title of [494] Hāfiz Khan. Rustamdil Khan, the dismissed faujdār of Karnātak-Bijapuri, was appointed naib-Subahdār of Haidarabad, *vice* Dāud Khan and received an increment of 500 *zāt* (same tr.) to his rank of 2-*hazāri* (1,000 tr.). Chin Qalich Khan Bahādur, nāzim of Bijapur, got the faujdāri *vice* him. He was a 4-*hazāri* (same tr.), and now got an increment of 2,000 tr. and 5 lakhs of *dām* as *in'ām*.

On Tuesday, the 13th March 1705/28th Zil. Q., news came from Ahmadābād that Jahānzeb Bānu Begam, wife of Shah 'Ālijah, had died. Some trusty female friends, who had access to her, said, "a pimple of the size of a lentil appeared on the nipple of her right bosom. For some time medicine was taken, yet the swelling grew wide and thick and its inflammation at times caused a burning fever. The doctors applied medicines. At last Monsieur Martin, the Frenchman, said "There is a skilful woman-surgeon (*hāziqa*) among my relatives at Delhi. If she is summoned and after examining the patient tells me the details of the case, she will be quickly cured." After her arrival, the Begam said to her foster-brother (*Koka*), "Summon her, and inquire about her age and habit of drinking wine." The Koka after inquiry reported, "She is 40 years old, and drinks wine." The Begam said, "It is certain that I shall not be able to save myself from this disease which is daily increasing. I don't wish that my body should be touched by a sinner." Although the Shāh pressed her, it had no effect. The disease lingered for two years, and at last she died." In all two lakhs of rupees were spent in furnishing the corpse, shrouding it, distributing money and food [495] (to beggars), sending the corpse to Delhi, and burying it in the cemetery of Khwāja Qutbuddin Bakhtiār. The Shāh gave up hearing music and seeing dances, of which he was very fond from his youth. All her jewels were sent to Bidār Bakht. Her other things and cash were made over to the officers of Najib-un-nisā Begam.

Sayyid Āsālat Khan, an officer serving under the Crown Prince, came to Court by command. At the Prince's request he received an increment of 500 *zāt* (200 tr.) making him a 1½-*hazāri* (700 tr.). Ya'qub Khan at the recommendation of Ibrāhim Khan became faujdār of Pakhli Dhamtur *vice* Rahmāndād Khan and got an increment of a *hazār* troopers. Kānhoji Shirké, a 5-*hazāri* (same tr.), got an increment of a *hazār zāt*. Murid Khan, son of Himmat Khan, became qiladār of the port of Surat, *vice* Dilir Khan deceased. Hāmid Khan Bahādur quarrelling with Firuz Jang Khan came to Court. He was a 2-*hazāri* (1,000 tr.), and now regained the 500 *zāt* (same tr.) which had been reduced. Vāsudeo, zamindār of Chandankerā, got his first *mansab* (a 3-*hazāri zāt*) and an elephant. Raja Shāhu, by command, went to and came back from the house of Firuz Jang with the troops of Hamiduddin Khan Bahādur. [496] Monday, the 4th June, 1705/2nd Safar had been fixed for giving leave to Kām Bakhsh to go to Haidarabad. But the Emperor postponed it. Chin Qalich Khan Bahādur Subahdār of Bijapur, got in addition the posts of (faujdār of) Nasratābād Sakkhar and Mudgal *vice* Burhānullah Khan and Kāmil Khan; Saif Khan got the qiladāri and faujdāri of 'Āzamnagar and Talkokan *vice* Chin Qalich Khan, with an increment of 500 *zāt* (1,300 tr.). Mirzā Safavi Khan was married to the daughter of Mu'azzam Khan deceased; he was given a robe with a *sarpech* and 12,000 rupees in cash. Bakhshi-ul-mulk Nasrat Jang Khan was presented with a ring with a ruby set in it, worth 5,000 rupees. 'Ināyetullah Khan's wife was presented with a pearl *badhi* worth 8,000 rupees and other jewels. Hamiduddin Khan Bahādur's daughter was presented with an *udrāj* and *makri* with two pearls. Sipahdār Khan, nāzim of Allahabad, a 4-*hazāri* (3,000 tr.), got an increment of a *hazār zāt*. Fathullah Khan Bahādur 'Ālamgirshahi got the thānahdāri of Lauhgarh *vice* Alah Yār Khan, with an increment of 200 tr. On Sunday, the 2nd September/4th Jamad. A., a *farmān* was issued calling Shah 'Ālijāh to Court. On Sunday, the 9th September, 1705/1st Jamad. S., the subahdārship of the Panjāb was given to the Crown Prince, *vice* Zabardast Khan. The subahdāri of Burhānpur and Aurangabad was given to Shah 'Ālijāh *vice* Bidār Bakht. Ibrāhim [497] Khan, dismissed Subahdār of Kashmir, became Subahdār of Ahmadabad *vice* the agents of Shāh 'Ālijāh. A 5-*hazāri* (same tr.) he got an increment of a *hazār zāt* (same tr.). Zabardast Khan, his son, became Subahdār of Ajmir *vice* the agents of Shāh 'Ālijāh. A *hazāri,* he got an increment of 500 (1,000 tr.). Mun'im Khan diwān of the establishment of the Crown Prince and of the Subah of Kābul, became deputy governor of the Panjāb on behalf of the Prince, and faujdār of Jammu on his own behalf. A *hazāri* (500 tr.), he got 500 *zāt* (same tr.) more. Nawāzish Khan became Subahdār of Kashmir. Mu'izzuddin, Subahdār of Multān and Tatta became (also) faujdār of Lakhi jungle *vice* Zabardast Khan. Hayātullah Khan son of Chin Qalich Khan Bahādur was presented with an elephant and a jewelled dagger. Mirzā Safavi Khan became third Bakhshi. Tarbiyat Khan, Mir Atish, was made qil'adār of Nabishāhdurg and Muhiābād up to the river Bhimā. He got a *hazār* tr. *seh-bandi*. Bāqi Khan, son of Bāqi Khan, uncle of Hamiduddin Khan, became qiladār of Agra *vice* Kāmgār Khan. A 1½-*hazāri,* he got 500 *zāt* (300 tr.) as an increment. Tarbiyat Khan, Mir Atish, got in addition the dāroghaship of the Deccan artillery *vice* Mansur Khan. His son Muhammad Ishāq was appointed his deputy. Wazārat Khan 'Arab Shaikh Muhammad, diwān of Kām Bakhsh, was sent to settle Haiderabad.

On Friday, the 16th November, 1705/10th Shabān, [498] the subahdāri of Mālwā was ordered to be continued to Bidār Bakht. Mukhtār Khan nāzim of Agra, in reward for the conquest of Sansani, a possession of the rebel Rājarām Jāt, which was captured for the second time on

Tuesday, the 9th October, 1705/2nd Rajab, got an addition of 500 *zat* to his rank of 3-*hazāri*. The Emperor learnt that Durgādas Rathor, who had left the army of Shah 'Ālijāh, had returned. He was ordered to be restored to the rank of 3-*hazāri* (2-*hazār* tr.).

I shall now turn to the siege of Wāgin-gerā. The intervening space was covered in three months and a few days, and on Thursday, the 8th February, 1705/4th Shawwal, the army arrived near it. Chin Qalich Khan Bahādur, son of Khan Firuz Jang, nāzim of Bijapur and jāgirdār of this country, who had hastened with the advanced detachment by command, took up a position a quarter of a *kos* from the fort, in company with Muhammad Āmin Khan Bahādur, Tarbiyat Khan Bahādur and the officers of the artillery. The Emperor's camp (*dāira*) was located at a distance of a *kos*. Everyday the enemy sallied forth and fought the imperialists. And as some thousand active musketeers and vigorous troopers, Hindu and Muslim, mostly of the Sayyid and other tribes, and servants of the best of Khalifas were opposed to them, severe struggles took place. The big guns from the top of the hill caused tumultuous slaughter; rockets followed each other vehemently. One morning Chin Qalich Khan Bahādur, Muhammad Āmin Khan [499] Bahādur, Tarbiyat Khan Bahādur, 'Aziz Khan Ruhila, and Ikhlās Khan Miāna, on the look out for opportunities, seized a hillock named Lāl Tikri, the capture of which would greatly weaken the enemy. The enemy learning of it, came in a large body, and so stoned the occupants of the hillock that they could not stand. The heroes waited for an opportunity to encircle the infantry. But the work did not prosper and they turned back. Although Kām Bakhsh and the Āmir-ul-umarā were sent, the efforts of the warriors did not succeed. The Emperor after the retreat ordered them to give up the endeavour from that side and try to promote the work from other sides.

That day, when Chin Qalich Khan Bahādur and Muhammad Āmin Khan Bahādur were riding out with a party to select the places for the trenches, by chance a cannon-ball fell upon them. Two legs of the horse of one and a foreleg of the horse of the other were blown away; but the two generals got down in safety. The Emperor on hearing of it sent with his personal (servant) Āmir Khan two Arab horses with gold *sāz* for the two generals and one precious perfumed pastile of amber for Chin Qalich Khan and gratified them. In short, the heroes planned to run trenches between Lāl Tikri and the hillock opposite the *petta* and Dhedāpur, Muhammad Āmin Khan Bahādur established an outpost for repelling the enemy between Lāl Tikri and the place of the trenches. Sultān Husain, surnamed Malang, with the men of the Prince kept his hold on the conquered hillock for some time. [500] And similarly, Bāqr Khan, son of Ruhullah Khan boldly maintained himself long on another hillock. These two parties encountered the enemy day and night, and checked their assault. In spite of the daily crowding of the enemy against these men, it seemed likely for the work to succeed soon, when the news spread that the Marathas were coming to aid the enemy. On Thursday, the 8th March, 1705/23rd Zil. Q. Dhanā Jādav and Hindu Rāo with five or six thousand troopers arrived near the imperial army. As the families of many (of them) were living in the protection of this fort, they kept the imperial army in play, and carried off the families by the other side of the hill. They advised the chief of Wāgingerā thus,—"With all our joint armies and materials, you and we cannot oppose the Emperor. If your hill be of iron, it would be dissolved and if your fort be of brass, it would be overthrown by him. Don't ruin your country. Don't overthrow your zamindāri. Don't rely too much on your remaining property. Save your army from being scattered." Regarding the Marathas as his helpers in his evil day, he had kept them attached to him by means of a daily subsidy of some thousands of rupees. The money went out of the purse of this luckless man, but what came from them (the Marathas) in return? The Marathas at his instigation, appeared on some occasions from the various sides of the camp, but being broken they fled to the hills. Several times great feats were performed through the forward movement of Muhammad Āmin Khan Bahādur, Hamiduddin Khan Bahadur, Āmānullah Khan [501] and other heroes. In the meantime, the rebel chief made overtures for peace. He gave a letter containing a prayer for safety and some other requests to 'Abdul Ghani Kashmiri, a hawking grocer, who had no (merchandise) under his arm save fraud and duplicity and had attained to (influence on) the chief by tricks and deception. As that unclean fellow was not one of the grandees known to the Emperor, he brought the letter to Hedāyetkesh, the general news-reader, who had once had an occasion to speak to him and said, "I had gone to take a walk towards the fort, and was delayed by having to perform the evening prayer. At that time some men of the Berad Chief arrived and carried me away bound. He after some inquiry wrote and gave me this letter".

Hedāyetkesh reported the matter to the Emperor, who in spite of his prudence, experience, the indications of the approaching end of the siege, and knowledge of the worth of that worthless fellow, said that the prayers would be granted. The Prince was ordered to be the mediator for these affairs. The rebel chief sent to the Court his brother Som Singh, who desired the zamindāri, the name of Pidiā and a *mansab* for him; he got rewards and a *mansab* on coming. Muhatasham Khan, son of Shaikh Mir, a debtor of the Kashmiri, who was living without a *mansab* and making no exertions (in the siege) and had been through the deception of that unclean creature appointed as qiladār, was taken inside the fort with some men after being given a *mansab*. [502] Som Singh spread the tale that Pidiā had turned mad and fled from the fort. The Kashmiri brought a message from his mother that the wretch had fled with the Maratha devils, that Som Singh might now be permitted to come to the fort and engage in the duties of zamindār, and that the fort would be vacated in a week. It was done. The Kashmiri was given a *mansab* of 3-hundred. Hedāyetkesh for a few days got the title of Hādi Khan and promotion. The fire of the trenches was stopped. The generals were summoned to Court. As the deceiver had imagined that according to his fraud and promises the Emperor would march away and his jugglery and hypocrisy would succeed but the affair did not result as he had expected,—he delayed in evacuating the fort and admitting the imperialists, and opened the door of disturbance with the desire of fighting. He knew not what enormous materials for ensuring the success of the work the Emperor had kept in view during the negotiations for peace and what mass of water had been poured [by him on the tree of] his object during the few days that the fire of slaughter was extinguished!

To put it shortly, in this interval of delay Bakhshi-ul-mulk Zulfiqār Khan Bahādur Nasrat Jang who had been ordered to come to Court from Burhānpur with treasure, quickly arrived with Rao Dalpat, Rām Singh and a strong force; Dāud Khan who was acting at Jinji as nāib of Nasrat Jang arrived speedily with Bahādur Khan and a large party; Yusuf Khan, qiladār of Qamarnagar and Kāmyāb Khan

[503] qiladār of Gulbargā and other faujdārs and qiladārs with excellent corps arrived. The Emperor ordered Nasrat Jang to capture the fort and punish the enemy. The day following the interview, the Khan went to view the fort on the side of the hillock of Sultān Husain and Bāqr Khan. The enemy firing muskets from their perches in the *petta,* advanced to fight, and were beaten, many being slain, and the rest fleeing to their holes, and firmly holding the wall of the *petta.* In this day's fight many of the followers of Rao Dalpat, after fighting valiantly, were slain or wounded. Jamshid Khan Bijapuri was killed by a cannon-ball. Nasrat Jang firmly planted himself a short distance from that wall. By order Hamiduddin Khan Bahādur, Tarbiyat Khan Bahādur and others joined Nasrat Jang. Chin Qalich Khan sat down between the trenches and Lāl Tikri to punish the enemy. After a few days he was ordered to patrol round the fort with Muhammad Āmin Khan and other Mughals, and Bakhshi-ul-mulk Mirzā Sadruddin Muhammad Khan Safavi, to keep his place hot for him. Meantime Nasrat Jang had captured some wells situated on the skirt of the hill whence the enemy used to draw water, and by setting up palisades (*katgara*) and making head-covers (? "tortoises" or wide shields), had come close to the wall. Till at last on Friday, the 27th April, 1705/14th Muharram [504] relying on God and the Emperor, he appointed for the assault Dāud Khan with his brothers from one side, and Hamiduddin Khan Bahādur, Tarbiyat Khan Bahādur and other heroes from another; while he himself stood on horseback to support them. The heroes, eager for honour, ran on foot from both sides; the enemy who fought while fleeing could not resist the onset. Vacating the *pettah* they fled to the fort. The victors, traversing the ups and downs for one *kos* on foot, slaying and breaking the enemy, firmly established themselves. When the accursed Berads and Marathas saw these victories, the Berad chief knew that he had no refuge save in flight, and stationing a body of musketeers to check the imperialists during the day, fled out of the other side of the hill with the Marathas, the companions of his days of adversity. Towards evening the party of musketeers set fire to the houses and property (*mān*) and fled. The conflagration and the disappearance of the unfortunates revealed the real circumstance. Dāud Khan, Mansur Khan, and others ran towards the chief's house, and found it empty. Before his flight he had confined Muhtasham

Khan in his house. After the conquest of the fort the door [505] was opened to the Khan. This great victory fell to the lot of Nasrat Jang through the grace and good fortune of the Emperor.

Next day, when Nasrat Jang interviewed the Emperor he was rewarded with a jewelled sword, a horse with gold *sāz* and an elephant with silver accoutrements; Dāud Khan with a sword and a horse; his brother Bahādur Khan with an increment of 100 tr. and the granting of kettledrums; Rao Dalpat was rewarded by the promotion of his sons, and Rām Singh by an increment of 500. Hamiduddin Khan Bahādur's exertions were rewarded with an increment of 300 tr. and a special robe, and those of Tarbiyat Khan Bahādur with an increment of 200 tr. and the granting of *naubat;* Matlab Khan and Āmānullah Khan each received an increment of 200 tr. and the *naubat*. Saifullah Khan, Mir Tuzuk, who was that day wounded in the arm with a musket-ball, received 100 mohars. Next day Āmir Khan (close to the Emperor's person), Bakhshi-ul-mulk Mirzā Sadruddin Muhammad Khan (Safavi), and 'Ināyetullah Khan, the chief of ministers, each received a promotion of 500. Khwāja 'Ambar got the title of Khidmatgār Khan, Khwaja Bakhtāwar the title of Khan and [506] each of them got an increment of a 100 *zāt* (5 tr.). Qāzi Ākrām Khan became, by an increment of 100, a *hazāri,* Chin Qalich Khan Bahādur and Muhammad Āmin Khan Bahādur, who had gone to patrol in the neighbourhood, done excellent work, and worked hard in the pursuit of the enemy, were summoned to Court after the enemy's escape. The first by an increment of *hazār zāt* became a 5-*hazāri* (same tr.) and received 1 kror and 50 lakh *dām* as in'ām, an enamelled sword, and an elephant. The second received a sword and the increment of 500, which made him a 4-*hazāri* (1,200 tr.). Sayyid Sarfarāz Khan was given back the 500 tr. formerly deducted, and thus became a 6-*hazāri* (5,000 tr.), and also received a special robe and 1,000 mohars as reward. Faridun Khan and Hasan Khan, sons of Jamshid Khan deceased, received, the first 500 *zāt* (300 tr.), the second 500 (200 tr.) as increment, and thus each became a $1\frac{1}{2}$-*hazāri*. Mughals and other clans, Hindu and Muslim, of the forces of the two Khan Bahādurs, were favoured with promotion, horses, swords, and daggers.

In short, a great celebration was made for the victory. The Muslims universally rejoiced. The peasants and commonalty, the high people and Sayyids of this country became composed and happy at the extirpation of the wicked infidel. The fort was renamed *Rahman-Bakhsh Kherā.*

[507] THE STAY OF THE ARMY AT DEWAPUR.

As the chief object of conquering this country was to spread Islamic practices in an infidels' land and to improve the condition of all the slaves, Chin Qalich Khan was sent with a portion of the army to hasten and settle the neighbourhood, reassure and compose the ryots, who had fled far away in terror and hidden themselves, and send messages of their being treated with justice and favour, in order to induce them to return to their old homes and engage in cultivation (*again*): and to exact tributes from some refractory chiefs or to punish them. In view of furthering these works, the return of the timid inhabitants to Rahman-Bakhsh-Kherā, the building of a fort and a mosque here, and the passing of the rainy season, the Emperor ordered that some place should be selected in the neighbourhood which was suitable for the imperial camp. The officers chose Dewāpur, 3 *kos* from Rahman-Bakhsh-Kherā, near the Krishnā. The Emperor reached the place in one march. It was a truly charming seat, the cause of comfort and repose to the people. Thanks to the Emperor, repose was enjoyed. During the stay here, the tributes that had been collected reached the Emperor; the peasantry returned to their homes and engaged in tillage; the rebels were chastised. Under the supervision of Khwāja Mas'aud Mahalli, a strong fort and a beautiful mosque were built, the superintendent being rewarded with the title of Mas'aud Khan. At this time, [508] Bakhshenda-Bakhsh Kondānā, having been recovered by the enemy through the cowardice of the qiladār and the tricks of the enemy, the Emperor sent Hamiduddin Khan Bahādur and Tarbiyat Khan Bahādur with a party of heroes, after favouring them with proper promotions and rewards and helping them with money, to hasten there.

ACCOUNT OF THE EMPEROR'S ILLNESS

Owing to the fickleness of fortune, every soundness of health is closely linked to some kind of illness, and every happiness goes hand in hand with some misery. At this time, when the people had acquired a little repose, suddenly a strange disorder and bewildering distress took place, owing to the illness of the Emperor who was the life of the world and the cause of the repose of men. * * *

At first His Majesty, through his natural strength of mind and firmness of purpose, did not allow himself to be overcome by the disease, and so did not give up the transaction of business, but sometimes like the sun in the eastern sky, he showed his face at the small door of the Court (of Justice). The prayers of men reached his knowledge through the medium of petitions and letters, and he used to write suitable answers firmly with his own hand. Thereafter, through the severity of the illness and the increase of the pain, extreme depression seized him, and at times he became unconscious. It seemed likely, that through this terrible [509] occurrence, the kingdom and the faith would break up. The people preferred their own death to their lives, but could not get it (death). Great agitation seized the camp. Wild and heart-sickening rumours began to spread. Fools formed the unlucky ambition of boldly practising oppression in this disorderly country, where the enemy lay in ambush everywhere in search of opportunities.

For ten or twelve days this state continued; till at last the life-giver of the world breathed new lives into the bodies of the frightened people; and the removal of the Emperor's illness gave peace and safety to the world. The turbulent enemy and evil-natured wrong-doers scattered the dust of despair on their heads. Āmir Khan used to narrate, "One day in extreme pain the Emperor muttered,

> 'By the time you reach your 80th or 90th year,
> You will have met with many afflictions from Time (or Fortune);
> And when from that point you reach the stage of a hundred years,
> Death will assume the shape of your life.'

The low moan reached my ears, I quickly said to him 'Peace be with Your Majesty! Shaikh Ganja has composed all these couplets merely as the preface to the following couplet :—

> 'Then, it is better for you to be cheerful,
> For in cheerfulness you can remember God!'

The Emperor said 'Recite again'. I recited it a number of times. He ordered me to show it written. I did so. He read it for a time. The Giver of mercy to the helpless, the Remover of the pain of troubled hearts, bestowed strength on the Cause of the world's comfort, and [510] next morning the Emperor came to the Court of the oppressed. The people got back their lives. The Emperor said 'Your couplet gave me perfect recovery and brought wonderful strength to my weak heart'. The methods which doctor Hāziq Khan employed in the Emperor's treatment were worthy of the ancient doctors. Praised be God, and again praised be God! This lucky man was, in reward of his excellent services, weighed against gold and presented with a *sarpech*. The Emperor after gaining relief from the use of China root (*Smilax China*) which had done great good to his constitution, sent away, to guard his own subah, Chin Qalich Khan Bahādur, who in excess of agitation had quickly reached the camp. On Tuesday the 23rd October, 1705/16th Rajab, the Emperor set out for Bahādurgarh in a pālki (*takht*). The rest of this month (Rajab) and the whole of the next (Shabān) were spent in the journey. On the way, Qāzi Ākrām Khan died. He was unparallelled in legal knowledge and uprightness. The Emperor in recognition of his merits used to speak of him under the name of 'the late most learned man'.

CHAPTER L.

50TH YEAR OF THE REIGN : 1117 A. H.

6th December, 1705—25th November, 1706.

* * * [511] On Thursday the 6th December, 1705/1st Ramzan the imperial camp reached Bahādurgarh. As the officers, appointed to recover Bakhshenda-Bakhsh had only made a tour and circuit and putting off the accomplishment of their purpose to another time, had returned to Court, Zulfiqar Khan Bahādur Nasrat Jang, who after the capture of Rahman-Bakhsh-Khera had been sent towards Aurangābād in pursuit of the thieves, was summoned to Court, and had interview at Bahādurgarh.

On the 23rd January 1706/19th Shawwāl* when the imperial army began its march for Ahmadnagar, the Khan (Nasrat Jang) after being suitably favoured, was sent against Bakhshenda-Bakhsh. In addition to his own troops, Tarbiyat Khan Bahādur, zil'adār of this quarter, obeyed orders (by joining Nasrat Jang). Shāhu, son of the infidel Sambhā, who was residing within the gulālbār, was ordered to accompany the army of Nasrat Jang. On Friday the 25th January, 1706/21st Shawwal, for some political reasons, his tent was ordered to be pitched close to the *dāira* of the Khan and he was presented with a special robe and two costly *udrāj*. The imperial camp returned to Ahmadnagar, after the lapse of 22 years, on Sunday, 20th January/16th Shawwal. [512]

On Thursday the 21st March, 1706/17th Zil. H. informants reported to the Emperor that Nasrat Jang had recaptured Bakhshenda-Bakhsh, and expelled the beaten garrison without arms and accoutrements. Prince 'Ālijāh, who had been engaged in governing Gujrat, on hearing of the Emperor's illness, had in his excess of love and devotion applied for permission to come to Court. By order, he arrived and had audience on the 25th March, 1706/21st Zil. H. Bidār Bakht was ordered to put down the enemy who had spread towards the province of Gujrat, on account of the delay in the arrival of Ibrāhim Khan who had been

* The printed text wrongly gives *Sha'bān*.

transferred from Kashmir to the Subahdāri of Gujrat. In the place of the Shāhzāda, the subahdārship of Burhānpur was entrusted to Najābat Khan, and the defence of Mālwā to Khan-i-'Ālam. News reached the Emperor from Delhi that Gauharārā Begam, his younger sister, had died. He was [513] deeply grieved, and repeatedly said, "Of the children of Shah Jahān, she and I alone were left". * * *

He gratified her dependants with many kinds of consolation and favour. He appointed Hāfiz Khan, her mirsāmān, as diwān of Lahore *vice* Muhammad Āslam Khan. Sayyid Muhammad, grandson of Qāzi Muhammad Āslam deceased who was the Emperor's *ustād*, was appointed Sadr of the same Subah. Khwāja Zakriā and Khwāja Yahyā, sons of Sarbuland Khan Khwāja Musa and daughter's sons of Prince Muhammad Mu'izzudin, had audience and received robes and cash gifts. Tarbiyat Khan Bahādur's daughter received ornaments worth 4,000 rupees to the delight of her father. Chin Qalich Khan Bahādur became faujdār of Firuz-Nagar *vice* Yusuf Khan, and also faujdār of Tālikota *vice* Qudratullah Khan. Muhammad Muhasan, brother's son of Bakhshi-ul-mulk Mirzā Safavi Khan having newly come from Persia, interviewed the Emperor. Āmat-ul-Hamid, daughter of Hamiduddin Khan Bahādur was presented with ornaments worth 2,000 rupees. Sarāfrāz Khan, a 6-*hazāri* (5-*hazār* tr.) was rewarded for the pursuit of Pidiā Nāik with the increment of a *hazār* troopers. Jagiā, deshmukh of Nasratābād, a 2½-*hazāri* (1,500 tr.) received an increment of [514] 5-*sadi*. Mullā Haidar, *ustād* of Muhammad 'Azim, and Qāzi of Delhi, had been summoned to Court to be made Qāzi of the imperial camp. He now arrived and got the high post. At Nasrat Jang's request, the zamindāri of Mau-maidāna was given to his officer Raja Ram Singh Hada *vice* Rao Budh Singh. This Emperor, so gracious in the material and spiritual spheres alike, had been permitted by Shaikh Abdul Latif, the chief of saints, to put away from himself the surname of Abul Faiyāz ("the father of bounties"), and now, out of kindness and favour to 'Alijāh, that prince was directed by His Majesty to add this title to his own name.*

* The printed text is defective, having omitted, at the beginning of this sentence, the words *Faiyāz-i-surat wa ma'ni āz* and thus made a mess of it. The Bihar Ms. supplies the omission.

Khudābanda Khan, Khan-i-sāmān, a $2\frac{1}{2}$-*hazāri* (1,000 tr.), got an increment of 500 *zāt* (200 tr.). The enemy who were commanded to be henceforth written of as 'thieves', appeared two *kos* from the camp. The Emperor ordered Khan-i-'Alam, Bakhshi-ul-mulk Sadruddin Muhammad Khan Safavi, and others to go and chastise them. As they, in the thick of the battle, sent reports of the numerical superiority of the enemy to the Emperor, he sent Hamiduddin Khan Bahādur and Matlab Khan to their aid, after presenting them with amulets for safety. The enemy were beaten back. Khan-i-'Alam and Munawwar Khan were sent to Shah 'Ālijāh, with the present of swords. [515] A ring set with an emerald, carved with the name of Chin Qalich Khan Bahādur was sent to him. Bāqi Khan, qiladār of Agra, a 2-*hazāri* (600 tr.), got an increment of 500 *zāt*, and said in gratitude,—

"The work succeeds through the Emperor's favour; Bāqi (1, he and 2, the rest) is a mere pretext (as the doer of it)!"

Gaitiārā Begam and 'Iffat-ārā Begam, daughters of Shah 'Ālijāh, and Bakht-un-nisā Begam, daughter of Bidār Bakht, came to Court : each was presented with ornaments varying in price from eight to ten thousand rupees. Nasrat Jang Khan hastened with light kit, for punishing the 'thieves' near Aurangabad sending his baggage to Court with Rām Singh Hādā. Ābul Khair Khan, faujdār and qiladār of Junnar, son of 'Abdul 'Aziz Khan, who had received his father's title, became administrator (*wali*) of the tomb of Miān Shaikh 'Abdul Latif, situated in the Daulatmaidān quarter of Burhānpur. Qamruddin Khan, son of Muhammad Āmin Khan, was presented with a yamani *sarpech*, and Muhammad Hasan, son of Mukhlis Khan deceased, with a jewelled ring. On Tuesday, the 18th June, 1706/17th Rabi. A., a round box full of jewels and one bundle of special dresses were sent to Sultāns Dādār Bakhsh and Dāwar Bakhsh, in condolence for the deaths of their parents, Izid Bakhsh and Mihr-un-nisā Begam, the daughter of the Emperor. On Sunday the 30th June/29th Rabi. A., at the end of the night the Emperor learnt that Buland Ākhtar had died. Khwāja Ma'saud Khan was sent to convey his three sons and the ladies [516] of his harem to the fort of Ahmadnagar. Jewels and mourning robes were presented to Chamni Begam, the daughter, and to Sultān Fatihā Qaribā and other sons of the deceased,

Satvā Daflé, who was at Islāmpuri, died. On Thursday the 25th July, 1706, Tarbiyat Khan Bahādur was sent towards Rahman-Bakhsh-Kherā to chastise the 'thieves'. Ābu Nasar Khan (son of Shāista Khan), an officer serving in Bengal, became Subahdār of Oudh *vice* Mirzā Khan-i-'Alam deceased. A 3-*hazāri* (2,000 tr.), he received an increment of 500 tr. Siw Singh, qiladār and faujdār of Rāiri, became qiladār and faujdār of Nabishāhdurg, *vice* Lodi Khan, and also qiladār of Chākna *vice* 'Abdullah, thānadār of Shirwal. A 1½-*hazāri* (1,000 tr.), he received an increment of 500 *zāt* (300 tr.). 'Azzuddin, son of Mu'izzuddin, and Muhammad Karim, son of Muhammad 'Azim, had been enjoying daily allowances; each was presented with forty lakhs of *dām*. The Crown Prince sent the robe of appointment for the post of his Court agent to Muhammad Ikhlās-kesh, (whose name, through the grace of the Emperor had been prefaced by the holy word 'Muhammad' and thus rendered famous as Muhammad Ikhlās), and the latter made his bow to the Emperor.

Mehtar Mubārak, messenger of the king of Balkh, had audience, and presented as peshkash, twelve horses and five mules. Two *dālis* of robes, an elephant, and a horse were sent to Mu'izzuddin Bahadur in reward of his conquest of Malik Ghazi. Muhammad Razā, son of 'Ali Mardān Khan Haidarābadi became qiladār of Rāmgarh *vice* his deceased father. [517] A *hazāri* (200 tr.), he received an increment of 200 tr. Māndhātā, son of Rao Kānhu, an officer under Nasrat Jang, was appointed in company with Yasin Khan to conquer the forts Hanumant-garh and Parichhitgarh, within the promised period of one year. 'Ināyetullah Khan, *mutasaddi* of *tan* and *khālsa,* used to stand on the carpet. The Emperor granted him the honour of standing within the railing (*katra*). Mehtar Mubārak, the envoy, on the day of taking *congee,* received a robe, a dagger, an elephant, and 5,000 rupees in cash. Yusuf Khan, qiladār and faujdār of Qamarnagar, became qiladār and faujdār of Imtiāzgarh *vice* Chin Qalich Khan Bahādur. A *hazāri* (600 tr.), he received an increment of 500 tr. Zinat-un-nisā Begam had bled herself. The price of *tasadduq* was sent to her, *viz.,* 2,000 rupees from the Emperor; 2,500 rupees from Shah 'Ālijāh; 1,000 rupees from Kām Bakhsh. Hamiduddin Khan Bahādur showed the Emperor some *sarpeches* of *chikan*-work which he graciously accepted. * * *

CHAPTER LI.

51ST YEAR OF THE REIGN : 1118 A.H.

26th November, 1706—20th February, 1707.

*   *   *   *

* * * [518] Muhammad Āmin Khan Bahādur with his comrades, having returned safe and laden with spoil from the chastisement of the enemy, was received in audience. He was honoured with the title of Chin Bahādur, 'Aziz Khan Bahādur Ruhela, was exalted by the addition, to his name, of the word "Chaghtāi" which was the designation of honour of his father Bahādur Khan. Mirzā Beg, son of Nasrat Khan deceased, who had brought to Court the articles of the crown Prince's peshkash, was presented with a jewelled dagger and sent back. With him were sent to the Prince, a jewelled dagger, waist-*muttakā,* and *punchhi* worth 50,000 rupees.

Muhammad Āmin Khan Chin Bahādur, a 4-*hazāri* (1,200 tr.) received an increment of 300 tr. 'Aziz Khan Bahādur Chaghtāi, a 2½-*hazāri* received an increment of 500 *zāt;* Sulaimān Khan, son of Khizir Khan Batani, a 1½-*hazāri,* got an increment of 500. Khwāja Khan, brother's son and (own) son-in-law of Siādat Khan Ughlān, a 1½-*hazāri* (500 tr:), had a hundred troopers added to his rank. A marriage was settled between the daughter of Āmir Khan deceased and Sultān 'Azzuddin, son of Mu'izzuddin. Ten thousand rupees were given to her for expenses. Chin Qalich Khan Bahādur, nāzim of Bijapur, was summoned [519] to Court, and had audience. Mun'im Khan, nāib Subahdār of Lahore, a *hazāri,* got an increment of 500 *zāt* (100 tr.).

DEATH OF THE EMPEROR :

*   *   *   *

After accomplishing holy war by wresting the spacious land of Deccan from the hands of hellish infidels, and conquering the forts of this region, on Sunday, the 20th

January, 1706/16th Shawwal [520] he alighted at Ahmadnagar. After one year of residence there, owing to the fickleness of fortune, he fell severely ill at the end of the month of Shawwāl of the 51st regnal year (26th December, 1706—23rd January, 1707). But * * he recovered from the illness. According to his usual custom, he came to the "Court of the oppressed" several times and engaged in the business of the State. In the course of this time, Shah 'Ālijāh was sent to remedy the disorders of the subah of Mālwā, and Kām Bakhsh started for Bijapur as Subahdār. After a space of four or five days, a severe fever attacked His Majesty, and for three days, although the severity of it continued, he by exerting his natural strength of purpose and loftiness of spirit came to the Court (*'adālatgāh*) at every one of the five hours of prayer, for the purpose of offering his prayers with the congregation, reciting God's name and performing (other) religious duties; and he did not neglect a single item (of worship). In these days he frequently recited this couplet:

> "In a twinkle, in a minute, in a breath,
> The condition of the world changes."

[521] In the afternoon of Thursday, the Emperor was shown a petition of Hamiduddin Khan Bahādur proposing the giving away of an elephant as *tasadduq*, and begging that 4,000 rupees, the price of the elephant, might be entrusted to the Qāzi-ul-qazāt Mullā Haidar for distribution among the poor. The Emperor wrote the letter *sād* (*'correct'*) on it. On the top (of the sheet), while he was in a condition which was almost that of the parting of life, he wrote "Convey this worthless person (*khāksār*) to the first stage". On the morning of Friday, the 20th February, 1707/28th Zil. Q. 1118, the Emperor came out and went to his bed-room (*khābgāh*) to perform his morning prayer, and engaged in reciting God's names, and in spite of his being overcome by unconsciousness and difficulty of breathing, his fingers moved in counting the beads of the rosary and (his tongue) in repeating the phrase "There is no deity save God". When nearly one quarter of the day was over, in accordance with his own wish,—he used to say that it is a great boon to die on a Friday,—he passed away. * * *

The Qāzi, scholars, and pious men engaged in furnishing and shrouding his corpse for burial, in the terms of his last will, [522] performed the funeral prayer, and kept his body in the khābgāh, till at last at the request of Zinat-un-nisā Began, second daughter of the Emperor, Prince Muhammad 'Āzam, who had been halting twenty-five *kos* from the imperial camp, arrived on Saturday, the 22nd February, 1707/30th Zil. Q., and went into the deepest mourning.

On Monday, the 24th February, the Prince in extreme grief carried the corpse on his own shoulders up to the hall of justice, by way of escorting it reverently, and then sent it away. According to His Majesty's last will, he was buried in the courtyard of the tomb of Shaikh Zainuddin [at Rauza, near Daulatabad] in a sepulchre built by the Emperor in his own lifetime. * * *

[523] This place, called Khuldābād, is eight *kos* from Aurangābād and three *kos* from Daulatābād. The red stone platform (*chabutra*) over his grave, not exceeding three yards in length, two and a half yards in breadth, and a few fingers in height, has a cavity in the middle. It has been filled with earth, in which fragrant herbs have been planted. * * * He is (now) remembered under the title of *Khuld-makān*.

* * * *

Through the numberless blessings of the angelic soul of this repository of Divine pardon, (after his death) not a trace appeared of those disturbances and ruin which descend on mankind during world-convulsing changes, and so the people reposed on the cushion of comfort exactly as they had passed their days in peace and happiness during the lifetime of this ever-living soul. God's pardon and mercy be on him! The period of his life was 91 years and 13 days (lunar) and that of his reign 50 years, 2 months and 27 days. It is impossible for me to say anything that can truly number the years of this Unique One of the Celestial Court. What can we speak of the life of a man who has been gifted with the life eternal? For ever-awake hearts like him, it is the rule to avoid the word 'death'. *Verses* :—

The pious have never died and will never die.
When applied to such men the name of death is
properly speaking 'translation'.

That passionate pursuer of perfection, Muhammad Ikhlās (*kesh*) used to narrate, "In the night preceding that Friday on which [524] His Majesty went to visit the garden of divine pardon, 'Ināyetullah Khan and myself were distracted and depressed in mind and body at the imminence of such a great calamity; we took sorts by opening the poems of 'the Tongue of the Invisible' (the *Diwān-i-Hāfiz*) at haphazard and our eyes fell on the following *ghazal* :—

So long as any trace or name of the tavern and
the wine will remain (on earth),
My head will be the dust on the road of the Magi.
On the soil that will bear the mark of the sole
of thy foot,
For years to come masters of sight (truly-sighted
men) will prostrate themselves in adoration.
When thou passest by my tomb, cheer up,
It will be a place of pilgrimage to the drunkards
of the world (= Sufis).

"Despair seized our souls, we passed the night in distraction of mind and anguish of heart. Next morning when one watch (three hours) of the day was over, the inevitable event took place. The night of the following Saturday (*i.e.*, the night of the Friday, according to the Christian almanac) we came together again. Mullā Haidar, the Qāzi of the imperial army, arrived as a guest; we told him that we had taken sorts out of the *Diwān-i-Hāfiz*. However much we tried, we could not recollect the verses.

We called for our books, but our baggage had been already packed up. Our company broke up. I fell asleep, when I dreamt that I was passing by a grave; a holy man (*Hazrat*) appeared with half his body standing out of the grave; he spoke to me,

'The verses you have forgotten are these—
When thou passest by my tomb, cheer up,
It will be a place of pilgrimage to the drunkards
(= Sufis) of the world.' "

Verses.

He never dies whose heart is (ever) awake with love.
My eternity has been inscribed on the pages of the world

[525] The noble character of this perfect Sovereign. As his blessed nature dictated, he was characterized by perfect devotion to the rites of the Faith; he followed the teaching of the great Imām Abu Hanifā (God be pleased with him!), and established and enforced to the best of his power the five foundations of Islām (five daily prayers). He was ever performing the purificatory lavation (before prayer) and repeating the blessed words (of the Prophet) and other holy sayings and prayers. He used to perform the obligatory prayers for the time (of the day) in the masjid or without a masjid, in congregation, and all the *sunnan* and *nawāfil* and the dearly loved (*mustahabbāt*) ceremonies publicly and with perfect humility. Fasting every month on the 12th and 13th days from the new moon (the brightest days), every week on Monday, Thursday and Friday, he used to perform the Friday prayer in the congregation mosque (Jām'i) in the company of all the Muslims and the community of the faithful.

The sacred nights he used to pass in wakefulness. With the light of the grace of God, he kindled the lamp of the church and the State. In his excessive quest of truth, in the sanctum sanctorum of the mosque of his royal residence, at nights he held converse with the men of God. In his private chamber, he never reposed on a cushion (*masnad*). He used to pay the canonical *zakat* (contribution to the poor of 2½ per cent every year) on the income that he had drawn and spent for his own food and clothing before his accession, in ways which were free from scruple or doubt, and whatever during his kingship he had added to the former by setting apart certain villages of Delhi and two or three salt-producing *mahals* for his privy purse; calculating the *zakat* on the income of his royal sons also, he used to send the amounts to the needy. The blessed month of Ramzān [526] he spent in fasting (in the day-time), and to the very end of that month he used to remain busy up to midnight in performing the Sunnan prayer and the tarāwih* and in chanting the entire *Qurān* in full congregation along with crowds of pious and learned men. On the 10th day of the month of Muharram (*'Ashurah*), he resided in the mosque in continual prayer. The performance of the ceremonies prescribed for the pilgrimage to Mecca—which was an obligation of the faith and the goal of his heart's desire—had outwardly

* Twenty or more genuflexions made after the last prayer of Ramzān.

to be postponed by him owing to certain obstructions and difficulties; but in order to atone for it, he conferred so many favours (money) on the pilgrims going to the two Holy Cities that it was equivalent to the Great Hajj itself. And during his reign he used to send large amounts of money, for some years annually, at others once in two or three years, to the pious men living in retreat in those Holy Cities, and a large number of men in those holy places were permanently employed by him on daily stipends to act as his deputies in walking round the Ka'ba, bowing (to the Prophet's tomb), reading the two copies of the *Qurān* written by this pious Emperor with his own hand and presented to Medina, counting the beads, repeating the Islamic credo and performing other acts of worship.

The characteristic qualities of scholars and the morals of perfect men, as they ought to be, were truly found in this Emperor of angelic character. His Majesty from the dawning of his understanding, being fully aware of the [canonical] duties and prohibitions, out of the perfect continence of his passions, never partook of any thing except the canonically sanctioned pleasures.

All the agents of pleasure and entertainment, such as sweet-voiced singers or charming players on musical instruments, were gathered in large numbers round his throne, and in the first few years of his reign he occasionally listened to their music and had a perfect expert's knowledge of this art; yet out of extreme abstinence he [later on] totally gave up listening to music [527].

Those of the court chanters, singers and musicians who repented of their sinful art, he made happy by the grant of daily stipends and land as "aid to living". Mirzā Mukarram Khan Safavi, who was an expert in the musical art, once said to His Majesty "What is Your Majesty's view of music?" The Emperor answered (in Arabic) "It is *mubah*,* neither good nor bad". The Khan asked, "Then what kind of it is in your opinion most worthy to be heard?" The Emperor replied, "I cannot listen to music without flutes, (*be-mazāmir*) especially *pakhāwaj*, but that is unanimously prohibited (*harām*); so I have left off hearing singing too".

* *Mubah*, literally "allowed", *i.e.*, an action which a person, according to the Muslim Canon law, may do or let alone, it being attended with neither praise nor blame; indifferent. (*Encyclopaedia of Islam*, iv. 322.)

He never wore garments declared impure by the Canon [such as robes of unmixed silk yarn], and not at all used vessels of gold or silver. In his company, no improper word such as of slander or obscenity or falsehood was spoken. His courtiers were instructed that when speaking or reading they should substitute some elegant word for every word that had any suspicion of being objectionable. Out of his love for doing justice, everyday, with open forehead and tender heart, he used to stand up two or three times, and grant justice to plaintiffs who used to find access in crowds without any obstruction to his court of justice and owing to the excessive kindness of His Majesty, used to state their plaints without the least fear or despair : and if in pleading their suits, they used any bombast (hyperbole in praise or censure) or exaggeration (or straining any point) of language or wrong pronunciation (or wrong expression), he did not at all get angry, and no lowering of anybody's dignity was ever seen on His Majesty's part. Many times his courtiers urged him to prevent (the plaintiffs) from displaying too much boldness (of speech). But he used to reply "From hearing [528] such words and the occurrence of such cases, the (sovereign's) character acquires an angelic patience". Never did he do any act which was without benefit to the populace. The tribe of harlots was expelled from Delhi, and the same order was published in all the provinces and all sides of the imperial dominions.

The work of the Censor of Morals was carried out to the full among the general public, both high and low. In administering such a vast empire he never had recourse to any punishment except the *hadud* and *siyāsat* authorized by the Islamic Holy Law (*Shara'*) and never issued an order for the killing of a man through the force of anger or the vehemence of passion, and none else had the power to do such deeds. By reason of his recognition of the dignity of others and his appreciation of merit, he used to honour Sayyids, Shaikhs and learned scholars (*ulamā*). Through the auspices of this hearty endeavour, the Hanafi creed (*i.e.*, the Orthodox Sunni faith) has gained such strength and currency in the great country of Hindustan as was never seen in the times of any of the preceding sovereigns. By one stroke of the pen, the Hindu clerks (writers) were dismissed from the public employment. Large numbers of the places of worship of the infidels and great temples of these wicked people have been thrown down and desolated. Men who can see only the outside of things are filled with wonder at the successful accomplishment of such a seemingly difficult task. And on the sites of the temples lofty mosques have been built. His Majesty personally taught the credo to many of the infidels who came to him, guided by their good fortune, with a view to being converted to Islam, and he bestowed on them robes of honour and other [529] favours.

About the middle of his reign he decided to levy the *jaziya* tax on the Hindus, as ordained by the Shara' and it was enforced throughout his empire; and this rare piece of good work (*hasnāt-i-gharib*) had not been done in Hindustan and the Hindus had not been degraded to such a degree in any other period. He used to spend so much money in religious alms (*khairāt*), beneficent public works, (like the building of public inns, *mubarrāt*), and pensions (*idrārāt*), that the expenditure of former rulers had not reached even a hundredth part of it: In the blessed month of Ramzān he used to distribute among the needy 60,000 rupees and in other months smaller amounts than that. Numerous free kitchens (*balghurkhānah* or *langar khānah*) for feeding the weak and the poor were established in Delhi and other provinces; wherever there was no inn or *sarāi* for the accommodation of travellers before, they were built by him. The repair of (old) mosques throughout the empire was carried out at the expense of his Government, and they were also supplied with a staff of *imām, mu'azzin* and *khātib* (for each), so that a huge amount of money was spent on this work. In all the cities and regions of this vast kingdom, he assigned adequate subsistence-allowances in the form of daily stipends and land grants (*imlāk*) to (Islamic) scholars and teachers, and provided food-money (cost of maintenance) for their students according to their condition and number.

All the aim of his exalted heart was devoted to making the general Muslim public act according to the legal decisions and precedents of the theological scholars (*ulamā*) of the Hanafi school; but seeing that these rulings as found in the existing law-books were confused (*lit.* mixed) on account of the diversity of opinion among the qāzis and muftis and the weakness (*i.e.,* little weight or authority) of the traditions, and the contradictory nature of the declarations of those ancient authorities—and above all as these rulings were not embodied in one book, so that till many law books were [530] collected and men (in India) could acquire adequate mastery of the science of jurisprudence, it was impossible to make a correct extract (of the Qurānic precept applicable to the particular case),—(therefore) the heart of this Emperor, the asylum of the Faith, was set on this that a syndicate of celebrated theologians and well-known scholars of Hindustan should go through the long authoritative books on jurisprudence, which had been collected in the imperial library, extract the rulings of muftis, and compile one comprehensive book out of them all, so that all may find out the authoritative rulings (on their cases) with ease. This great work was entrusted to a board presided over by that highest of scholars Shaikh Nizām (of Bhāgalpur in Bihār) and all the scholars engaged in the work were given good pay and subsistence. About two lakhs of rupees were spent in preparing this book, which was entitled the *Fatāwa-i-'Ālamgiri*, and which rendered the world independent of all other books on jurisprudence.

Among His Majesty's many favours to the public was the abolition of the taxes on grain and other food-stuffs, the charge for road-patrols (*rāhdāri*), the excise duty on cloth and other articles subject to the *sāir* (octroi), especially the duty on tobacco, which last article yielded a vast revenue and the excise-officers used to practise astonishing outrages on the modesty of women* in searching their persons, under the suspicion of its being smuggled.

Another of his gracious concessions was the remission throughout his dominions (of certain cesses)† on the Muslims in particular and the aforesaid items on the people in general, the total annual yield of which taken together exceeded thirty lakhs of rupees. He also abolished the rule of realising from his mansabdars the unspent Government advances to their grandfathers and other kinsmen, which under the standing practice of the finance department used before his time to be recovered by gradual deduction from the pay of their mansabs, and credited to the Exchequer, and which every year brought in a large total. [531] His Majesty also forbade the practice of escheating to the State the property of the dead nobles who had left behind them no debt due to Government, but he let their heirs succeed to their legacy,—whereas in former reigns the imperial collectors used strictly to confiscate such property and this rule proved a source of suffering to the surviving relatives. The Emperor also sent

* For examples, see Manucci's *Storia do Mogor*, ii. 175, Khafi Khan, ii. 88.

† For a list of the cesses (*ābwābs*) remitted by him, see J. Sarkar's *Mughal Administration*, Ch. V, Sec. 8 and 9.

his *farmāns* to every subah ordering that the taxes (*hāsilāt*) should be collected only in accordance with the rules of the Holy Qurānic Law.

The military activities that His Majesty had performed both before his accession to the throne and after it, have been embodied in the course of the occurrences described in this auspicious history. Here I shall write only a little about the wonderful firmness of His Majesty, which was witnessed when the imperial army (of Shāh Jahān) invaded Balkh, and 'Abdul 'Aziz Khan opposed him in battle. A hostile force, more numerous than ants and locusts, completely encircled the imperial army and engaged in fighting; in the very heat of the engagement, the time of the *zuhar* prayer arrived; His Majesty disregarding the dissuasions of his officers, alighted from his mount, adorned the ranks of prayer in congregation, and performed the *namāzes,* obligatory, *sunnat* and *nafl,* with firmness* and perfect composure of mind. 'Abdul 'Aziz Khan, as soon as he heard of this act of bravery, was overpowered by the force of the verse "Help is from God", and gave up the fight, saying, "To quarrel with such a man is to ruin one's self".

Among the admirable pursuits of His Majesty, which adorned him with divinely bestowed conditions (*hālāt-i-wahabiya,* ecstasy?) was his diligent study of religious books, such as the Commentaries on the Qurān, the Traditions of the Prophet, and works on jurisprudence, [532] the writings of Imām Muhammad Ghazāli : selections from the books of Shaikh Sharf Yahia of Maner, Shaikh Zain-ud-din, Qutb Muhi Shirāzi, and other books of the same class, which he perused constantly.

Another of his brilliant characteristics was the memorising of the Word of God : although from the beginning of his fortunate life he had committed to memory certain of the chapters (*sura*) of the *Qurān* as the result of his following the guidance of chanters, yet the *Qurān* was completely memorised by him only after his accession to the throne, with great exertion and angelic persistence. The date of his commencing this work of memorising will be found from the numerical value of the letters in the blessed sentence *Sanqarek—falātansi* (=1071 A.H.) and the date of completion from the phrase *Lawh-i-mahfuz* (=1078).

---

* *Ba-ta'dil-i-ārākan,* (1) on equal terms with the nobles (the pillars of the State), or (2) with the firmness of pillars.

The hand-writing of His Majesty in the *naskh* style was exceedingly firm and wellformed, and he showed great energy in writing it. Two copies of the Holy *Qurān* transcribed with his own hand—on the tablet (*lawh*), marginal lines in gold and silver, and binding of which 7,000 rupees had been spent,—he had presented to Medina. He could also write the *nastāliq* and *shikastah* hands very well.

He possessed great skill in prose composition and letter-writing, and was well-versed in prose and poetry (literature). But holding firmly to the precept of the holy verse: "It is the erring who follow the poets", (*Qurān,* xxvi. 224), he did not incline to the hearing of useless poetry. How then could he be expected to listen to adulatory verses? But poems breathing moral advice (he liked). *Verses* [533].

In order to please God the High and Splendid, I have not
Turned my eyes on any *ghazāl* (fawn-like beauty)
nor my ears on any *ghazal* (erotic ode).

It is beyond the power of the pen to embrace all the noble traits of the character of this Choice One of the Age, and to recount them. (Verses omitted) * * *

ACCOUNT OF THIS HOLY EMPEROR'S CHILDREN

This perfect-natured Sovereign brought up his sons in such a way that through his outward and inward exertions they became endowed with high accomplishments and orthodox learning and came to possess an abundant share of virtue, submissiveness to God, abstinence from uncanonical acts, the science and practice of kingship and generalship, and skill in many useful arts.

Guided by the Emperor, they committed the *Qurān* to memory and acquired some amount of polite learning (under twelve heads), gained skill in writing different kinds of hand, and mastered the Turki and Persian languages. So, too, all the females of his harem (daughters) under his direction learnt the necessary rules and doctrines of religion, and all engaged in the worship of God, reading and transcribing the *Qurān,* and the acquisition of virtues and provision for the next world.

The Lord had given His Majesty five sons and five daughters. [534] Here I shall give a brief account of each of them, although the affairs of the Emperor's sons and daughters have been narrated among the events of the life of this Emperor in the *'Ālamgirnāmah* and this history of mine.

Sons:—1. Prince Muhammad Sultān, borne by Nawāb Bāi, 4th Ramzān, 1049/19th December, 1639. He was noted for his noble manners and admirable qualities; memorised the *Qurān*, could read and write Arabic, Persian and Turki sufficiently well. In the wars of His Majesty, this Prince performed brilliant exertions and gave proofs of his valour. Died in the 20th year of His Majesty's reign.

2. Prince Muhammad Mu'azzam Shāh 'Ālam Bahādur, born on the last day of Rajab, 1053/4th October, 1643, from the womb of the same queen as the above. This epitome of the "Book of Night and Day", owing to his blessed character and the teaching of His Majesty, from the dawn of his reason, acquired noble traits of character and manly accomplishments. When young he memorised the *Qurān*. He has mastered the art of reading the *Qurān* with the correct intonation; and he chants the verses with such a clear melodious voice, that [535] the listener's ears are never satiated with hearing it. Before reading the verses, one verse is [*cor. from ms.*] the *manzil* (? phase, stage)* with regard to this Chosen One of the Times. He spent the time of his youth mostly in acquiring learning and united theoretical knowledge to practice. For his knowledge of the Prophet's traditions, the trustworthy men of the age call him "the foremost master of the *Hadis*". He has such a minute and accurate knowledge of canon law that he can extract the Qurānic or *Hadis* rule applicable to any case (very quickly). He speaks Arabic so correctly and elegantly that even the Arabs of Arabia praise it; and he has a perfect knowledge of the Turki and Persian tongues; in writing various kinds of hand he can serve as a master and guide to others. He spends most nights in wakefulness, performing the *nafl*, the daily tasks, the chanting of the *Qurān*, the reading of books on the *Hadis*, commentaries on the *Qurān*, Canon Law, and right conduct (*saluk*). The morning

---

* *Māqabil-i-āyāt-khāndan āyite bud* [Ms. reads *āst*] *manzil dar shān-i-ān barguzidah-i-rozgār*. Does the variant in the printed text mean that he earnt the Qurānic verses one by one?

prayer (*fajar*) he offers at daybreak, and sits on a prayer carpet (*musalla*) elevated one spear's length, sometimes two spears' lengths.

Next he appears at the window (of *darshan*) and delights the eyes of the people waiting to see him, and listens to the petitions of oppressed persons seeking justice; here he stays as long as may be required on each particular day. Then he sits in the Hall of Private Audience and conducts the administration of the revenue and the Government on the reports of the High Diwāns, Bakhshis and other officers. After the prayer (of noon), he retires to the harem and takes his meal and repose for his health's sake. After offering the *'asar namāz,* he remedies the pain in the hearts of the oppressed. Before sunset, the officers in charge of the armoury present the weapons before His Majesty. [536]

After the sun has set, kindling the lamps of adoration, he performs the *'ashā* prayer at one-third of the night past, and then retires to bed . . . May the gracious God keep the shadow of this great monarch for ever on the heads of the people of the world!

3. Prince Muhammad 'Āzam, born on 28th June 1653/12th Shabān 1063, to Dilras Bānu Begam, the daughter of Shāh Nawāz Khan Safavi. The lustre of greatness shone from the first lunar station of his forehead and the star of intelligence glittered from the horizon of his life.

By the excellent training of His Majesty (Aurangzib) he ascended to the pinnacle of perfection and gained an abundance of accomplishments and excellent qualities. That Emperor used to be extremely delighted with this Prince's noble character and excellent manners. He had a wonderful brilliancy and firmness; in contests of quick repartee and discovering the aptest word he was everywhere very nimble-witted.

He had attained to the status of a comrade of his father, who often used to say "Between this pair of matchless friends, a separation is imminent". On the 18th Rabi.A./8th June, 1707, three months and twenty days after the Emperor 'Ālamgir's death, he died after fighting bravely in battle (against Shah 'Ālam I, at Jājau.) [537].

4. Muhammad Ākbar, born on the 12th Zil. H., 1067/11th September, 1657, to the Begam (Dilras Bānu). Under the teaching of his father, he acquired sublime accomplishments. His death took place in Irān in the 48th

year of 'Ālamgir's reign. He had run away from the side of his august father to the wilderness of disappointment, but two things prove that his end was good : the first is,—"The Emperor used to say that Ākbar never gave up attending the congregated prayer with the (Sunni) community and he had not the least fear of the enemies of the faith (*i.e.*, the Persian Shia's). Secondly, it was his fortune to be buried at the holy Mashhad at the place where the shoes are left behind by pilgrims to the tomb of the eighth Imām Musā." It would not be inapt to quote here the "letter by order" (*hasb-ul-hukm*) which the wise minister 'Ināyetullah Khan wrote by command to Prince Bidār Bakht : "When Muni'm Khan, the Court agent of the eldest Prince Shah 'Ālam, on being appointed his diwān, got his *congee* for Kābul, advice was sent through him to his master urging him not to be negligent towards the mischievous vain intentions of *Ākbar-i-ābtar,** who has ruined his present world and the next, and is residing at Farāh† near Qandahār, and by the advice of the ruler of that country (the Shāh of Persia) would not go away elsewhere. He is waiting there in the expectation that if the inevitable thing to which flesh is subject (namely the death of Aurangzib) should take place through the stroke of misfortune, and Shāh 'Ālam would move out of Kābul to Hindustan, Ākbar would then enter Kābul and Multān with the help of the Persian (king), that deceitful carrion-eating demon (*ghul*).‡ (In Arabic) "The evil example of those who take unto themselves other gods besides Allah". (*Qurān*, xxv. 3.)

"To this grandson who will (soon) be with his august father 'Ālijāh (Muhammad 'Āzam) let me say by way of

---

* *Akbar* is an Arabic superlative meaning the greatest, while *abtar* is its antithesis, meaning the worst. So, after this prince's rebellion his imperial father ordered his name to be written in all official papers as *abtar* and also as the Rebel (*Bāghi*). The Shah of Persia refused to give military aid to Akbar in a war with his father, (which was an act of impiety), but promised to lend him a Persian army after his father's death, for contesting the throne with his brothers, which was a common thing in Islamic and other history.

† *Farāh* is south-west of the Mughal province of Kābul, which then included Ghazni but not Qandahār, and Akbar's presence just beyond the frontier was a standing menace to the peace of Hindustan. (See Sarkar's *Studies in Aurangzib's Reign*, Ch. VI and *House of Shivaji*, Ch. XI.)

‡ *Ghul* is Persian for the *ignis fatuus*, "Will of the wisp", who lured travellers into the wilderness at night by his false light, killed them and then ate the corpses, digging them out of graves. Spelt in English as *ghoul*. (See *Encyclopaedia of Islam*, ii. 165.)

§ This letter to Bidār Bakht has been given in an incorrect form in the printed text. I have translated the full original letter as given in 'Ināyetullah's *Ahkam* (my transcript of the Rampur State Library Ms, collated with the Safdar Nawab Ms. of Patna.)

parting advice (*wasiyyat*) that as far as possible [538] he should follow the policy of concord and abstain from fighting and quarrelling, because to quarrel is to ruin one's own self, and a strange revolution will take place. Take pity on the people, because the poor faithful community will be trodden down (in a war of succession). (Arabic) "And the end is for the pious and the next world is better and more lasting than this. Do what you choose." (*Qurān,* xxi. 132; lxxxvii. 17; xli. 40.)

5. Prince Muhammad Kām Bakhsh, born on the 24th February, 1667/10th Ramzān, 1077 A.H., to Bāi Udipuri. Brought up by the Emperor, he memorised the Qurān, and studied the standard books more than all his brothers, and acquired a great knowledge of the Turki language and skill in writing various kinds of hand. How can I embrace within the limits of my writing his bravery and liberality, which were characteristic of these excellent princes? On 3rd Zil. Q., 1120/3rd January, 1709, two years after Aurangzib's death, he fell, fighting like a Rustam or an Āsfandiyār.

DAUGHTERS:

1. Zeb-un-nisā Begam, born on the 10th Shawwāl, 1047/15th February, 1638 (text wrong by one year), to Begam (Dilras Bānu). Through the auspicious upbringing of the God-knowing Emperor ('Ālamgir) she learnt the *Qurān* by rote, for which she received from the Emperor a reward of 30,000 gold coins. She completely mastered the Arabic and Persian languages, and in writing various kinds of hand, such as *nastāliq, naskh* [539], and *shikastah* correctly, she had full competence. She appreciated the value of learning and skill; and all her heart was set on the collection, copying and reading of books and she turned her kind attention to improving the lot of scholars and gifted men. The result was that she collected a library the like of which no man has seen; and large numbers of theologians, scholars, pious men, poets, scribes and calligraphists by this means came to enjoy the bounty of this lady hidden in the harem of grandeur; *e.g.,* Mullā Safi-ud-din Ārdbili by her order took up his residence in Kashmir and engaged in making a translation (into Persian) of the "Great Commentary on the Qurān", which came to be entitled *Zeb-ut-tafāsir,* "The ornament of commentaries". Other tracts

and books have been composed in her honoured name. She died in her father's life-time, in the 46th year of his reign, 1113, (26th May, 1702).

2. Ziṇat-un-nisā Begam, born 1st Shabān, 1053/5th October, 1643, to Begam Dilras Bānu. Her father brought her up in the knowledge of the doctrines and the necessary rules of the Faith. Vast numbers of people received their livelihood from her bounty.

3. Badar-un-nisā Begam, born on 29th Shawwāl, 1057/17th November, 1647, to Nawāb Bāi. Her father made her memorize [540] the *Qurān*, and read books on the Faith. She spent her life in doing pious deeds. She died on 28th Zil. Q., in the 13th year of his reign/9th April, 1670.

4. Zubdat-un-nisā Begam, born on 26th Ramzān, 1061/2nd September, 1651, to Dilras Bānu Begam. She employed herself in adoring the Creator and thus gaining boundless rewards; was married to Sipihr Shukoh, the son of Dārā Shukoh, and died in the same year as her father, (in February, 1707).

5. Mihr-un-nisā Begam, born on 3rd Safar 1072/18th September, 1661, to Āurangābādi Mahal. She died in the 50th year of her father's reign, 1116 A.H./ 1706 A.D. She was the wife of Izid Bakhsh, the son of Murād Bakhsh. God be pleased with them!

GLOSSARY

Āghābāni—must not be mistaken for *Agha-Khani,* that title being a 19th century creation. I suggest *Āghā-bāshi,* chief of the Āghās or a certain class of Turkish Court officials or inferior officers up to the grade of captain. *Encyclopædia of Islam,* i. 180.

Āhadi—'gentleman trooper', or soldier on a higher pay and status than the ordinary and serving directly under the Emperor. IR. 10, 43. BL. 250.

Āima—land granted either rent-free or subject to a small quit-rent, to learned and religious persons of the Muslim faith or for religious and charitable uses in relation to Islam. WL. 13.

Ākhta-begi—master of the horse. IR. 21.

Anant—a bracelet of gold, usually in the form of a snake with its tail entering into its mouth, (named after the Anant snake on which Vishnu reclines.)

Ārgajā—a perfume of a yellowish colour, compounded of several ingredients. FB. 30.

Ārsi—a small mirror set on a thumb-ring. FB. 29.

'Arz-i-mukarrar—confirmation of an order (for appointment, promotion, etc.), by reporting the order to the Emperor a second time. IR. 13, 18.

'Asa—a long stick or mace, coated with silver, carried before a man of rank. WL. 34.

'Atr of fitna—scent or essence of the flower *fitna* (which see).

Bahlia—infantry armed with muskets ; (mostly Rajputs of Oudh) see Crooke's *N. W. Provinces,* 212-213. WL. 46 calls them *Baheria,* "a clan of Rajputs in Jaunpur and Chunar".

Bait-ul-māl—the public treasury into which payments on various accounts are made, and according to the sources from which they are derived, applicable to the support of different classes of persons ; an escheat property that falls to the Crown on failure of heirs goes into it. WL. 48.

Bakāwal—head cook, superintendent of a kitches. FB. 118.

Bālāband—(1) turban-ornament, IR. 29. (2) a coat of a particular kind. FB. 91.

Bālādast (khil'at)—(probably) a superior kind of *khil'at.*

Barq-āndāz—Match-lockmen. IR. 20, 166.

Bayutāt—short for 'diwan-i-bayutat', an officer who registered the property of deceased persons, in order to secure the payment of the dues of the State as well as to safeguard the property for the heirs. SK. 53.

Bāz—(p. 67), a mistake for tār. See Shamsher.

Bāzuband—a bracelet or an amulet worn on the arm. FB. 90.

Beldār—a digger. IR. 178.

Bid-i-mushk—musk-willow, celebrated for its fragrance. FB. 155.

Chabutra of Kotwāl—platform in front of the police-prefect's office, where criminals or their severed heads were exposed to public view. SK. 66-71.
Chādar—(1) a missile of spreading fire. IR. 131.
Chakmaq—battle-axe, IR. 81.
Chāmar—fly-whisk, usually made of the tail of the Yak cow.
Chār-qab—"*chār-qubā* is a vest without sleeves. It covers only the breast and the back and reaches up to the shoulders. The front and the arms are covered with frills made of (small) pearls". (Letter *c.* 10 Dec. 1784 of the Maratha envoy in Delhi. *Dilliyethil M. Rajkaranen,* i. No. 133.)
Chaugharā—a small box with four partitions for holding betel-leaf, nut, chunam, and spices, or for perfumes. FB. 336.
Chauki-i-khās—the special watch or guard placed round the Emperor's person.
Haft chauki—the patrol conducted by noblemen round the Emperor's residence, one on each day of the week. IR. 188. BL. 257.
Chobdār—a mace-bearer, a servant whose business is to announce the arrival of company. FB. 332.

Daftardār—Registrar, recorder. FB.· 384.
Dāgh—branding of horses at muster. IR. 46.
Dām—a small coin of which 40 made a rupee. IR. 6.
Dāna-kesh—a kind of embroidered neck-cloth, worn in cold weather over the cloak. FB. 372.
Dangal—crowd, party.
Dārogha—superintendent or chief of a department or office.
Dār-ul-inshā—"writing office", Secretariat.
Deorhi—literally a gate ; the audience or office held in the front room or portico. FB. 410.
Dhakdhaki—*dhuk-dhuki,* an ornament worn on the breast. FB. 401.
Dhup—a straight sword. Usually Deccani. IR. 76.
Diwān—(1) Hall of Audience. (2) Revenue minister.
Do-āspā—a trooper with two horses and receiving higher pay than the ordinary. IR. 23.
Do-balgha—
Do-dāmi—flowered muslin, the flowers worked with a needle. FB. 391.
Doli—also *dola,* a sort of sedan in which women are carried, inferior to a palki. WL. 147.
Do-patta—a kind of veil in which there are two breadths, a sheet for covering the body when sleeping. FB. 391.
Do-shāla—two shawls sewn together ; (a single shawl is never worn by Indians.) FB. 394.

Ek-lari—an ornament (necklace) with one string only.

Fath-pech—a mode of tying the turban. FR. 535. Probably here, a cloth for tying the beard (*fatha*).
Filkhānah—Elephant stables, also the department of elephants.
Fitna—a species of mimosa or acacia, bearing flowers and having a powerful scent. FB. 535

Fota—a cloth which they wrap round the middle when going to bathe. FB. 539.

Gaj-mānik—see BL. 118. An excrescence resembling a large pearl on the forehead of a first-class elephant. FB. 609, "it is a popular idea among the Hindus that the finest gems (*mānik*) and pearls (*moti*) are to be found in the heads of elephants and serpents."

Gajnal—a small gun, mounted on an elephant. IR. 135.

Ghor-nal—a long musket or swivelgun fired from horse-back. IR. 111 has *Ghor-dahan*.

Ghusal-khānah—literary "bath-room", but in Mughal history applied as the popular name to the Emperor's hall of private audience, because in the new palace of Agra fort built by Shah Jahan this hall occupied the site of Akbar's bath-room (now demolished). It is a fanciful theory of some European writers that the Mughal hall of private audience was so called because every Emperor gave audience to his select grandees when he was washing! This theory is due to the false analogy of Louis XIV of France giving audience to his nobles when he was rising from his bed (whence the term *levee*), and the nobles handed to His Majesty his soap and towel!!! It is true that Akbar allowed the highest officers to report *urgent* business to him when he was bathing. Abd. Hamid, *Padishah-namah*, IA. 148.

Gulālbār—outer enclosure of the Emperor's own residential tents. IR. 199.

Huqqa—hand-grenade. IR. 282.

'Ilaqa—lace-work (FB. 526) or pearls strung in the form of a border.

Inā'm—literally, a present or gift ; in this book, a cash gift over and above the pay of a person's mansab. BL. 271. Later (esp. in the Deccan) it came to mean a rent free grant of land. WL. 217-218.

Jahalam—correctly *Jihlam*, the vizor of a helmet, (Steingass spells it as *chahlam*). IR. 68.

Jilau-khānah—yard for the parade of led horses. BL. 142 *n*.

Jamdhār—a kind of dagger. IR. 86. EG. Plate I. no. 27.

Jā-namāz-khānah—the Emperor's prayer-room the materials of which were kept in an anteroom of the palace ; chapel.

Jigha—an ornament of gold and jewels worn in the helmet. FB. 308. crest, *aigrette*.

Jhumka—the bell-shaped pendant of an ear-ring. FB. 306.

Kajāwah—a camel's saddle ; a kind of camel's litter in which female travel. FB. 561.

Kalgi—an ornament on the turban.

Kamar-band—a girdle, a long piece of cloth girt round the loins FB. 581.

Kangan—also Kankan, an ornament worn on the wrists by wome bracelet. FB. 586.

Karah—a ring worn on the wrists, ankles etc. FB. 570.
Karori—collector of the Government dues of a certain area (originally estimated to yield one kror of dam or Rs. 2,50,000), or market place. SK. 86.
Khās—literally, special ; superior kind of articles made for the Emperor's use, or articles already used by the Emperor.
Khatam-bandi-khānah—department of setting shells. FB. 356 gives a different meaning.
Khawās—a domestic servant, a page.
Khil'at—robe of honour conferred by the Emperor and other high persons.
Khil'at-khānah—department or factory for the manufacture and storing of robes of honour.
Khush-āspā—possessing excellent or superior horses.
Khush-manzil—an officer whose duty was to select good places for the Emperor's halt during his marches ; he fixed the limits of each stage of the journey.
Khutba—the royal titles as proclaimed from the pulpit before prayers.
Kirkirāq-khānah—ward-robe of a peculiar kind. Full description in Sarkar's *Mughal Administration*, p. 193.

Langri—(misspelt as *langar*), a large shallow metal pan used for kneading bread in or serving rice. FB. 650.
Latkan—drops worn in the ear. FB. 642.

Mahalla—parade of an officer's contingent of troops. IR. 46.
Māhi marātib—*māhi o marātib*, or fish and standard, the highest insignia of distinction. IR. 31-33.
Makri—an ornament for the ear resembling a spider's web.
Mānik—gem.
Mashk—leather-bag.
Masnad—royal seat, usually a cushion or carpet raised above the floor.
Mir Tuzuk—chief marshal, an officer whose duty it is to preserve order in a march or procession. FB. 722.
Misl—station, department ; here encampment.
Mufti—assistant to the Qazi or judge ; he consulted the old Arabic works on jurisprudence and stated the abstract law bearing on the case to the Qazi, who pronounced the sentence. SK. 27.
Muttakā—cushion or couch. FB. 665.
Muzāwwar—? probably, a retaining wall or buttress (*pushta*).

Naqdi—troops paid in cash. IR. 14, 20.
Naqqār-khānah—band-room.
Nazar—present made to a superior.
Nāzir—superintendent of an office, esp. the harem.
Niāz—offering made usually in fulfilment of a vow, or by way of dedication or prayer.
Nimchāh—A short sword. IR. 75, 112.
Nisār—literally sacrifice ; money waved round the head of the Emperor and then scattered among the people to ensure God's blessings for his health or victory.

Pakhwāz—a kind of drum, a timbrel. FB. 201.
Pān—betel-leaf, chewed in India.
Parastār—(1) servant-girl, (2) concubine, sometimes also married wife.
Par-i-kaling—feather of the heron, used as a crest.
Parkhāna—
Parm-narm—
Peshdast—office assistant, head clerk (?)
Phul-katārā—a kind of dagger.
Prahar—one quarter of the day or night, 3 hours.
Punchhi—an ornament like a fish-tail.

Qur—The Turkish standard of balls and the Yak cow's tail fixed on a rod and borne aloft ; imperial insignia ; the officer in charge of these was called the *Qur-begi.*

Rahkala—wheeled field-piece. IR. 135, 139, 140.
Rāk—Shalwār—*Shalwār* means trousers. If *rāk* be taken as *rak* (or vein, *rag*), it would mean striped trousers.

Sadr—civil judge (and royal almoner.) SK. 28.
Sadr-us-sadur—the chief Civil Judge and Almoner, i.e., supervisor of the religious endowments of the Emperors. SK. 29.
Sihra—a wreath worn on the head by a bridegroom and a bride at the marriage ceremony.
Sarbāri—a porter who carries loads on his head, but on p. 135, chief.
Sarf-i-khās—literally privy purse, the Emperor's private expenditure.
Sarpech—an ornament in front of a turban. FB. 464.
Sawār—(1) trooper, (2) additional men assigned to a mansabdar as a mark of distinction. IR. 5-8.
Sāz—trappings, harness, accoutrements, ornament.
Sehbandi—militia, or irregular troops enlisted for assisting in revenue collection.
Shāgird-peshā—menials.
Shamsher-band-o-baz (p. 67)—wrongly printed and translated. The correct words are *Shamsher-bandi-e-tār-i-nuqra,* "a sword-belt decorated with silver filigree work". IR. 75 is doubtful about it.
Shutar-nal—a long piece fired from the back of a camel.
Smarani—a small rosary or string of beads for prayer. FB. 477.
Sukh-sajyā-khānah—department or store of cosy beds for the Emperor.
Suzani—a kind of coverlet, sometimes ornamented with needle work.

Tabar-dār—wood-cutter, a man plying an axe.
Takht-i-rawān—literally, portable throne, litter for the Emperor's riding.
Talāir—?
Tashiha—verification at muster. IR. 53.
Tan—short for *tankhwa.*
Tankhwā—cash payment of officers, usually by an order on a treasury as distinguished from *jagir* or payment by the assignment of the land-revenue of a marked place.
Tāqah—a single silken garment. Steingass, 806.

Thān—one entire piece of cloth, sometimes 20 or 40 yards.
Top-khānah—the artillery department, which included all fire arms, not only cannon, but also muskets and rockets whether handled by horsemen or infantry.
Tora—a bag containing a thousand rupees. FB. 250.
Tuighun falcon—not mentioned among the various classes and breeds of falcons kept by Akbar. BL. 293-295.
Tuman tugh—a kind of standard. IR. 31, 34.

Wāla-shāhi—the household troops, or men raised and paid by the Emperor out of his privy purse. IR. 40.

Zamburak—a long musket fired from a camel's back, and resting on a prong. IR. 135.
Zarah—or *Zirih,* a kind of armour. IR. 66. Coat of chain mail, EG. 120.
Zāt—the personal rank of a mansabdar, as distinct from his sawar or trooper rank. IR. 5.

Note.—Words commonly used in Muslim religious practices and Persian and Arabic literature are not included in this list. The following works will supply fuller information or authority on my translation :

Abbreviations—

BL—Eng. trans. of the *Ain-i-Akbari,* vol. I, by Blochmann (1873.)
EG—Egerton's *Handbook of Indian Arms,* (London, 1880.)
FB—Forbes's *Dictionary, Hindustani and English,* 2nd ed. (London, 1866.)
IR—W. Irvine's *Army of the Indian Moghuls,* (London, 1903.)
SK.—Jadunath Sarkar's *Mughal Administration,* 3rd ed. (1935.)
WL—Wilson's *Glossary of Judicial and Revenue Terms,* (London, 1855.)

INDEX

The reference is to the pages of this translation.